Writing and Reasoning Across Disciplines

A Reader for RHET 1302

The University of Texas at Dallas
School of Arts and Humanities

 **Learning Solutions**

Boston   Burr Ridge, IL   Dubuque, IA   New York   San Francisco   St. Louis
Bangkok   Bogotá   Caracas   Lisbon   London   Madrid
Mexico City   Milan   New Delhi   Seoul   Singapore   Sydney   Taipei   Toronto

WRITING AND REASONING ACROSS DISCIPLINES
A Reader for RHET 1302

Copyright © 2009 by The McGraw-Hill Companies, Inc. All rights reserved. Printed in the United States of America. Except as permitted under the United States Copyright Act of 1976, no part of this publication may be reproduced or distributed in any form or by any means, or stored in a data base retrieval system, without prior written permission of the publisher.

1 2 3 4 5 6 7 8 9 0 DIG DIG 0 9

ISBN-13: 978-0-697-78636-4
ISBN-10: 0-697-78636-6

Learning Solutions Manager: Richard Barchak
Primis Sponsoring Editor: Joan L. McNamara
Production Editor: Tina Hermsen
Photo Credit: Randy Anderson
Cover Design: Michelle Long
Printer/Binder: Digital Impressions

Contents

Science, Technology, and Society

Media Ecology

Literacy and Artistic Expression

Historical Moments

Acknowledgments

Editor
Dr. John Gooch, Director of Rhetoric and Writing
School of Arts and Humanities
The University of Texas at Dallas

Co-Editor
Rashmi Ramachandran
School of Arts and Humanities
The University of Texas at Dallas

Rhetoric Program Contributors
Jordan Canfield
Ryan Fletcher
Matthew Kies
Abigail Manuel
Shellie McCullough
Jeff Pettineo
Claude Pruitt
Rachael Sullivan
Barbara Vance

Law, Politics, and Economics

Alan M. Dershowitz (1938–) was born in Brooklyn, New York, and received a B.A. from Brooklyn College in 1959. Awarded a Bachelor of Laws (L.L.B.) in 1962 from Yale Law School, Dershowitz distinguished his ability to analyze law while serving as editor-in-chief of the *Yale Law Journal*. At age 25, Dershowitz joined the faculty at Harvard Law School. His writing has appeared in publications such as *The New York Times Magazine*, *The Washington Post*, *The Wall Street Journal*, *The Harvard Law Review* and the *Yale Law Journal*. Dershowitz's books include *Taking Liberties* (1989), *What Israel Means to Me* (2006), and *The Case Against Israel's Enemies: Exposing Jimmy Carter and Others Who Stand in the Way of Peace* (2008). Dershowitz is currently the Felix Frankfurter Professor of Law at Harvard Law School and is highly regarded in scholarly and legal communities for his strong activism with regard to civil and human rights. The following essay was originally published in the *Harvard Law Bulletin* in 1989.

Shouting "Fire!"

Alan M. Dershowitz

Justice Oliver Wendell Holmes' classic example of unprotected speech—falsely shouting "Fire!" in a crowded theater—has been invoked so often, by so many people, in such diverse contexts, that it has become part of our national folk language.   1

But in spite of its hallowed position in both the jurisprudence of the First Amendment and the arsenal of political discourse, it is and was an inapt analogy, even in the context in which it was originally offered. It has lately become— despite, perhaps even because of, the frequency and promiscuousness of its invocation—little more than a caricature of logical argumentation.   2

The case that gave rise to the "Fire!"—in-a-crowded-theater analogy— *Schenck v. United States,* involved the prosecution of Charles Schenck, who was the general secretary of the Socialist party in Philadelphia, and Elizabeth Baer, who was its recording secretary. In 1917 a jury found Schenck and Baer guilty of attempting to cause insubordination among soldiers who had been drafted to fight in the first World War. They and other party members had circulated leaflets urging draftees not to "submit to intimidation" by fighting in a war being conducted on behalf of "Wall Street's chosen few." Schenck admitted, and the Court found, that the intent of the pamphlet's "impassioned language" was to "influence" draftees to resist the draft. Interestingly, however, Justice Holmes noted that nothing in the pamphlet suggested that the draftees should use unlawful or violent means to oppose conscription.   3

Justice Holmes acknowledged that "in many places and in ordinary times the defendants, in saying all that was said in the circular, would have been within their constitutional rights." "But," he added, "the character of every act depends   4 upon the circumstances in which it is done." And to illustrate that truism he went on to say,

> The most stringent protection of free speech would not protect a man in falsely shouting fire in a theater, and causing a panic. It does not even protect a man from an injunction against uttering words that may have all the effect of force.

The example of shouting "Fire!" obviously bore little relationship to the facts 5 of the Schenck case. The Schenck pamphlet contained a substantive political message. It urged its draftee readers to *think* about the message and then—if they so chose—to act on it in a lawful and nonviolent way. The man who shouts "Fire!" in a crowded theater is neither sending a political message nor inviting his listener to think about what he has said and decide what to do in a rational, calculated manner. On the contrary, the message is designed to force action *without* contemplation. The message "Fire!" is directed not to the mind and the conscience of the listener but, rather, to his adrenaline and his feet. It is a stimulus to immediate *action*, not thoughtful reflection. It is—as Justice Holmes recognized in his follow-up sentence—the functional equivalent of "uttering words that may have all the effect of force."

Indeed, in that respect the shout of "Fire!" is not even speech, in any mean- 6 ingful sense of that term. It is a *clang* sound, the equivalent of setting off a non-verbal alarm. Had Justice Holmes been more honest about his example, he would have said that freedom of speech does not protect a kid who pulls a fire alarm in the absence of a fire. But that obviously would have been irrelevant to the case at hand. The proposition that pulling an alarm is not protected speech certainly leads to the conclusion that shouting the word *fire* is also not protected. But the core analogy is the non-verbal alarm, and the derivative example is the verbal shout. By cleverly substituting the derivative shout for the core alarm, Holmes made it possible to analogize one set of words to another—as he could not have done if he had begun with the self-evident proposition that setting off an alarm bell is not free speech.

The analogy is thus not only inapt but also insulting. Most Americans do not 7 respond to political rhetoric with the same kind of automatic acceptance expected of schoolchildren responding to a fire drill. Not a single recipient of the Schenck pamphlet is known to have changed his mind after reading it. Indeed, one draftee, who appeared as a prosecution witness, was asked whether reading a pamphlet asserting that the draft law was unjust would make him "immediately decide that you must erase that law." Not surprisingly, he replied, "I do my own thinking." A theatergoer would probably not respond similarly if asked how he would react to a shout of "Fire!"

Another important reason why the analogy is inapt is that Holmes emphasizes 8 the factual falsity of the shout "Fire!" The Schenck pamphlet, however, was not factually false. It contained political opinions and ideas about the causes of the war and about appropriate and lawful responses to the draft. As the Supreme Court recently reaffirmed (in *Falwell v. Hustler*), "The First Amendment recognizes no such thing as a 'false' idea." Nor does it recognize false opinions about the causes or cures for war.

A closer analogy to the facts of the Schenck case might have been provided 9 by a person's standing outside a theater, offering the patrons a leaflet advising them that in his opinion the theater was structurally unsafe, and urging them not to enter but to complain to the building inspectors. That analogy, however, would not have served Holmes's argument for punishing Schenck. Holmes needed an analogy that would appear relevant to Schenck's political speech, but one that would invite the conclusion that censorship was appropriate.

Analogies are, by their nature, matters of degree. Some are closer to the core 10 example than others. But any attempt to analogize political ideas in a pamphlet, ugly parody in a magazine, offensive movies in a theater, or controversial newspaper articles to the very different act of shouting "Fire!" in a crowded theater is either self-deceptive or self-serving.

The government does, of course, have some arguable legitimate bases for sup- 11 pressing speech that bear no relationship to shouting "Fire!" It may ban the publication of nuclear-weapon codes, information about troop movements, and the identity of undercover agents. It may criminalize extortion threats and conspiratorial agreements. These expressions may lead directly to serious harm, but the mechanisms of causation are very different from that at work when an alarm is sounded. One may also argue—less persuasively, in my view—against protecting certain forms of public obscenity and defamatory statements. Here, too, the mechanisms of causation are very different. None of these exceptions to the First Amendment's exhortation that the government "shall make no law . . . abridging the freedom of speech, or of the press" is anything like falsely shouting "Fire!" in a crowded theater; they all must be justified on other grounds.

A comedian once told his audience, during a stand-up routine, about the time 12 he was standing around a fire with a crowd of people and got in trouble for yelling "Theater, theater!" That, I think, is about as clever and productive a use as anyone has ever made of Holmes's flawed analogy.

Thomas Gale Moore is a Senior Fellow at the Hoover Institution at Stanford University in Palo Alto, California. Moore specializes in international trade, deregulation, and privatization. Before coming to the Hoover Institution, Moore was professor of economics at Michigan State University as well as a member of President Ronald Reagan's Council of Economic Advisers from 1985 to 1989. His publications include *Climate of Fear: Why We Shouldn't Worry about Global Warming* (Cato Institute, 1998), *In Sickness or in Health: The Kyoto Protocol versus Global Warming* (Hoover Essays in Public Policy, 2000), *Global Warming: A Boon to Humans and Other Animals* (Hoover Essays in Public Policy, 1995), and *Environmental Terrorism* (Hoover Essays in Public Policy, 1994). Moore's numerous articles on economic, political, and law issues appear in a wide variety of popular and academic publications.

Happiness Is a Warm Planet

Thomas Gale Moore

President Clinton convened a conference on global warming yesterday, as the White House agonizes over its posture at the forthcoming talks in Kyoto, Japan, on a worldwide global warming treaty. Mr. Clinton is eager to please his environmentalist supporters, but industry, labor and members of the Senate have told the administration that this treaty would wreck the economy, cost millions of jobs and provoke a flight of investment to more hospitable climes.   1

A crucial point gets lost in the debate: Global warming, if it were to occur, would probably *benefit* most Americans.   2

If mankind had to choose between a warmer or a cooler climate, we would certainly choose the former: Humans, nearly all other animals and most plants would be better off with higher temperatures. The climate models suggest, and so far the record confirms, that under global warming nighttime winter temperatures would rise the most, and daytime summer temperatures the least. Most Americans prefer a warmer climate to a colder one—and that preference is justified. More people die of the cold than of the heat; more die in the winter than the summer. Statistical evidence suggests that the climate predicted for the end of the next century might reduce U.S. deaths by about 40,000 annually.   3

In addition, less snow and ice would reduce transportation delays and accidents. A warmer winter would cut heating costs, more than offsetting any increase in air conditioning expenses in the summer. Manufacturing, mining and most services would be unaffected. Longer growing seasons, more rainfall and higher concentrations of carbon dioxide would benefit plant growth. Already there is evidence that trees and other plants are growing more vigorously. Although some locales may become too dry, too wet or too warm, on the whole mankind should benefit from an upward tick in the thermometer.   4

What about the economic effects? In the pessimistic view of the Intergovernmental Panel on Climate Change, the costs of global warming might be as high as 1.5 percent of the U.S. gross domestic product by the end of the next century. The cost of reducing carbon dioxide emissions, however, would be much higher. William Cline of the Institute for International Economics has calculated that the cost of cutting emissions by one-third from current levels by 2040 would be 3.5 percent of worldwide GDP. The IPCC also reviewed various estimates of losses from stabilizing emissions at 1990 levels, a more modest objective, and concluded that the cost to the U.S. economy would be at least 1.5 percent of GDP by 2050, with the burden continuing to increase thereafter.   5

The forecast cost of warming is for the end of the next century, not the middle. Adjusting for the time difference, the cost to the U.S. from a warmer climate at midcentury, according to the IPCC, would be at most 0.75 percent of GDP, meaning that the costs of holding carbon dioxide to 1990 levels would be twice the gain from preventing any climate change. But the benefit-cost calculus is even worse. The administration is planning to exempt Third World nations, such as China, India and Brazil, from the requirements of the treaty. Under such a scheme, Americans would pay a huge price for virtually no benefit.   6

And even if the developing countries agreed to return emissions to 1990 levels, greenhouse gas concentrations would not be stabilized. Since for many decades more carbon dioxide would be added to the atmosphere than removed through natural processes, the buildup would only slow; consequently temperatures would continue to go up. Instead of saving the full 0.75 percent of GDP by keeping emissions at 1990 levels, we would be saving much less.   7

It is true that whatever dangers global warming may pose, they will be most pronounced in the developing world. It is much easier for rich countries to adapt to any long-term shift in weather than it is for poor countries, which tend to be much more dependent on agriculture. Poor countries lack the resources to aid their flora and fauna in adapting, and many of their farmers earn too little to survive a shift to new conditions. But the best insurance for these poor countries is an increase in their wealth, which would diminish their dependence on agriculture and make it easier for them to adjust to changes in weather, including increases in precipitation and possible flooding or higher sea level. Subjecting Americans to high taxes and onerous regulations will help neither them—we could buy less from them—nor us.   8

The optimal way to deal with potential climate change is not to embark on a futile attempt to prevent it, but to promote growth and prosperity so that people will have the resources to deal with the normal set of natural disasters. Based on the evidence, including historical records, global warming is likely to be good for most of mankind. The additional carbon, rain and warmth should promote the plant growth necessary to sustain an expanding world population. Global change is inevitable; warmer is better; richer is healthier.   9

Barbara Jordan (1936–1996) was born in Houston, Texas. She earned her B.A. from Texas Southern University in 1956 and her law degree from Boston University School of Law in 1959. Jordan was the first African American to be elected to the Texas Senate since Reconstruction, where she served for five years (1967–1972). She then became the first African American woman from a Southern state to be elected to the United States House of Representatives. In 1974, Jordan was appointed to the House Judiciary Committee where she enthralled the nation with her speech calling for the impeachment of President Nixon. Jordan left the Senate in 1979 but remained politically active. Until the early 1990s, Jordan taught at the Lyndon B. Johnson School of Public Affairs at the University of Texas. The recipient of numerous awards, including the Presidential Medal of Honor in 1994, perhaps the most prestigious award was given to Jordan posthumously. Following her death on January 17, 1996, Jordan's body lay in state in the LBJ Library on the campus of the University of Texas at Austin. She is buried in the Texas State Cemetery, the first black woman to be interred on its grounds.

Statement on the Articles of Impeachment

Barbara Jordan

Thank you, Mr. Chairman.

Mr. Chairman, I join my colleague Mr. Rangel in thanking you for giving the junior members of this committee the glorious opportunity of sharing the pain of this inquiry. Mr. Chairman, you are a strong man, and it has not been easy but we have tried as best we can to give you as much assistance as possible. 1 2

Earlier today, we heard the beginning of the Preamble to the Constitution of the United States: "We, the people." It's a very eloquent beginning. But when that document was completed on the seventeenth of September in 1787, I was not included in that "We, the people." I felt somehow for many years that George Washington and Alexander Hamilton just left me out by mistake. But through the process of amendment, interpretation, and court decision, I have finally been included in "We, the people." 3

Today I am an inquisitor. An hyperbole would not be fictional and would not overstate the solemnness that I feel right now. My faith in the Constitution is whole; it is complete; it is total. And I am not going to sit here and be an idle spectator to the diminution, the subversion, the destruction, of the Constitution. 4

"Who can so properly be the inquisitors for the nation as the representatives of the nation themselves?" "The subjects of its jurisdiction are those offenses which proceed from the misconduct of public men." And that's what we're talking about. In other words, [the jurisdiction comes] from the abuse or violation of some public trust. 5

It is wrong, I suggest, it is a misreading of the Constitution for any member here to assert that for a member to vote for an article of impeachment means that 6

Barbara Charline Jordan, "Statement on the Articles of Impeachment," delivered July 25, 1974, House Judiciary Committee.

that member must be convinced that the President should be removed from office. The Constitution doesn't say that. The powers relating to impeachment are an essential check in the hands of the body of the legislature against and upon the encroachments of the executive. The division between the two branches of the legislature, the House and the Senate, assigning to the one the right to accuse and to the other the right to judge, the framers of this Constitution were very astute. They did not make the accusers and the judgers—and the judges the same person.

We know the nature of impeachment. We've been talking about it awhile now. It is chiefly designed for the President and his high ministers to somehow be called into account. It is designed to "bridle" the executive if he engages in excesses. "It is designed as a method of national inquest into the conduct of public men." The framers confided in the Congress the power if need be, to remove the President in order to strike a delicate balance between a President swollen with power and grown tyrannical, and preservation of the independence of the executive.

7

The nature of impeachment: a narrowly channeled exception to the separation-of-powers maxim. The Federal Convention of 1787 said that. It limited impeachment to high crimes and misdemeanors and discounted and opposed the term "maladministration." "It is to be used only for great misdemeanors," so it was said in the North Carolina ratification convention. And in the Virginia ratification convention: "We do not trust our liberty to a particular branch. We need one branch to check the other."

8

"No one need be afraid"—the North Carolina ratification convention—"No one need be afraid that officers who commit oppression will pass with immunity." "Prosecutions of impeachments will seldom fail to agitate the passions of the whole community," said Hamilton in the Federalist Papers, number 65. "We divide into parties more or less friendly or inimical to the accused." I do not mean political parties in that sense.

9

The drawing of political lines goes to the motivation behind impeachment; but impeachment must proceed within the confines of the constitutional term "high crime[s] and misdemeanors." Of the impeachment process, it was Woodrow Wilson who said that "Nothing short of the grossest offenses against the plain law of the land will suffice to give them speed and effectiveness. Indignation so great as to overgrow party interest may secure a conviction; but nothing else can."

10

Common sense would be revolted if we engaged upon this process for petty reasons. Congress has a lot to do: Appropriations, Tax Reform, Health Insurance, Campaign Finance Reform, Housing, Environmental Protection, Energy Sufficiency, Mass Transportation. Pettiness cannot be allowed to stand in the face of such overwhelming problems. So today we are not being petty. We are trying to be big, because the task we have before us is a big one.

11

This morning, in a discussion of the evidence, we were told that the evidence which purports to support the allegations of misuse of the CIA by the President is thin. We're told that that evidence is insufficient. What that recital of the evidence this morning did not include is what the President did know on June the 23rd, 1972.

12

The President did know that it was Republican money, that it was money from the Committee for the Re-Election of the President, which was found in the possession of one of the burglars arrested on June the 17th. What the President did know on the 23rd of June was the prior activities of E. Howard Hunt, which included his participation in the break-in of Daniel Ellsberg's psychiatrist, which included Howard Hunt's participation in the Dita Beard ITT affair, which included Howard Hunt's fabrication of cables designed to discredit the Kennedy Administration. 13

We were further cautioned today that perhaps these proceedings ought to be delayed because certainly there would be new evidence forthcoming from the President of the United States. There has not even been an obfuscated indication that this committee would receive any additional materials from the President. The committee subpoena is outstanding, and if the President wants to supply that material, the committee sits here. The fact is that on yesterday, the American people waited with great anxiety for eight hours, not knowing whether their President would obey an order of the Supreme Court of the United States. 14

At this point, I would like to juxtapose a few of the impeachment criteria with some of the actions the President has engaged in. Impeachment criteria: James Madison, from the Virginia ratification convention. "If the President be connected in any suspicious manner with any person and there be grounds to believe that he will shelter him, he may be impeached." 15

We have heard time and time again that the evidence reflects the payment to defendants money. The President had knowledge that these funds were being paid and these were funds collected for the 1972 presidential campaign. We know that the President met with Mr. Henry Petersen 27 times to discuss matters related to Watergate, and immediately thereafter met with the very persons who were implicated in the information Mr. Petersen was receiving. The words are: "If the President is connected in any suspicious manner with any person and there be grounds to believe that he will shelter that person, he may be impeached." 16

Justice Story: "Impeachment" is attended—"is intended for occasional and extraordinary cases where a superior power acting for the whole people is put into operation to protect their rights and rescue their liberties from violations." We know about the Huston plan. We know about the break-in of the psychiatrist's office. We know that there was absolute complete direction on September 3rd when the President indicated that a surreptitious entry had been made in Dr. Fielding's office, after having met with Mr. Ehrlichman and Mr. Young. "Protect their rights." "Rescue their liberties from violation." 17

The Carolina ratification convention impeachment criteria: those are impeachable "who behave amiss or betray their public trust." Beginning shortly after the Watergate break-in and continuing to the present time, the President has engaged in a series of public statements and actions designed to thwart the lawful investigation by government prosecutors. Moreover, the President has made public announcements and assertions bearing on the Watergate case, which the evidence will show he knew to be false. These assertions, false assertions, impeachable, those who misbehave. Those who "behave amiss or betray the public trust." 18

James Madison again at the Constitutional Convention: "A President is impeachable if he attempts to subvert the Constitution." The Constitution charges the President with the task of taking care that the laws be faithfully executed, and yet the President has counseled his aides to commit perjury, willfully disregard the secrecy of grand jury proceedings, conceal surreptitious entry, attempt to compromise a federal judge, while publicly displaying his cooperation with the processes of criminal justice. "A President is impeachable if he attempts to subvert the Constitution." 19

If the impeachment provision in the Constitution of the United States will not reach the offenses charged here, then perhaps that 18th-century Constitution should be abandoned to a 20th-century paper shredder. 20

Has the President committed offenses, and planned, and directed, and acquiesced in a course of conduct which the Constitution will not tolerate? That's the question. We know that. We know the question. We should now forthwith proceed to answer the question. It is reason, and not passion, which must guide our deliberations, guide our debate, and guide our decision. 21

I yield back the balance of my time, Mr. Chairman. 22

John Grisham (1955–) is a best-selling author of legal thrillers, a former lawyer, and a politician. Born in Arkansas but raised in Mississippi, Grisham earned his B.S. and law degree from the University of Mississippi. He spent ten years practicing law and was elected as a Democrat in 1983 to the Mississippi House of Representatives, where he served for seven years. Grisham's first novel A *Time to Kill* was published in 1988. Success soon followed and over the next decade, Grisham became one of the top-selling authors in the world. His most famous novels include *The Firm* (1991), *The Pelican Brief* (1992), *The Client* (1993), and *A Painted House* (2002). Worldwide, Grisham's novels have sold more than 250 million copies. Grisham is married and has two children. The family divides its time between homes in Mississippi and Virginia.

Somewhere for Everyone

John Grisham

In the small southern towns of my childhood no one talked about the homeless. In fact, the word "homeless" as a description for very poor people was never used. They were called hungry or needy, or they were winos or hobos, but never homeless. They, whoever and wherever they were, were rarely seen, and it was always assumed that someone else, probably a relative, would eventually take care of them.   1

Years later, during one of my first visits to New York City, I was accosted by an angry panhandler. Like the rest of the crowd, I tried to ignore him. But for some reason he chose to follow me. We exchanged insults for a block as my pace quickened, and I half expected him to produce a weapon of some sort. I escaped in the crowd, and he was left to torment someone else.   2

The incident did nothing to arouse my concern for the homeless, but it did make me notice and avoid street beggars. And since nearly everyone else avoided them, too, I was certain the problem would simply go away.   3

For a brief period back in the '80s, homelessness was the chic issue of the pretty people. It was worthy of galas and fund-raisers and cover stories. Now, as a cause, it has fallen on hard times, and the glamour crusades have moved to new fronts. But homelessness is a problem that is not going away. There are more homeless this year than last, and the number keeps growing. The new welfare overhaul our politicians are so proud of is sending more poor people into the streets. Many homeless people actually work, but not where they prefer. They are relegated to minimum-wage jobs with few hours and no benefits. The cost of housing is high, so they have a choice: sleep under a bridge or fight for a spot in a shelter.   4

About 40 percent of the homeless are substance abusers, and this number is expected to increase as rehab programs dwindle. (Don't be so quick to pass judg-   5

John Grisham, "Somewhere for Everyone," *Newsweek,* February 9, 1998. Reprinted by permission of The Gernert Company, agent for John Grisham ment and say, "Serves them right. If they're gonna abuse drugs and alcohol, they belong on the streets." Let's not kid ourselves. If teenagers from good families and executives with big jobs can succumb to alcohol and drugs, what can we expect from people who live on the streets?) Many of the homeless are mothers with children, and shelters are not always equipped to handle them. Tonight many thousands of children will find a place to sleep without a decent bed, shelter or roof. They will sleep in the trunks of old cars, and in parks I wouldn't walk through in daylight, and in abandoned buildings in inner-city combat zones.

There is now a new and growing threat. Some cities are in the midst of an   6
effort to criminalize homelessness. Attempts have been made to outlaw panhandling, sleeping on park benches and sidewalks, eating near fountains and leaving personal property on public property. Some of these ill-advised ordinances have been struck down, so the cities selectively enforce existing laws. A panhandler may be charged with blocking pedestrian traffic or loitering. A wino sleeping in a park may be charged with public drunkenness. A homeless man relieves himself in an alley and he's charged with public exposure.

Sweeps have become routine in some cities. The police target certain areas of   7
a city. They remove those who are begging or otherwise appear unsightly and simply deposit them into another, less fashionable section of town. Or they arrest them and grind them through the overworked criminal justice system.

Everyone has to be somewhere. The problem of homelessness is not solved   8
by removing the victims from our view. The issue borders on the brink of hopelessness.

I didn't know this a year ago. I had other causes and concerns and supported   9
other charities. Then inspiration hit. Ideas for novels often fall from the sky, striking like lightning and causing sleep loss. (Others take years to piece together.) I thought of a story about a young lawyer who has a violent encounter with a street person, and who survives, and for the first time in his busy young life stops and notices the less fortunate. In short order he becomes a street lawyer, a public-interest advocate for the poor. Adding a few of the usual twists and turns, I could make the story work. Problem was, I knew nothing about street law.

In the spring of '97 my research took me into the world of the homeless. I   10
made the two-hour drive from my comfortable home in the Virginia countryside to the streets of D.C., and there I met real poverty lawyers. I went to shelters where people lived packed together, their meager assets locked away in small trunks. I met women whose children had been taken away because they couldn't feed and clothe them. I met young mothers still clinging to their kids, terrified they would lose their shelter space and land in the streets. In a church basement I chatted with street people happy to be eating a warm meal, most of them uncertain where they would sleep in a few hours. I almost froze on a park bench one night as I tried to strike up a conversation with a homeless man who suspected I was from the IRS. I talked politics with a panhandler near the Capitol. He finally asked me to leave because I was hurting his business. I listened to hymns being sung at a women's center as it closed for the day. The ladies said their goodbyes and drifted away, half

of them headed for shelters, the rest destined for alleys and parks. I interviewed volunteers and social workers, and I'm still amazed at their compassion.

I cried only once. I was in a soup kitchen one night, trying but failing to appear inconspicuous, when a young mother rushed in with three children, an infant and twin boys. She was running from something, but no one seemed to care. Her boys were about 4 dressed in rags and bone thin, and they attacked a tray of peanut butter sandwiches as if they hadn't seen food in a month. A volunteer fixed them a plate with cookies, an apple, a cup of vegetable soup and more sandwiches. They ate furiously, their eyes darting in all directions as if someone might stop them. They stuffed themselves because they knew the uncertainties of tomorrow. 11

Little street soldiers, preparing for the coming battles. Is this the Third World, I asked myself? Or is this America? 12

Vicente Navarro is a professor of health policy, sociology, and public policy, and editor-in-chief of the *International Journal of Health Services*. His research focuses on the impact that the globalization of the world economy has on social structures and social policy. He received his Ph.D. from Johns Hopkins University, where he currently teaches in the Bloomberg School of Public Health. "The Middle Class—a Useful Myth" was first published in the March 23, 1992 issue of *The Nation*.

The Middle Class—a Useful Myth

Vicente Navarro

The new conventional wisdom among political pundits is that the Democratic Party has been too concerned with the minorities and the poor and has not paid enough attention to the middle class. The Democrats' political redemption, the commentators say, can occur only if the party concentrates on the needs of the middle class—needs that are assumed to be different from those of the minorities and the poor. In this political discourse, the pundits' concern for the middle class has an antiminority flavor. Indeed, this appeal to the middle class—which supposedly includes the majority of Americans—is profoundly ideological.   1

Actually, the majority of Americans belong not to the middle class but to the working class: that is, their financial identity is defined by hourly wages. According to Prof. Erik Olin Wright of the University of Wisconsin, one of the most respected scholars in the analysis of social class structure, manual, supervised, unskilled and semiskilled workers represent more than 50 percent of the adult working population. They are the core of the working class, and they and their dependents represent the majority of the population. Most members of the working class are white, although minorities (predominantly black and Hispanic) and women are the fastest-growing sector of that class.   2

A majority of the working population do not identify themselves as middle class. According to the 1983 class self-identification survey of the National Opinion Research Center, more people defined themselves as working class (48 percent) than as middle class (43 percent). This differential is even higher among Americans under 35, 50 percent of whom defined themselves as working class in the 1983–88 period, compared with 42 percent among those over 35.   3

The majority of poor people belong to the working class, and their problems do not differ from those of the nonpoor sector of that class. One example is health insurance. Fifty-two percent of the working poor in this country do not have health insurance of any type. If they get sick, because they cannot afford health care they might die. Experts have estimated that 100,000 deaths occur annually because people cannot afford health care. Lack of health care causes three times more deaths   4 than AIDS. In 1990, 56 percent of the population and 75 percent of the working class indicated that they have problems paying their medical bills. The overwhelming majority of Americans, poor and nonpoor, do not have comprehensive health coverage. They do not have coverage, for example, for long-term care, for which the average annual cost is $27,243.

The solution to the problems of the poor, working and non-working, is not, as the "middle class versus the poor" theorists seem to believe, to design different solutions for the middle class. The solution is to create programs, such as a comprehensive national health program without co-payments and deductibles, that would benefit the entire working class, which has been hurt the most by Reagan/Bush administration policies (supported, for the most part, by the Democrat-controlled Congress). These policies have facilitated a reduction by almost 50 percent in hourly health insurance benefits, from $1.63 per hour in 1980 to 85 cents per hour in 1989. In addition, employer-financed contributions to family coverage fell from 51 percent in 1980 to 34 percent in 1988. Because of these policies, today 28 percent of Americans have at one point or another during a period of more than two years gone without health insurance. While the working poor are the sector of the population hurt most, the majority of the uninsured are nonpoor. The problems in this supposedly "kinder, gentler" America, however, are the same for both groups of our working population. But the middle-class discourse ignores this reality; instead, its aim is to divide rather than unite the working class—the actual majority of this country. By referring to a mythical middle-class majority as an entity separate from "the others," the divisive message is clear. The "others" are presented as minorities, and racism is called on to do the rest. Terms used in political discourse are indeed never innocent.

5

Barbara Ehrenreich (1941–   ) was born in Butte, Montana, and earned a Ph.D. from Rockefeller University in 1968. Ehrenreich has worked as a college professor, editor, and columnist for such magazines as *Mother Jones* and *Time*. Her books include *The Hearts of Men: American Dreams and the Flight from Commitment* (1983), *Blood Rites: Origins and History of the Passions of War* (1997), and *Nickel-and-Dimed: On (Not) Getting By in America* (2001). Among other honors and prizes, Ehrenreich won a National Magazine Award in 1980 and a Guggenheim Fellowship in 1987. The following selection is an excerpt from *Nickel and Dimed* that first appeared in *Harper's* Magazine in January, 1999.

Nickel-and-Dimed: On (Not) Getting By in America

Barbara Ehrenreich

At the beginning of June 1998 I leave behind everything that normally soothes the ego and sustains the body—home, career, companion, reputation, ATM card— for a plunge into the low-wage workforce. There, I become another, occupationally much diminished "Barbara Ehrenreich"—depicted on job-application forms as a divorced homemaker whose sole work experience consists of housekeeping in a few private homes. I am terrified, at the beginning, of being unmasked for what I am: a middle-class journalist setting out to explore the world that welfare mothers are entering, at the rate of approximately 50,000 a month, as welfare reform kicks in. Happily, though, my fears turn out to be entirely unwarranted: during a month of poverty and toil, my name goes unnoticed and for the most part unuttered. In this parallel universe where my father never got out of the mines and I never got through college, I am "baby," "honey," "blondie," and, most commonly, "girl."

My first task is to find a place to live. I figure that if I can earn $7 an hour— which, from the want ads, seems doable—I can afford to spend $500 on rent, or maybe, with severe economies, $600. In the Key West area, where I live, this pretty much confines me to flophouses and trailer homes—like the one, a pleasing fifteen-minute drive from town, that has no air-conditioning, no screens, no fans, no television, and, by way of diversion, only the challenge of evading the landlord's Doberman pinscher. The big problem with this place, though, is the rent, which at $675 a month is well beyond my reach. All right, Key West is expensive. But so is New York City, or the Bay Area, or Jackson Hole, or Telluride, or Boston, or any other place where tourists and the wealthy compete for living space with the people who clean their toilets and fry their hash browns.[1] Still, it is a shock to realize that "trailer trash" has become, for me, a demographic category to aspire to.

[1]According to the Department of Housing and Urban Development, the "fair-market rent" for an efficiency is $551 here in Monroe County, Florida. A comparable rent in the five boroughs of New York City is $704; in San Francisco, $713; and in the heart of Silicon Valley, $808. The fair-market rent for an area is defined as the amount that would be needed to pay rent plus utilities for "privately owned, decent, safe, and sanitary rental housing of a modest (non-luxury) nature with suitable amenities."

So I decide to make the common trade-off between affordability and convenience, and go for a $500-a-month efficiency thirty miles up a two-lane highway from the employment opportunities of Key West, meaning forty-five minutes if there's no road construction and I don't get caught behind some sun-dazed Canadian tourists. I hate the drive, along a roadside studded with white crosses commemorating the more effective head-on collisions, but it's a sweet little place—a cabin, more or less, set in the swampy back yard of the converted mobile home where my landlord, an affable TV repairman, lives with his bartender girlfriend. Anthropologically speaking, a bustling trailer park would be preferable, but here I have a gleaming white floor and a firm mattress, and the few resident bugs are easily vanquished.

Besides, I am not doing this for the anthropology. My aim is nothing so mistily subjective as to "experience poverty" or find out how it "really feels" to be a long-term low-wage worker. I've had enough unchosen encounters with poverty and the world of low-wage work to know it's not a place you want to visit for touristic purposes; it just smells too much like fear. And with all my real-life assets—bank account, IRA, health insurance, multiroom home—waiting indulgently in the background, I am, of course, thoroughly insulated from the terrors that afflict the genuinely poor.

No, this is a purely objective, scientific sort of mission. The humanitarian rationale for welfare reform—as opposed to the more punitive and stingy impulses that may actually have motivated it—is that work will lift poor women out of poverty while simultaneously inflating their self-esteem and hence their future value in the labor market. Thus, whatever the hassles involved in finding child care, transportation, etc., the transition from welfare to work will end happily, in greater prosperity for all. Now there are many problems with this comforting prediction, such as the fact that the economy will inevitably undergo a downturn, eliminating many jobs. Even without a downturn, the influx of a million former welfare recipients into the low-wage labor market could depress wages by as much as 11.9 percent, according to the Economic Policy Institute (EPI) in Washington, D.C.

But is it really possible to make a living on the kinds of jobs currently available to unskilled people? Mathematically, the answer is no, as can be shown by taking $6 to $7 an hour, perhaps subtracting a dollar or two an hour for child care, multiplying by 160 hours a month, and comparing the result to the prevailing rents. According to the National Coalition for the Homeless, for example, in 1998 it took, on average nationwide, an hourly wage of $8.89 to afford a one-bedroom apartment, and the Preamble Center for Public Policy estimates that the odds against a typical welfare recipient's landing a job at such a "living wage" are about 97 to 1. If these numbers are right, low-wage work is not a solution to poverty and possibly not even to homelessness.

It may seem excessive to put this proposition to an experimental test. As certain family members keep unhelpfully reminding me, the viability of low-wage work could be tested, after a fashion, without ever leaving my study. I could just pay myself $7 an hour for eight hours a day, charge myself for room and board, and total up the numbers after a month. Why leave the people and work that I love? But I am an experimental scientist by training. In that business, you don't just sit at a desk and theorize; you plunge into the everyday chaos of nature, where surprises lurk in the most mundane measurements. Maybe, when I got into it, I would discover some hidden economies in the world of the low-wage worker. After all, if 30 percent of the workforce toils for less than $8 an hour, according to the EPI, they may have found some tricks as yet unknown to me. Maybe—who knows?—I would even be able to detect in myself the bracing psychological effects of getting out of the house, as promised by the welfare wonks at places like the Heritage Foundation. Or, on the other hand, maybe there would be unexpected costs—physical, mental, or financial—to throw off all my calculations. Ideally, I should do this with two small children in tow, that being the welfare average, but mine are grown and no one is willing to lend me theirs for a month-long vacation in penury. So this is not the perfect experiment, just a test of the best possible case: an unencumbered woman, smart and even strong, attempting to live more or less off the land.

On the morning of my first full day of job searching, I take a red pen to the want ads, which are auspiciously numerous. Everyone in Key West's booming "hospitality industry" seems to be looking for someone like me—trainable, flexible, and with suitably humble expectations as to pay. I know I possess certain traits that might be advantageous—I'm white and, I like to think, well-spoken and poised—but I decide on two rules: One, I cannot use any skills derived from my education or usual work—not that there are a lot of want ads for satirical essayists anyway. Two, I have to take the best-paid job that is offered me and of course do my best to hold it; no Marxist rants or sneaking off to read novels in the ladies' room. In addition, I rule out various occupations for one reason or another: Hotel front-desk clerk, for example, which to my surprise is regarded as unskilled and pays around $7 an hour, gets eliminated because it involves standing in one spot for eight hours a day. Waitressing is similarly something I'd like to avoid, because I remember it leaving me bone-tired when I was eighteen, and I'm decades of varicosities and back pain beyond that now. Telemarketing, one of the first refuges of the suddenly indigent, can be dismissed on grounds of personality. This leaves certain supermarket jobs, such as deli clerk, or housekeeping in Key West's thousands of hotel and guest rooms. Housekeeping is especially appealing, for reasons both atavistic and practical: it's what my mother did before I came along, and it can't be too different from what I've been doing part-time, in my own home, all my life.

So I put on what I take to be a respectful-looking outfit of ironed Bermuda shorts and scooped-neck T-shirt and set out for a tour of the local hotels and supermarkets. Best Western, Econo Lodge, and HoJo's all let me fill out application forms, and these are, to my relief interested in little more than whether I am a legal resident of the United States and have committed any felonies. My next stop is Winn-Dixie, the supermarket, which turns out to have a particularly onerous application process, featuring a fifteen-minute "interview" by computer since, apparently, no human on the premises is deemed capable of representing the corporate point of view. I am conducted to a large room decorated with posters illustrating how to look "professional" (it helps to be white and, if female, permed) and warning of the slick promises that union organizers might try to tempt me with. The interview is multiple choice: Do I have anything, such as child-care problems, that might make it hard for me to get to work on time? Do I think safety on the job is the responsibility of management? Then, popping up cunningly out of the blue: How many dollars' worth of stolen goods have I purchased in the last year? Would I turn in a fellow employee if I caught him stealing? Finally, "Are you an honest person?"

Apparently, I ace the interview, because I am told that all I have to do is show up in some doctor's office tomorrow for a urine test. This seems to be a fairly general rule: if you want to stack Cheerio boxes or vacuum hotel rooms in chemically fascist America, you have to be willing to squat down and pee in front of some health worker (who has no doubt had to do the same thing herself). The wages Winn-Dixie is offering—$6 and a couple of dimes to start with—are not enough, I decide, to compensate for this indignity.[2]

I lunch at Wendy's, where $4.99 gets you unlimited refills at the Mexican part of the Superbar, a comforting surfeit of refried beans and "cheese sauce." A teenage employee, seeing me studying the want ads, kindly offers me an application form, which I fill out, though here, too, the pay is just $6 and change an hour. Then it's off for a round of the locally owned inns and guesthouses. At "The Palms," let's call it, a bouncy manager actually takes me around to see the rooms and meet the existing housekeepers, who, I note with satisfaction, look pretty much like me—faded ex-hippie types in shorts with long hair pulled back in braids. Mostly, through, no one speaks to me or even looks at me except to proffer an application form. At my last stop; a palatial B&B, I wait twenty minutes to meet "Max," only to be told that there are no jobs now but there should be one soon, since "nobody lasts more than a couple weeks." (Because none of the people I talked to knew I was a reporter, I have changed their names to protect their privacy and, in some cases perhaps, their jobs.)

Three days go by like this, and, to my chagrin, no one out of the approximately twenty places I've applied calls me for an interview. I had been vain enough to worry about coming across as too educated for the jobs I sought, but no one even seems interested in finding out how overqualified I am. Only later will I realize that the want ads are not a reliable measure of the actual jobs available at any particular time. They are, as I should have guessed from Max's comment, the employers' insurance policy against the relentless turnover of the low-wage workforce. Most of the big hotels run ads almost continually, just to build a supply of applicants to replace the current workers as they drift away or are fired, so finding a job is just a matter of being at the right place at the right time and flexible enough to take whatever is being offered that day. This finally happens to me at one of the big discount hotel chains, where I go, as usual, for housekeeping and am sent, instead, to try out as a waitress at the attached "family restaurant," a dismal spot with a counter and about thirty tables that looks our on a parking garage and features such tempting fare as "Pollish [sic] sausage and BBQ sauce" on 95-degree days. Phillip, the dapper young West Indian

10

11

12

---

[2]According to the *Monthly Labor Review* (November 1996), 28 percent of work sites surveyed in the service industry conduct drug tests (corporate workplaces have much higher rates), and the incidence of testing has risen markedly since the eighties. The rate of testing is highest in the South (56 percent of work sites polled), with the Midwest in second place (50 percent). The drug most likely to be detected—marijuana, which can be detected in urine for weeks—is also the most innocuous, while heroin and cocaine are generally undetectable three days after use. Prospective employees sometimes try to cheat the tests by consuming excessive amounts of liquids and taking diuretics and even masking substances available through the Internet.

who introduces himself as the manager, interviews me with about as much enthusiasm as if he were a clerk processing me for Medicare, the principal questions being what shifts can I work and when can I start. I mutter something about being woefully out of practice as a waitress, but he's already on to the uniform: I'm to show up tomorrow wearing black slacks and black shoes; he'll provide the rustcolored polo shirt with HEARTHSIDE embroidered on it, though I might want to wear my own shirt to get to work, ha ha. At the word "tomorrow," something between fear and indignation rises in my chest. I want to say, "Thank you for your time, sir, but this is just an experiment, you know, not my actual life."

So begins my career at the Hearthside, I shall call it, one small profit center within a global discount hotel chain, where for two weeks I work from 2:00 till 10:00 P.M. for $2.43 an hour plus tips.[3] In some futile bid for gentility, the management has barred employees from using the front door, so my first day I enter through the kitchen, where a red-faced man with shoulder-length blond hair is throwing frozen steaks against the wall and yelling, "Fuck this shit!" "That's just Jack," explains Gail, the wiry middle-aged waitress who is assigned to train me. "He's on the rag again"—a condition occasioned, in this instance, by the fact that the cook on the morning shift had forgotten to thaw out the steaks. For the next eight hours, I run after the agile Gail, absorbing bits of instruction along with fragments of personal tragedy. All food must be trayed, and the reason she's so tired today is that she woke up in a cold sweat thinking of her boyfriend, who killed himself recently in an upstate prison. No refills on lemonade. And the reason he was in prison is that a few DUIs caught up with him, that's all, could have happened to anyone. Carry the creamers to the table in a monkey bowl, never in your hand. And after he was gone she spent several months living in her truck, peeing in a plastic pee bottle and reading by candlelight at right, but you can't live in a truck in the summer, since you need to have the windows down, which means anything can get in, from mosquitoes on up.

At least Gail puts to rest any fears I had of appearing overqualified. From the first day on, I find that of all the things I have left behind, such as home and identity, what I miss the most is competence. Not that I have ever felt utterly competent in the writing business, in which one day's success augurs nothing at all for the next. But in my writing life, I at least have some notion of procedure: do the research, make the outline, rough out a draft, etc. As a server, though, I am beset by requests like bees: more iced tea here, ketchup over there, a to-go box for table fourteen, and where are the high chairs, anyway? Of the twenty-seven tables, up to six are usually mine at any time, though on slow afternoons or if Gail is off, I sometimes have the whole place to myself. There is the touch-screen computer-ordering system to master, which is, I suppose, meant to minimize server-cook contact, but in practice requires constant verbal fine-tuning: "That's gravy on the mashed, okay? None on the meatloaf," and so forth—while the cook scowls as if I were inventing these refinements just to tor-

13

14

---

[3]According to the Fair Labor Standards Act, employers are not required to pay "tipped employees," such as restaurant servers, more than $2.13 an hour in direct wages. However, if the sum of tips plus $2.13 an hour falls below the minimum wage, or $5.15 an hour, the employer is required to make up the difference. This fact was not mentioned by managers or otherwise publicized at either of the restaurants where I worked.

ment him. Plus, something I had forgotten in the years since I was eighteen: about a third of a server's job is "side work" that's invisible to customers—sweeping, scrubbing, slicing, refilling, and restocking. If it isn't all done, every little bit of it, you're going to face the 6:00 P.M. dinner rush defenseless and probably go down in flames. I screw up dozens of times at the beginning, sustained in my shame entirely by Gail's support—"It's okay, baby, everyone does that sometime"—because, to my total surprise and despite the scientific detachment I am doing my best to maintain, I care.

The whole thing would be a lot easier if I could just skate through it as Lily Tomlin   15
in one of her waitress skits, but I was raised by the absurd Booker T. Washingtonian precept that says: If you're going to do something, do it well. In fact, "well" isn't good enough by half. Do it better than anyone has ever done it before. Or so said my father, who must have known what he was talking about because he managed to pull himself, and us with him, up from the mile-deep copper mines of Butte to the leafy suburbs of the Northeast, ascending from boilermakers to martinis before booze beat out ambition. As in most endeavors I have encountered in my life, doing it "better than anyone" is not a reasonable goal. Still, when I wake up at 4:00 A.M. in my own cold sweat, I am not thinking about the writing deadlines I'm neglecting; I'm thinking about the table whose order I screwed up so that one of the boys didn't get his kiddie meal until the rest of the family had moved on to their Key Lime pies. That's the other powerful motivation I hadn't expected—the customers, or "patients," as I can't help thinking of them on account of the mysterious vulnerability that seems to have left them temporarily unable to feed themselves. After a few days at the Hearthside, I feel the service ethic kick in like a shot of oxytocin, the nurturance hormone. The plurality of my customers are hard-working locals—truck drivers, construction workers, even housekeepers from the attached hotel—and I want them to have the closest to a "fine dining" experience that the grubby circumstances will allow. No "you guys" for me; everyone over twelve is "sir" or "ma'am." I ply them with iced tea and coffee refills; I return, mid-meal, to inquire how everything is; I doll up their salads with chopped raw mushrooms, summer squash slices, or whatever bits of produce I can find that have survived their sojourn in the cold-storage room mold-free.

There is Benny, for example, a short, tight-muscled sewer repairman, who can-   16
not even think of eating until he has absorbed a half hour of air-conditioning and ice water. We chat about hyperthermia and electrolytes until he is ready to order some finicky combination like soup of the day, garden salad, and a side of grits. There are the German tourists who are so touched by my pidgin "Willkommen" and "Ist alles gut?" that they actually tip. (Europeans, spoiled by their trade-union-ridden, high-wage welfare states, generally do not know that they are supposed to tip. Some restaurants, the Hearthside included, allow servers to "grat" their foreign customers, or add a tip to the bill. Since this amount is added before the customers have a chance to tip or not tip, the practice amounts to an automatic penalty for imperfect English.) There are the two dirt-smudged lesbians, just off their construction shift, who are impressed enough by my suave handling of the fly in the piña colada that they take the time to praise me to Stu, the assistant manager. There's Sam, the kindly retired cop, who has to plug up his tracheotomy hole with one finger in order to force the cigarette smoke into his lungs.

Sometimes I play with the fantasy that I am a princess who, in penance for some 17 tiny transgression, has undertaken to feed each of her subjects by hand. But the non-princesses working with me are just as indulgent, even when this means flouting management rules—concerning, for example, the number of croutons that can go on a salad (six). "Put on all you want," Gail whispers, "as long as Stu isn't looking." She dips into her own tip money to buy biscuits and gravy for an out-of-work mechanic who's used up all his money on dental surgery, inspiring me to pick up the tab for his milk and pie. Maybe the same high levels of agape can be found throughout the "hospitality industry." I remember the poster decorating one of the apartments I looked at, which said "If you seek happiness for yourself you will never find it. Only when you seek happiness for others will it come to you," or words to that effect—an odd sentiment, it seemed to me at the time, to find in the dank one-room basement apartment of a bellhop at the Best Western. At the Hearthside, we utilize whatever bits of autonomy we have to ply our customers with the illicit calories that signal our love. It is our job as servers to assemble the salads and desserts, pouring the dressings and squirting the whipped cream. We also control the number of butter patties our customers get and the amount of sour cream on their baked potatoes. So if you wonder why Americans are so obese, consider the fact that waitresses both express their humanity and earn their tips through the covert distribution of fats.

Ten days into it, this is beginning to look like a livable lifestyle. I like Gail, 18 who is "looking at fifty" but moves so fast she can alight in one place and then another without apparently being anywhere between them. I clown around with Lionel, the teenage Haitian busboy, and catch a few fragments of conversation with Joan, the svelte fortyish hostess and militant feminist who is the only one of us who dares to tell Jack to shut the fuck up. I even warm up to Jack when, on a slow night and to make up for a particularly unwarranted attack on my abilities, or so I imagine, he tells me about his glory days as a young man at "coronary school"—or do you say "culinary"?—in Brooklyn, where he dated a knock-out Puerto Rican chick and learned everything there is to know about food. I finish up at 10:00 or 10:30, depending on how much side work I've been able to get done during the shift, and cruise home to the tapes I snatched up at random when I left my real home—Marianne Faithfull, Tracy Chapman, Enigma, King Sunny Ade, the Violent Femmes—just drained enough for the music to set my cranium resonating but hardly dead. Midnight snack is Wheat Thins and Monterey Jack, accompanied by cheap white wine on ice and whatever AMC has to offer. To bed by 1:30 or 2:00, up at 9:00 or 10:00, read for an hour while my uniform whirls around in the landlord's washing machine, and then it's another eight hours spent following Mao's central instruction, as laid out in the Little Red Book, which was: Serve the people.

I could drift along like this, in some dreamy proletarian idyll, except for two 19 things. One is management. If I have kept this subject on the margins thus far it is because I still flinch to think that I spent all those weeks under the surveillance of men (and later women) whose job it was to monitor my behavior for signs of sloth, theft, drug abuse, or worse. Not that managers and especially "assistant managers" in low-wage settings like this are exactly the class enemy. In the restaurant business, they are mostly former cooks or servers, still capable of pinch-hitting in the kitchen or on the floor, just as in hotels they are likely to be former clerks, and paid a salary of only about $400 a week. But everyone knows they have crossed over to the other side, which is, crudely put, corporate as opposed to human. Cooks want to prepare tasty meals; servers want to serve them graciously; but managers are there for only one reason—to make sure that money is made for some theoretical entity that exists far away in Chicago or New York, if a corporation can be said to have a physical existence at all. Reflecting on her career, Gail tells me ruefully that she had sworn, years ago, never to work for a corporation again. "They don't cut you no slack. You give and you give, and they take."

Managers can sit—for hours at a time if they want—but it's their job to see   20
that no one else ever does, even when there's nothing to do, and this is why, for servers, slow times can be as exhausting as rushes. You start dragging out each little chore, because if the manager on duty catches you in an idle moment, he will give you something far nastier to do. So I wipe, I clean, I consolidate ketchup bottles and recheck the cheesecake supply, even tour the tables to make sure the customer evaluation forms are all standing perkily in their places—wondering all the time how many calories I burn in these strictly theatrical exercises. When, on a particularly dead afternoon, Stu finds me glancing at a *USA Today* a customer has left behind, he assigns me to vacuum the entire floor with the broken vacuum cleaner that has a handle only two feet long, and the only way to do that without incurring orthopedic damage is to proceed from spot to spot on your knees.

On my first Friday at the Hearthside there is a "mandatory meeting for all restau-   21
rant employees," which I attend, eager for insight into our overall marketing strategy and the niche (your basic Ohio cuisine with a tropical twist?) we aim to inhabit. But there is no "we" at this meeting. Phillip, our top manager except for an occasional "consultant" sent out by corporate headquarters, opens it with a sneer: "The break room—it's disgusting. Butts in the ashtrays, newspapers lying around, crumbs." This windowless little room, which also houses the time clock for the entire hotel, is where we stash our bags and civilian clothes and take our half-hour meal breaks. But a break room is not a right, he tells us. It can be taken away. We should also know that the lockers in the break room and whatever is in them can be searched at any time. Then comes gossip; there has been gossip; gossip (which seems to mean employees talking among themselves) must stop. Off-duty employees are henceforth barred from eating at the restaurant, because "other servers gather around them and gossip." When Phillip has exhausted his agenda of rebukes, Joan complains about the condition of the ladies' room and I throw in my two bits about the vacuum cleaner. But I don't see any backup coming from my fellow servers, each of whom has subsided into her own personal funk; Gail, my role model, stares sorrowfully at a point six inches from her nose. The meeting ends when Andy, one of the cooks, gets up, muttering about breaking up his day off for this almighty bullshit.

Just four days later we are suddenly summoned into the kitchen at 3:30 P.M., even   22
though there are live tables on the floor. We all—about ten of us—stand around Phillip, who announces grimly that there has been a report of some "drug activity" on the night shift and that, as a result, we are now to be a "drug-free" workplace,

meaning that all new hires will be tested, as will possibly current employees on a random basis. I am glad that this part of the kitchen is so dark, because I find myself blushing as hard as if I had been caught toking up in the ladies' room myself: I haven't been treated this way—lined up in the corridor, threatened with locker searches, peppered with carelessly aimed accusations—since junior high school. Back on the floor, Joan cracks, "Next they'll be telling us we can't have sex on the job." When I ask Stu what happened to inspire the crackdown, he just mutters about "management decisions" and takes the opportunity to upbraid Gail and me for being too generous with the rolls. From now on there's to be only one per customer, and it goes out with the dinner, not with the salad. He's also been riding the cooks, prompting Andy to come out of the kitchen and observe—with the serenity of a man whose customary implement is a butcher knife—that "Stu has a death wish today."

Later in the evening, the gossip crystallizes around the theory that Stu is himself the drug culprit, that he uses the restaurant phone to order up marijuana and sends one of the late servers out to fetch it for him. The server was caught, and she may have ratted Stu out or at least said enough to cast some suspicion on him; thus accounting for his pissy behavior. Who knows? Lionel, the busboy, entertains us for the rest of the shift by standing just behind Stu's back and sucking deliriously on an imaginary joint.   23

The other problem, in addition to the less-than-nurturing management style, is that this job shows no sign of being financially viable. You might imagine, from a comfortable distance, that people who live, year in and year out, on $6 to $10 an hour have discovered some survival stratagems unknown to the middle class. But no. It's not hard to get my co-workers to talk about their living situations, because housing, in almost every case, is the principal source of disruption in their lives, the first thing they fill you in on when they arrive for their shifts. After a week, I have compiled the following survey: 24

- Gail is sharing a room in a well-known downtown flophouse for which she and a roommate pay about $250 a week. Her roommate, a male friend, has begun hitting on her, driving her nuts, but the rent would be impossible alone.
- Claude, the Haitian cook, is desperate to get out of the two-room apartment he shares with his girlfriend and two other, unrelated, people. As far as I can determine, the other Haitian men (most of whom only speak Creole) live in similarly crowded situations.
- Annette, a twenty-year-old server who is six months pregnant and has been abandoned by her boyfriend, lives with her mother, a postal clerk.
- Marianne and her boyfriend are paying $170 a week for a one-person trailer.
- Jack, who is, at $10 an hour, the wealthiest of us, lives in the trailer he owns, paying only the $400-a-month lot fee.
- The other white cook, Andy, lives on his dry-docked boat, which, as far as I can tell from his loving descriptions, can't be more than twenty feet long. He offers to take me out on it, once it's repaired, but the offer comes with inquiries as to my marital status, so I do not follow up on it.

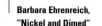

- Tina and her husband are paying $60 a night for a double room in a Days Inn. This is because they have no car and the Days Inn is within walking distance of the Hearthside. When Marianne, one of the breakfast servers, is tossed out of her trailer for subletting (which is against the trailer-park rules), she leaves her boyfriend and moves in with Tina and her husband.
- Joan, who had fooled me with her numerous and tasteful outfits (hostesses wear their own clothes), lives in a van she parks behind a shopping center at night and showers in Tina's motel room. The clothes are from thrift shops.[4]

It strikes me, in my middle-class solipsism, that there is gross improvidence in some of these arrangements. When Gail and I are wrapping silverware in napkins—the only task for which we are permitted to sit—she tells me she is thinking of escaping from her roommate by moving into the Days Inn herself. I am astounded: How can she even think of paying between $40 and $60 a day? But if I was afraid of sounding like a social worker, I come out just sounding like a fool. She squints at me in disbelief, "And where am I supposed to get a month's rent and a month's deposit for an apartment?" I'd been feeling pretty smug about my $500 efficiency, but of course it was made possible only by the $1,300 I had allotted myself for start-up costs when I began my low-wage life: $1,000 for the first month's rent and deposit, $100 for initial groceries and cash in my pocket, $200 stuffed away for emergencies. In poverty, as in certain propositions in physics, starting conditions are everything.

There are no secret economies that nourish the poor; on the contrary, there are a host of special costs. If you can't put up the two months' rent you need to secure an apartment, you end up paying through the nose for a room by the week. If you have only a room, with a hot plate at best, you can't save by cooking up huge lentil stews that can be frozen for the week ahead. You eat fast food, or the hot dogs and styrofoam cups of soup that can be microwaved in a convenience store. If you have no money for health insurance—and the Hearthside's niggardly plan kicks in only after three months—you go without routine care or prescription drugs and end up paying the price. Gail, for example, was fine until she ran out of money for estrogen pills. She is supposed to be on the company plan by now, but they claim to have lost her application form and need to begin the paperwork all over again. So she spends $9 per migraine pill to control the headaches she wouldn't have, she insists, if her estrogen supplements were covered. Similarly, Marianne's boyfriend lost his job as a roofer because he missed so much time after getting a cut on his foot for which he couldn't afford the prescribed antibiotic.

My own situation, when I sit down to assess it after two weeks of work, would not be much better if this were my actual life. The seductive thing about waitressing is that you don't have to wait for payday to feel a few bills in your pocket, and my tips usually cover meals and gas, plus something left over to stuff into the kitchen drawer I use as a bank. But as the tourist business slows in the summer heat, I sometimes leave work with only $20 in tips (the gross is higher, but servers share about 15 per-

25

26

27

[4]I could find no statistics on the number of employed people living in cars or vans, but according to the National Coalition for the Homeless's 1997 report "Myths and Facts About Homelessness," nearly one in five homeless people (in twenty-nine cities across the nation) is employed in a full- or part-time job.

cent of their tips with the busboys and bartenders). With wages included, this amounts to about the minimum wage of $5.15 an hour. Although the sum in the drawer is piling up, at the present rate of accumulation it will be more than a hundred dollars short of my rent when the end of the month comes around. Nor can I see any expenses to cut. True, I haven't gone the lentil-stew route yet, but that's because I don't have a large cooking pot, pot holders, or a ladle to stir with (which cost about $30 at Kmart, less at thrift stores), not to mention onions, carrots, and the indispensable bay leaf. I do make my lunch almost every day—usually some slow-burning, high-protein combo like frozen chicken patties with melted cheese on top and canned pinto beans on the side. Dinner is at the Hearthside, which offers its employees a choice of BLT, fish sandwich, or hamburger for only $2. The burger lasts longest, especially if it's heaped with gut-puckering jalapeños, but by midnight my stomach is growling again.

So unless I want to start using my car as a residence, I have to find a second, or alternative, job. I call all the hotels where I filled out housekeeping applications weeks ago—the Hyatt, Holiday Inn, Econo Lodge, HoJo's, Best Western, plus a half dozen or so locally run guesthouses. Nothing. Then I start making the rounds again, wasting whole mornings waiting for some assistant manager to show up, even dipping into places so creepy that the front-desk clerk greets you from behind bulletproof glass and sells pints of liquor over the counter. But either someone has exposed my real-life housekeeping habits—which are, shall we say, mellow—or I am at the wrong end of some infallible ethnic equation: most, but by no means all, of the working housekeepers I see on my job searches are African Americans, Spanish-speaking, or immigrants from the Central European post-Communist world, whereas servers are almost invariably white and monolingually English-speaking. When I finally get a positive response, I have been identified once again as server material. Jerry's, which is part of a well-known national family restaurant chain and physically attached here to another budget hotel chain, is ready to use me at once. The prospect is both exciting and terrifying, because, with about the same number of tables and counter seats, Jerry's attracts three or four times the volume of customers as the gloomy old Hearthside. 28

Picture a fat person's hell, and I don't mean a place with no food. Instead there is everything you might eat if eating had no bodily consequences—cheese fries, chicken-fried steaks, fudge-laden desserts—only here every bite must be paid for, one way or another, in human discomfort. The kitchen is a cavern, a stomach leading to the lower intestine that is the garbage and dishwashing area, from which issue bizarre smells combining the edible and the offal: creamy carrion, pizza barf, and that unique and enigmatic Jerry's scent—citrus fart. The floor is slick with spills, forcing us to walk through the kitchen with tiny steps, like Susan McDougal in leg irons. Sinks everywhere are clogged with scraps of lettuce, decomposing lemon wedges, waterlogged toast crusts. Put your hand down on any counter and you risk being stuck to it by the film of ancient syrup spills, and this is unfortunate, because hands are utensils here, used for scooping up lettuce onto salad plates, lifting out pie slices, and even moving hash browns from one plate to another. The regulation poster in the single unisex restroom admonishes us to wash our hands thoroughly and even offers 29 instructions for doing so, but there is always some vital substance missing—soap, paper towels, toilet paper—and I never find all three at once. You learn to stuff your pockets with napkins before going in there, and too bad about the customers, who must eat, though they don't realize this, almost literally out of our hands.

The break room typifies the whole situation: there is none, because there are no breaks at Jerry's. Fox six to eight hours in a row, you never sit except to pee. Actually, there are three folding chairs at a table immediately adjacent to the bathroom, but hardly anyone ever sits here, in the very rectum of the gastro-architectural system. Rather, the function of the peritoilet area is to house the ashtrays in which servers and dishwashers leave their cigarettes burning at all times, like votive candles, so that they don't have to waste time lighting up again when they dash back for a puff. Almost everyone smokes as if his or her pulmonary well-being depended on it— the multinational mélange of cooks, the Czech dishwashers, the servers, who are all American natives—creating an atmosphere in which oxygen is only an occasional pollutant. My first morning at Jerry's, when the hypoglycemic shakes set in, I complain to one of my fellow servers that I don't understand how she can go so long without food. "Well, I don't understand how you can go so long without a cigarette," she responds in a tone of reproach—because work is what you do for others; smoking is what you do for yourself. I don't know why the antismoking crusaders have never grasped the element of defiant self-nurturance that makes the habit so endearing to its victims—as if, in the American workplace, the only thing people have to call their own is the tumors they are nourishing and the spare moments they devote to feeding them.

Now, the Industrial Revolution is not an easy transition, especially when you have to zip through it in just a couple of days. I have gone from craft work straight into the factory, from the air-conditioned morgue of the Hearthside directly into the flames. Customers arrive in human waves, sometimes disgorged fifty at a time from their tour buses, peckish and whiny. Instead of two "girls" on the floor at once, there can be as many as six of us running around in our brilliant pink-and-orange Hawaiian shirts. Conversations, either with customers or fellow employees, seldom last more than twenty seconds at a time. On my first day, in fact, I am hurt by my sister servers' coldness. My mentor for the day is an emotionally uninflected twenty-three-year-old, and the others, who gossip a little among themselves about the real reason someone is out sick today and the size of the bail bond someone else has had to pay, ignore me completely. On my second day, I find out why. "Well, it's good to see you again," one of them says in greeting. "Hardly anyone comes back after the first day." I feel powerfully vindicated—a survivor—but it would take a long time, probably months, before I could hope to be accepted into this sorority.

I start out with the beautiful, heroic idea of handling the two jobs at once, and for two days I almost do it: the breakfast/lunch shift at Jerry's, which goes till 2:00, arriving at the Hearthside at 2:10, and attempting to hold out until 10:00. In the ten minutes between jobs, I pick up a spicy chicken sandwich at the Wendy's drive-through window, gobble it down in the car, and change from khaki slacks to black, from Hawaiian to rust polo. There is a problem, though. When during the 3:00 to 4:00 p.m. dead time I finally sit down to wrap silver, my flesh seems to bond to the

30

31

32

seat. I try to refuel with a purloined cup of soup, as I've seen Gail and Joan do dozens of times, but a manager catches me and hisses "No eating!" though there's not a customer around to be offended by the sight of food making contact with a server's lips. So I tell Gail I'm going to quit, and she hugs me and says she might just follow me to Jerry's herself.

But the chances of this are minuscule. She has left the flophouse and her annoying roommate and is back to living in her beat-up old truck. But guess what? she reports to me excitedly later that evening: Phillip has given her permission to park overnight in the hotel parking lot, as long as she keeps out of sight, and the parking lot should be totally safe, since it's patrolled by a hotel security guard! With the Hearthside offering benefits like that, how could anyone think of leaving?

Gail would have triumphed at Jerry's, I'm sure, but for me it's a crash course in exhaustion management. Years ago, the kindly fry cook who trained me to waitress at a Los Angeles truck stop used to say: Never make an unnecessary trip; if you don't have to walk fast, walk slow; if you don't have to walk, stand. But at Jerry's the effort of distinguishing necessary from unnecessary and urgent from whenever would itself be too much of an energy drain. The only thing to do is to treat each shift as a one-time-only emergency: you've got fifty starving people out there, lying scattered on the battlefield, so get out there and feed them! Forget that you will have to do this again tomorrow, forget that you will have to be alert enough to dodge the drunks on the drive home tonight—just burn, burn, burn! Ideally, at some point you enter what servers call "a rhythm" and psychologists term a "flow state," in which signals pass from the sense organs directly to the muscles, bypassing the cerebral cortex, and a Zen-like emptiness sets in. A male server from the Hearthside's morning shift tells me about the time he "pulled a triple"—three shifts in a row, all the way around the clock—and then got off and had a drink and met this girl, and maybe he shouldn't tell me this, but they had sex right then and there, and it was like, beautiful.

But there's another capacity of the neuromuscular system, which is pain. I start tossing back drugstore-brand ibuprofen pills as if they were vitamin C, four before each shift, because an old mouse-related repetitive-stress injury in my upper back has come back to full-spasm strength, thanks to the tray carrying. In my ordinary life, this level of disability might justify a day of ice packs and stretching. Here I comfort myself with the Aleve commercial in which the cute blue-collar guy asks: If you quit after working four hours, what would your boss say? And the not-so-cute blue-collar guy, who's lugging a metal beam on his back, answers: He'd fire me, that's what. But fortunately, the commercial tells us, we workers can exert the same kind of authority over our painkillers that our bosses exert over us. If Tylenol doesn't want to work for more than four hours, you just fire its ass and switch to Aleve.

True, I take occasional breaks from this life, going home now and then to catch up on e-mail and for conjugal visits (though I am careful to "pay" for anything I eat there), seeing The Truman Show with friends and letting them buy my ticket. And I still have those what-am-I-doing-here moments at work, when I get so homesick for the printed word that I obsessively reread the six-page menu. But as the days go by, my old life is beginning to look exceedingly strange. The e-mails and phone messages addressed to my former self come from a distant race of people with exotic concerns and far too much time on their hands. The neighborly market I used to cruise for produce now looks forbiddingly like a Manhattan yuppie emporium. And when I sit down one morning in my real home to pay bills from my past life, I am dazzled at the two- and three-figure sums owed to outfits like Club Body Tech and Amazon.com.

Management at Jerry's is generally calmer and more "professional" than at the Hearthside, with two exceptions. One is Joy, a plump, blowsy woman in her early thirties, who once kindly devoted several minutes to instructing me in the correct one-handed method of carrying trays but whose moods change disconcertingly from shift to shift and even within one. Then there's B.J., a.k.a. B.J.-the-bitch, whose contribution is to stand by the kitchen counter and yell, "Nita, your order's up, move it!" or, "Barbara, didn't you see you've got another table out there? Come on, girl!" Among other things, she is hated for having replaced the whipped-cream squirt cans with big plastic whipped-cream-filled baggies that have to be squeezed with both hands—because, reportedly, she saw or thought she saw employees trying to inhale the propellant gas from the squirt cans, in the hope that it might be nitrous oxide. On my third night, she pulls me aside abruptly and brings her face so close that it looks as if she's planning to butt me with her forehead. But instead of saying, "You're fired," she says, "You're doing fine." The only trouble is I'm spending time chatting with customers: "That's how they're getting you." Furthermore I am letting them "run me," which means harassment by sequential demands: you bring the ketchup and they decide they want extra Thousand Island; you bring that and they announce they now need a side of fries; and so on into distraction. Finally she tells me not to take her wrong. She tries to say things in a nice way, but you get into a mode, you know, because everything has to move so fast.[5]

I mumble thanks for the advice, feeling like I've just been stripped naked by the crazed enforcer of some ancient sumptuary law: No chatting for you, girl. No fancy service ethic allowed for the serfs. Chatting with customers is for the beautiful young college-educated servers in the downtown carpaccio joints, the kids who can make $70 to $100 a night. What had I been thinking? My job is to move orders from tables to kitchen and then trays from kitchen to tables. Customers are, in fact, the major obstacle to the smooth transformation of information into food and food into money—they are, in short, the enemy. And the painful thing is that I'm beginning to see it this way myself. There are the traditional asshole types—frat boys who down multiple Buds and then make a fuss because the steaks are so emaciated and the fries so sparse—as well as the variously impaired—due to age, diabetes, or literacy issues—who require patient nutritional counseling. The worst, for some reason, are the Visible Christians—like the ten-person table, all jolly and sanctified after Sunday-night service, who run me mercilessly and then leave me $1 on a $92 bill. Or the guy with

37

38

---

[5]In *Workers in a Lean World: Unions in the International Economy* (Verso, 1997). Kim Moody cites studies finding an increase in stress-related workplace injuries and illness between the mid-1980s and the early 1990s. He argues that rising stress levels reflect a new system of "management by stress," in which workers in a variety of industries are being squeezed to extract maximum productivity, to the detriment of their health.

the crucifixion T-shirt (SOMEONE TO LOOK UP TO) who complains that his baked potato is too hard and his iced tea too icy (I cheerfully fix both) and leaves no tip. As a general rule, people wearing crosses or WWJD? (What Would Jesus Do?) buttons look at us disapprovingly no matter what we do, as if they were confusing waitressing with Mary Magdalene's original profession.

I make friends, over time, with the other "girls" who work my shift: Nita, the 39 tattooed twenty-something who taunts us by going around saying brightly, "Have we started making money yet?" Ellen, whose teenage son cooks on the graveyard shift and who once managed a restaurant in Massachusetts but won't try out for management here because she prefers being a "common worker" and not "ordering people around." Easy-going fiftyish Lucy, with the raucous laugh, who limps toward the end of the shift because of something that has gone wrong with her leg, the exact nature of which cannot be determined without health insurance. We talk about the usual girl things—men, children, and the sinister allure of Jerry's chocolate peanut-butter cream pie—though no one, I notice, ever brings up anything potentially expensive, like shopping or movies. As at the Hearthside, the only recreation ever referred to is partying, which requires little more than some beer, a joint, and a few close friends. Still, no one here is homeless, or cops to it anyway, thanks usually to a working husband or boyfriend. All in all, we form a reliable mutual-support group: If one of us is feeling sick or overwhelmed, another one will "bev" a table or even carry trays for her. If one of us is off sneaking a cigarette or a pee,[6] the others will do their best to conceal her absence from the enforcers of corporate rationality.

But my saving human connection—my oxytocin receptor, as it were—is George, 40 the nineteen-year-old, fresh-off-the-boat Czech dishwasher. We get to talking when he asks me, tortuously, how much cigarettes cost at Jerry's. I do my best to explain that they cost over a dollar more here than at a regular store and suggest that he just take one from the half-filled packs that are always lying around on the break table. But that would be unthinkable. Except for the one tiny earring signaling his allegiance to some vaguely alternative point of view, George is a perfect straight arrow—crew-cut, hardworking, and hungry for eye contact. "Czech Republic," I ask, "or Slovakia?" and he seems delighted that I know the difference. "Václav Havel," I try. "Velvet Revolution, Frank Zappa?" "Yes, yes, 1989," he says, and I realize we are talking about history.

My project is to teach George English. "How are you today, George?" I say at the 41 start of each shift. "I am good, and how are you today, Barbara?" I learn that he is not paid by Jerry's but by the "agent" who shipped him over—$5 an hour, with the agent getting the dollar or so difference between that and what Jerry's pays dishwashers. I learn also that he shares an apartment with a crowd of other Czech "dishers," as he

[6]Until April 1998, there was no federally mandated right to bathroom breaks. According to Marc Linder and Ingrid Nygaard, authors of *Void Where Prohibited: Rest Breaks and the Right to Urinate on Company Time* (Cornell University Press, 1997), "The right to rest and void at work is not high on the list of social or political causes supported by professional or executive employees, who enjoy personal workplace liberties that millions of factory workers can only daydream about. . . . While we were dismayed to discover that workers lacked an acknowledged legal right to void at work, [the workers] were amazed by outsiders' naive belief that their employers would permit them to perform this basic bodily function when necessary. . . . A factory worker, not allowed a break for six-hour stretches, voided into pads worn inside her uniform; and a kindergarten teacher in a school without aides had to take all twenty children with her to the bathroom and line them up outside the stall door when she voided."

calls them, and that he cannot sleep until one of them goes off for his shift, leaving a vacant bed. We are having one of our ESL sessions late one afternoon when B.J. catches us at it and orders "Joseph" to take up the rubber mats on the floor near the dishwashing sinks and mop underneath. "I thought your name was George," I say loud enough for B.J. to hear as she strides off back to the counter. Is she embarrassed? Maybe a little, because she greets me back at the counter with "George, Joseph— there are so many of them!" I say nothing, neither nodding nor smiling, and for this I am punished later when I think I am ready to go and she announces that I need to roll fifty more sets of silverware and isn't it time I mixed up a fresh four-gallon batch of blue-cheese dressing? May you grow old in this place, B.J., is the curse I beam out at her when I am finally permitted to leave. May the syrup spills glue your feet to the floor.

I make the decision to move closer to Key West. First, because of the drive. Second and third, also because of the drive: gas is eating up $4 to $5 a day, and although Jerry's is as high-volume as you can get, the tips average only 10 percent, and not just for a newbie like me. Between the base pay of $2.15 an hour and the obligation to share tips with the busboys and dishwashers, we're averaging only about $7.50 an hour. Then there is the $30 I had to spend on the regulation tan slacks worn by Jerry's servers—a setback it could take weeks to absorb. (I had combed the town's two downscale department stores hoping for something cheaper but decided in the end that these marked-down Dockers, originally $49, were more likely to survive a daily washing.) Of my fellow servers, everyone who lacks a working husband or boyfriend seems to have a second job: Nita does something at a computer eight hours a day; another welds. Without the forty-five-minute commute, I can picture myself working two jobs and having the time to shower between them. 42

So I take the $500 deposit I have coming from my landlord, the $400 I have earned toward the next month's rent, plus the $200 reserved for emergencies, and use the $1,100 to pay the rent and deposit on trailer number 46 in the Overseas Trailer Park, a mile from the cluster of budget hotels that constitute Key West's version of an industrial park. Number 46 is about eight feet in width and shaped like a barbell inside, with a narrow region—because of the sink and the stove—separating the bedroom from what might optimistically be called the "living" area, with its two-person table and half-sized couch. The bathroom is so small my knees rub against the shower stall when I sit on the toilet; and you can't just leap out of the bed, you have to climb down to the foot of it in order to find a patch of floor space to stand on. Outside, I am within a few yards of a liquor store, a bar that advertises "free beer tomorrow," a convenience store, and a Burger King—but no supermarket or, alas, laundromat. By reputation, the Overseas park is a nest of crime and crack, and I am hoping at least for some vibrant, multicultural street life. But desolation rules night and day, except for a thin stream of pedestrian traffic heading for their jobs at the Sheraton or 7-Eleven. There are not exactly people here but what amounts to canned labor, being preserved from the heat between shifts. 43

In line with my reduced living conditions, a new form of ugliness arises at Jerry's. First we are confronted—via an announcement on the computers through which we 44 input orders—with the new rule that the hotel bar is henceforth off-limits to restaurant employees. The culprit, I learn through the grapevine, is the ultra-efficient gal who trained me—another trailer-home dweller and a mother of three. Something had set her off one morning, so she slipped out for a nip and returned to the floor impaired. This mostly hurts Ellen, whose habit it is to free her hair from its rubber band and drop by the bar for a couple of Zins before heading home at the end of the shift, but all of us feel the chill. Then the next day, when I go for straws, for the first time I find the dry-storage room locked. Ted, the portly assistant manager who opens it for me, explains that he caught one of the dishwashers attempting to steal something, and, unfortunately, the miscreant will be with us until a replacement can be found—hence the locked door. I neglect to ask what he had been trying to steal, but Ted tells me who he is—the kid with the buzz cut and the earring. You know, he's back there right now.

I wish I could say I rushed back and confronted George to get his side of the story. I wish I could say I stood up to Ted and insisted that George be given a translator and allowed to defend himself, or announced that I'd find a lawyer who'd handle the case pro bono. The mystery to me is that there's not much worth stealing in the dry-storage room, at least not in any fenceable quantity: "Is Gyorgi here, and am having 200—maybe 250—ketchup packets. What do you say?" My guess is that he had taken—if he had taken anything at all—some Saltines or a can of cherry-pie mix, and that the motive for taking it was hunger.   45

So why didn't I intervene? Certainly not because I was held back by the kind of moral paralysis that can pass as journalistic objectivity. On the contrary, something new—something loathsome and servile—had infected me, along with the kitchen odors that I could still sniff on my bra when I finally undressed at night. In real life I am moderately brave, but plenty of brave people shed their courage in concentration camps, and maybe something similar goes on in the infinitely more congenial milieu of the low-wage American workplace. Maybe, in a month or two more at Jerry's, I might have regained my crusading spirit. Then again, in a month or two I might have turned into a different person altogether—say, the kind of person who would have turned George in.   46

But this is not something I am slated to find out. When my month-long plunge into poverty is almost over, I finally land my dream job—housekeeping. I do this by walking into the personnel office of the only place I figure I might have some credibility, the hotel attached to Jerry's, and confiding urgently that I have to have a second job if I am to pay my rent and, no, it couldn't be front-desk clerk. "All right," the personnel lady fairly spits, "So it's housekeeping," and she marches me back to meet Maria, the housekeeping manager, a tiny, frenetic Hispanic woman who greets me as "babe" and hands me a pamphlet emphasizing the need for a positive attitude. The hours are nine in the morning till whenever, the pay is $6.10 an hour, and there's one week of vacation a year. I don't have to ask about health insurance once I meet Carlotta, the middle-aged African-American woman who will be training me. Carla, as she tells me to call her, is missing all of her top front teeth.   47

On that first day of housekeeping and last day of my entire project—although I don't yet know it's the last—Carla is in a foul mood. We have been given nine-   48 teen rooms to clean, most of them "checkouts," as opposed to "stay-overs," that require the whole enchilada of bed-stripping, vacuuming, and bathroom-scrubbing. When one of the rooms that had been listed as a stay-over turns out to be a check-out, Carla calls Maria to complain, but of course to no avail. "So make up the mother-fucker," Carla orders me, and I do the beds while she sloshes around the bathroom. For four hours without a break I strip and remake beds, taking about four and a half minutes per queen-sized bed, which I could get down to three if there were any rea-son to. We try to avoid vacuuming by picking up the larger specks by hand, but often there is nothing to do but drag the monstrous vacuum cleaner—it weighs about thirty pounds—off our cart and try to wrestle it around the floor. Sometimes Carla hands me the squirt bottle of "BAM" (an acronym for something that begins, ominously, with "butyric"; the rest has been worn off the label) and lets me do the bathrooms. No service ethic challenges me here to new heights of performance. I just concen-trate on removing the pubic hairs from the bathtubs, or at least the dark ones that I can see.

I had looked forward to the breaking-and-entering aspect of cleaning the stay-overs, the chance to examine the secret, physical existence of strangers. But the con-tents of the rooms are always banal and surprisingly neat—zipped up shaving kits, shoes lined up against the wall (there are no closets), flyers for snorkeling trips, maybe an empty wine bottle or two. It is the TV that keeps us going, from *Jerry* to *Sally* to *Hawaii Five-O* and then on to the soaps. If there's something especially arresting, like "Won't Take No for an Answer" on *Jerry,* we sit down on the edge of a bed and gig-gle for a moment as if this were a pajama party instead of a terminally dead-end job. The soaps are the best, and Carla turns the volume up full blast so that she won't miss anything from the bathroom or while the vacuum is on. In room 503, Marcia confronts Jeff about Lauren. In 505, Lauren taunts poor cuckolded Marcia. In 511, Helen offers Amanda $10,000 to stop seeing Eric, prompting Carla to emerge from the bathroom to study Amanda's troubled face. "You take it, girl," she advises. "I would for sure." 49

The tourists' rooms that we clean and, beyond them, the far more expensively appointed interiors in the soaps, begin after a while to merge. We have entered a better world—a world of comfort where every day is a day off, waiting to be filled up with sexual intrigue. We, however, are only gate-crashers in this fantasy, forced to pay for our presence with backaches and perpetual thirst. The mirrors, and there are far too many of them in hotel rooms, contain the kind of person you would normally find pushing a shopping cart down a city street—bedraggled, dressed in a damp hotel polo shirt two sizes too large, and with sweat dribbling down her chin like drool. I am enor-mously relieved when Carla announces a half-hour meal break, but my appetite fades when I see that the bag of hot-dog rolls she has been carrying around on out cart is not trash salvaged from a checkout but what she has brought for her lunch. 50

When I request permission to leave at about 3:30, another housekeeper warns me that no one has so far succeeded in combining housekeeping at the hotel with serving at Jerry's: "Some kid did it once for five days, and you're no kid." With that helpful information in mind, I rush back to number 46, down four Advils (the name brand this time), shower, stooping to fit into the stall, and attempt to compose myself 51 for the oncoming shift. So much for what Marx termed the "reproduction of labor power," meaning the things a worker has to do just so she'll be ready to work again. The only unforeseen obstacle to the smooth transition from job to job is that my tan Jerry's slacks, which had looked reasonably clean by 40-watt bulb last night when I handwashed my Hawaiian shirt, prove by daylight to be mottled with ketchup and ranch-dressing stains. I spend most of my hour-long break between jobs attempting to remove the edible portions with a sponge and then drying the slacks over the hood of my car in the sun.

I can do this two-job thing, is my theory, if I can drink enough caffeine and avoid getting distracted by George's ever more obvious suffering.[7] The first few days after being caught he seemed not to understand the trouble he was in, and our chirpy little conversations had continued. But the last couple of shifts he's been listless and unshaven, and tonight he looks like the ghost we all know him to be, with dark half-moons hanging from his eyes. At one point, when I am briefly immobilized by the task of filling little paper cups with sour cream for baked potatoes, he comes over and looks as if he'd like to explore the limits of our shared vocabulary, but I am called to the floor for a table. I resolve to give him all my tips that night and to hell with the experiment in low-wage money management. At eight, Ellen and I grab a snack together standing at the mephitic end of the kitchen counter, but I can only manage two or three mozzarella sticks and lunch had been a mere handful of McNuggets. I am not tired at all, I assure myself, though it may be that there is simply no more "I" left to do the tiredness monitoring. What I would see, if I were more alert to the situation, is that the forces of destruction are already massing against me. There is only one cook on duty, a young man named Jesus ("Hay-Sue," that is) and he is new to the job. And there is Joy, who shows up to take over in the middle of the shift, wearing high heels and a long, clingy white dress and fuming as if she'd just been stood up in some cocktail bar.

Then it comes, the perfect storm. Four of my tables fill up at once. Four tables is nothing for me now, but only so long as they are obligingly staggered. As I bev table 27, tables 25, 28, and 24 are watching enviously. As I bev 25, 24 glowers because their bevs haven't even been ordered. Twenty-eight is four yuppyish types, meaning everything on the side and agonizing instructions as to the chicken Caesars. Twenty-five is a middle-aged black couple, who complain, with some justice, that the iced tea isn't fresh and the tabletop is sticky. But table 24 is the meteorological event of the century: ten British tourists who seem to have made the decision to absorb the American experience entirely by mouth. Here everyone has at least two drinks—iced tea and milk shake, Michelob and water (with lemon slice, please)—and a huge promiscuous orgy of breakfast specials, mozz sticks, chicken strips, quesadillas, burgers with cheese and without, sides of hash browns with cheddar, with onions, with gravy, seasoned fries, plain fries, banana splits. Poor Jesus! Poor me! Because when I arrive with their first tray of food—after three prior trips just to refill bevs—Princess Di refuses to eat her chicken strips with her pancake-and-sausage

52

53

---

[7] In 1996, the number of persons holding two or more jobs averaged 7.8 million, or 6.2 percent of the workforce. It was about the same rate for men and for women (6.1 versus 6.2), though the kinds of jobs differ by gender. About two-thirds of multiple jobholders work one job full-time and the other part-time. Only a heroic minority—4 percent of men and 2 percent of women—work two full-time jobs simultaneously. (From John F. Stinson Jr., "New Data on Multiple Jobholding Available from the CPS," in the Monthly Labor Review, March 1997.)

special, since, as she now reveals, the strips were meant to be an appetizer. Maybe the others would have accepted their meals, but Di, who is deep into her third Michelob, insists that everything else go back while they work on their "starters." Meanwhile, the yuppies are waving me down for more decaf and the black couple looks ready to summon the NAACP.

Much of what happened next is lost in the fog of war. Jesus starts going under. The little printer on the counter in front of him is spewing out orders faster than he can rip them off, much less produce the meals. Even the invincible Ellen is ashen from stress. I bring table 24 their reheated main courses, which they immediately reject as either too cold or fossilized by the microwave. When I return to the kitchen with their trays (three trays in three trips), Joy confronts me with arms akimbo: "What is this?" She means the food—the plates of rejected pancakes, hash browns in assorted flavors, toasts, burgers, sausages, eggs. "Uh, scrambled with cheddar," I try, "and that's . . ." "NO," she screams in my face. "Is it a traditional, a super-scramble, an eye-opener?" I pretend to study my check for a clue, but entropy has been up to its tricks, not only on the plates but in my head, and I have to admit that the original order is beyond reconstruction. "You don't know an eye-opener from a traditional?" she demands in outage. All I know, in fact, is that my legs have lost interest in the current venture and have announced their intention to fold. I am saved by a yuppie (mercifully not one of mine) who chooses this moment to charge into the kitchen to bellow that his food is twenty-five minutes late. Joy screams at him to get the hell out of her kitchen, please, and then turns on Jesus in a fury, hurling an empty tray across the room for emphasis. 54

I leave. I don't walk out, I just leave. I don't finish my side work or pick up my credit-card tips, if any, at the cash register or, of course, ask Joy's permission to go. And the surprising thing is that you *can* walk out without permission, that the door opens, that the thick tropical night air parts to let me pass, that my car is still parked where I left it. There is no vindication in this exit, no fuck-you surge of relief, just an overwhelming, dank sense of failure pressing down on me and the entire parking lot. I had gone into this venture in the spirit of science, to test a mathematical proposition, but somewhere along the line, in the tunnel vision imposed by long shifts and relentless concentration, it became a test of myself, and clearly I have failed. Not only had I flamed out as a housekeeper/server, I had even forgotten to give George my tips, and, for reasons perhaps best known to hardworking, generous people like Gail and Ellen, this hurts. I don't cry, but I am in a position to realize, for the first time in many years, that the tear ducts still there, and still capable of doing their job. 55

When I moved out of the trailer park, I gave the key to number 46 to Gail and arranged for my deposit to be transferred to her. She told me that Joan is still living in her van and that Stu had been fired from the Hearthside. I never found out what happened to George. 56

In one month, I had earned approximately $1,040 and spent $517 on food, gas, toiletries, laundry, phone, and utilities. If I had remained in my $500 efficiency, I would have been able to pay the rent and have $22 left over (which is $78 less than the cash I had in my pocket at the start of the month). During this time I bought no clothing except for the required slacks and no prescription drugs or medical care (I did finally buy some 57 vitamin B to compensate for the lack of vegetables in my diet). Perhaps I could have saved a little on food if I had gotten to a supermarket more often, instead of convenience stores, but it should be noted that I lost almost four pounds in four weeks, on a diet weighted heavily toward burgers and fries.

How former welfare recipients and single mothers will (and do) survive in the low-wage workforce, I cannot imagine. Maybe they will figure out how to condense their lives—including child-raising, laundry, romance, and meals—into the couple of hours between full-time jobs. Maybe they will take up residence in their vehicles, if they have one. All I know is that I couldn't hold two jobs and I couldn't make enough money to live on with one. And I had advantages unthinkable to many of the long-term poor— health, stamina, a working car, and no children to care for and support. Certainly nothing in my experience contradicts the conclusion of Kathryn Edin and Laura Lein, in their recent book *Making Ends Meet: How Single Mothers Survive Welfare and Low-Wage Work*, that low-wage work actually involves more hardship and deprivation than life at the mercy of the welfare state. In the coming months and years, economic conditions for the working poor are bound to worsen, even without the almost inevitable recession. As mentioned earlier, the influx of former welfare recipients into the low-skilled workforce will have a depressing effect on both wages and the number of jobs available. A general economic downturn will only enhance these effects, and the working poor will of course be facing it without the slight, but nonetheless often saving, protection of welfare as a backup.   58

The thinking behind welfare reform was that even the humblest jobs are morally uplifting and psychologically buoying. In reality they are likely to be fraught with insult and stress. But I did discover one redeeming feature of the most abject low-wage work— the camaraderie of people who are, in almost all cases, far too smart and funny and caring for the work they do and the wages they're paid. The hope, of course, is that someday these people will come to know what they're worth, and take appropriate action.   59

Gender and Cultural Studies

Margaret Atwood (1939–) studied at the University of Toronto (B.A. 1961), Radcliffe College (M.A. 1962), and did graduate work at Harvard University (1962–63, 1965–67). She began her career as a lecturer at the University of British Columbia in Vancouver and at Williams University in Montreal, and was an editor at House of Anansi Press. Since 1972, she has been a writer-in-residence at the University of Toronto (1972-73), the University of Alabama, Tuscaloosa (1985), New York University (1986), and Macquarie University, Australia (1987). She is a member of PEN, the Royal Society of Canada, and the American Academy of Arts and Sciences, and has received numerous awards and honorary degrees for her work. She is a prolific writer; her work includes novels, poetry, short stories, nonfiction, and radio and television plays. A few of her best-known books are the novels *The Edible Women* (1969), *Surfacing* (1972), *The Handmaid's Tale* (1985), and *Cat's Eye* (1988), and the short story collections *Dancing Girls and Other Stories* (1977) and *Bluebeard's Egg and Other Stories* (1983). Atwood's fictional works often blend fiction, history, science fiction, the gothic, and realism; her nonfiction works tend to be acerbic political pieces with a decidedly feminist stance. Atwood is one of the few Canadian authors to enjoy a widespread popularity in the United States; in Canada she has achieved celebrity status.

The Female Body

Margaret Atwood

> . . . entirely devoted to the subject of "The Female Body." Knowing how well you have written on this topic . . . this capacious topic . . .
> —letter from *Michigan Quarterly Review*

1.

I agree, it's a hot topic. But only one? Look around, there's a wide range. Take my own, for instance.   1

I get up in the morning. My topic feels like hell. I sprinkle it with water, brush parts of it, rub it with towels, powder it, add lubricant. I dump in the fuel and away goes my topic, my topical topic, my controversial topic, my capacious topic, my limping topic, my nearsighted topic, my topic with back problems, my badly behaved topic, my vulgar topic, my outrageous topic, my aging topic, my topic that is out of the question and anyway still can't spell, in its oversized coat and worn winter boots, scuttling along the sidewalk as if it were flesh and blood, hunting for what's out there, an avocado, an alderman, an adjective, hungry as ever.   2

2.

The basic Female Body comes with the following accessories: garter belt, panti-girdle, crinoline, camisole, bustle, brassiere, stomacher, chemise, virgin zone, spike heels, nose ring, veil, kid gloves, fishnet stockings, fichu, bandeau, Merry   3

Widow, weepers, chokers, barrettes, bangles, beads, lorgnette, feather boa, basic black, compact, Lycra stretch one-piece with modesty panel, designer peignoir, flannel nightie, lace teddy, bed, head.

3.

The Female Body is made of transparent plastic and lights up when you plug it in. 4 You press a button to illuminate the different systems. The circulatory system is red, for the heart and arteries, purple for the veins; the respiratory system is blue; the lymphatic system is yellow; the digestive system is green, with liver and kidneys in aqua. The nerves are done in orange and the brain is pink. The skeleton, as you might expect, is white.

The reproductive system is optional, and can be removed. It comes with or 5 without a miniature embryo. Parental judgment can thereby be exercised. We do not wish to frighten or offend.

4.

He said, I won't have one of those things in the house. It gives a young girl a false 6 notion of beauty, not to mention anatomy. If a real woman was built like that she'd fall on her face.

She said, If we don't let her have one like all the other girls she'll feel singled 7 out. It'll become an issue. She'll long for one and she'll long to turn into one. Repression breeds sublimation. You know that.

He said, It's not just the pointy plastic tits, it's the wardrobes. The wardrobes 8 and that stupid male doll, what's his name, the one with the underwear glued on.

She said, Better to get it over with when she's young. He said, All right, but 9 don't let me see it.

She came whizzing down the stairs, thrown like a dart. She was stark naked. 10 Her hair had been chopped off, her head was turned back to front, she was missing some toes and she'd been tattooed all over her body with purple ink in a scrollwork design. She hit the potted azalea, trembled there for a moment like a botched angel, and fell.

He said, I guess we're safe. 11

5.

The Female Body has many uses. It's been used as a door knocker, a bottle opener, as 12 a clock with a ticking belly, as something to hold up lampshades, as a nutcracker, just squeeze the brass legs together and out comes your nut. It bears torches, lifts victorious wreaths, grows copper wings and raises aloft a ring of neon stars; whole buildings rest on its marble heads.

It sells cars, beer, shaving lotion, cigarettes, hard liquor; it sells diet plans and 13 diamonds, and desire in tiny crystal bottles. Is this the face that launched a thousand products? You bet it is, but don't get any funny big ideas, honey, that smile is a dime a dozen.

It does not merely sell, it is sold. Money flows into this country or that country, 14
flies in, practically crawls in, suitful after suitful, lured by all those hairless pre-teen
legs. Listen, you want to reduce the national debt, don't you? Aren't you patriotic?
That's the spirit. That's my girl.

She's a natural resource, a renewable one luckily, because those things wear out 15
so quickly. They don't make 'em like they used to. Shoddy goods.

6.

One and one equals another one. Pleasure in the female is not a requirement. 16
Pair-bonding is stronger in geese. We're not talking about love, we're talking about
biology. That's how we all got here, daughter.

Snails do it differently. They're hermaphrodites, and work in threes.   17

7.

Each Female Body contains a female brain. Handy. Makes things work. Stick pins in 18
it and you get amazing results. Old popular songs. Short circuits. Bad dreams.

Anyway: each of these brains has two halves. They're joined together by a thick 19
cord; neural pathways flow from one to the other, sparkles of electric information
washing to and from. Like light on waves. Like a conversation. How does a woman
know? She listens. She listens in.

The male brain, now, that's a different matter. Only a thin connection. Space 20
over here, time over there, music and arithmetic in their own sealed compartments.
The right brain doesn't know what the left brain is doing. Good for aiming though,
for hitting the target when you pull the trigger. What's the target? Who's the target?
Who cares? What matters is hitting it. That's the male brain for you. Objective.

This is why men are so sad, why they feel so cut off, why they think of them- 21
selves as orphans cast adrift, footloose and stringless in the deep void. What void?
she asks. What are you talking about? The void of the universe, he says, and she says
Oh and looks out the window and tries to get a handle on it, but it's no use, there's
too much going on, too many rustlings in the leaves, too many voices, so she says,
Would you like a cheese sandwich, a piece of cake, a cup of tea? And he grinds his
teeth because she doesn't understand, and wanders off, not just alone but Alone, lost
in the dark, lost in the skull, searching for the other half, the twin who could
complete him.

Then it comes to him: he's lost the Female Body! Look, it shines in the gloom, 22
far ahead, a vision of wholeness, ripeness, like a giant melon, like an apple, like a
metaphor for "breast" in a bad sex novel; it shines like a balloon, like a foggy noon, a
watery moon, shimmering in its egg of light.

Catch it. Put it in a pumpkin, in a high tower, in a compound, in a chamber, in 23
a house, in a room. Quick, stick a leash on it, a lock, a chain, some pain, settle it
down, so it can never get away from you again.

Margaret Atwood (1939–) studied at the University of Toronto (B.A. 1961), Radcliffe College (M.A. 1962), and did graduate work at Harvard University (1962–63, 1965–67). She began her career as a lecturer at the University of British Columbia in Vancouver and at Williams University in Montreal, and was an editor at House of Anansi Press. Since 1972, she has been a writer-in-residence at the University of Toronto (1972-73), the University of Alabama, Tuscaloosa (1985), New York University (1986), and Macquarie University, Australia (1987). She is a member of PEN, the Royal Society of Canada, and the American Academy of Arts and Sciences, and has received numerous awards and honorary degrees for her work. She is a prolific writer; her work includes novels, poetry, short stories, nonfiction, and radio and television plays. A few of her best-known books are the novels *The Edible Women* (1969), *Surfacing* (1972), *The Handmaid's Tale* (1985), and *Cat's Eye* (1988), and the short story collections *Dancing Girls and Other Stories* (1977) and *Bluebeard's Egg and Other Stories* (1983). Atwood's fictional works often blend fiction, history, science fiction, the gothic, and realism; her nonfiction works tend to be acerbic political pieces with a decidedly feminist stance. Atwood is one of the few Canadian authors to enjoy a widespread popularity in the United States; in Canada she has achieved celebrity status.

Fiction: Happy Endings

Margaret Atwood

A

John and Mary fall in love and get married. They both have worthwhile and remunerative jobs which they find stimulating and challenging. They buy a charming house. Real estate values go up. Eventually, when they can afford live-in help, they have two children, to whom they are devoted. The children turn out well. John and Mary have a stimulating and challenging sex life and worthwhile friends. They go on fun vacations together. They retire. They both have hobbies which they find stimulating and challenging. Eventually they die. This is the end of the story.   1

B

Mary falls in love with John but John doesn't fall in love with Mary. He merely uses her body for selfish pleasure and ego gratification of a tepid kind. He comes to her apartment twice a week and she cooks him dinner, you'll notice that he doesn't even consider her worth the price of a dinner out, and after he's eaten the dinner he fucks her and after that he falls asleep; while, she does the dishes so he won't think she's untidy, having all those dirty dishes lying around, and puts on fresh lipstick so she'll look good when he wakes up, but when he wakes up he doesn't even notice, he puts on his socks and his shorts and his pants and his shirt and his tie and his shoes, the reverse order from the one in which he took them off. He doesn't take off Mary's clothes, she takes them off herself, she acts as if she's dying for it every time,   2 not because she likes sex exactly, she doesn't but she wants John to think she does because if they do it often enough surely he'll get used to her, he'll come to depend on her and they will get married, but John goes out the door with hardly so much as a good-night and three days later he turns up at six o'clock and they do the whole thing over again.

Mary gets run down. Crying is bad for your face everyone knows that and so does Mary but she can't stop. People at work notice. Her friends tell her John is a rat, a pig, a dog, he isn't good enough for her, but she can't believe it. Inside John, she thinks is another John, who is much nicer. This other John will emerge like a butterfly from a cocoon, a Jack from a box, a pit from a prune if the first John is only squeezed hard enough.

One evening John complains about the food. He has never complained about the food before. Mary is hurt.

Her friends tell her they've seen him in a restaurant with another woman, whose name is Madge. It's not even Madge that finally gets to Mary: it's the restaurant. John has never taken Mary to a restaurant. Mary collects all the sleeping pills and aspirins she can find, and takes them and half a bottle of sherry. You can see what kind of a woman she is by the fact that it's not even whiskey. She leaves a note for John. She hopes he'll discover her and get her to the hospital in time and repent and then they can get married, but this fails to happen and she dies.

John marries Madge and everything continues as in A.

C

John, who is an older man, falls in love with Mary, and Mary, who is only twenty-two, feels sorry for him because he's worried about his hair falling out. She sleeps with him even though she's not in love with him. She met him at work. She's in love with someone called James, who is twenty-two also and not yet ready to settle down.

John on the contrary settled down a long time ago: this is what is bothering him. John has a steady respectable job and is getting ahead in his field, but Mary isn't impressed by him, she's impressed by James, who has a motorcycle, being free. Freedom isn't the same for girls, so in the meantime Mary spends Thursday evenings with John. Thursdays are the only days John can get away.

John is married to a woman named Madge and they have two children, a charming house which they bought just before the real estate values went up, and hobbies which they find stimulating and challenging, when they have the time. John tells Mary how important she is to him, but of course he can't leave his wife because a commitment is a commitment. He goes on about this more than is necessary and Mary finds it boxing, but older men can keep it up longer so on the whole she has a fairly good time.

One day James breezes in on his motorcycle with some top grade California hybrid and James and Mary get higher than you'd believe possible and they climb into bed. Everything becomes very underwater, but along comes John, who has a key to Mary's apartment. He finds them stoned and entwined. He's hardly in any position to be jealous, considering Madge, but nevertheless he's overcome with despair. Finally he's middle-aged, in two years he'll be bald as an egg and he can't stand it. He purchases a handgun, saying he needs it for target practice—this is the thin part of the plot, but it can be dealt with later—and shoots the two of them and himself.

Madge, after a suitable period of mourning, marries an understanding man 11 called Fred and everything continues as in A, but under different names.

D

Fred and Madge have no problems. They get along exceptionally well and are good 12 at working out any little difficulties that may arise. But their charming house is by the seashore and one day a giant tidal wave approaches. Real estate values go down. The rest of the story is about what caused the tidal wave and how they escape from it. They do, though thousands drown. Some of the story is about how the thousands drown, but Fred and Madge are virtuous and lucky. Finally on high ground they clasp each other, wet and dripping and grateful, and continue as in A.

E

Yes, but Fred has a bad heart. The rest of the story is about how kind and under- 13 standing they both are until Fred dies. Then Madge devotes herself to charity work until the end of A. If you like, it can be "Madge," "cancer," "guilty and confused," and "birdwatching."

F

If you think this is all too bourgeois, make John a revolutionary and Mary a coun- 14 terespionage agent and see how far that gets you. You'll still end up with A, though in between you may get a lustful brawling saga of passionate involvement, a chroni-cle of our times, sort of.

You'll have to face it, the endings are the same however you slice it. Don't be 15 deluded by any other endings, they're all fake, either deliberately fake, with mali-cious intent to deceive, or just motivated by excessive optimism if not by downright sentimentality.

The only authentic ending is the one provided right here: 16

John and Mary die. John and Mary die. John and Mary die. 17

So much for endings. Beginnings are always more fun. True connoisseurs, 18 however, are known to favor the stretch in between, since it's the hardest to do anything with.

That's about all that can be said for plots, which anyway are just one thing after 19 another, a what and a what and a what.

Now try How and Why. 20

Ursula Kroeber Le Guin (1929–   ) was born on October 21 in Berkeley, California. She received an A.B. from Radcliffe College in 1951 and an A.M. from Columbia University in 1952. A resident of Portland, Oregon, Le Guin studied Renaissance history and married a history professor. She has written novels; worked as an instructor of French; lectured; and written essays, poetry, and children's books. Le Guin sees her writing as spanning several modes, including science fiction, fantasy, realism, and magic realism. Her work offers social analysis but does not advocate specific social reforms.

Le Guin has won Nebula and Hugo awards for short fiction. She emphasizes a broad definition of humanity in her fiction as well as the need for individual morality. In her Earthsea trilogy (*A Wizard of Earthsea*, 1968; *The Tombs of Atuan*, 1971; *The Farthest Shore*, 1972; and another sequel, *Tehanu: The Last Book of Earthsea*, 1990), Le Guin presents a balanced cosmology not based on a Christian ethos, as are the works of C. S. Lewis, but rather a holistic version based on respect for the universe. Her many works include *The Left Hand of Darkness* (1969; new ed. 1984) and *The Dispossessed: An Ambiguous Utopia* (1974). Le Guin has also coedited *The Norton Book of Science Fiction: North American Science Fiction, 1960–1990* (1993).

Is Gender Necessary Redux

Ursula K. Le Guin

IS GENDER NECESSARY?
1976

In the mid-1960s the women's movement was just beginning to move again, after a fifty-year halt. There was a groundswell gathering. I felt it, but I didn't know it was a groundswell; I just thought it was something wrong with me. I considered myself a feminist; I didn't see how you could be a thinking woman and not be a feminist; but I had never taken a step beyond the ground gained for us by Emmeline Pankhurst and Virginia Woolf.[1]

Along about 1967, I began to feel a certain unease, a need to step on a little farther, perhaps, on my own. I began to want to define and understand the meaning of sexuality and the meaning of gender, in my life and in our society. Much had gathered in the unconscious—both personal and collective—which must either be brought up into consciousness, or else turn destructive. It was that same need, I think, that had led Beauvoir to write *The Second Sex*, and Friedan to write *The Feminine*

RECONSIDERATIONS
1987:

1

[1] Feminism has enlarged its ground and strengthened its theory and practice immensely, and enduringly, in these past twenty years; but has anyone actually taken a step "beyond" Virginia Woolf? The image, implying an ideal of "progress," is not one I would use now.

2

From *Dancing at the Edge of the World: Thoughts on Words, Women, Places* by Ursula K. Le Guin. Copyright © 1989 by Ursula K. Le Guin. Used by permission of Grove Press, Inc.

Mystique, and that was, at the same time, leading Kate Millett and others to write their books, and to create the new feminism. But I was not a theoretician, a political thinker or activist, or a sociologist. I was and am a fiction writer. The way I did my thinking was to write a novel. That novel, *The Left Hand of Darkness*, is the record of my consciousness, the process of my thinking.

Perhaps, now that we have all[2] moved on to a plane of heightened consciousness about these matters, it might be of some interest to look back on the book, to see what it did, what it tried to do, and what it might have done, insofar as it is a "feminist"[3] book. (Let me repeat that last qualification, once. The fact is that the real subject of the book is not feminism or sex or gender or anything of the sort; as far as I can see, it is a book about betrayal and fidelity. That is why one of its two dominant sets of symbols is an extended metaphor of winter, of ice, snow, cold: the winter of journey. The rest of this discussion will concern only half, the lesser half, of the book.)[4]

It takes place on a planet called Gethen, whose human inhabitants differ from us in their sexual physiology. Instead of our continuous sexuality, the Gethenians have an oestrus period, called *kemmer*. When they are not in kemmer, they are sexually inactive and impotent; they are also androgynous. An observer in the book describes the cycle:

> In the first phase of kemmer [the individual] remains completely androgynous. Gender, and potency, are not attained in isolation. . . . Yet the sexual impulse is tremendously strong in this phase, controlling the entire personality. . . . When the individual finds a partner in kemmer, hormonal secretion is further stimulated (most importantly by touch—secretion? scent?) until in one partner either a male or female hormonal dominance is established. The genitals engorge or shrink accordingly, foreplay intensifies, and the partner, triggered by the change, takes on the other sexual role (apparently without exception). . . . Normal individuals have no predisposition to either sexual role in kemmer; they do not know whether they will be the

[2] Well, quite a lot of us, anyhow.

[3] Strike the quotation marks from the word *feminist*, please.

[4] This parenthesis is overstated; I was feeling defensive, and resentful that critics of the book insisted upon talking only about its "gender problems," as if it were an essay not a novel. *"The fact is that the real subject of the book is. . . ."* This is bluster. I had opened a can of worms and was trying hard to shut it. "The fact is," however, that there are other aspects to the book, which are involved with its sex/gender aspects quite inextricably.

3

4

5

male or the female, and have no choice in the matter. . . . The culminant phase of kemmer . . . lasts from two to five days, during which sexual drive and capacity are at maximum. It ends fairly abruptly, and if conception has not taken place, the individual returns to the latent phase and the cycle begins anew. If the individual was in the female role and was impregnated, hormonal activity of course continues, and for the gestation and lactation periods this individual remains female. . . . With the cessation of lactation the female becomes once more a perfect androgyne. No physiological habit is established, and the mother of several children may be the father of several more.

Why did I invent these peculiar people? Not just so that the book could contain, halfway through it, the sentence, "The king was pregnant"—though I admit that I am fond of that sentence. Not, certainly not, to propose Gethen as a model for humanity. I am not in favor of genetic alteration of the human organism—not at our present level of understanding. I was not recommending the Gethenian sexual setup: I was using it. It was a heuristic device, a thought-experiment. Physicists often do thought-experiments. Einstein shoots a light ray through a moving elevator; Schrödinger puts a cat in a box. There is no elevator, no cat, no box. The experiment is performed, the question is asked, in the mind. Einstein's elevator, Schrödinger's cat, my Gethenians, are simply a way of thinking. They are questions, not answers; process, not stasis. One of the essential functions of science fiction, I think, is precisely this kind of question-asking: reversals of an habitual way of thinking, metaphors for what our language has no words for as yet, experiments in imagination.

6

The subject of my experiment, then, was something like this: Because of our lifelong social conditioning, it is hard for us to see clearly what, besides purely physiological form and function, truly differentiates men and women. Are there real differences in temperament, capacity, talent, psychic processes, etc.? If so, what are they? Only comparative ethnology offers, so far, any solid

7

evidence on the matter, and the evidence is incomplete and often contradictory. The only going social experiments that are truly relevant are the kibbutzim and the Chinese communes, and they too are inconclusive—and hard to get unbiased information about. How to find out? Well, one can always put a cat in a box. One can send an imaginary, but conventional, indeed rather stuffy, young man from Earth into an imaginary culture which is totally free of sex roles because there is no, absolutely no, physiological sex distinction. I eliminated gender, to find out what was left. Whatever was left would be, presumably, simply human. It would define the area that is shared by men and women alike.

I still think that this was a rather neat idea. But as an experiment, it was messy. All results were uncertain; a repetition of the experiment by someone else, or by myself seven years later, would probably[5] give quite different results. Scientifically, this is most disreputable. That's all right; I am not a scientist. I play the game where the rules keep changing.

Among these dubious and uncertain results, achieved as I thought, and wrote, and wrote, and thought, about my imaginary people, three appear rather interesting to me.

First: The absence of war. In the 13,000 years of recorded history on Gethen, there has not been a war. The people seem to be as quarrelsome, competitive, and aggressive as we are; they have fights, murders, assassinations, feuds, forays, and so on. But there have been no great invasions by peoples on the move, like the Mongols in Asia or the Whites in the New World: partly because Gethenian populations seem to remain stable in size, they do not move in large masses, or rapidly. Their migrations have been slow, no one generation going very far. They have no nomadic peoples, and no societies which live by expansion and aggression against other societies. Nor have they formed large, hierarchically governed nation-states, the mobilizable entity that is the essential factor in modern war. The basic social unit all over the planet is a group of from 200 to

8

9

10

[5] Strike the word *probably* and replace it with *certainly.*

800 people, called a "hearth," a structure founded less on economic convenience than on sexual necessity (there must be others in kemmer at the same time), and therefore more tribal than urban in nature, though overlaid and interwoven with a later urban pattern. The hearth tends to be communal, independent, and somewhat introverted. Rivalries between hearths, as between individuals, are channeled into a socially approved form of aggression called *shifgrethor,* a conflict without physical violence, involving one-upsmanship, the saving and losing of face—conflict ritualized, stylized, controlled. When *shifgrethor* breaks down there may be physical violence, but it does not become mass violence, remaining limited, personal. The active group remains small. The dispersive trend is as strong as the cohesive. Historically, when hearths gathered into a nation for economic reasons, the cellular pattern still dominated the centralized one. There might be a king and a parliament, but authority was not enforced so much by might as by the use of *shifgrethor* and intrigue, and was accepted as custom, without appeal to patriarchal ideals of divine right, patriotic duty, etc. Ritual and parade were far more effective agents of order than armies or police. Class structure was flexible and open; the value of the social hierarchy was less economic than aesthetic, and there was no great gap between rich and poor. There was no slavery or servitude. Nobody owned anybody. There were no chattels. Economic organization was rather communistic or syndicalistic than capitalistic, and was seldom highly centralized.

During the time span of the novel, however, all this is changing. One of the two large nations of the planet is becoming a genuine nation-state, complete with patriotism and bureaucracy. It has achieved state capitalism and the centralization of power, authoritarian government, and a secret police; and it is on the verge of achieving the world's first war.

11

Why did I present the first picture, and show it in the process of changing to a different one?

12

I am not sure. I think it is because I was trying to show a balance—and the delicacy of a balance. To me the "female principle" is, or at least historically has been, basically anarchic. It values order without constraint, rule by custom not by force. It has been the male who enforces order, who constructs power-structures, who makes, enforces, and breaks laws. On Gethen, these two principles are in balance: the decentralizing against the centralizing, the flexible against the rigid, the circular against the linear. But balance is a precarious state, and at the moment of the novel the balance, which had leaned toward the "feminine," is tipping the other way[6].

Second: The absence of exploitation. The Gethenians do not rape their world. They have developed a high technology, heavy industry, automobiles, radios, explosives, etc., but they have done so very slowly, absorbing their technology rather than letting it overwhelm them. They have no myth of Progress at all. Their calendar calls the current year always the Year One, and they count backward and forward from that.

In this, it seems that what I was after again was a balance: the driving linearity of the "male," the pushing forward to the limit, the logicality that admits no boundary—and the circularity of the "female," the valuing of patience, ripeness, practicality, livableness. A model for this balance, of course, exists on Earth: Chinese civilization over the past six millennia. (I did not know when I wrote the book that the parallel extends even to the calendar; the Chinese historically never had a linear dating system, such as ours that dates from the birth of Christ.)[7]

Third: The absence of sexuality as a continuous social factor. For four-fifths of the month, a Gethenian's sexuality plays no part at all in his social life (unless he's pregnant); for the other one-fifth, it dominates him absolutely. In kemmer, one must have a partner, it is imperative. (Have you ever lived in a small apartment with a tabby-cat in heat?) Gethenian society fully accepts this imperative. When a Gethenian has to make love,

[6] At the very inception of the whole book, I was interested in writing a novel about people in a society that had never had a war. That came first. The androgyny came second. (Cause and effect? Effect and cause?) I would now rewrite this paragraph this way: The "female principle" has historically been anarchic; that is, anarchy has been historically identified as female. The domain allotted to women—"the family," for example—is the area of order without coercion, rule by custom not by force. Men have reserved the structures of social power to themselves (and those few women whom they admit to it on male terms, such as queens, prime ministers); men make the wars and peaces, men make, enforce, and break the laws. On Gethen, the two polarities we perceive through our cultural conditioning as male and female are neither, and are in balance: consensus with authority, decentralizing with centralizing, flexible with rigid, circular with linear, hierarchy with network. But it is not a motionless balance, there being no such thing in life, and at the moment of the novel, it is wobbling perilously.

13

14

[7] A better model might be some of the pre-Conquest cultures of the Americas, though not those hierarchical and imperialistic ones approvingly termed, by our hierarchical and imperialistic standards, "high." The trouble with the Chinese model is that their civilisation instituted and practiced male domination as thoroughly as the other "high" civilisations. I was thinking of a Taoist ideal, not of such practices as bride-selling and foot-binding, which we are trained to consider unimportant, nor of the deep misogyny of Chinese culture, which we are trained to consider normal.

15

he does make love, and everybody expects him to, and approves of it.[8]

But still, human beings are human beings, not cats. Despite our continuous sexuality and our intense self-domestication (domesticated animals tend to be promiscuous, wild animals pairbonding, familial, or tribal in their mating), we are very seldom truly promiscuous. We do have rape, to be sure—no other animal has equaled us there. We have mass rape, when an army (male, of course) invades; we have prostitution, promiscuity controlled by economics; and sometimes ritual abreactive promiscuity controlled by religion; but in general we seem to avoid genuine license. At most we award it as a price to the Alpha Male, in certain situations; it is scarcely ever permitted to the female without social penalty. It would seem, perhaps, that the mature human being, male or female, is not satisfied by sexual gratification without psychic involvement, and in fact may be afraid of it, to judge by the tremendous variety of social, legal, and religious controls and sanctions exerted over it in all human societies. Sex is a great mana, and therefore the immature society, or psyche, sets great taboos about it. The maturer culture, or psyche, can integrate these taboos or laws into an internal ethical code, which, while allowing great freedom, does not permit the treatment of another person as an object. But, however irrational or rational, there is always a code.

Because the Gethenians cannot have sexual intercourse unless both partners are willing, because they cannot rape or be raped, I figured that they would have less fear and guilt about sex than we tend to have; but still it is a problem for them, in some ways more than for us, because of the extreme, explosive, imperative quality of the oestrous phase. Their society would have to control it, though it might move more easily than we from the taboo stage to the ethical stage. So the basic arrangement, I found, is that of the kemmerhouse, in every Gethenian community, which is open to anyone in kemmer, native or stranger, so that he can find a partner.[9] Then there are various customary (not legal)

[8] I would now write this paragraph this way: . . . For four-fifths of the month, sexuality plays no part at all in a Gethenian's social behavior; for the other one-fifth, it controls behavior absolutely. In kemmer, one must have a partner, it is imperative. (Have you ever lived in a small apartment with a tabby-cat in heat?) Gethenian society fully accepts this imperative. When Gethenians have to make love, they do make love, and everybody else expects it and approves of it.

16

17

[9] Read: so that they can find sexual partners.

institutions, such as the kemmering group, a group
who choose to come together during kemmer as
a regular thing; this is like the primate tribe, or
group marriage. Or there is the possibility of vow-
ing kemmering, which is marriage, pairbonding
for life, a personal commitment without legal
sanction. Such commitments have intense moral
and psychic significance, but they are not controlled by Church or State. Finally, there are two
forbidden acts, which might be taboo or illegal or
simply considered contemptible, depending on
which of the regions of Gethen you are in: first,
you don't pair off with a relative of a different generation (one who might be your own parent or
child); second, you may mate, but not vow kemmering, with your own sibling. These are the old
incest prohibitions. They are so general among
us—and with good cause, I think, not so much
genetic as psychological—that they seemed likely to be equally valid on Gethen.

These three "results," then, of my experiment,
I feel were fairly clearly and successfully worked
out, though there is nothing definitive about them.

In other areas where I might have pressed for
at least such plausible results, I see now a failure
to think things through, or to express them clearly. For example, I think I took the easy way in
using such familiar governmental structures as a
feudal monarchy and a modern-style bureaucracy for the two Gethenian countries that are the
scene of the novel. I doubt that Gethenian gov-
ernments, rising out of the cellular "hearth," would
resemble any of our own so closely. They might
be better, they might be worse, but they would
certainly be different.

I regret even more certain timidities or
ineptnesses I showed in following up the psychic
implications of Gethenian physiology.[10] Just for
example, I wish I had known Jung's work, when I
wrote the book: so that I could have decided
whether a Gethenian had *no* animus or anima, or
both, or an animum. . . . But the central failure
in this area comes up in the frequent criticism I
receive, that the Gethenians seem like *men*,
instead of menwomen.

18

19

20

[10] For another example (and Jung wouldn't have
helped with this, more likely hindered) I quite unnec-
essarily locked the Gethenians into heterosexuality. It
is a naively pragmatic view of sex that insists that sexual partners must be of opposite sex! In any kemmerhouse homosexual practice would, of course, be
possible and acceptable and welcomed—but I never
thought to explore this option; and the omission, alas,
implies that sexuality is heterosexuality. I regret this
very much.

This rises in part from the choice of pronoun. I call Gethenians "he," because I utterly refuse to mangle English by inventing a pronoun for "he/she."[11] "He" is the generic pronoun, damn it, in English. (I envy the Japanese, who, I am told, do have a he/she pronoun.) But I do not consider this really very important.[12] The pronouns wouldn't matter at all if I had been cleverer at *showing* the "female" component of the Gethenian characters in *action*.[13] Unfortunately, the plot and structure that arose as I worked the book out cast the Gethenian protagonist, Estraven, almost exclusively into roles which we are culturally conditioned to perceive as "male"—a prime minister (it takes more than even Golda Meir and Indira Gandhi to break a stereotype), a political schemer, a fugitive, a prison-breaker, a sledge-hauler. . . . I think I did this because I was privately delighted at watching, not a man, but a manwoman, do all these things, and do them with considerable skill and flair. But, for the reader, I left out too much. One does not see Estraven as a mother, with his children, in any role which we automatically perceive as "female": and therefore, we tend to see him as a man. This is a real flaw in the book, and I can only be very grateful to those readers, men and women, whose willingness to participate in the experiment led them to fill in that omission with the work of their own imagination, and to see Estraven as I saw him, as man and woman, familiar and different, alien and utterly human.[14]

It seems to be men, more often than women, who thus complete my work for me: I think because men are often more willing to identify as they read with poor, confused, defensive Genly, the Earthman, and therefore to participate in his painful and gradual discovery of love.

Finally, the question arises, is the book a Utopia? It seems to me that it is quite clearly not; it poses no *practicable* alternative to contemporary society, since it is based on an imaginary, radical change in human anatomy. All it tries to do is open up an alternative viewpoint, to widen the imagination, without making any definite suggestions as to what might be seen from the new viewpoint.

21

[11] This "utter refusal" of 1968 restated in 1976 collapsed, utterly, within a couple of years more. I still dislike invented pronouns, but I now dislike them less than the so-called generic pronoun

he/him/his, which does in fact exclude women from discourse; and which was an invention of male grammarians, for until the sixteenth century the English generic singular pronoun was they/them/their, as it still is in English and American colloquial speech. It should be restored to the written language, and let the pedants and pundits squeak and gibber in the streets.

In a screenplay of *The Left Hand of Darkness* written in 1985, I referred to Gethenians not pregnant or in kemmer by the invented pronouns a/un/a's, modelled on a British dialect. These would drive the reader mad in print, I suppose; but I have read parts of the book aloud using them, and the audience was perfectly happy, except that they pointed out that the subject pronoun, "a" pronounced "uh" [ə]sounds too much like "I" said with a Southern accent.

[12] I now consider it very important.

[13] If I had realised how the pronouns I used shaped, directed, controlled my own thinking, I might have been "cleverer."

[14] I now see it thus: Men were inclined to be satisfied with the book, which allowed them a safe trip into androgyny and back, from a conventionally male viewpoint. But many women wanted it to go further, to dare more, to explore androgyny from a woman's point of view as well as a man's. In fact, it does so, in that it was written by a woman. But this is admitted directly only in the chapter "The Question of Sex," the only voice of a woman in the book. I think women were justified in asking more courage of me and a more rigorous thinking through of implications.

22

23

The most it says is, I think, something like this: If we were socially ambisexual, if men and women were completely and genuinely equal in their social roles, equal legally and economically, equal in freedom, in responsibility, and in self-esteem, then society would be a very different thing. What our problems might be, God knows; I only know we would have them. But it seems likely that our central problem would not be the one it is now: the problem of exploitation—exploitation of the woman, of the weak, of the earth. Our curse is alienation, the separation of yang from yin.[15] Instead of a search for balance and integration, there is a struggle for dominance. Divisions are insisted upon, interdependence is denied. The dualism of value that destroys us, the dualism of superior/inferior, ruler/ruled, owner/owned, user/used, might give way to what seems to me, from here, a much healthier, sounder, more promising modality of integration and integrity.

[15] —and the moralisation of yang as good—of yin as bad.

Gloria Anzaldua (1942–   ) was born in Jesus Maria of the Valley, which is located within Texas's Rio Grande Valley. Anzaldua earned an M.A. from the University of Texas at Austin in 1973. She has taught at the University of California at Santa Cruz, Georgetown University, and Colorado University. Her books include the collection of essays and poems, *Borderlands/La Frontera: The New Mestiza* (1987), several children's books, and a novel, *La Prieta* (1997). Among other distinctions, she has won a National Endowment for the Arts fiction award and the Sappho Award of Distinction. "How to Tame a Wild Tongue" is taken from *Borderlands*.

How to Tame a Wild Tongue

Gloria Anzaldua

"We're going to have to control your tongue," the dentist says, pulling out all the metal from my mouth. Silver bits plop and tinkle into the basin. My mouth is a motherlode. 1

The dentist is cleaning out my roots. I get a whiff of the stench when I gasp. "I can't cap that tooth yet, you're still draining," he says. 2

"We're going to have to do something about your tongue," I hear the anger rising in his voice. My tongue keeps pushing out the wads of cotton, pushing back the drills, the long thin needles. "I've never seen anything as strong or as stubborn," he says. And I think, how do you tame a wild tongue, train it to be quiet, how do you bridle and saddle it? How do you make it lie down? 3

"Who is to say that robbing a people of its language is less violent than war?"
—Ray Gwyn Smith[1]

I remember being caught speaking Spanish at recess—that was good for three licks on the knuckles with a sharp ruler. I remember being sent to the corner of the classroom for "talking back" to the Anglo teacher when all I was trying to do was tell her how to pronounce my name. "If you want to be American, speak 'American.' If you don't like it, go back to Mexico where you belong." 4

"I want you to speak English. *Pa' hallar buen trabajo tienes que saber hablar el inglés bien. Qué vale toda tu educación si todavia hablas inglés con un* 'accent,' my mother would say, mortified that I spoke English like a Mexican. At Pan American University, I, and all Chicano students were required to take two speech classes. Their purpose: to get rid of our accents. 5

Attacks on one's form of expression with the intent to censor are a violation of the First Amendment. *El Anglo con cara de inocente nos arrancó la lengua.* Wild tongues can't be tamed, they can only be cut out. 6

OVERCOMING THE TRADITION OF SILENCE

Abogadas, escupimos el oscuro.
Peleando con nuestra propia sombra
el silencio nos sepulta.

En boca cerrada no entran moscas. "Flies don't enter a closed mouth" is a saying   7
I kept hearing when I was a child. *Ser habladora* was to be a gossip and a liar, to talk
too much. *Muchachitas bien criadas,* well-bred girls don't answer back. *Es una falta
de respeto* to talk back to one's mother or father. I remember one of the sins I'd recite
to the priest in the confession box the few times I went to confession: talking back
to my mother, *hablar pa' 'trás, repelar. Hocicona, repelona, chismosa,* having a big
mouth, questioning, carrying tales are all signs of being *mal criada.* In my culture they
are all words that are derogatory if applied to women—I've never heard them applied
to men.

The first time I heard two women, a Puerto Rican and a Cuban, say the word   8
"*nosotras,*" I was shocked. I had not known the word existed. Chicanas use *nosotros*
whether we're male or female. We are robbed of our female being by the masculine
plural. Language is a male discourse.

And our tongues have become
dry   the wilderness has
dried out our tongues   and
we have forgotten speech.
                —Irena Klepfisz[2]

Even our own people, other Spanish speakers *nos quieren poner candados en la*   9
boca. They would hold us back with their bag of *reglas de academia.*

OYÉ COMO LADRA: EL LENGUAJE DE LA FRONTERA

Quien tiene boca se equivoca.
        —Mexican saying

"*Pocho,* cultural traitor, you're speaking the oppressor's language by speaking English,   10
you're ruining the Spanish language," I have been accused by various Latinos and
Latinas. Chicano Spanish is considered by the purist and by most Latinos deficient,
a mutilation of Spanish.

But Chicano Spanish is a border tongue which developed naturally. Change,   11
evolución, enriquecimiento de palabras nuevas por invención o adopción have created variants of Chicano Spanish, *un nuevo lenguaje. Un lenguaje que corresponde a un modo de
vivir.* Chicano Spanish is not incorrect, it is a living language.

For a people who are neither Spanish nor live in a country in which Spanish is   12
the first language; for a people who live in a country in which English is the reigning
tongue but who are not Anglo; for a people who cannot entirely identify with either
standard (formal, Castillian) Spanish nor standard English, what recourse is left to

them but to create their own language? A language which they can connect their identity to, one capable of communicating the realities and values true to themselves—a language with terms that are neither *español ni inglés*, but both. We speak a patois, a forked tongue, a variation of two languages.

Chicano Spanish sprang out of the Chicanos' need to identify ourselves as a distinct people. We needed a language with which we could communicate with ourselves, a secret language. For some of us, language is a homeland closer than the Southwest—for many Chicanos today live in the Midwest and the East. And because we are a complex, heterogeneous people, we speak many languages. Some of the languages we speak are: 13

1. Standard English
2. Working class and slang English
3. Standard Spanish
4. Standard Mexican Spanish
5. North Mexican Spanish dialect
6. Chicano Spanish (Texas, New Mexico, Arizona, and California have regional variations)
7. Tex-Mex
8. *Pachuco* (called *caló*)

My "home" tongues are the languages I speak with my sister and brothers, with my friends. They are the last five listed, with 6 and 7 being closest to my heart. From school, the media and job situations, I've picked up standard and working class English. From Mamagrande Locha and from reading Spanish and Mexican literature, I've picked up Standard Spanish and Standard Mexican Spanish. From *los recién llegados*, Mexican immigrants, and *braceros*, I learned the North Mexican dialect. With Mexicans I'll try to speak either Standard Mexican Spanish or the North Mexican dialect. From my parents and Chicanos living in the Valley, I picked up Chicano Texas Spanish, and I speak it with my mom, younger brother (who married a Mexican and who rarely mixes Spanish with English), aunts and older relatives.   14

With Chicanas from *Nuevo México* or *Arizona* I will speak Chicano Spanish a little, but often they don't understand what I'm saying. With most California Chicanas I speak entirely in English (unless I forget). When I first moved to San Francisco, I'd rattle off something in Spanish, unintentionally embarrassing them. Often it is only with another Chicana *tejana* that I can talk freely.   15

Words distorted by English are known as anglicisms or *pochismos*. The *pocho* is an anglicized Mexican or American of Mexican origin who speaks Spanish with an accent characteristic of North Americans and who distorts and reconstructs the language according to the influence of English.[3] Tex-Mex, or Spanglish, comes most naturally to me. I may switch back and forth from English to Spanish in the same sentence or in the same word. With my sister and my brother Nune and with Chicano *tejano* contemporaries I speak in Tex-Mex.   16

From kids and people my own age I picked up *Pachuco. Pachuco* (the language of the zoot suiters) is a language of rebellion, both against Standard Spanish and Standard English. It is a secret language. Adults of the culture and outsiders cannot understand it. It is made up of slang words from both English and Spanish. *Ruca* means   17 girl or woman, *vato* means guy or dude, *chale* means no, *simón* means yes, *churro* is sure, talk is *periquiar, pigionear* means petting, *que gacho* means how nerdy, *ponte águila* means watch out, death is called *la petona*. Through lack of practice and not having others who can speak it, I've lost most of the *Pachuco* tongue.

CHICANO SPANISH

Chicanos, after 250 years of Spanish/Anglo colonization have developed significant differences in the Spanish we speak. We collapse two adjacent vowels into a single syllable and sometimes shift the stress in certain words such as *maíz/maiz, cobete/cuete*. We leave out certain consonants when they appear between vowels: *lado/lao, mojado/mojao*. Chicanos from South Texas pronounced *f* as *j* as in *jue (fue)*. Chicanos use "archaisms," words that are no longer in the Spanish language, words that have been evolved out. We say *semos, trufe, baiga, ansina,* and *naiden*. We retain the "archaic" *j* as in *jalar*, that derives from an earlier *h*, (the French *halar* or the Germanic *halon* which was lost to standard Spanish in the 16th century), but which is still found in several regional dialects such as the one spoken in South Texas. (Due to geography, Chicanos from the Valley of South Texas were cut off linguistically from other Spanish speakers. We tend to use words that the Spaniards brought over from Medieval Spain. The majority of the Spanish colonizers in Mexico and the Southwest came from Extremadura—Herrian Cortés was one of them—and Andalucia. Andalucians pronounce *ll* like a *y*, and their *d*'s tend to be absorbed by adjacent vowels: *tirado* becomes *tirao*. They brought *el lenguaje popular, dialectos y regionalismos*.[4])

18

Chicanos and other Spanish speakers also shift *ll* to *y* and *z* to *s*.[5] We leave out initial syllables, saying *tar* for *estar, toy* for *estoy, hora* for *ahora (cubanos* and *puertorriqueños* also leave out initial letters of some words). We also leave out the final syllable such as *pa* for *para*. The intervocalic *y*, the *ll* as in *tortilla, ella, botella*, gets replaced by *tortia* or *tortiya, ea, botea*. We add an additional syllable at the beginning of certain words: *atocar* for *tocar, agastar* for *gastar*. Sometimes we'll say *lavaste las vacijas*, other times *lavates* (substituting the *ates* verb endings for the *aste*).

19

We use anglicisms, words borrowed from English: *bola* from ball, *carpeta* from carpet, *máchina de lavar* (instead of *lavadora*) from washing machine. Tex-Mex argot, created by adding a Spanish sound at the beginning or end of an English word such as *cookiar* for cook, *watchar* for watch, *parkiar* for park, and *rapiar* for rape, is the result of the pressures on Spanish speakers to adapt to English.

20

We don't use the word *vosotros/as* or its accompanying verb form. We don't say *claro* (to mean yes), *imagínate,* or *me emociona,* unless we picked up Spanish from Latinas, out of a book, or in a classroom. Other Spanish-speaking groups are going through the same, or similar, development in their Spanish.

21

LINGUISTIC TERRORISM

Deslenguadas. Somos los del español deficiente. We are your linguistic nightmare, your linguistic aberration, your linguistic *mestizaje,* the subject of your *burla*. Because we speak with tongues of fire we are culturally crucified. Racially, culturally and linguistically *somos huérfanos*—we speak an orphan tongue.

22

Chicanas who grew up speaking Chicano Spanish have internalized the belief that we speak poor Spanish. It is illegitimate, a bastard language. And because we

23

internalize how our language has been used against us by the dominant culture, we use our language differences against each other.

Chicana feminists often skirt around each other with suspicion and hesitation. 24
For the longest time I couldn't figure it out. Then it dawned on me. To be close to another Chicana is like looking into the mirror. We are afraid of what we'll see there. *Pena.* Shame. Low estimation of self. In childhood we are told that our language is wrong. Repeated attacks on our native tongue diminish our sense of self. The attacks continue throughout our lives.

Chicanas feel uncomfortable talking in Spanish to Latinas, afraid of their cen- 25
sure. Their language was not outlawed in their countries. They had a whole life-time of being immersed in their native tongue; generations, centuries in which Spanish was a first language, taught in school, heard on radio and TV, and read in the newspaper.

If a person, Chicana or Latina, has a low estimation of my native tongue, she 26
also has a low estimation of me. Often with *mexicanas y latinas* we'll speak English as a neutral language. Even among Chicanas we tend to speak English at parties or conferences. Yet, at the same time, we're afraid the other will think we're *agringadas* because we don't speak Chicano Spanish. We oppress each other trying to out Chicano each other, vying to be the "real" Chicanas, to speak like Chicanos. There is no one Chicano language just as there is no one Chicano experience. A mono-lingual Chicana whose first language is English or Spanish is just as much a Chicana as one who speaks several variants of Spanish. A Chicana from Michigan or Chicago or Detroit is just as much a Chicana as one from the Southwest. Chicano Spanish is as diverse linguistically as it is regionally.

By the end of this century, Spanish speakers will comprise the biggest minority 27
group in the U.S., a country where students in high schools and colleges are encour-aged to take French classes because French is considered more "cultured." But for a language to remain alive it must be used.[6] By the end of this century English, and not Spanish, will be the mother tongue of most Chicanos and Latinos.

So, if you want to really hurt me, talk badly about my language. Ethnic iden- 28
tity is twin skin to linguistic identity—I am my language. Until I can take pride in my language, I cannot take pride in myself. Until I can accept as legitimate Chicano Texas Spanish, Tex-Mex and all the other languages I speak, I cannot accept the legitimacy of myself. Until I am free to write bilingually and to switch codes without having always to translate, while I still have to speak English or Spanish when I would rather speak Spanglish, and as long as I have to accommodate the English speakers rather than having them accommodate me, my tongue will be illegitimate.

I will no longer be made to feel ashamed of existing. I will have my voice: Indian, 29
Spanish, white. I will have my serpent's tongue—my woman's voice, my sexual voice, my poet's voice. I will overcome the tradition of silence.

My fingers
move sly against your palm
Like women everywhere, we speak in code. . . .
—Melanie Kaye/Kantrowitz[7]

"VISTAS," CORRIDOS, Y COMIDA: MY NATIVE TONGUE

In the 1960s, I read my first Chicano novel. It was *City of Night* by John Rechy, a gay   30
Texan, son of a Scottish father and a Mexican mother. For days I walked around in
stunned amazement that a Chicano could write and could get published. When I
read *I Am Joaquin*[8] I was surprised to see a bilingual book by a Chicano in print. When
I saw poetry written in Tex-Mex for the first time, a feeling of pure joy flashed through
me. I felt like we really existed as a people. In 1971, when I started teaching High
School English to Chicano students, I tried to supplement the required texts with
works by Chicanos, only to be reprimanded and forbidden to do so by the principal. He claimed that I was supposed to teach "American" and English literature.
At the risk of being fired, I swore my students to secrecy and slipped in Chicano short
stories, poems, a play. In graduate school, while working toward a Ph.D., I had to
"argue" with one advisor after the other, semester after semester, before I was allowed
to make Chicano literature an area of focus.

Even before I read books by Chicanos or Mexicans, it was the Mexican movies   31
I saw at the drive-in—the Thursday night special of $1.00 a carload—that gave me
a sense of belonging. "*Vámonos a las vistas,*" my mother would call out and we'd all—
grandmother, brothers, sister, and cousins—squeeze into the car. We'd wolf down
cheese and bologna white bread sandwiches while watching Pedro Infante in melodramatic tear-jerkers like *Nosotros los pobres,* the first "real" Mexican movie (that was
not an imitation of European movies). I remember seeing *Cuando los hijos se van* and
surmising that all Mexican movies played up the love a mother has for her children and what ungrateful sons and daughters suffer when they are not devoted to
their mothers. I remember the singing-type "westerns" of Jorge Negrete and Miguel
Aceves Meía. When watching Mexican movies, I felt a sense of homecoming as well
as alienation. People who were to amount to something didn't go to Mexican movies,
or *baíes* or tune their radios to *bolero, rancherita,* and *corrido* music.

The whole time I was growing up, there was *norteño* music sometimes called   32
North Mexican border music, or Tex-Mex music, or Chicano music, or *cantina* (bar)
music. I grew up listening to *conjuntos,* three- or four-piece bands made up of folk
musicians playing guitar, *bajo sexto,* drums, and button accordion, which Chicanos
had borrowed from the German immigrants who had come to Central Texas and
Mexico to farm and build breweries. In the Rio Grande Valley, Steve Jordan and
Little Joe Hernández were popular, and Flaco Jiménez was the accordion king. The
rhythms of Tex-Mex music are those of the polka, also adapted from the Germans,
who in turn had borrowed the polka from the Czechs and Bohemians.

I remember the hot, sultry evenings when *corridos*—songs of love and death   33
on the Texas-Mexican borderlands—reverberated out of cheap amplifiers from the
local *cantinas* and wafted in through my bedroom window.

Corridos first became widely used along the South Texas Mexican border during   34
the early conflict between Chicanos and Anglos. The *corridos* are usually about
Mexican heroes who do valiant deeds against the Anglo oppressors. Pancho Villa's
song, "*La cucaracha,*" is the most famous one. *Corridos* of John F. Kennedy and his
death are still very popular in the Valley. Older Chicanos remember Lydia Mendoza,
one of the great border *corrido* singers who was called *la Gloria de Tejas.* Her "*El tango*

negro," sung during the Great Depression, made her a singer of the people. The everpresent *corridos* narrated one hundred years of border history, bringing news of events as well as entertaining. These folk musicians and folk songs are our chief cultural mythmakers, and they made our hard lives seem bearable.

I grew up feeling ambivalent about our music. Country-western and rock-and-roll 35
had more status. In the 50s and 60s, for the slightly educated and *agringado* Chicanos, there existed a sense of shame at being caught listening to our music. Yet I couldn't stop my feet from thumping to the music, could not stop humming the words, nor hide from myself the exhilaration I felt when I heard it.

There are more subtle ways that we internalize identification, especially in 36
the forms of images and emotions. For me food and certain smells are tied to my identity, to my homeland. Woodsmoke curling up to an immense blue sky; woodsmoke perfuming my grandmother's clothes, her skin. The stench of cow manure and the yellow patches on the ground; the crack of a .22 rifle and the reek of cordite. Homemade white cheese sizzling in a pan, melting inside a folded *tortilla.* My sister Hilda's hot, spicy *menudo, chile colorado* making it deep red, pieces of *panza* and hominy floating on top. My brother Carito barbecuing *fajitas* in the backyard. Even now and 3,000 miles away, I can see my mother spicing the ground beef, pork, and venison with *chile.* My mouth salivates at the thought of the hot steaming *tamales* I would be eating if I were home.

SI LE PREGUNTAS A MI MAMÁ, "¿QUÉ ERES?"

> "Identity is the essential core of who
> we are as individuals, the conscious
> experience of the self inside."
> —Kaufman[9]

Nosotros los Chicanos straddle the borderlands. On one side of us, we are constantly 37
exposed to the Spanish of the Mexicans, on the other side we hear the Anglos' incessant clamoring so that we forget our language. Among ourselves we don't say *nosotros los americanos, o nosotros los españoles, o nosotros los hispanos.* We say *nosotros los mexicanos* (by *mexicanos* we do not mean citizens of Mexico; we do not mean a national identity, but a racial one). We distinguish between *mexicanos del otro lado* and *mexicanos de este lado.* Deep in our hearts we believe that being Mexican has nothing to do with which country one lives in. Being Mexican is a state of soul—not one of mind, not one of citizenship. Neither eagle nor serpent, but both. And like the ocean, neither animal respects borders.

> *Dime con quien andas y te diré quien eres.*
> (Tell me who your friends are and I'll tell you who you are.)
> —Mexican saying

Si le preguntas a mi mamá, "¿Qué eres?" te dirá, "Soy mexicana." My brothers 38
and sister say the same. I sometimes will answer "*soy mexicana*" and at others will say "*soy Chicana*" *o* "*soy tejana.*" But I identified as "*Raza*" before I ever identified as "*mexicana*" or "Chicana."

As a culture, we call ourselves Spanish when referring to ourselves as a linguistic group and when copping out. It is then that we forget our predominant Indian genes. We are 70 to 80% Indian.[10] We call ourselves Hispanic[11] or Spanish-American or Latin American or Latin when linking ourselves to other Spanish-speaking peoples of the Western hemisphere and when copping out. We call ourselves Mexican-American[12] to signify we are neither Mexican nor American, but more the noun "American" than the adjective "mexican" (and when copping out).   39

Chicanos and other people of color suffer economically for not acculturating. This voluntary (yet forced) alienation makes for psychological conflict, a kind of dual identity—we don't identify with the Anglo-American cultural values and we don't totally identify with the Mexican cultural values. We are a synergy of two cultures with various degrees of Mexicanness or Angloness. I have so internalized the borderland conflict that sometimes I feel like one cancels out the other and we are zero, nothing, no one. *A veces no soy nada ni nadie. Pero hasta cuando no lo soy, lo soy.*   40

When not copping out, when we know we are more than nothing, we call ourselves Mexican, referring to race and ancestry: *mestizo* when affirming both our Indian and Spanish (but we hardly ever own our Black ancestry); Chicano when referring to a politically aware people born and/or raised in the U.S.: *Raza* when referring to Chicanos; *tejanos* when we are Chicanos from Texas.   41

Chicanos did not know we were a people until 1965 when Cesar Chavez and the farmworkers united and *I Am Joaquín* was published and *la Raza Unida* party was formed in Texas. With that recognition, we became a distinct people. Something momentous happened to the Chicano soul—we became aware of our reality and acquired a name and a language (Chicano Spanish) that reflected that reality. Now that we had a name, some of the fragmented pieces began to fall together—who we were, what we were, how we had evolved. We began to get glimpses of what we might eventually become.   42

Yet the struggle of identities continues, the struggle of borders is our reality still. One day the inner struggle will cease and a true integration take place. In the meantime, *tenemos que hacerla lucha. ¿Quién está protegiendo los ranchos de mi gente? ¿Quién está tratando de cerrar la fisura entre la india y el blanco en nuestra sangre? El Chicano, sí, el Chicano que anda como un ladrón en su propia casa.*   43

Los Chicanos, how patient we seem, how very patient. There is the quiet of the Indian about us.[13] We know how to survive. When other races have given up their tongue, we've kept ours. We know what it is to live under the hammer blow of the dominant *norteamericano* culture. But more than we count the blows, we count the days the weeks the years the centuries the eons until the white laws and commerce and customs will rot in the deserts they've created, lie bleached. *Humildes* yet proud, *quietos* yet wild, *nosotros los mexicanos*-Chicanos will walk by the crumbling ashes as we go about our business. Stubborn, persevering, impenetrable as stone, yet possessing a malleability that renders us unbreakable, we, the *mestizas* and *mestizos,* will remain.   44

ENDNOTES

1. Ray Gwyn Smith, *Moorland Is Cold Country*. Unpublished book.

2. Irena Klepfisz, "*Di rayze aheym*/The Journey Home," *The Tribe of Dina: A Jewish Women's Anthology*, eds. Melanie Kaye/Kantrowitz and Irena Klepfisz (Montpelier, VT: Sinister Wisdom Books, 1986) 49.

3. R.C. Ortega. *Dialectología Del Barrio*, trans. Hortencia S. Alwan (Los Angeles, CA: R.C. Ortega Publisher & Bookseller, 1977) 132.

4. Eduardo Hernandéz-Chávez, Andrew D. Cohen, and Anthony F. Beltramo, *El Lenguaje de los Chicanos: Regional and Social Characteristics of Language Used By Mexican Americans* (Arlington, VA: Center for Applied Linguistics, 1975) 39.

5. Hernandéz-Chávez xvii.

6. Irena Klepfisz, "Secular Jewish Identity: Yidishkayt in America," *The Tribe of Dina*, 43.

7. Melanie Kaye/Kantrowitz, "Sign," *We Speak in Code: Poems and Other Writings* (Pittsburgh, PA: Motheroot Publications, Inc., 1980) 85.

8. Rodolfo Gonzales, *I Am Joaquín/Yo Soy Joaquín* (New York, NY: Bantam Books, 1972). It was first published in 1967.

9. Kaufman 68.

10. Chávez 88–90.

11. "Hispanic" is derived from *Hispanis* (*España*, a name given to the Iberian Peninsula in ancient times when it was a part of the Roman Empire) and is a term designated by the U.S. government to make it easier to handle us on paper.

12. The Treaty of Guadalupe Hidalgo created the Mexican-American in 1848.

13. Anglos, in order to alleviate their guilt for dispossessing the Chicano, stressed the Spanish part of us and perpetrated the myth of the Spanish Southwest. We have accepted the fiction that we are Hispanic, that is Spanish, in order to accommodate ourselves to the dominant culture and its abhorrence of Indians. Chávez 88–91.

Judith Ortiz Cofer (1952–   ) was born in Hormigueros, Puerto Rico, and grew up in New Jersey. She earned an M.A. from Florida Atlantic University in 1977. Cofer has taught at many colleges and universities, including the University of Michigan and the University of Georgia. Her books include the novel *The Line of the Sun* (1989) and *Woman in Front of the Sun: On Becoming a Writer* (2000). Among other awards and honors, she has won the Pushcart Prize for her nonfiction, and an O. Henry Award for her short story "Nada." "The Myth of the Latin Woman" was first published in 1992 in *Glamour* magazine and collected in *The Latin Deli: Prose and Poetry* (1993).

The Myth of the Latin Woman

Judith Ortiz Cofer

On a bus trip to London from Oxford University where I was earning some gradu-   1
ate credits one summer, a young man, obviously fresh from a pub, spotted me and
as if struck by inspiration went down on his knees in the aisle. With both hands over
his heart he broke into an Irish tenor's rendition of "María" from *West Side Story*. My
politely amused fellow passengers gave his lovely voice the round of gentle applause
it deserved. Though I was not quite as amused, I managed my version of an English
smile: no show of teeth, no extreme contortions of the facial muscles—I was at this
time of my life practicing reserve and cool. Oh, that British control, how I coveted
it. But María had followed me to London, reminding me of a prime fact of my life:
you can leave the Island, master the English language, and travel as far as you can,
but if you are a Latina, especially one like me who so obviously belongs to Rita
Moreno's gene pool, the Island travels with you.

This is sometimes a very good thing—it may win you that extra minute of some-   2
one's attention. But with some people, the same things can make *you* an island—not
so much a tropical paradise as an Alcatraz, a place nobody wants to visit. As a Puerto
Rican girl growing up in the United States and wanting like most children to
"belong," I resented the stereotype that my Hispanic appearance called forth from
many people I met.

Our family lived in a large urban center in New Jersey during the sixties, where   3
life was designed as a microcosm of my parents' casas on the island. We spoke in
Spanish, we ate Puerto Rican food bought at the bodega, and we practiced strict
Catholicism complete with Saturday confession and Sunday mass at a church where
our parents were accommodated into a one-hour Spanish mass slot, performed by a
Chinese priest trained as a missionary for Latin America.

As a girl I was kept under strict surveillance, since virtue and modesty were, by   4
cultural equation, the same as family honor. As a teenager I was instructed on how
to behave as a proper señorita. But it was a conflicting message girls got, since the
Puerto Rican mothers also encouraged their daughters to look and act like women
and to dress in clothes our Anglo friends and their mothers found too "mature" for

our age. It was, and is, cultural, yet I often felt humiliated when I appeared at an American friend's party wearing a dress more suitable to a semiformal than to a playroom birthday celebration. At Puerto Rican festivities, neither the music nor the colors we wore could be too loud. I still experience a vague sense of letdown when I'm invited to a "party" and it turns out to be a marathon conversation in hushed tones rather than a fiesta with salsa, laughter, and dancing—the kind of celebration I remember from my childhood.

I remember Career Day in our high school, when teachers told us to come dressed as if for a job interview. It quickly became obvious that to the barrio girls, "dressing up" sometimes meant wearing ornate jewelry and clothing that would be more appropriate (by mainstream standards) for the company Christmas party than as daily office attire. That morning I had agonized in front of my closet, trying to figure out what a "career girl" would wear because, essentially except for Marlo Thomas on TV, I had no models on which to base my decision. I knew how to dress for school: at the Catholic school I attended we all wore uniforms; I knew how to dress for Sunday mass, and I knew what dresses to wear for parties at my relatives' homes. Though I do not recall the precise details of my Career Day outfit, it must have been a composite of the above choices. But I remember a comment my friend (an Italian-American) made in later years that coalesced my impressions of that day. She said that at the business school she was attending the Puerto Rican girls always stood out for wearing "everything at once." She meant, of course, too much jewelry, too many accessories. On that day at school, we were simply made the negative models by the nuns who were themselves not credible fashion experts to any of us. But it was painfully obvious to me that to the others, in their tailored skirts and silk blouses, we must have seemed "hopeless" and "vulgar." Though I now know that most adolescents feel out of step much of the time, I also know that for the Puerto Rican girls of my generation that sense was intensified. The way our teachers and classmates looked at us that day in school was just a taste of the culture clash that awaited us in the real world, where prospective employers and men on the street would often misinterpret our tight skirts and jingling bracelets as a come-on.

Mixed cultural signals have perpetuated certain stereotypes—for example, that of the Hispanic woman as the "Hot Tamale" or sexual firebrand. It is a one-dimensional view that the media have found easy to promote. In their special vocabulary, advertisers have designated "sizzling" and "smoldering" as the adjectives of choice for describing not only the foods but also the women of Latin America. From conversations in my house I recall hearing about the harassment that Puerto Rican women endured in factories where the "boss men" talked to them as if sexual innuendo was all they understood and, worse, often gave them the choice of submitting to advances or being fired.

It is custom, however, not chromosomes, that leads us to choose scarlet over pale pink. As young girls, we were influenced in our decisions about clothes and colors by the women—older sisters and mothers who had grown up on a tropical island where the natural environment was a riot of primary colors, where showing your skin was one way to keep cool as well as to look sexy. Most important of all, on the island, women perhaps felt freer to dress and move more provocatively, since, in most cases, they were protected by the traditions, mores, and laws of a Spanish/Catholic system of morality and machismo whose main rule was: *You may look at my sister, but if you touch her I will kill you*. The extended family and church structure could provide a young woman with a circle of safety in her small pueblo on the island; if a man "wronged" a girl, everyone would close in to save her family honor.

This is what I have gleaned from my discussions as an adult with older Puerto Rican women. They have told me about dressing in their best party clothes on Saturday nights and going to the town's plaza to promenade with their girlfriends in front of the boys they liked. The males were thus given an opportunity to admire the women and to express their admiration in the form of *piropos*: erotically charged street poems they composed on the spot. I have been subjected to a few piropos while visiting the Island, and they can be outrageous, although custom dictates that they must never cross into obscenity. This ritual, as I understand it, also entails a show of studied indifference on the woman's part; if she is "decent," she must not acknowledge the man's impassioned words. So I do understand how things can be lost in translation. When a Puerto Rican girl dressed in her idea of what is attractive meets a man from the mainstream culture who has been trained to react to certain types of clothing as a sexual signal, a clash is likely to take place. The line I first heard based on this aspect of the myth happened when the boy who took me to my first formal dance leaned over to plant a sloppy overeager kiss painfully on my mouth, and when I didn't respond with sufficient passion said in a resentful tone: "I thought you Latin girls were supposed to mature early"—my first instance of being thought of as a fruit or vegetable—I was supposed to *ripen*, not just grow into womanhood like other girls.

8

It is surprising to some of my professional friends that some people, including those who should know better, still put others, "in their place." Though rarer, these incidents are still commonplace in my life. It happened to me most recently during a stay at a very classy metropolitan hotel favored by young professional couples for their weddings. Late one evening after the theater, as I walked toward my room with my new colleague (a woman with whom I was coordinating an arts program), a middle-aged man in a tuxedo, a young girl in satin and lace on his arm, stepped directly into our path. With his champagne glass extended toward me, he exclaimed, "Evita!"

9

Our way blocked, my companion and I listened as the man half-recited, half-bellowed "Don't Cry for Me, Argentina." When he finished, the young girl said: "How about a round of applause for my daddy?" We complied, hoping this would bring the silly spectacle to a close. I was becoming aware that our little group was attracting the attention of the other guests. "Daddy" must have perceived this too, and he once more barred the way as we tried to walk past him. He began to shout-sing a ditty to the tune of "La Bamba"—except the lyrics were about a girl named María whose exploits all rhymed with her name and gonorrhea. The girl kept saying "Oh, Daddy" and looking at me with pleading eyes. She wanted me to laugh along with the others. My companion and I stood silently waiting for the man to end his offensive song. When he finished, I looked not at him but at his daughter. I advised her calmly never to ask her father what he had done in the army. Then I walked between them and to

10

my room. My friend complimented me on my cool handling of the situation. I confessed to her that I really had wanted to push the jerk into the swimming pool. I knew that this same man—probably a corporate executive, well educated, even worldly by most standards—would not have been likely to regale a white woman with a dirty song in public. He would perhaps have checked his impulse by assuming that she could be somebody's wife or mother, or at least *somebody* who might take offense. But to him, I was just an Evita or a María: merely a character in his cartoon-populated universe.

Because of my education and my proficiency with the English language, I have   11
acquired many mechanisms for dealing with the anger I experience. This was not true for my parents, nor is it true for the many Latin women working at menial jobs who must put up with stereotypes about our ethnic group such as: "They make good domestics." This is another facet of the myth of the Latin woman in the United States. Its origin is simple to deduce. Work as domestics, waitressing, and factory jobs are all that's available to women with little English and few skills. The myth of the Hispanic menial has been sustained by the same media phenomenon that made "Mammy" from *Gone with the Wind* America's idea of the black woman for generations; María, the housemaid or counter girl, is now indelibly etched into the national psyche. The big and the little screens have presented us with the picture of the funny Hispanic maid, mispronouncing words and cooking up a spicy storm in a shiny California kitchen.

This media-engendered image of the Latina in the United States has been doc-   12
umented by feminist Hispanic scholars, who claim that such portrayals are partially responsible for the denial of opportunities for upward mobility among Latinas in the professions. I have a Chicana friend working on a Ph.D. in philosophy at a major university. She says her doctor still shakes his head in puzzled amazement at all the "big words" she uses. Since I do not wear my diplomas around my neck for all to see, I too have on occasion been sent to that "kitchen," where some think I obviously belong.

One such incident that has stayed with me, though I recognize it as a minor   13
offense, happened on the day of my first public poetry reading. It took place in Miami in a boat-restaurant where we were having lunch before the event. I was nervous and excited as I walked in with my notebook in my hand. An older woman motioned me to her table. Thinking (foolish me) that she wanted me to autograph a copy of my brand new slender volume of verse, I went over. She ordered a cup of coffee from me, assuming that I was the waitress. Easy enough to mistake my poems for menus, I suppose. I know that it wasn't an intentional act of cruelty, yet of all the good things that happened that day, I remember that scene most clearly, because it reminded me of what I had to overcome before anyone would take me seriously. In retrospect I understand that my anger gave my reading fire, that I have almost always taken doubts in my abilities as a challenge—and that the result is, most times, a feeling of satisfaction at having won a convert when I see the cold, appraising eyes warm to my words, the body language change, the smile that indicates that I have opened some avenue for communication. That day I read to that woman and her lowered eyes told me that she was embarrassed at her little faux pas, and when I willed her to look up

at me, it was my victory, and she graciously allowed me to punish her with my full attention. We shook hands at the end of the reading, and I never saw her again. She has probably forgotten the whole thing but maybe not.

Yet I am one of the lucky ones. My parents made it possible for me to acquire a stronger footing in the mainstream culture by giving me the chance at an education. And, books and art have saved me from the harsher forms of ethnic and racial prejudice that many of my Hispanic *compañeras* have had to endure. I travel a lot around the United States, reading from my books of poetry and my novel, and the reception I most often receive is one of positive interest by people who want to know more about my culture. There are, however, thousands of Latinas without the privilege of an education or the entrée into society that I have. For them life is a struggle against the misconceptions perpetuated by the myth of the Latina as whore, domestic or criminal. We cannot change this by legislating the way people look at us. The transformation, as I see it, has to occur at a much more individual level. My personal goal in my public life is to try to replace the old pervasive stereotypes and myths about Latinas with a much more interesting set of realities. Every time I give a reading, I hope the stories I tell, the dreams and fears I examine in my work, can achieve some universal truth which will get my audience past the particulars of my skin color, my accent, or my clothes. 14

I once wrote a poem in which I called us Latinas "God's brown daughters." This poem is really a prayer of sorts, offered upward, but also, through the human-to-human channel of art, outward. It is a prayer for communication, and for respect. In it, Latin women pray "in Spanish to an Anglo God/with a Jewish heritage," and they are "fervently hoping/that if not omnipotent,/at least He be bilingual." 15

Elizabeth Wong (1958–) was born in South Gate, an industrial city just south of downtown Los Angeles, to Chinese immigrant parents who valued hard work but experienced employment limitations due to racial prejudice. Her father died when she was five years old. The family later lived in Chinatown and Monterey Park. Continually feeling a misfit in Chinatown, Wong read avidly for comfort and escape, as she describes in the following essay. She went on to study journalism at the University of Southern California where she completed her B.A. in 1980. After working ten years in TV and print journalism in California and Connecticut, she began writing plays. She entered the M.F.A. playwriting program at the Tisch School of the Arts at New York University in 1989, although she continued as a contributing columnist for the *Los Angeles Times* opinion pages. She has written eight full-length plays, seven short plays, and seven plays for children. Her best-known plays include *Letters to a Revolutionary Student* (1993), the first American play commenting on the Tiananmen Square massacre, and *Kimchee and Chitlins: A Serious Comedy about Getting Along* (1996), dealing with the news coverage of the black boycott of Korean-owned stores in New York City. She has taught as an adjunct visiting professor or guest lecturer at many universities, including the University of Southern California, Loyola University, and Emory University. She has been an artist-in-residence at Harvard University, Bowdoin College, and the University of Washington, among others. In the essay below, Wong describes her forced enrollment in Chinese school and her childhood feelings of exclusion from both the Chinese-American and mainstream American cultures in which she lived.

The Struggle to Be an All-American Girl

Elizabeth Wong

It's still there, the Chinese school on Yale Street where my brother and I used to 1 go. Despite the new coat of paint and the high wire fence, the school I knew ten years ago remains remarkably, stoically the same.

Every day at five P.M., instead of playing with our fourth- and fifth-grade 2 friends or sneaking out to the empty lot to hunt ghosts and animal bones, my brother and I had to go to Chinese school. No amount of kicking, screaming, or pleading could dissuade my mother, who was solidly determined to have us learn the language of our heritage.

Forcibly, she walked us the seven long, hilly blocks from our home to school, 3 depositing our defiant tearful faces before the stern principal. My only memory of him is that he swayed on his heels like a palm tree, and he always clasped his impatient twitching hands behind his back. I recognized him as a repressed maniacal child killer, and knew that if we ever saw his hands we'd be in big trouble.

We all sat in little chairs in an empty auditorium. The room smelled like 4 Chinese medicine, an imported faraway mustiness. Like ancient mothballs or dirty closets. I hated that smell. I favored crisp new scents. Like the soft French perfume that my American teacher wore in public school.

There was a stage far to the right, flanked by an American flag and the flag of the Nationalist republic of China, which was also red, white and blue but not as pretty.   5

Although the emphasis at the school was mainly language—speaking, reading, writing—the lessons always began with an exercise in politeness. With the entrance of the teacher, the best student would tap a bell and everyone would get up, kowtow, and chant, "Sing san ho," the phonetic for "How are you, teacher?"   6

Being ten years old, I had better things to learn than ideographs copied painstakingly in lines that ran right to left from the tip of a *moc but*, a real ink pen that had to be held in an awkward way if blotches were to be avoided. After all I could do the multiplication tables, name the satellites of Mars, and write reports on *Little Women* and *Black Beauty*. Nancy Drew, my favorite book heroine, never spoke Chinese.   7

The language was a source of embarrassment. More times than not, I had tried to disassociate myself from the nagging loud voice that followed me wherever I wandered in the nearby American supermarket outside Chinatown. The voice belonged to my grandmother, a fragile woman in her seventies who could outshout the best of the street vendors. Her humor was raunchy, her Chinese rhythmless, patternless. It was quick, it was loud, it was unbeautiful. It was not like the quiet, lilting romance of French or the gentle refinement of the American South. Chinese sounded pedestrian. Public.   8

In Chinatown, the comings and goings of hundreds of Chinese on their daily tasks sounded chaotic and frenzied. I did not want to be thought of as mad, as talking gibberish. When I spoke English, people nodded at me, smiled sweetly, said encouraging words. Even the people in my culture would cluck and say that I'd do well in life. "My, doesn't she move her lips fast," they would say, meaning that I'd be able to keep up with the world outside Chinatown.   9

My brother was even more fanatical than I about speaking English. He was especially hard on my mother, criticizing her, often cruelly, for her pidgin speech—smatterings of Chinese scattered like chop suey in her conversation. "It's not 'What it is,' Mom," he'd say in exasperation. "It's 'What *is* it, what *is* it, what *is* it!" Sometimes Mom might leave out an occasional "the" or "a," or perhaps a verb of being. He would stop her in mid-sentence: "Say it again, Mom. Say it right." When he tripped over his own tongue, he'd blame it on her: "See, Mom, it's all your fault. You set a bad example."   10

What infuriated my mother most was when my brother cornered her on her consonants, especially "r." My father had played a cruel joke on Mom by assigning her an American name that her tongue wouldn't allow her to say. No matter how hard she tried, "Ruth" always ended up "Luth" or "Roof."   11

After two years of writing with a *moc but* and reciting words with multiples of meanings, I finally was granted a cultural divorce. I was permitted to stop Chinese school.   12

I thought of myself as multicultural. I preferred tacos to egg rolls; I enjoyed Cinco de Mayo more than Chinese New Year.   13

At last, I was one of you; I wasn't one of them.   14

Sadly, I still am.   15

Alice Walker (1944–   ), born and raised in Eatonton, Georgia, is an American novelist, short story writer, and poet. Walker tends in her fiction to deal with personal and family relationships, particularly among black women, and their struggles with racism and sexism. She received much acclaim for *The Color Purple* (1982), a novel about the trials and eventual triumph of a young black Southern woman in the early twentieth century. The novel won a Pulitzer Prize in 1983 and was subsequently made into a successful film. Walker was principally responsible for reviving the reputation of Harlem Renaissance great Zora Neale Hurston. "In Search of Our Mothers' Gardens" was first published in 1974 in *Ms.* Magazine.

In Search of Our Mothers' Gardens

Alice Walker

> I described her own nature and temperament. Told how they needed a larger life for their expression. . . . I pointed out that in lieu of proper channels, her emotions had overflowed into paths that dissipated them. I talked, beautifully I thought, about an art that would be born, an art that would open the way for women the likes of her. I asked her to hope, and build up an inner life against the coming of that day. I sang, with a strange quiver in my voice, a promise song.
>
> —*Jean Toomer*, "Avey," CANE

The poet speaking to a prostitute who falls asleep while he's talking—   1

When the poet Jean Toomer walked through the South in the early twenties,   2
he discovered a curious thing: black women whose spirituality was so intense, so deep, so *unconscious,* that they were themselves unaware of the richness they held. They stumbled blindly through their lives: creatures so abused and mutilated in body, so dimmed and confused by pain, that they considered themselves unworthy even of hope. In the selfless abstractions their bodies became to the men who used them, they became more than "sexual objects," more even than mere women: they became "Saints." Instead of being perceived as whole persons, their bodies became shrines: what was thought to be their minds became temples suitable for worship. These crazy Saints stared out at the world, wildly, like lunatics—or quietly, like suicides; and the "God" that was in their gaze was as mute as a great stone.

Who were these Saints? These crazy, loony, pitiful women?   3

Some of them, without a doubt, were our mothers and grandmothers.   4

In the still heat of the post-Reconstruction South, this is how they seemed to   5
Jean Toomer: exquisite butterflies trapped in an evil honey, toiling away their lives in an era, a century, that did not acknowledge them, except as "the *mule* of the world." They dreamed dreams that no one knew—not even themselves, in any coherent fashion—and saw visions no one could understand. They wandered or sat about

the countryside crooning lullabies to ghosts, and drawing the mother of Christ in charcoal on courthouse walls.

They forced their minds to desert their bodies and their striving spirits sought 6
to rise, like frail whirlwinds from the hard red clay. And when those frail whirlwinds fell, in scattered particles, upon the ground, no one mourned. Instead, men lit candles to celebrate the emptiness that remained, as people do who enter a beautiful but vacant space to resurrect a God.

Our mothers and grandmothers, some of them: moving to music not yet writ- 7
ten. And they waited.

They waited for a day when the unknown thing that was in them would be made 8
known; but guessed, somehow in their darkness, that on the day of their revelation they would be long dead. Therefore to Toomer they walked, and even ran, in slow motion. For they were going nowhere immediate, and the future was not yet within their grasp. And men took our mothers and grandmothers, "but got no pleasure from it." So complex was their passion and their calm.

To Toomer, they lay vacant and fallow as autumn fields, with harvest time never 9
in sight: and he saw them enter loveless marriages, without joy; and become prostitutes, without resistance; and become mothers of children, without fulfillment.

For these grandmothers and mothers of ours were not Saints, but Artists; driven 10
to a numb and bleeding madness by the springs of creativity in them for which there was no release. They were Creators, who lived lives of spiritual waste, because they were so rich in spirituality—which is the basis of Art—that the strain of enduring their unused and unwanted talent drove them insane. Throwing away this spirituality was their pathetic attempt to lighten the soul to a weight their work-worn, sexually abused bodies could bear.

What did it mean for a black woman to be an artist in our grandmothers' time? 11
In our great-grandmothers' day? It is a question with an answer cruel enough to stop the blood.

Did you have a genius of a great-great-grandmother who died under some igno- 12
rant and depraved white overseer's lash? Or was she required to bake biscuits for a lazy backwater tramp, when she cried out in her soul to paint watercolors of sunsets, or the rain falling on the green and peaceful pasturelands? Or was her body broken and forced to bear children (who were more often than not sold away from her)—eight, ten, fifteen, twenty children—when her one joy was the thought of modeling heroic figures of rebellion, in stone or clay?

How was the creativity of the black woman kept alive, year after year and cen- 13
tury after century, when for most of the years black people have been in America, it was a punishable crime for a black person to read or write? And the freedom to paint, to sculpt, to expand the mind with action did not exist. Consider, if you can bear to imagine it, what might have been the result if singing, too, had been forbidden by law. Listen to the voices of Bessie Smith, Billie Holiday, Nina Simone, Roberta Flack, and Aretha Franklin, among others, and imagine those voices muzzled for life. Then you may begin to comprehend the lives of our "crazy," "Sainted" mothers and grandmothers. The agony of the lives of women who might have been

Poets, Novelists, Essayists, and Short-Story Writers (over a period of centuries), who died with their real gifts stifled within them.

And, if this were the end of the story, we would have cause to cry out in my paraphrase of Okot p'Bitek's great poem: 14

> O, my clanswomen
> Let us all cry together!
> Come,
> Let us mourn the death of our mother,
> The death of a Queen
> The ash that was produced
> By a great fire!
> O, this homestead is utterly dead
> Close the gates
> With *lacari* thorns,
> For our mother
> The creator of the Stool is lost!
> And all the young women
> Have perished in the wilderness!

But this is not the end of the story, for all the young women—our mothers and   15
grandmothers, *ourselves*—have not perished in the wilderness. And if we ask ourselves why, and search for and find the answer, we will know beyond all efforts to erase
it from our minds, just exactly who, and of what, we black American women are.

One example, perhaps the most pathetic, most misunderstood one, can provide   16
a backdrop for our mothers' work: Phillis Wheatley, a slave in the 1700s.

Virginia Woolf, in her book *A Room of One's Own*, wrote that in order for a   17
woman to write fiction she must have two things, certainly: a room of her own (with
key and lock) and enough money to support herself.

What then are we to make of Phillis Wheatley, a slave, who owned not even   18
herself? This sickly, frail black girl who required a servant of her own at times—her
health was so precarious—and who, had she been white, would have been easily considered the intellectual superior of all the women and most of the men in the society of her day.

Virginia Woolf wrote further, speaking of course not of our Phillis, that "any   19
woman born with a great gift in the sixteenth century [insert "eighteenth century,"
insert "black woman," insert "born or made a slave"] would certainly have gone crazed,
shot herself, or ended her days in some lonely cottage outside the village, half witch,
half wizard [insert "Saint"], feared and mocked at. For it needs little skill and psychology to be sure that a highly gifted girl who had tried to use her gift for poetry
would have been so thwarted and hindered by contrary instincts [add "chains, guns,
the lash, the ownership of one's body by someone else, sub-mission to an alien religion"], that she must have lost her health and sanity to a certainty."

The key words, as they relate to Phillis, are "contrary instincts." For when we   20
read the poetry of Phillis Wheatley—as when we read the novels of Nella Larsen
or the oddly false-sounding autobiography of that freest of all black women writers,

Zora Hurston—evidence of "contrary instincts" is everywhere. Her loyalties were completely divided, as was, without question, her mind.

But how could this be otherwise? Captured at seven, a slave of wealthy, doting whites who instilled in her the "savagery" of the Africa they "rescued" her from . . . one wonders if she was even able to remember her homeland as she had known it, or as it really was. 21

Yet, because she did try to use her gift for poetry in a world that made her a slave, she was "so thwarted and hindered by . . . contrary instincts, that she . . . lost her health. . . ." In the last years of her brief life, burdened not only with the need to express her gift but also with a penniless, friendless "freedom" and several small children for whom she was forced to do strenuous work to feed, she lost her health, certainly. Suffering from malnutrition and neglect and who knows what mental agonies, Phillis Wheatley died. 22

So torn by "contrary instincts" was black, kidnapped, enslaved Phillis that her description of "the Goddess"—as she poetically called the Liberty she did not have—is ironically, cruelly humorous. And, in fact, has held Phillis up to ridicule for more than a century. It is usually read prior to hanging Phillis's memory as that of a fool. She wrote: 23

> The Goddess comes, she moves divinely fair,
> Olive and laurel binds her *golden* hair.
> Wherever shines this native of the skies,
> Unnumber'd charms and recent graces rise. [My italics]

It is obvious that Phillis, the slave, combed the "Goddess's" hair every morning; prior, perhaps, to bringing in the milk, or fixing her mistress's lunch. She took her imagery from the one thing she saw elevated above all others. 24

With the benefit of hindsight we ask, "How could she?" 25

But at last, Phillis, we understand. No more snickering when your stiff, struggling, ambivalent lines are forced on us. We know now that you were not an idiot or a traitor; only a sickly little black girl, snatched from your home and country and made a slave; a woman who still struggled to sing the song that was your gift, although in a land of barbarians who praised you for your bewildered tongue. It is not so much what you sang, as that you kept alive, in so many of our ancestors, *the notion of song*. 26

Black women are called, in the folklore that so aptly identifies one's status in society, "the *mule* of the world," because we have been handed the burdens that everyone else—*everyone* else—refused to carry. We have also been called "Matriarchs," "Superwomen," and "Mean and Evil Bitches." Not to mention "Castraters" and "Sapphire's Mama." When we have pleaded for understanding, our character has been distorted; when we have asked for simple caring, we have been handed empty inspirational appellations, then stuck in the farthest corner. When we have asked for love, we have been given children. In short, even our plainer gifts, our labors of fidelity and love, have been knocked down our throats. To be an artist and a black woman, 27 even today, lowers our status in many respects, rather than raises it: and yet, artists we will be.

Therefore we must fearlessly pull out of ourselves and look at and identify with our lives the living creativity some of our great-grandmothers were not allowed to know. I stress *some* of them because it is well known that the majority of our great-grandmothers knew, even without "knowing" it, the reality of their spirituality, even if they didn't recognize it beyond what happened in the singing at church—and they never had any intention of giving it up. 28

How they did it—those millions of black women who were not Phillis Wheatley, or Lucy Terry or Frances Harper or Zora Hurston or Nella Larsen or Bessie Smith; or Elizabeth Catlett, or Katherine Dunham, either—brings me to the title of this essay, "In Search of Our Mothers' Gardens," which is a personal account that is yet shared, in its theme and its meaning, by all of us. I found, while thinking about the far-reaching world of the creative black woman, that often the truest answer to a question that really matters can be found very close. 29

In the late 1920s my mother ran away from home to marry my father. Marriage, if not running away, was expected of seventeen-year-old girls. By the time she was twenty, she had two children and was pregnant with a third. Five children later, I was born. And this is how I came to know my mother: she seemed a large, soft, loving-eyed woman who was rarely impatient in our home. Her quick, violent temper was on view only a few times a year, when she battled with the white landlord who had the misfortune to suggest to her that her children did not need to go to school. 30

She made all the clothes we wore, even my brothers' overalls. She made all the towels and sheets we used. She spent the summers canning vegetables and fruits. She spent the winter evenings making quilts enough to cover all our beds. 31

During the "working" day, she labored beside—not behind—my father in the fields. Her day began before sunup, and did not end until late at night. There was never a moment for her to sit down, undisturbed, to unravel her own private thoughts; never a time free from interruption—by work or the noisy inquiries of her many children. And yet, it is to my mother—and all our mothers who were not famous—that I went in search of the secret of what has fed that muzzled and often mutilated, but vibrant, creative spirit that the black woman has inherited, and that pops out in wild and unlikely places to this day. 32

But when, you will ask, did my overworked mother have time to know or care about feeding the creative spirit? 33

The answer is so simple that many of us have spent years discovering it. We have constantly looked high, when we should have looked high—and low. 34

For example: in the Smithsonian Institution in Washington, D.C., there hangs a quilt unlike any other in the world. In fanciful, inspired, and yet simple and identifiable figures, it portrays the story of the Crucifixion. It is considered rare, beyond price. Though it follows no known pattern of quilt-making, and though it is made of bits and pieces of worthless rags, it is obviously the work of a person of powerful imagination and deep spiritual feeling. Below this quilt I saw a note that says it was made by "an anonymous Black woman in Alabama, a hundred years ago." 35

If we could locate this "anonymous" black woman from Alabama, she would 36
turn out to be one of our grandmothers—an artist who left her mark in the only materials she could afford, and in the only medium her position in society allowed her to use.

As Virginia Woolf wrote further, in *A Room of One's Own:* 37

Yet genius of a sort must have existed among women as it must have existed among the working class. [Change this to "slaves" and "the wives and daughters of sharecroppers."] Now and again an Emily Brontë or a Robert Burns [change this to "a Zora Hurston or a Richard Wright"] blazes out and proves its presence. But certainly it never got itself on to paper. When, however, one reads of a witch being ducked, of a woman possessed by devils [or "Sainthood"], of a wise woman selling herbs [our root workers], or even a very remarkable man who had a mother, then I think we are on the track of a lost novelist, a suppressed poet, of some mute and inglorious Jane Austen. . . . Indeed, I would venture to guess that Anon, who wrote so many poems without signing them, was often a woman. . . .

And so our mothers and grandmothers have, more often than not anonymously, 38
handed on the creative spark, the seed of the flower they themselves never hoped to see: or like a sealed letter they could not plainly read.

And so it is, certainly, with my own mother. Unlike "Ma" Rainey's songs, which 39
retained their creator's name even while blasting forth from Bessie Smith's mouth, no song or poem will bear my mother's name. Yet so many of the stories that I write, that we all write, are my mother's stories. Only recently did I fully realize this: that through years of listening to my mother's stories of her life, I have absorbed not only the stories themselves, but something of the manner in which she spoke, something of the urgency that involves the knowledge that her stories—like her life—must be recorded. It is probably for this reason that so much of what I have written is about characters whose counterparts in real life are so much older than I am.

But the telling of these stories, which came from my mother's lips as naturally as 40
breathing, was not the only way my mother showed herself as an artist. For stories, too, were subject to being distracted, to dying without conclusion. Dinners must be started, and cotton must be gathered before the big rains. The artist that was and is my mother showed itself to me only after many years. This is what I finally noticed:

Like Mem, a character in *The Third Life of Grange Copeland,* my mother adorned 41
with flowers whatever shabby house we were forced to live in. And not just your typical straggly country stand of zinnias, either. She planted ambitious gardens—and still does—with over fifty different varieties of plants that bloom profusely from early March until late November. Before she left home for the fields, she watered her flowers, chopped up the grass, and laid out new beds. When she returned from the fields she might divide clumps of bulbs, dig a cold pit, uproot and replant roses, or prune branches from her taller bushes or trees—until night came and it was too dark to see.

Whatever she planted grew as if by magic, and her fame as a grower of flowers 42
spread over three counties. Because of her creativity with her flowers, even my memories of poverty are seen through a screen of blooms—sunflowers, petunias, roses, dahlias, forsythia, spirea, delphiniums, verbena . . . and on and on.

And I remember people coming to my mother's yard to be given cuttings from her flowers; I hear again the praise showered on her because whatever rocky soil she landed on, she turned into a garden. A garden so brilliant with colors, so original in its design, so magnificent with life and creativity, that to this day people drive by our house in Georgia—perfect strangers and imperfect strangers—and ask to stand or walk among my mother's art.   43

I notice that it is only when my mother is working in her flowers that she is radiant, almost to the point of being invisible—except as Creator: hand and eye. She is involved in work her soul must have. Ordering the universe in the image of her personal conception of Beauty.   44

Her face, as she prepares the Art that is her gift, is a legacy of respect she leaves to me, for all that illuminates and cherishes life. She has handed down respect for the possibilities—and the will to grasp them.   45

For her, so hindered and intruded upon in so many ways, being an artist has still been a daily part of her life. This ability to hold on, even in very simple ways, is work black women have done for a very long time.   46

This poem is not enough, but it is something, for the woman who literally covered the holes in our walls with sunflowers: 47

> They were women then
> My mama's generation
> Husky of voice—Stout of
> Step
> With fists as well as
> Hands
> How they battered down
> Doors
> And ironed
> Starched white
> Shirts
> How they led
> Armies
> Headragged Generals
> Across mined
> Fields
> Booby-trapped
> Kitchens
> To discover books
> Desks
> A place for us
> How they knew what we
> *Must* know
> Without knowing a page
> Of it
> Themselves.

The iDeal Reader

Alice Walker, "In Search
of Our Mothers' Gardens"

Reading

© The McGraw–Hill
Companies, 2002

83

Guided by my heritage of a love of beauty and a respect for strength—in search   48
of my mother's garden, I found my own.

And perhaps in Africa over two hundred years ago, there was just such a mother;   49
perhaps she painted vivid and daring decorations in oranges and yellows and greens
on the walls of her hut; perhaps she sang—in a voice like Roberta Flack's—*sweetly*
over the compounds of her village; perhaps she wove the most stunning mats or told
the most ingenious stories of all the village storytellers. Perhaps she was herself a
poet—though only her daughter's name is signed to the poems that we know.

Perhaps Phillis Wheatley's mother was also an artist.   50

Perhaps in more than Phillis Wheatley's biological life is her mother's signa-   51
ture made clear.

Science, Technology, and Society

Dorothy Nelkin (1933–   ), born on July 30 in Boston, received a B.A. degree from Cornell University in 1954 before becoming a sociologist at New York University. She has also worked as a senior research associate in science, technology, and society at Cornell University; as a professor of sociology at Cornell and New York University; and an affiliated professor of law. Nelkin won a Guggenheim fellowship in 1983 and became a Russell Sage Fellow in 1984. She has written or co-written over a dozen books of nonfiction on labor, politics, technology, and science. Her books include *Nuclear Power and Its Critics: The Cayuga Lake Controversy* (1971), *The University and Military Research: Moral Politics at M.I.T.* (1972), *The Creation Controversy: Science or Scripture in the Schools* (1982); and *Selling Science: How the Press Covers Science and Technology* (1987).

The Mystique of Science in the Press

Dorothy Nelkin

On January 16, 1902, the editor of the *Nation* wrote a critical editorial on the popular appreciation of science. The public conceives of science as a "variant of the black art," of scientists as wizards and magicians, socially isolated from the society. "The scientist appears akin to the medicine man . . . "the multitude thinks of him as a being of quasi-supernatural and romantic powers. . . . There is in all this little resemblance to Huxley's definition of science as simply organized and trained common sense." To the extent that the public still holds such attitudes, one should not be surprised given the image of science in the press.

Science often appears in the press today as an arcane and incomprehensible subject, far from organized common sense. And scientists still appear to be remote but superior wizards, above ordinary people, culturally isolated from the society. Such heroic images are perhaps most apparent in press reports about prestigious scientists, especially Nobel laureates. But the mystique of science as a superior culture is also conveyed in the promotion of science literacy, in the coverage of scientific theories, and even in stories about scientific fraud. The result? Far from enhancing public understanding, such press coverage creates a distance between scientists and the public that, paradoxically, obscures the importance of science and its effect on our daily lives.

The Scientist as Star

Each year the press devotes increased attention to winners of the Nobel Prize. Most news magazines have doubled their coverage over the past decade; much of this extra space is being used simply for larger headlines and a greater number of photographs. In the accompanying text, the press, with stunning regularity, focuses on the recipient's national affiliations and stellar qualities, using language recycled from reports of the Olympic games. "Another strong U.S. show"; "Americans again this year receive a healthy share of the Nobel prizes"; "U.S. showed it is doing something right by scoring a near sweep of the 1980 Nobel Prize"; "The winning American style." These are the headlines one is likely to find in newspapers across the country.

From *Selling Science* by Dorothy Nelkin. Copyright © 1987 by W. H. Freeman and Company. Reprinted with permission.

Just as the papers count Olympic medals, so they keep a running count of the Nobel awards: one year "Americans won eight of eleven"; in another, "Eight Americans were recognized, tying a record set in 1972." "Since 1941," *U.S. News and World Report* announced to its readers in 1980, "the U.S. has had 126 Nobel winners in science, more than double the number won by second place Britain." The stories describe nations as rivals somehow competing in a Nobel race for national pride—an image that obfuscates the international cooperation that is supposed to, and often does, characterize scientific endeavors.

Following the style of sports writing or reports of Academy Awards, journalists emphasize the honor, the glory, and the supreme achievement of the prize: "The most prestigious prizes in the world. . . . They bring instant fame, flooding winners with speaking invitations, job offers, book contracts, and honorary degrees," runs a typical comment. In 1979 *Time* printed a large picture of the gold medal: "The Nobel Prize Winners are called to Mount Olympus; the recipients have worldwide respect."

Local or regional papers also cover Nobel winners like sports or movie stars but add a twist, seeking to find a local angle, however remote. Consider Ronald Hoffmann, who received the 1981 prize in chemistry. A Rochester, New York, paper mentioned that he was a "Kodak consultant." The *New York Daily News* reported that he had graduated from Stuyvesant High School in New York City and printed his picture from the high school yearbook with the caption: "Another example of an alumnus who has done well." A journalist on a Seattle newspaper found a local angle in the fact that one of Hoffmann's Ph.D. advisers was a professor at the University of Washington. Columbia University claimed Hoffmann as one of 39 laureates among its former faculty and alumni. In fact, university publications not infrequently provide counts of the prizes of their alumni and faculty as evidence that their institutions are vibrant and vital research centers. A Harvard publication boasts of "more than twice the number than from any other American university."

In one important respect, though, reports of Nobel awards differ markedly from sports writing. Coverage of sports stars often includes analyses of their training, their techniques, and the details of their accomplishments. However, except in the *New York Times* and specialized science journals, the coverage of Nobel scientists seldom includes details on the nature of the prizewinner's research or its scientific significance. To the extent that research is noted at all, it appears as an arcane, esoteric, mysterious activity that is beyond the comprehension of normal human beings. "How many people could identify with Mr. Hoffman's lecture subject: 'coupling carbenes and carbynes on mono-, di-, and tri-nuclear transmission metal centers' "? The presentation of science as arcane is reinforced by photographs of scientists standing before blackboards that are covered with complicated equations.

In their interviews with journalists, scientists themselves reinforce the mystification of science by emphasizing the extraordinary complexity of their work. Physicist Val Fitch describes his research: "It's really quite arcane." "I find it difficult to convey to my family just what it is I've been doing," said physicist James Cronin in an interview with a *Time* reporter in 1980. *Time* cited the words of a member of the Nobel committee to describe Cronin's work: "Only an Einstein could say what it means."

4

5

6

7

8

Just as science is described as divorced from normal activity, so the scientist, at least the male scientist, is portrayed in popular newspapers and magazines as socially removed, apart from, and above most normal human preoccupations. Science thus appears to be the activity of lonely geniuses whose success reflects their combination of inspiration and total dedication to their work. One scientist sees "in a most passive looking object" a "veritable cauldron of activity" that the rest of us are unaware of. Another "stumbled" on his find but then spent a year "probing" for errors. A frequent image is that of scientists spending twelve hours a day, seven days a week, at their work. Reporting on the effect of the prize on Sir Godfrey Hounsfield, one of the 1979 winners in medicine, a journalist from *Time* notes only one change in his life: "He plans to put a laboratory in his living room." Another reporter portrays prizewinning scientists as part of "an inner circle of scientific giants" who talk about science "the way other people talk about ball games." Being with them is "like sitting in a conversation with the angels."

That a prestigious scientist can behave like ordinary mortals is noted with an air of surprise. The caption of a *New York Times* photograph of Walter Gilbert (the Nobel Prize winning chemist who gave up his chair at Harvard to run the firm Biogen) notes his managerial skills: "[These] should not be underestimated just because he has a Nobel Prize." Writing of Nobel physicist Hans Bethe's concern about the buildup of nuclear weapons, a *New York Times* reporter remarks that "he ultimately places his faith not in technology but in human beings—a remarkable stance for a man who has dedicated his life to the pursuit of science." The fact that celebrated scientists often teach undergraduate classes or keep office hours is considered a newsworthy point: "Why would a world-class scientist waste time describing electrons to a fidgety mob of 400 students?"

While successful male scientists appear in the press as above the mundane world and totally absorbed in their work, the few women laureates have a very different image. Stories of female Nobel Prize winners appear not only in the science pages, but in such life style and women's magazines as *Vogue* and *McCall's*, which seldom cover science news.

McCall's described Maria Mayer, who shared the physics prize in 1963 for her theoretical work on the structure of the nucleus, as a "tiny, shy, touchingly devoted wife and mother," a woman "who makes people very happy at her home." Approaching the story in a personal style hard to imagine in the coverage of a male Nobelist, the reporter interviewed Mayer's husband, who observed: "She was once a terrible flirt but lovely and brighter than any girl I had ever met." She is, according to this article, "almost too good to be true"; "a brilliant scientist, her children were perfectly darling, and she was so darned pretty that it all seemed unfair." The reporter noted the "graceful union between science and femininity," but also emphasized the conflict between being a mother and a scientist, the guilt, the opportunities missed by not spending more time at home. Writing about Mayer's work, the journalist remarked that she explains it in a "startlingly feminine way" because she used the image of onion layers to describe the structure of the atom. The article then goes on to describe Mayer's reputation as "the faculty's most elegant hostess."

Science journalists used similar stereotypes in their descriptions. A *Science Digest*   13
article called "At Home with Maria Mayer" begins: "The first woman to win a Nobel
Prize in science is a scientist and a wife." It showed a picture of her, not at the
blackboard, but at her kitchen stove. Similarly, the *New York Times* headlined its article on Dorothy Hodgkin, who shared the prize for chemistry in 1966: "British
Grandmother Wins the Prize." And *Time* emphasized her "domesticity" and "elegance
of appearance."

The feminist movement did little to dispel such stereotypes. In 1977 Rosalyn   14
Yalow, winner of the prize in medicine, also received extensive coverage in women's
magazines. By *Vogue* she was characterized as "a wonderwoman, remarkable, able
to do everything, who works 70 hours a week, who keeps a kosher kitchen, who is
a happily married, rather conventional wife and mother." *Family Health*, a magazine that reaches 5.3 million readers, headlined an article: "She Cooks, She Cleans,
She Wins the Nobel Prize" and introduced Yalow as a "Bronx housewife." The
journalist expected to meet "a crisp, efficient, no nonsense type" but discovered that
"she looked as though she would be at home selling brownies for the PTA fund raiser."

Journalists had more difficulty fitting Barbara McClintock, recipient of the 1983   15
Nobel Prize in medicine, into this stereotype, and this in itself became news. *Newsweek*
called her "the Greta Garbo of genetics. At 81 she has never married, always preferring
to be alone." This article was published in the section called "Transition" (along with
the obituaries), although an item on McClintock also appeared on the "Medicine"
page. The *New York Times* covered McClintock in a long feature article. Its very first
paragraph observed that she is well known for baking with black walnuts.

The overwhelming message in these popular press accounts is that the successful   16
woman scientist must have the ability to do everything—to be feminine, motherly,
and to achieve as well. Far from being insulated and apart from ordinary mortals,
women scientists are admired for fitting in and for balancing domestic with professional
activities. As a remarkable exception to the usual coverage of scientists in the press,
the portraits of female Nobelists only highlight the prevailing image of science as an
arcane and superior profession, and points up the lack of attention to its substance.

To complete the image of the esoteric scientist, journalists often convey the need   17
of money and, above all, freedom to sustain science stars. A 1979 *Time* article is a typical example, attributing the prominence of American Nobel Prize winners to the
"heady air of freedom in U.S. academia and the abundant flow of grants. . . . Just
do your own thing, the bounteous government seemed to say." The writer compares
this tradition of freedom to the "rigid" British, the "ideological" Soviets, and the "herr
doctor" syndrome in Germany and France. Accepting the conventional (but ques-
tionable) wisdom among many scientists, he expresses concern that the pressure to
apply science to practical ends and to impose "cumbersome" regulations on experimental procedures will limit future triumphs. This reporter also argues that U.S.
science gains by insulation from humanistic pursuits: "The best minds have not been
overburdened with required studies that are remote from their interests." Scientists,
he suggests, do such specialized and important work that they operate outside a
common intellectual or cultural tradition.

Ironically, while treating scientists as somehow removed from the common   18
culture, journalists often turn them into authorities in areas well outside their
professional competence. Thus we frequently read of their opinions on nuclear power,
the arms race, the prospect for world peace. In 1981 *U.S. News* offered its readers the
opinions of past and present American Nobel winners on the question "What are
the greatest challenges facing the U.S. and the world at large and what can be done
to meet those challenges?" The answers, of course, varied, but the message underlying
the question was clear: science is a superior form of knowledge, and those who have
reached its pinnacle have some special insight into every problem.

Vivian Sobchack (1940–) is professor emeritus of the University of California, Los Angeles's School of Theater, Film, and Television, and was associate dean of the School of Theater, Film, and Television there. A prolific author who has written on a wide range of subjects including film genre, philosophy, and theory, her essays have been published in *Body & Society*, *Film Quarterly*, and *Film Comment*, among others. She has edited two volumes of work on visual media and culture and authored five books, including *Screening Space: The American Science Fiction Film*, *The Address of the Eye: A Phenomenology of Film Experience*, and *Carnal Thoughts: Embodiment and Moving Image Culture*.

"SUSIE SCRIBBLES" ON TECHNOLOGY, TECHNË, AND WRITING INCARNATE

Vivian Sobchack

Il y a d'abord le moment où le désire s'investit dans la pulsion graphique, aboutissant à un objet calligraphique.—Roland Barthes

Avoid haphazard writing materials.—Walter Benjamin

The following phenomenological meditations on the carnal activity of writing were provoked by an electronic doll. A contemporary version of eighteenth-century anthropomorphic writing automata, "Susie Scribbles" appeared on the shelves of Toys R Us quite a number of Christmases ago and sold for $119. Unable to resist, I bought her. Susie and the peculiarities of her existence raised significant questions about writing bodies and writing technologies—not only because her automaton's instrumentalism interrogated what writing is and how it is accomplished but also because the form in which this instrumentalism was embodied interrogated what is—or is not—"human" about writing. Susie was a quite large female doll, about two feet high, meant to look (her brochure says) about five years old. She came with her own writing desk, a ballpoint pen (with four color ink cartridges for, one supposes, expressive purposes), a pad of paper, and a robotic arm—along with a tape cassette that fit in a player inserted in her back, which, under the overalls and pink polo shirt, gave her arm electronic instructions and enabled her to sing (albeit without moving her lips) about how much fun she and her consumer playmate were having. Aside from the very idea of her, as well as my curiosity about why—in this electronic moment—an anthropomorphic writing machine would still be fashioned to write with a pen rather than at a computer, what first really fascinated me about Susie was her comportment. A bit limp in body so that she could be positioned at her desk to appear as if she were really looking down at the paper, she had to be latched to her desk chair in back at her shoulders. Fair-skinned, blond, and blue-eyed, she

1

had a facial expression that seemed to me somewhat anxious. Most disturbing, however, was her lack of neck muscle. Her five-year-old's head hung down over the writing pad abjectly at best, at worst as if her neck were broken. In sum, as both a "writing technology" and a simulacrum of the lived body, "Susie Scribbles" made substantial for me questions about the relations between technology and embodiment in the matter—and meaning—of writing. I will return to Susie and her accomplishments later, but first I want to explore the materiality of writing as it is more humanly experienced in its subjective and objective forms.

Within the context of phenomenological inquiry, Susie hyperbolizes—by hypostatizing—the material nature of both "writing bodies" and "bodies of writing" and thus reminds us that writing is never an abstraction. It is a concrete intentional *activity* as well as, in its various substantial forms, a concrete intentional *object*. Both activity and object, the phenomenon we call writing also sufficiently (if not necessarily) implicates an embodied and enworlded *subject*—the one who writes, and in writing, not only through labor brings some "thing" into material presence and social meaning that was not there before but also spatially and temporally lives the activity through her body in a specifically meaningful, because specifically material, way.[1] Which is to say that writing is as much about *mattering* as it is about *meaning*. Making things matter, however, requires both a *technology* and a *technique*. Although writing is itself a concrete as well as social mediation between subjective consciousness and the objective world of others, it is further mediated through the materiality of discrete instrumental forms. Although we may trace letters in the sand, chisel words into stone, or sign a childhood pact in the blood from our finger, today in our culture we usually write with pencils, pens, typewriters, and "word-processing" computers—technologies we differently (and to different degrees) *incorporate* into our bodies and our experience of writing.[2] These technologies not only demand different techniques to use them, but they also differently frame and transform the sense and matter of the activity, object, and subject of writing—and hence its experience and meaning. This is not to say that we all have the same experience of the use of a particular writing instrument, nor is it to say that our experience of a particular writing instrument is constant and may not vary with our task or our mood, nor is it to deny that our valuation of writing instruments and practices is always constituted in history and culture. It is to say, however, that our carnal use of particular and material writing instruments informs and contributes to the structure of our thought and its concrete expression.

EMBODIED TECHNOLOGIES

In "A Phenomenology of Writing by Hand" Daniel Chandler points out that a wide range of our experience of writing can be linked to five key features that inform the activity and product of writing but vary according to the substantial materiality of our writing implements: directness of inscription; uniformity of script; speed of transcription; linearity of composition; and boundedness of surface.[3] Glossing these features, Chandler writes:

Directness refers to suspension in time and indirection in space. Clearly the pen and the pencil involve the most direct inscription; the typewriter involves spatial indirection and the word processor involves both this and temporally suspended inscription (making it the least direct). *Uniformity* refers to whether letters are shaped by hand (as with the pen and pencil) or pre-formed (as with the typewriter and the word processor). *Speed* refers to the potential speed of transcription relative to other tools. Clearly the typewriter and the word processor are potentially faster than the pen and the pencil, at least for longhand. *Linearity* refers to the extent to which the tool allows one to jump around in a text: here the word processor is far less linear than other media. By *boundedness* I refer to limits on the "frame-size" of a particular writing and reading surface. In the case of the typewriter, these bounds include the carriage width and the visibility of the text only above the typing line. In the case of the word processor this also includes the carriage width of the printer, but more importantly the number of lines and characters per line which can be displayed on the screen. Here the pen and the pencil are clearly less bounded. (72)

Although this may seem a dry reduction of what we already know (or think 4 we know), Chandler points out that these five features all "relate to the handling of space and time both by the tool and by the writer, and, since, as phenomenologists argue, such relationships are fundamental to our structuring of experience, it is hardly surprising that they may be experienced as transforming influences" (72). Thus, in "The Writer's Technique in Thirteen Theses," Walter Benjamin's quite serious dictum to the writer, Benjamin prescribes that writers "[a]void haphazard writing materials. A pedantic adherence to certain papers, pens, inks is beneficial. No luxury, but an abundance of these utensils is necessary."[4] And in an interview entitled "Un rapport presque maniaque avec les instruments graphique," Roland Barthes obsessed about his "problems in finding the right kind of pen."[5]

For example, now that I use the computer for writing anything more than 5 notes or lists, contemplation of the "bumpy" callus on the third finger of my right hand fills me with a certain wonder. It brings back physical memories from childhood and adolescence: of tightly gripping a pencil or pen, of writer's cramp, of pressing into different textures of paper to meet various forms of reception and resistance. Even at the moment of composing these present thoughts on a computer (which demands only slight substantial bodily engagement, the light touch of my fingertips on the keys nearly overridden by the intense concentration of my gaze), that callus reminds me of my earlier and more physical connection with writing. Most particularly, I recall the specific feeling of a vague thought gaining force and focus and momentum to take shape and emerge through my arm and in the grip of my fingers in the material form of words—which occasionally surprised even me with their sudden substance and rare exactitude.[6] The callus on my finger also reminds me that there is a reciprocity between our bodies and our various writing technologies that co-constitute different experiences of *spatiality*. Unlike my upright posture at the typewriter or computer, when I wrote with pencil or pen, I generally curled my body forward toward the protective half-circle of my left arm—whether I was sitting at a desk or table, sprawling on floor or bed, or propped up with a pad resting against my knees, whether I was dreamily writing a poem or anxiously taking a test at school. This bodily circumscription of a lived space made intimate not only points to my right-handedness in a way that my use of both hands at the typewriter and computer keyboard does not, but it also suggests a form of spatial privatization that my incorporation of pencil or pen inscribed along with my meanings.[7] This is a space that Gaston Bachelard might have described as shell-like: that is, a space constituted and inhabited in a dialectical structure of intrusion and extrusion, a space that among other qualities allowed for what Bachelard calls, as a characteristic of the *poiësis* of the shell, "the mystery of slow, continuous formation."[8] Thus, paradoxically, even in school, under the monitoring eyes of others, writing by hand with pencil or pen was a private, enclosed, and intimate experience of material and social emergence—one that encompassed and protected a world from intrusion as it simultaneously extruded and expressed it.

This lived space expanded but lost a certain intimate intensity when I began   6 to use a typewriter—although I was a good enough typist that, for the most part, my experience of the machine, like that of my pencil or pen, was sufficiently transparent for me to incorporate and write through it. Writing at the typewriter felt a less private experience; sitting at the machine somehow demanded a correspondent spatial accommodation of the concrete and artifactual quality of the room itself: the sheets of paper next to me, the furniture and books surrounding me. These "things" became gently unfocused toward the horizons of my vision as I gazed at the paper in my typewriter, but they remained a very physical presence nonetheless, a complement to all of the concrete and often pleasurably resistant materials I was engaging: the striking keys, the keyboard, the paper to be inserted and pulled out and crumpled or laid on a growing pile of achievement, a bottle of "white out" for mistakes, and so on.

In contrast, when I sit at my computer, the space of my writing seems at once   7 more intimate yet more immense than the shell-like experience of writing with a pen, and it also feels less physically grounded in the breadth of a world than the experience of writing at a typewriter. My experience at the computer is more tunnel-like than shell-like, more blindered, occluded, and abstract than expansively material and physical. Its intimate space is less one of intrusion and extrusion than of exclusion, its physical sense less that of impression and expression than of nearly effortless and immaterial exchange in which my body seems more diffuse—my head and the screen vaguely if intensely conjoined, my hands and fingers and the keyboard and mouse lightly felt peripherals to a less than solidly felt core. Even if, as Chandler notes above of writing through the computer, physical inscription is delayed and thus, as he puts it, "indirect," my sense of intense direct engagement with my words is enhanced if almost decorporealized—this proportionate to my spatial existence while writing, which seems in many ways to deny the limitations and resistances of my quotidian material world. Michael Heim describes this spatial experience in *Electric Language: A Philosophical Study of Word Processing*: "Words dance on the screen. Sentences slide smoothly into place, make way for one another, while paragraphs ripple down the screen. Words become highlighted, vanish at the push of a button, then reappear instantly at will" in this "frictionless electric element."[9] (In this regard the callus on my finger also—and indelibly—reminds me that my body and the writing materials it engages are marked by different degrees of friction and resistance in the making of the mark. This is an issue even with "Susie Scribbles," who, although she will never get a callus, may "not work" since as her brochure notes, certain writing implements, "usually the markers with the broad cloth tips, . . . create too much friction for the hand.")

That callus, in calling me back from the computer into a more physical world   8
of writing and writing instruments, reminds me also that my incorporation of pencil and pen and their particular materiality gives rise not only to particular *spatial forms* but also to particular *temporal forms*—for me marked at their limits, on the one side, by an aesthetic languor that locates its pleasure as much in the manual forging and visual sight of the letters and words as in their semantic and communicative value, and, on the other side, by a physical fatigue felt in the hand. Writing by hand seems slow and languorous or slow and laborious. Indeed, as Heim observes of writing by hand: "A certain amount of drudgery has always attached to the task of putting words on paper" (192). Yet the labor involved in handwriting also physically imprints and invests the subject in its object to constitute a particular *material value*. Thus, Heim also tells us: "The graphic stamp, or personal character, of the writer is more than a merely subjective component of the element of handwriting. . . . The graphic stamp is the subjective side of a process which includes the physical resistance of the materials and a respect for materials arising from this resistance" (193). For example, fascinated by watching his children use old-fashioned "dip pens" when they were in elementary school in France and compelled to try it out himself, philosopher Don Ihde comments on his perceived sense of "the slowness of the writing process" and the painfulness of rewriting. But, as he points out, this slowness has its correlated compensations: "I also discovered that while one's mental processes raced well ahead of the actual writing, (mental) editing could take shape while under way. One could formulate or reformulate a sentence several times before completion." Furthermore, Ihde notes how his "fascination with the actual appearance of the script, whose lettering could be quite beautiful in that the curves and varying scribing could attain aesthetic quality," led him to a rediscovery of the "art" of that style of writing we associate with belles lettres.[10]

Ihde describes and contrasts his own various experiences with different writ-   9
ing technologies ("the dip ink pen, a typewriter and the word processor") within a broader consideration of the phenomeno-logic of our embodied relations with, as he puts it, "technologies-in-use." Although he emphasizes that technologies (here, writing technologies) do not *determine* the subject's intentional behavior, he also emphasizes that technologies are never neutral, and thus, to varying degrees, they inform our behavior: "Technologies, by providing a framework for action, do form intentionalities and inclinations within which use-patterns take dominant shape." Thus, he tells us: "I could not claim that the use of the dip pen 'determined' that I write in the style of *belles lettres*, but the propensity or inclination was certainly there" (141). Certainly, the reason for writing is a cultural factor in qualifying any stylistic possibility or influence imposed by the specific materiality of

writing. Nonetheless, inflected, of course, by their historical situation in various cultural contexts, different writing technologies, Ihde suggests, may "incline" us toward different compositional and stylistic possibilities "simply by virtue of which part of the writing experience is enhanced and which made difficult" (142). Heim notes this as well: "The manipulation of symbols, the arrangement of symbolic domains, has its own special time and motion" (138).

There are, then, even major differences between the material experience of writing with a pencil or pen, since each possesses its own discretion, its own spatial claims, temporal rhythms, and motions. I recall that, for me, writing with a pencil involved a temporal rhythm rather different from writing with a pen. It involved a freedom of scrawl nearly always informed by the possibility of erasure. Indeed, erasure, itself part of the process, brought to writing with a pencil a particular temporal punctuation wrought by a hand gesture remarkably isomorphic, in this culture, with nodding one's head "no," followed by a motion that brushed from the paper the rubbery remnants of words that no longer mattered—at least not as written expression. Writing with pen rather than pencil, I recall a different rhythm: somewhat slower at first, when the page was neat, so I wouldn't make the first nonerasable mistake, then gaining a freer, if slightly hostile, momentum as the page became increasingly marked—and measured—by the messiness of error and self-repudiation. Thus, as Ihde remarks, "to actually rewrite was painful, and were the object to be a composed letter, it would call for starting over, since there was no simple erasure" (141). At the beginning (whether of a letter, a singular composition, or a fresh, new school notebook whose blank white pages prompted my perfection and then paled at my slips of hand or mind), I was more *thoughtful* writing with a pen, more aware of the *permanent commitment* I was making—and marking. (This experience was heightened in the few instances when, like Ihde, I tried to write with a dip pen but was largely reduced with my use of a computer, where, until I print them out, I can command words to move elsewhere or to vanish and do not even have to brush or blow away their remains.) Using a pen, I had to *cross out* mistakes rather than *erase* them, the rubbery pleasure of materially removing them gone—replaced by (often angry) additive gestures that covered over their worldly matter with slashes and black and blue marks so that, as if dead and defaced bodies, later identification of the words would be impossible. When I moved to the typewriter, however, these assaults on my mistakes were transformed—on the one hand, by a careful and additive, brush-stroke coating of Wite-Out that Heim calls "the industrial chore of correcting errors by imposing one material substance over another" (132) but that I found rather pleasurable in its soothing and ritual antidote to my mistake; on the other hand, by the typewriter's striking keys "x-ing" over a repudiated expression in a satisfyingly brisk physical gesture and staccato rhythm: the rat-a-tat-tat (particularly of my electric typewriter) evoking less a slashing or black-and-blue battery than an efficient machine-gunning of the errant words into nonexistence.

As we incorporate writing technologies, we simultaneously excorporate and give material form to our thoughts and feelings; and, as there is spatial reciprocity between the subjective and objective poles of this process, so also is there *tempo-*

10

11

ral reciprocity. A journalist friend of mine who hates computers and almost always prefers to write with pencil or pen tells me that she feels not so much technologically challenged as *temporally challenged* by both electric and electronic writing technologies. "As it is," she says, "I can barely tolerate the impatient hum of the electric typewriter waiting for my fingers on the keys, a low insistent reminder that time is passing. How could I think at all with a hungry computer screen glaring at me all the time?"[11] The flashing or blinking computer cursor seems particularly insistent and demanding of a response. Thus, as Chandler notes, although "such a feeling of being pressured by the tool into behaviour with which one is uncomfortable is certainly not the experience of all writers . . . one must insist to those who dismiss it that it remains important for those who do experience it" (71). Furthermore, despite an occasionally broken pencil point or an empty ink cartridge, pencils and pens stay relatively unchanged and constant in their material instrumentality compared to computer word-processing programs and the temporal demands, distractions, and interruptions they impose on the writing process even as they make certain aspects of it "easier" and "faster."

"If our artifacts do not act on us," Elaine Scarry observes, "there is no point in having made them. We make material artifacts in order to interiorize them: we make things so that they will in turn remake us, revising the interior of embodied consciousness."[12] Thus, as writing technologies incorporated by my body, the pencil and pen in-formed not only the particular shape of my lived space and temporality but also the manner in which I approached my task of creating meaning and matter in the world. Here, as Ihde noted of his inclination to write belles lettres when he used the dip pen, the notion of *existential style* emerges—a style that "character-izes" the subject of writing as much as it does the written object. Writing's relation to existential style is, of course, most materially figured in the eccentricity and "personality" of one's handwriting. In this regard it is telling that the term *belles lettres* first emerged between 1630 and 1699, a period that marks the emergence of mechanical print culture. As Tamara Plakins Thornton notes: "Only at this point did script come to be defined as distinct from print. If print was the impersonal product of a machine, then script became the creation of the hand, physically—and conceptually—linked to the human being who produces it."[13]

Yet even so personal and nontechnological a matter as one's own handwriting may alter, along with one's manner, in response to a particular writing technology. Thus, although it has been hardly admitted in the discourse on writing, it is telling that along with Benjamin and Barthes a great many people favor certain kinds of writing instruments over others—even when several would seem to accomplish the same objective task equally well. When it comes to pencils, for example, I have always had a preference for those with no. 2 lead. A no. 1 pencil marks the page too lightly but not gently enough for me: it seems too hard and stingy and unforgiving at its tip. With pens, my range of preference (and desire) is broader— although, generally, whether fountain pen, ballpoint, or felt-tip, and whatever the color, I prefer a fine point. Only occasionally do these choices have something to do with my *objective* task. There's no discernible reason that I should prefer to take notes at a lecture with a ballpoint rather than a felt-tip pen, prefer a felt-tip for

12

13

writing lists, reserve a fountain pen for special and more formal writing. I have no accountant's justification for seeking out a fine point. Nor, barring specific instructions on certain standardized tests or evaluation forms, does there seem to be any objective rationale for my preference of a no. 2 rather than no. 1 pencil—particularly when my choice in lead pencils seems in direct contradiction to my choice in fine-tipped pens (the softer, more expansive lead of a no. 2 pencil making thicker marks than a no. 1).

This apparent contradiction makes *existential* as well as *cultural* sense and, from a phenomenological perspective, is not a contradiction at all. It has direct bearing on the manufacture of my writing, the manner and style of my activity, the project that I am going about, and that objective matter called "writing" that I bring into being. As a child of my culture, with its sanctioned hierarchy of formality that begins with the pencil and moves from pen to typewriter/word processor to published print, I have always found writing with a pencil a relatively casual and dashing affair, writing with a pen relatively more committed and often even stately and formal.[14] Yet it is also materially and carnally true that the lighter imprint and stingy hardness of a no. 1 pencil does not coincide with the sloppy expansiveness and freeing allowance that, for me, is enabled by the softer lead and less resistant tip of a no. 2 pencil. (I have always tended to write theme outlines and impassioned poetry in pencil.) However, when I write more indelibly in ink, "committing" pen to paper (when do we ever use the term *commit* in relation to pencil, typewriter, or word processor?), I constitute the enabling possibility not only to physically *use* but also to materially *make* the "fine point." It is as though my thoughts go through an enhanced process of discrimination and refinement so that they are able to emerge physically through the precise and refined materiality of the pen nib. Indeed, before I switched to the typewriter and then to the computer, I preferred to write expository prose with a pen.

Now, of course, because of its ease, I write my essays and books on the computer—and, reminded by a certain quickening within my callus, I shudder at the thought of all the labor involved were I to have to use a pencil or pen or even my electric typewriter (which has been relegated for years now to somewhere in the back of my hall closet). Indeed, much has been made of this "ease" in writing on the computer—particularly by critics who note that facilitation of the physical process of writing and the ability to easily manipulate and alter text encourage not only the sloppy expansiveness I associate with the casual impermanence of the pencil but also the endless qualifications that move toward the ever finer points that, for me, were first correlated to fine-point pens. Thus, there's a tendency to write "long" on the computer, to lose sight (literally) of how many "pages" (material sheets of paper) there are—or should be—in relation to a given project. In relation to this expanded capacity to write, O. B. Hardison Jr. notes that "the thrust of computer writing is continuous movement ('scrolling') from one screen to the next,"[15] and Heim points out that scrolling, however expansively openended, is also a mode of concealment that "hides the calculational capacity of computers which makes it possible to assign pages to the text in an infinite variety of formats, before or dur-

14

15

ing the printout" (129).[16] And in regard to the way in which this expansiveness leads also to an increase in ever "finer points" of qualification, Ihde notes the reappearance of what he calls the "'Germanic tome,' the highly footnoted and documented scholarly treatise now made easier by the various footnoting programs favored by scholars already so inclined" (142). Ihde goes on to note that publishers increasingly complain about the growth of manuscript length over the contracted length since the advent of word processing. Writing on a computer, I find myself including more citations and adding more qualifying or expansive content footnotes than I would have before this technology—and this not because I am suddenly reading or thinking more than ever but because both writing and footnoting are easier to accomplish. Indeed, these days, how many of us who write on a computer no longer have a material sense of "the page" and, often writing over our assigned limits, practice a computational sleight of hand by reducing not the length of the essay but the size of the font?

16   In sum, my "style" of writing has correspondingly changed with the technologies of writing I have adopted or abandoned. Moving from pencil and pen to typewriter as my primary technology, I wrote more prose than poetry, and my prose became somewhat more staccato. Moving from typewriter to computer, I, too, tended to form lengthier sentences and found myself using a larger range of emphases—underlining, italics, boldface, different fonts—that corresponded to the inflections of my *voice* and *mood* in a way that neither handwriting nor the typewriter could so variously accommodate. Nonetheless, whereas these more modern technologies have amplified certain aspects of writing for me, such as the speed of composition or editorial freedom and fluidity, they have reduced others—particularly the *physical sense* of writing. The typewriter and, even more so, the computer have diminished my experience of language coursing through my body to make both its—and my—mark on a resistant and resilient worldly surface.

17   Whatever particular aspects of experience are amplified or reduced through various writing technologies, the point to be made here is that my existential style and my writing style are correlated—and insofar as I incorporate different technologies of writing I am also incorporated by them. Chandler cites one writer who "goes so far as to suggest that he feels not simply that the pen is an extension of the hand, but that he himself becomes an extension of the pen: 'Words flow from a pen, not from a mind. . . . I *become* my pen; my entire organism becomes an extension of this writing instrument. Consciousness is focused in the point of the pen'" (69). Certainly I am not merely subjected to the material demands of pencil, pen, typewriter, or computer, and I can struggle against and override the responses they most easily provoke from me. Nonetheless, in what phenomenologists call the "natural attitude" (natural because it is historically and culturally "naturalized" into transparency—and, barring reflection—lived at a "zero-degree" of awareness), insofar as I privilege in practice a given writing technology, I will tend to succumb to its material demands and most likely form an existential habit of living according to its spatial, temporal, bodily, and technical coordinates.

EMBODIED TECHNIQUES

As these observations indicate, a phenomenology of the material and technological experience of writing attempts to describe and bring to awareness the dynamic and essentially correlational structure of that experience as it entails the existential activity of writing, the intentional objects that emerge in material form as the means of writing and the written matter, and an embodied and enworlded subject who is the writer—activity, object, and subject all enabled and mediated through a particular writing technology that spatially and temporally qualifies the embodied manner and objective style in which we write. However, given that phenomenological description of an existential kind recognizes that it is always also qualified by history and culture, it should further describe the ways in which the meaning of writing and its material technologies are historically and culturally enworlded—in particular embodied techniques and the meanings that in-form them.

18

Here, it is particularly telling and warrants further elaboration that the electronic writing doll "Susie Scribbles" came in two other embodiments than a "five-year-old" Caucasian female: one an African American male child, the other a furry brown teddy bear. Insofar as we understand that writing by hand serves simultaneously as an indexical sign of subjectivity, a symbolic sign of class, and a pragmatic form of social empowerment, these selective embodiments of writing automata are uncanny not only for their mechanical aptitude. They are also uncanny for their material revelation of certain kinds of beliefs about what (and who) constitutes appropriate writing and, as well, about the "inappropriate appropriation of writing"—beliefs that hold that certain writers, deemed lacking in significant (and therefore signifying) intentionality and subjectivity, are merely automatons engaged in appropriating and "aping" the appropriate writing of their accomplished betters. In this regard and in relation to those automaton scribblers who appeared on the toy store shelf—a female child, a black male child, and a culturally declawed animal—it is worth noting the unmarked absence of a white male child automaton. Thus, we might suppose that for the enlightened men at Wonderama Toys in (of all places) Edison, New Jersey, who conceived these writing automata, embodying the human ability to write not only in agencyless machines but also in the forms of supposedly less rational, less powerful, and inferior "others" both materializes an "uncanny" oxymoron and amplifies the very "not-human" nature of automatic writing.[17] It also functions, from the transparent perspective and legacy of Enlightenment (white male) humanism, as both self-aggrandizing and self-congratulatory. Indeed, as Annette Michelson writes of another and more "accomplished" female automaton "invented by Edison" in a fiction, the white girl, black boy, and furry teddy bear all sit at their writing desks as a "palimpsest of inscription"—each not only inscribing but also inscribed as both an "unreasoning and reasonable facsimile, generated by reason" itself.[18]

19

Thus far, I have scrupulously avoided discussion of writing as a discrete form of *symbolic* communication—nor have I yet discussed it as acculturated through an embodied *technique*. My emphasis has been instead on the radical physical activ-

20

ity and experience of the lived body in the act of writing and its entailment of material and technological means to make some "thing" that matters out of no "thing" at all. Indeed, closer phenomenological scrutiny reveals that the particular activity and thing we call writing and understand as a discrete order of symbolic communication is, in its very discretion, a secondary apprehension built on the primary ground of the material lived body making its meaningful mark on the world as a necessary condition of its very existence. This primary kind of symbolic activity is an activity more general than discrete, and it can be best described as a radical and emergent semiosis of the lived body that has, makes, and marks meaning in the world and to others. That is, always marking its existential situation by its punctual material presence and always in intentional movement that is tropic and choice-making, the lived body in its material presence and social existence constitutes the "original" diacritical mark and "magic" marker: it concretely and visibly produces in its very being the first formation of what we term—both humanly and alphabetically—"character."[19]

Some specific illustration might prove helpful here, and I will thus enlist Sean, a five-year-old neighbor just beginning school at the time I interviewed him. Accompanied by his younger brother, Sean stopped pedaling his tricycle when I asked him what writing was. Not at all surprised by the question, he told me that he knew—and then proceeded to arch and move his right arm in a set of limited but fluid and morphologically regular curves across the air. "Does your little brother write too?" I asked. "No," Sean said. "He's only three. He scribbles." "Well, what's the difference between writing and scribbling?" I asked. Sean then demonstrated scribbling—this time moving his arm back and forth across the air in a more mechanical, rigid, and jagged fashion than he had before.[20] I then asked Sean "what" he could write. He responded by telling me first his name followed by a discrete pronouncement of its letters, and then he announced a list of separate and disconnected words. After a brief moment of silence he companionably offered up the fact that he had written *spiderwebs* the other day. I am quite certain that he was not talking about the word as the sum of its letters but rather that he had not as yet made a clear distinction between writing and drawing.[21] Indeed, both Sean's sure distinction between writing and scribbling and his confident conflation of writing and drawing raise a major question about the general meaning and matter of writing: "Where does scribble end and writing as communication, or drawing as representation, begin?"[22] Finally, at the end of a lengthier conversation than I can recount here, I asked Sean what writing was "good for," and, although he understood my question as one about function and value, he groped for an answer he couldn't quite find. Instead, he told me his little brother had a magic pencil that turned scribbling into writing. "All you have to do," he told me, "is to scribble on this magic pad with this magic pencil, say 'abracadabra,' and real writing will be there instead of just squiggly lines." Definitely aware of the nature of writing as a bodily activity and a material object requiring a technique for its production, vaguely aware of some kind of instant and magical material transformation accomplished by writing, this five-year-old's concept of writing was founded—and, more significantly, focused—on its physical and material aspects.

21

Sean's initiation into writing, then, is grounded in bodily action and the specific techniques involved in making material marks that matter—whatever their vaguely apprehended use value or "reason" for being. On the one hand, Sean illustrates the bodily *originality* of writing, of making one's mark, simultaneously in and on the world. On the other, his cultural initiation into the activity of writing came (just as mine had) by way of institutionalized instruction and bodily imitation, an instruction and imitation focused on *technique*. That is, the act of writing was brought into focus for Sean through a *bodily tuition*: a discrete set of objective steps that were to be physically followed prior to any clear understanding he might have of what he was doing or why he was doing it (that is, why this particular mode of bringing matter into the world mattered). Thus, like all the writers who have come before him, Sean's generalized physical activity and pleasure of making and leaving any kind of marks on the world as an existential assertion of presence have been historically and culturally regulated into specific and highly objectified forms. Indeed, only with time and practice will Sean's larger inscriptional body movements become objectively contained by and regulated "in the hand."[23] The movements and techniques of "penmanship" will become incorporated into Sean's bodily schema and, once habituated, will eventually seem less alien and laborious than "natural."

In "Handwriting as an Act of Self-Definition" Thornton comments on the history and literature of techniques for writing by hand, pointing not only to "the exquisitely engraved penmanship manuals of the eighteenth century or the copybooks of the Victorian era" but also, of course, to the "Palmer method" that dominated the teaching of handwriting well into the twentieth century, articulating a mechanical and repetitive standard consonant with the Taylorism and Fordism that marked assembly-line production in the machine age. Thornton writes:

> Mr. Palmer promised to deliver a tireless arm that could compete with the typewriter, but what really attracted educators were his handwriting drills. . . . Sometimes they began with "preparatory calisthenics." Then, at the teacher's command, . . . students executed row after row of ovals and "push-pulls." School officials were blunt about the value of these drills. The lessons they conveyed—conformity to standard models, obedience to authority—would reform juvenile delinquents, assimilate foreigners, and acclimate working-class children to their futures in the typing pool or on the factory line.[24]

In this regard the brochure for the more contemporary "Susie Scribbles" is illuminating. Sitting at her desk with her "magic" pen and pad and her electronically controlled writing arm, Susie is regarded by those who made her not only as a play toy but also as "a learning assistant." Thus, the brochure first tells us (in somewhat righteous tones): "Remember that Susie Scribbles is about five years old and will write at that level by design. We would not want a toy writing better than a child." And then it continues (shades of Palmer embedded in its Montessori patience): "Susie Scribbles can assist your child in learning, but repetition is the key to learning, and always remember that each child learns at their own speed."

22

23

24

Monique Wittig's autobiographical novel *The Opoponax* wonderfully, meticu-   25
lously, and painfully describes not only the young child's original focus on writing
in its materiality and concrete grounding in bodily action rather than in the symbolic meaning of what one is writing but also the culture's focus on the technology and techniques of writing as a form of social control rather than on writing as
the matter of both personal and social expression. Wittig tells us of her young alter
ego:

> Catherine Legrand can't write. She presses on the paper with the black pen-
> cil. She makes letters that stick out on both sides beyond the two lines you are
> supposed to write inside of, they stick out above and below, they touch the
> other lines, they are not straight. Mademoiselle says, Begin again. First you
> make d's and a's, then r's. The bellies of the s's are always too big, the r's fall
> forward on their canes.[25]

This description of the concrete (let alone bodily) shape of letters, as well as   26
a perceived sense of their objective recalcitrance, is extended in a later, and excruciating, passage that conjoins writing's concrete materiality with both technology
and proscribed bodily technique:

> You write in your notebook with a pen which you dip into purple ink. The
> point scrapes the paper, the two ends come apart, it is like writing on a blot-
> ter, afterward the nib is full of little hairs. You take them off with your fingers.
> You start writing again. There are more hairs. You rub the pen on your smock.
> You wipe it on the skin of your hand. You separate the two parts of the nib so
> you can get your finger between them and clean them. The pointed ends do
> not go back together again, so that now you write double. . . . Mademoiselle
> gets mad. That makes the third [time] today, you must pay attention and hold
> your pen like this. . . . Mademoiselle leans over her shoulder to guide her
> hand. . . . You hold the pen between your thumb and index finger. Your
> index finger is bent at a right angle and presses against the round end the
> point is stuck into. Your thumb is a little less bent. The index finger is always
> sliding onto the inky point. . . . You have to press the index finger against
> the end of the pen with all your might so it won't slide off. The thumb is also
> pressed to the end to keep the pen tight between the fingers, which then you
> can't use. Your whole arm even hurts. . . . Anyway Catherine Legrand is a
> pig. Mademoiselle tells her so waving her notebook. . . . There are ink
> stains and fingerprints on the notebook. This is because when you dip the pen
> into the inkwell it either comes out full of ink or else without enough ink. In
> the first case the ink immediately drips onto the notebook just as you are get-
> ting ready to write. In the second case you press the nib of the pen onto the
> paper too hard and it makes holes. After this there is no point even trying to
> make the letters as you know how to do with a pencil. Françoise Pommier
> writes slowly and carefully. At the top of her notebook she pushes a clean blot-
> ter along the line, holding it in place with the hand that is not writing. She
> raises her head when she has finished the page. . . . Pascale Delaroche
> makes a blot. She gives a little cry. . . . Reine Dieu's notebook . . . has a
> lot of blots and holes like Catherine Legrand's. It also has doodles around
> which Reine Dieu has written the letters as she was asked to do. She has tried
> to erase something here and there. This makes a funny mess with hills and val-
> leys which you want to touch. Between the hills is dirty. Mademoiselle gets
> mad again and even throws Reine Dieu's notebook under the table.[26]

Catherine Legrand's (and Monique Wittig's) writing lessons with her dip pen elaborately flesh out, yet also serve as ironic commentary on, Ihde's adult encounter with the same writing instrument when he is in France with his school-age children. Certainly, Catherine's writing lessons dramatize the materiality and technique that ultimately ground Ihde's adult understanding and valuation of the art and craft of belles lettres, but their extreme objectification (as well as hers by Mademoiselle) disallows her the pleasure of making her mark.[27] In *Electric Language* Heim writes: "The resistance of materials in handwriting enhances the sense of felt origination. . . . The stamp of characteristic ownership marks written thought as my own, acquired through the struggle with experience and with recalcitrant materials. Handwritten formulation thereby enhances a sense of personal experience or an integrity pertaining to the private, personal self " (186). Catherine Legrand's writing lessons would seem to counter this description—although Monique Wittig goes on to become "a writer" (albeit, in the context of her classroom experience, one who describes herself as an objectified third person).

Wittig's text also throws into relief the less restrictive penmanship lessons a five-year-old American boy more recently gave me out of the classroom and against the empty slate of a spring sky. I remember his sure bodily distinction between writing and scribbling, his untroubled confusion of writing and drawing, and his inability to tell me what writing "was good for." It is not only in French schools that writing is first taught as a technology and technique, as a means of mattering rather than as a matter of meaning. Indeed, it is in this fact that our Enlightenment heritage might be made to seem strange. Although I can't quite think of how else to teach a child to write concretely, I can think how fundamental Enlightenment dualisms separated spirit and mind from the material body (figured now by Susie's effectively "broken" neck). Is it any wonder that this separation led to the objectification and mechanization of human subjectivity and greatly influenced the notion and instruction of writing as an objective technique? Furthermore, given this historical and cultural separation of meaning and matter, of consciousness and the body, insofar as it always also inscribes and makes matter an "existential style," I can understand how writing by hand would always also *confound* this objectification and remain, in a problematic way, *auratic*.[28] Thus, it is telling that in the mid-1700s, the period that marks the rise of scientific materialism and the move into mechanical typography and print culture, we find both a complementarity and a contradiction in, on the one hand, the privilege enjoyed by belles lettres as a form of writing that embodies reflexive consciousness and individual sensibility and, on the other hand, a significant increase and interest in mechanical writing automata embodied as human beings.[29]

One particular example of such Enlightenment writing automata is worth considering in relation to "Susie Scribbles," the electronic doll who sits at her desk several centuries later. Invented by Pierre Jaquet-Droz and his son Henri-Louis and first exhibited in 1774 in Neuchâtel, Switzerland, where it is still in working order and exhibited today, Susie's Enlightenment equivalent was known as "The Scribe." Taking the form of a Caucasian boy aged about three, the mechanical child was accompanied and matched by a twin "brother" known as "The

27

28

29

Draughtsman," who did not write but drew pictures. (Here, in an uncanny way, Sean's lingering confusion of writing and drawing is at once bifurcated and "twinned" as a difference that is, nonetheless, the same.) Gaby Wood describes the pair at the beginning of *Edison's Eve*:

> These prodigies, who look no older than toddlers, are dressed . . . in identical velvet jackets and silk pantaloons. Their faces are doll-like and blank; their bare feet dangle some way off the ground. The first boy begins by dipping his quill pen in a tiny ink well at the side of his desk. He shakes it twice, then methodically moves his hand across the paper and starts to trace the letters in his message. Meanwhile his twin works on a sketch. He slowly draws a head in profile, then drops his chin and blows away the dust from his pencil.[30]

A picture shows "The Scribe" seated like "Susie" at his own writing desk in a posture almost identical to hers; indeed, he looks amazingly like her—but for his differently fashioned clothing, his bare feet,[31] and the quill rather than ballpoint pen he holds in his fingers.

    Such anthropomorphic automata were particularly valued for the exactitude of their lifelike qualities: for example, intricate mechanisms made "a girl's chest rise and fall at regular intervals in perfect imitation of breathing" and made "the eyes move and animate[d] the head," turning it round so it looked left and right and down and up again.[32] Correlatively, however, human beings of the period were often celebrated for their mechanical and autonomic "clockwork" qualities. Thus, philosopher Julien Offray de La Mettrie could write in 1748, "The human body is a machine which winds its own springs. It is the living image of perpetual movement."[33] This contradiction and complementarity between anthropomorphic automata and automated human bodies and the conundrum of their "reversibility" continues historically to the present day. In the context of a discussion on the bourgeois fascination with anthropomorphic automata in the nineteenth century, Susan Buck-Morss tells us: "This reversal epitomizes that which Marx considered characteristic of the capitalist-industrial mode of production: Machines that bring the promise of the naturalization of humanity and the humanization of nature result instead in the mechanization of both."[34] We are no less fascinated by notions of these human-machine exchanges, reversals, and reifications today—hence not only Susie in Toys R Us sold as an "interactive" teaching toy and fun-loving companion (with handwriting no better than a five-year-old's) but also, and more transparently, computers that catch viruses and humans who possess "artificial intelligence." Thus, how far have we come (or not) from de La Mettrie and the eighteenth century when our dominant techno-logic considers the human body, according to contemporary philosopher Jean-François Lyotard's provocative phenomenological critique, "as the *hardware* of the complex technical device that is human thought"?[35]

EMBODYING *TECHNĒ*

We can see in this historical and cultural trajectory how the matter of technology elides a humanly embodied meaning that matters and how mechanical technique becomes institutionalized and "industrialized" in penmanship classes where chil-

30

31

32

The iDeal Reader

Vivian Sobchack, "'Susie
Scribbles:' Technology,
Technë, and Writing
Incarnate"

Reading

© The McGraw–Hill
Companies, 2008

107

dren learn to suppress the idiosyncrasies of their uniquely embodied "existential
style," their very "originality." A paradox emerges, however: today, precisely
because of this social suppression of writerly idiosyncrasy and the valuation of
"originality" and "spontaneity" amidst the institutionalized and technological
management of our lives, unlike some of our historical predecessors we tend to
think that "painstaking penmanship betrays a deficient imagination."[36] Indeed, as
Thornton suggests, since the onset of mechanical typography and print culture
there has been an essential ambiguity about the relationship between the technological and mass production of writing and the lived body engaged in writing as an
act of self-expression. Ever more troubling in highly technologized cultures that
depend on standardization, an ongoing argument exists "between the forces of
conformity and those of individuality" about "the nature of the self."[37]

In this sense, however much we may deny it, we are hardly yet post-
Enlightenment or postindustrial, even as we are post-postmodern. "Susie
Scribbles" is a concrete extension of the Enlightenment objectification of both
writing and human being and the nineteenth century's valuation of assembly-line
standardization, conformity, and repetition—which, among other things, gave us
first the typewriter, then the word processor, and now "repetitive stress injury."[38]
Susie is a specific anthropomorphic and electronic writing machine aimed not at
provoking intellectual reflection and amusing adults but at constituting "good parents" and at "engaging" and "instructing" children on what it is to write.
Materially, despite her Oshkosh B'Gosh overalls and her blonde ponytail, Susie
bears great resemblance—if a different "clockwork"—to the automata that have
preceded her from the 1740s on. Indeed, if one looks at pictures and diagrams of
past automated writing dolls, Susie's robotic arm mechanism, albeit directed electronically, is hardly that different from theirs. Yet, for all her similarity, Susie dif-
fers significantly from her forebears. It is not only that in a nonphilosophical
culture she is not perceived as a philosophical toy or that her cloyingly sweet voice
and horrid taped laughter and song keep insisting aloud how much "fun" she and
the child-consumer will have writing "together." Whereas the first thing written
by her Enlightenment predecessor, "The Scribe," was a provocative "I think,
therefore I am," followed by "Our mechanisms defy time,"[39] the first thing Susie
writes is the toll-free telephone number of a "help line" in Edison, New Jersey, that
one can call if she breaks down. These things give one pause, of course, as does her
drawing of the two "C" batteries that give her the charge of her artificial life.
Despite these differences, however, it is the very *similarity* of Susie to her childish
ancestors that marks her real—and radical—*difference* from them. That is, it seems
both culturally logical and technologically natural that Enlightenment automata
wrote with quill pens in their mechanical hands. The dip pen was then a common
writing technology. Thus we must ask, Why, in an electronically driven and
obsessed culture, does Susie write with a pen at all? Why is she not seated at a little word processor or computer? Why is a pen, even a plastic ballpoint with four
color ink cartridges, the preferred instrument for an electronic doll in an electronic culture? Indeed, if one thinks historically backward, we might ask if there

33

have been any writing dolls that, when it was a common mode of writing, sat at a typewriter? Although I don't know for sure, I rather think not.

The answers to these questions lie, I believe, quite precisely, *in the hand*. That   34
Susie still writes with a pen in an electronic culture demonstrates that we know deeply, and with the knowledge of the lived body, that writing is not merely a learned mechanical technique. Rather, and more significantly, it is always also *auratic* insofar as it is enabled not just by a material body but by a *lived body* that, however regulated, cannot avoid inscribing its singular intentionality in acts and marks of *expressive improvisation*.[40] Even after years of discipline in penmanship classes, in that pen and pencil enable the broadest and most idiosyncratic expression of the lived body making matter from "no-thing"—that is, transforming meaning to matter and making matter mean—pen and pencil are the technologies that best extend the idiosyncrasies of the *hand* and most fully and materially mark the embodied, intentional, and contingent *excess* of what writing is over its objectification, standardization, and mechanization. Although one might be mildly amused at its transparent social commentary, there would be no fascination, nothing *uncanny*, in seeing an anthropomorphic writing machine write *through* a nonanthropomorphic writing machine—particularly those like the typewriter or the computer, which have greatly reduced the unique *graphological excess* that brings into being and matter an embodied *existential style*.[41]

Thus, in a review of Thornton's *Handwriting in America*, although Thomas   35
Mallon applauds the author's tracking of changes in methods and styles of penmanship, as well as her discussions of the history of handwriting analysis (which began in the romantic period) and the "twentieth-century showdown between characterological and physiological notions of handwritten individuality," he also chides Thornton for not considering the contemporary moment and "what has been lost or gained by our cultural shift toward mouse and screen." Mallon points out that although "the fax and E-mail have brought back letter-writing to an encouraging extent," they have marked the "limits of that revival, too." As both writers and readers, he says, we know that "you can't seal E-mail with a kiss, and the latest laptops protect us from even our own bodily fluids: the Macintosh Power Books have eliminated trackballs in favor of trackpads, so the sweat from one's thumb won't gum up the works." In contrast to electronic writing (even of an amorous kind), Mallon notes how the power and value of handwritten love letters emerge from the exchange of indexical signs of the physical proximity of the lovers' bodies to the page and from the graphological transfer and display of a "physical motion and intensity"—which does let them see you sweat or weep. Whatever an individual lover's method of penmanship, the embodied movement that made his or her expression matter was, as Mallon concludes, "connected to all those other movements that would make him, once he appeared in the flesh, yours truly."[42] (And, here, I might point out that Susie untruly—that is, mechanically albeit electronically—prints "I love you" on her writing pad to anyone and everyone who, dare I say it, turns her on.)

Our handwriting is singular—and it has taken on an increasingly auratic and   36
precious quality as it has become increasingly scarce. Susie's difference from her

mechanical ancestors is that, in an electronic culture, she further hyperbolizes the mystery not of writing as a technical enterprise but as an expression of the human hand. Thus, however hidden it is by her Oshkosh B'Goshes and saccharine songs and ignored by the adults who buy her, Susie is a philosophical toy after all. She and her forebears affirm across time that although writing is a technique and employs technology, it is always also something *more*. And in so doing, they charge us to reframe "the question concerning technology" to accommodate the intentional and lived body-subject in the act of writing not only the word but also the world and herself. As Heidegger reminds us, technology consists not merely of objective tools, nor is technique merely their objective application. "Technology is . . . no mere means," he tells us. "Technology is a way of revealing." Thus, he returns us to the Greek notion of *technë*: "the name not only for the activities and skills of the craftsman, but also for the arts of the mind and the fine arts. *Technë* belongs to bringing-forth, to *poiësis*; it is something poetic."[43] Furthermore, *technë* is a way and manner of knowing. Making, bringing forth, and revealing are integral not only to the existence of matter but also to why and how some "thing" is known and understood as "mattering."

Necessarily and materially implicated in both this bringing forth and its particular modes of knowing is an embodied and intentional subject. Unlike Susie (the intentionless simulacrum who laughs without mirth and writes without mattering), this lived body subjectively incorporates and excorporates objective technologies and, in what Scarry calls a "consensual materialism," brings into material being both the variety of herself and multiple worlds.[44] Thus, even seated before a computer printing my thoughts in a tenpoint Geneva font that reveals nothing idiosyncratic of my hand, I am never reduced to a mere writing machine and never completely forget or forgo the mystery of the human hand's ability to reveal and bring forth an expression of human being. Even here, before my computer screen, even if in a relatively reduced way, my writing materially reveals itself as an existential style as well as a cultural habit. Indeed, my lived body is "continuous with the modes of reproduction that it also disrupts."[45] As I write, my choices of font and diacritical marks begin to signify something in excess of the digitized regularity of my words on the screen. (By the time you read this in a printed book, however, press editors surely will have further reduced my idiosyncrasies, pleading a "house style" that takes precedence over my original authorial style as it once was manifest in typographical and diacritical "preferences.") In sum, objectively material means (*technology*) and the tropology of subjective desire (*poiësis*) are bound in an irreducible intentional relation as a revelatory bringing forth (*technë*) that, in its diverse historical and personal practices, makes matter meaningful and meaning matter.

I have no idea whether, seated at their little desks and writing mechanically, historical versions of Susie provoked first in the children of their owners and later in their child owners an overwhelming urge to rip apart the "signifying scene." But I rather think so. Even though I am an adult who certainly respects a doll for which I paid $119 and who has read the brochure admonishing me to "remember that Susie is a machine" and, therefore, that I should not "abuse" her, I nonethe-

37

38

less admit to wanting to take off Susie's pink long-sleeved polo shirt and to wrench her robotic writing arm from its socket "to see how it works." (I rather think, to the disappointment and horror of the adults who bought it for them, this is the only real interactivity the young owners of this supposedly "interactive" toy ever actually experience.) Although, on the surface, this urge "to see how it works" seems grounded in a sense of technology as mere *mechanical means*, I would suggest it reveals a much deeper curiosity about the radical *bringing forth* of both action and matter. Indeed, writing "by hand" (even, or especially, when it's mechanical) keeps alive the question of the animate and the inanimate, the lived body and the material "thing" that merely simulates a lived body, which is not only a material object but also an intentional and sentient subject. It is apposite here that "The Scribe" not only wrote the simulated assertion, "I think, therefore I am," but also wrote, as Wood tells us, "a more ironic tribute: 'I do not think . . . do I therefore not exist?' The writer, a mere machine, is able to communicate the fact that it cannot think. Clearly, however, it does exist: and if it is able to communicate that fact that it cannot think, is it possible that it can think after all? Might the machine be lying?"[46]

Given this question of the animate and the inanimate, the auratic lived body and its uncanny simulation, it is hardly surprising that children are usually so deeply disappointed after they have ripped apart their mechanical but animated playthings and found no *objective* and *technical* correlative to the *subjective* and deeply *poetic* curiosity they themselves have about the world and human being. Either in animatronic operation or dissected in a childish autopsy, Susie's robotic writing arm would tell us nothing *truly material* to either the meaning of writing or the matter of the hand. In fact, our fascination with the anthropomorphic writing machine lies precisely in its inability to tell us anything truly material to writing—even as it writes and "brings forth" meaning in material form. Ripping apart Susie's signifying scene would reveal nothing significant—either about signifying or about mattering. Susie is, after all, just a machine. Despite her technical facility for mechanical mimesis, she lacks precisely the ability to respond to what we really want to know: that is, how the intentionality, subjective desire, and existential style of the lived body come to materiality and matter through the *poiësis* of *technë* rather than the mechanics and automation of technique.

NOTES

1. In terms of material "things," the "matter" of writing does not necessarily entail an intentional subject. (Hence, as will be discussed later, the fascination with writing produced by automata.) But for the matter of writing to mean, for writing not only to necessarily "be" but for it to be sufficiently "what" it is, it must entail an intentional subject. In this regard Margaret Morse, "Television Graphics and the Virtual Body: Words on the Move," in her *Virtualities: Television, Media Art and Cyberspace* (Bloomington: Indiana University Press, 1998), aptly points out that "much of the nomenclature of both writing and typographics—*hand, face, character*—are metonymies of the absent human body and of the subjectivity which we presume is responsible for them" (72).

2. I don't mention here the experience or techniques of writing with a brush in other cultures. Such an activity, with its particular materials and techniques, would have its own spatial, temporal, and bodily phenomeno-logic. Indeed, in contemporary Western culture writing has often been viewed by theorists (most male) as a form of sadistic incision, as violently aggressive; considering the use of a brush, one could understand its action on a surface as quite different: additive, caressive, nonviolent. See Andrew Brown, *Roland Barthes: The Figures of Writing* (Oxford: Clarendon Press, 1992), for discussion of this issue in relation to Barthes; Brown also mentions the felt-tipped pen as a writing instrument that does not aggressively scratch or impress the paper (170, 192–93).

3. Daniel Chandler, "The Phenomenology of Writing by Hand," *Intelligent Tutoring Media* 3, nos. 2/3 (May/Aug. 1992). Subsequent references will be cited in the text. See also Chandler's *The Act of Writing: A Media Theory Approach* (Great Britain: University of Wales, Aberystwyth, 1995), esp. chap. 6, "Writing Tools," 132–88.

4. Walter Benjamin, "One-Way Street," trans. Edmund Jephcott, in *Walter Benjamin: Selected Writings, Volume 1, 1913–1926*, ed. Marcus Bullock and Michael W. Jennings (Cambridge, MA: Harvard University Press, 1996), 458.

5. Brown, *Roland Barthes*, 192–93. Brown draws from an interview with Barthes—"Un rapport preseque maniaque avec les instruments graphique" [An Almost Maniacal Rapport with Writing Instruments], which was collected in the French edition of *Le Grain de la voix: Entretiens, 1962–1980* (Paris: Seuil, 1981), 170–74—to quote the epigraph that begins this essay: "Il y a d'abord le moment où le désire s'investit dans la pulsion graphique, aboutissant à un objet calligraphique" [There is a moment when desire infuses the graphic impulse, ending up in a calligraphic object] (translation mine). Brown also criticizes what he sees as an unfair reduction of this sentence by others to "J'aime écrire à la main" (193).

6. On writing as the movement of a thought through the body (albeit from a distinctively male perspective) see Charles Grivel, "Travel Writing," in *Materialities of Communication*, ed. Hans Ulrich Gumbrecht and K. Ludwig Pfeiffer, trans. William Whobrey (Stanford, CA: Stanford University Press, 1994), 254–55.

7. Lisa Jensen, "Confessions of a Computer Phobe," *Santa Cruz (California) Good Times*, Dec. 13, 1990, writes: "Trying to coax inspiration from my own elusive muse is far too private a process to be scrutinized by the prying terminal eye" (23).

8. Gaston Bachelard, *The Poetics of Space*, trans. Maria Jolas (New York: Beacon, 1969), 106.

9. Michael Heim, *Electric Language: A Philosophical Study of Word Processing* (New Haven, CT: Yale University Press, 1987), 152. Subsequent references will be cited in the text.

10. Don Ihde, *Technology and the Lifeworld: From Garden to Earth* (Bloomington: Indiana University Press, 1990), 141. Subsequent references will be cited in the text.

11. Jensen, "Confessions of a Computer Phobe," 23.

12. Elaine Scarry, "The Merging of Bodies and Artifacts in the Social Contract," in *Culture on the Brink: Ideologies of Technology*, ed. Gretchen Bender and Timothy Druckrey (Seattle: Bay Press, 1994), 97.

13. Tamara Plakins Thompson, "Handwriting as an Act of Self-Definition," *Chronicle of Higher Education*, Aug. 15, 1997, B7. Although print has existed since the Gutenberg press, insofar as broad cultural understandings of writing by hand are concerned Thompson also points out: "As late as the 17th century, men and women hardly recognized an association between an individual and his or her script. Only in the early 18th century did the English legal authority Geoffrey Gilbert advance the new idea that 'men are distinguished by their handwriting as well as by their faces'" (B7).

14. Daniel Chandler, in an email to me (Aug. 7, 1997), mentions this notion of "the culturally-sanctioned hierarchy of formality" associated with these writing implements in Western culture.

15. O. B. Hardison Jr., *Disappearing through the Skylight: Culture and Technology in the Twentieth Century* (New York: Penguin, 1989), 259.

16. For a more "popular" discussion of scrolling see ibid., 259–346.

17. Mary Ann Doane, in "Technology's Body," in *Feminist Anthology in Early Cinema*, ed. Jennifer M. Bean and Diane Negra (Durham, NC: Duke University Press, 2002), aptly summarizes the "theory of evolution that opposes the more advanced, civilized, and neurotic exemplar of the human species to a primitive—that is, racial other—defined in terms of an immediacy of the body and unrestricted sexuality"; and she continues: "In Freud, a metonymic chain is constructed that links infantile sexuality, female sexuality, and racial otherness" (542). Also illuminating in this regard is Donna J. Haraway, *Simians, Cyborgs, and Women: The Reinvention of Nature* (New York: Routledge, 1991).

18. See Annette Michelson, "On the Eve of the Future: The Reasonable Facsimile and the Philosophical Toy," in *October: The First Decade, 1976–1986*, ed. Annette Michelson, Rosalind Krauss, Douglas Crimp, and Joan Copjec (Cambridge, MA: MIT Press, 1987), 432. (In this brilliant essay about philosophical toys, cinema, and the bodies of women, Michelson writes of the android female Hadaly, invented by Thomas Alva Edison, in Villier de l'Isle-Adam's 1889 fiction, *L'eve future*.)

19. For further elaboration of the origins of semiosis in the lived body and its diacritical activity see my "The Lived Body and the Emergence of Language," in *Semiotics around the World: Synthesis in Diversity (Proceedings of the Fifth Congress of the International Association for Semiotic Studies, Berkeley, 1994)*, ed. Irmengard Rauch and Gerald F. Carr (Berlin: Mouton de Gruyter, 1997), 1051–54; and my *The Address of the Eye: A Phenomenology of Film Experience* (Princeton, NJ: Princeton University Press, 1992), 71–76.

20. On the possible meanings of scribbling at a much more sophisticated level than Sean's see Brown, *Roland Barthes*, esp. chap. 4, "The Scribbler," 152–209.

21. Régis Debray, in "The Three Ages of Looking," trans. Eric Rauth, *Critical Inquiry* 21 (spring 1995), notes "the ambiguity of *graphisme* itself [the translator retaining the French word 'because it signifies graphics or the graphic arts as well as handwriting or script'], which accounts for the double meaning of the Greek verb *graphein*, to draw and to write" (541). For extended discussion of the unclear distinction between writing and drawing see also James Elkins, *On Pictures and the Words That Fail Them* (Cambridge, UK: Cambridge University Press, 1998). Elkins asks: "How do we know when we are looking at writing, and not pictures? What criteria are brought into play, and how are they related to the more elaborate structures that preoccupy linguistics?" And he concludes: "Any picture can be understood as failed or incomplete writing, and the same is true of any writing" (130–31).

22. Brown, *Roland Barthes*, 178. Also of interest here is Barthes's wide-ranging work on the connection between the body and signification. In relation to the specific issue of writing, scribbling, and drawing see his essay, "Cy Twombly: Works on Paper," in *The Responsibility of Forms: Critical Essays on Music, Art, and Representation*, trans. Richard Howard (New York: Hill and Wang, 1985), esp. 158–62.

23. See Jonathan Goldberg, *Writing Matter: From the Hands of the English Renaissance* (Stanford, CA: Stanford University Press, 1990). Goldberg traces a genealogy of the "relationship between the hand writing and handwriting" in the Renaissance as an increasing separation and objectification of the hand from the whole—and subjective—body in relation to the instrumental production of script (236). I am grateful to Sarah Jain for directing me to this text.

24. Thornton, "Handwriting as an Act of Self-Definition," B7.

25. Monique Wittig, *The Opoponax*, trans. Helen Weaver (Plainfield, VT: Daughters, 1966), 24.

26. Wittig, *The Opoponax*, 31–33.

27. The exquisite torture of this objective technical training is contradicted by a simultaneous cultural belief in the value of the subjective idiosyncrasies of handwriting and graphology; on this contradiction see Roxanne Panchasi, "Graphology and the Science of Individual Identity in Modern France," *Configurations* 4, no. 1 (1996): 1–31.

28. Elaborating on Walter Benjamin's use of the term, Samuel Weber describes *aura* as "*the singular leave-taking of the singular*, whose singularity is no longer that of an original moment but of its posthumous aftershock." Certainly, writing by hand (the "singular leave-taking of the singular") and the handwritten object (the letter that stands as and for the "singular leave-taking of the singular" and is, in relation to the original moment of writing, its "posthumous aftershock") are auratic. See Samuel Weber, "Mass Mediauras, or: Art, Aura and Media in the Work of Walter Benjamin," in *Mass Mediauras: Form, Technics, Media*, ed. Alan Cholodenko (Stanford, CA: Stanford University Press, 1996), 104–5.

29. Although anthropomorphic automata date back to ancient Greek, Chinese, and Arabic cultures and, in Europe, to the medieval and Renaissance periods, the mid-1700s sees a marked proliferation of such fabrications. See, e.g., Jean-Claude Beaune, "The Classical Age of Automata: An Impressionistic Survey from the Sixteenth to the Nineteenth Century," trans. Ian Patterson, in *Fragments for a History of the Human Body, Part One*, ed. Michel Feher, Ramona Naddaff, and Nadia Tazi (New York: Zone, 1989), 430–80. For a recent history of these and later attempts at "mechanical life" see also Gaby Wood, *Edison's Eve: A Magical History of the Quest for Mechanical Life* (New York: Knopf, 2002).

30. Wood, *Edison's Eve*, xiii.

31. Wood, in *Edison's Eve*, writes: "The Jaquet-Droz figures conduct their marvellous activities barefoot, illustrating a belief, held by their contemporary Jean-Jacques Rousseau, that children would learn more freely if unhampered by shoes" (xx).

32. Jasia Reichardt, *Robots: Fact, Fiction, and Prediction* (London: Penguin, 1978), 14. For illustrations of writing automata see 13–15.

33. Quoted from his essay "L'Homme Machine," in Julie Wosk, *Breaking Frame: Technology and the Visual Arts in the Nineteenth Century* (New Brunswick, NJ: Rutgers University Press, 1992), 81. (I am indebted to Jennifer Gonzalez for this reference.)

34. Susan Buck-Morss, *The Dialectics of Seeing: Walter Benjamin and the Arcades Project* (Cambridge, MA: MIT Press, 1991), 363. Relevant here is Benjamin on late-nineteenth-century bourgeois culture: "You have no idea how these automatons and dolls become repugnant, how one breathes relief in meeting a fully natural being in this society" (363).

35. Jean-François Lyotard, "Can Thought Go On without a Body?" trans. Bruce Boone and Lee Hildreth, in *Materialities of Communication*, ed. Hans Ulrich Gumbrecht and K. Ludwig Pfeiffer, trans. William Whobrey (Stanford, CA: Stanford University Press, 1994), 291 (emphasis added). It is worth noting that the same technologic that informs Lyotard's description of the human body as the "hardware" of thought also informs its description as the completely disposable and despised "wetware" of "neuromancers." See, e.g., William Gibson's influential novel, *Neuromancer* (New York: Ace, 1984).

36. Thomas Mallon, "Minding Your 'P's' and 'Q's,' " review of *Handwriting in America: A Cultural History*, by Tamara Plakins Thornton, *New Yorker*, Feb. 3, 1997, 79.

37. Thornton, "Handwriting as an Act of Self-Definition," B7.

38. Writing of the historical recognition of "occupational diseases," Carolyn Steedman, in *Dust: The Archive and Cultural History* (New Brunswick, NJ: Rutgers University Press, 2002), notes the emergence of what we now call "repetitive stress injury" in the 1920s, when "the British Association of Women Clerks focused a century of complaints about writers' cramp among clerical workers, in their attempts to have it scheduled as an industrial sick-

ness with no limit of compensation. But theirs were arguments about the physical effect of minutely repeated movements of hand and arm; the comparison was with telegraphists (telegraphists' cramp was a scheduled industrial disease for which benefit might be claimed indefinitely under the National Insurance legislation of 1911) and with comptometers" (33n14).

39. Wood, *Edison's Eve*, xiv, xvii.

40. This relation between various representational and expressive technologies and "the hand," between the mechanical and the improvisational, are quite wonderfully elaborated in two works by phenomenological sociologist David Sudnow. See his *Ways of the Hand: The Organization of Improvised Conduct* (Cambridge, MA: Harvard University Press, 1978); and *Talk's Body: A Meditation between Two Keyboards* (New York: Knopf, 1979). In the latter Sudnow contrasts touch typing with jazz improvisation on a piano keyboard.

41. In regard to graphological excess and its marking of existential style, it bears noting that idiosyncrasies in typewriting usually belong less to the human user than to the machine (hence, police work occasionally involves finding a particular typewriter so as to find the person who might have composed something incriminating on it). In contrast, the computer as a writing machine is much more standardized: no keys to chip, no misalignments of letters, etc. However, as mentioned previously, writing on a computer "builds in" some small level of "personal choice" and "expressive potential" that exceeds the typewriter insofar as the writer can use a broader number and variety of typefaces, font sizes, and diacritical marks through which to express existential style. E-mail writers in particular have developed a novel mode of using diacritical marks to indicate existential tone: the ironic wink, peals of laughter, etc. Nonetheless, whatever graphological excess the computer allows over what the typewriter can provide, it still does not afford the personal expression of the "expressive hand" as do pencil and pen.

42. Mallon, "Minding Your 'P's' and 'Q's,'" 81.

43. Martin Heidegger, "The Question Concerning Technology," trans. William Lovitt, in *Martin Heidegger: Basic Writings*, ed. David Farrell Krell (New York: Harper and Row, 1977), 294.

44. Scarry, "Merging of Bodies," 97.

45. Brown, *Roland Barthes*, 185.

46. Wood, *Edison's Eve*, 8.

Stephen Jay Gould (1941–   ) was born in New York City and earned a Ph.D. from Columbia University in 1967. He has been a professor of zoology at Harvard University since 1967, specializing in evolutionary theory, geology, and the history of science. Among his numerous awards and honors is a MacArthur Foundation Prize Fellowship. His best-selling books include *Ever Since Darwin: Reflections in Natural History* (1977) and *The Mismeasure of Man* (1981). Gould also contributes frequently to periodicals, and has written a monthly column for *Natural History* called "This View of Life" since 1974. "Sex, Drugs, Disasters, and the Extinction of Dinosaurs" is taken from Gould's book *The Flamingo's Smile: Reflections in Natural History* (1985).

Sex, Drugs, Disasters, and the Extinction of Dinosaurs

Stephen Jay Gould

Science, in its most fundamental definition, is a fruitful mode of inquiry, not a list of enticing conclusions. The conclusions are the consequence, not the essence.

My greatest unhappiness with most popular presentations of science concerns their failure to separate fascinating claims from the methods that scientists use to establish the facts of nature. Journalists, and the public, thrive on controversial and stunning statements. But science is, basically, a way of knowing—in P. B. Medawar's apt words, "the art of the soluble." If the growing corps of popular science writers would focus on *how* scientists develop and defend those fascinating claims, they would make their greatest possible contribution to public understanding.

Consider three ideas, proposed in perfect seriousness to explain that greatest of all titillating puzzles—the extinction of dinosaurs. Since these three notions invoke the primally fascinating themes of our culture—sex, drugs, and violence—they surely reside in the category of fascinating claims. I want to show why two of them rank as silly speculation, while the other represents science at its grandest and most useful.

Science works with testable proposals. If, after much compilation and scrutiny of data, new information continues to affirm a hypothesis, we may accept it provisionally and gain confidence as further evidence mounts. We can never be completely sure that a hypothesis is right, though we may be able to show with confidence that it is wrong. The best scientific hypotheses are also generous and expansive: They suggest extensions and implications that enlighten related, and even far distant, subjects. Simply consider how the idea of evolution has influenced virtually every intellectual field.

Useless speculation, on the other hand, is restrictive. It generates no testable hypothesis, and offers no way to obtain potentially refuting evidence. Please note that I am not speaking of truth or falsity. The speculation may well be true; still, if it provides, in principle, no material for affirmation or rejection, we can make nothing of it. It must simply stand forever as an intriguing idea. Useless speculation turns in on itself and leads nowhere; good science, containing both seeds for its poten-

1

2

3

4

5

tial refutation and implications for more and different testable knowledge, reaches out. But, enough preaching. Let's move on to dinosaurs, and the three proposals for their extinction.

1. **Sex:** Testes function only in a narrow range of temperature (those of mammals hang externally in a scrotal sac because internal body temperatures are too high for their proper function). A worldwide rise in temperature at the close of the Cretaceous period caused the testes of dinosaurs to stop functioning and led to their extinction by sterilization of males.

2. **Drugs:** Angiosperms (flowering plants) first evolved toward the end of the dinosaurs' reign. Many of these plants contain psychoactive agents, avoided by mammals today as a result of their bitter taste. Dinosaurs had neither means to taste the bitterness nor livers effective enough to detoxify the substances. They died of massive overdoses.

3. **Disasters:** A large comet or asteroid struck the Earth some 65 million years ago, lofting a cloud of dust into the sky and blocking sunlight, thereby suppressing photosynthesis and so drastically lowering world temperatures that dinosaurs and hosts of other creatures became extinct.

Before analyzing these three tantalizing statements, we must establish a basic   6
ground rule often violated in proposals for the dinosaurs' demise. *There is no separate problem of the extinction of dinosaurs.* Too often we divorce specific events from their wider contexts and systems of cause and effect. The fundamental fact of dinosaur extinction is its synchrony with the demise of so many other groups across a wide range of habitats, from terrestrial to marine.

The history of life has been punctuated by brief episodes of mass extinction. A   7
recent analysis by University of Chicago paleontologists Jack Sepkoski and Dave Raup, based on the best and most exhaustive tabulation of data ever assembled, shows clearly that five episodes of mass dying stand well above the "background" extinctions of normal times (when we consider all mass extinctions, large and small, they seem to fall in a regular 26-million-year cycle). The Cretaceous debacle, occurring 65 million years ago and separating the Mesozoic and Cenozoic eras of our geological time scale, ranks prominently among the five. Nearly all the marine plankton (single-celled floating creatures) died with geological suddenness; among marine invertebrates, nearly 15 percent of all families perished, including many previously dominant groups, especially the ammonites (relatives of squids in coiled shells). On land, the dinosaurs disappeared after more than 100 million years of unchallenged domination.

In this context, speculations limited to dinosaurs alone ignore the larger phe-   8
nomenon. We need a coordinated explanation for a system of events that includes the extinction of dinosaurs as one component. Thus it makes little sense, though it may fuel our desire to view mammals as inevitable inheritors of the Earth, to guess that dinosaurs died because small mammals ate their eggs (a perennial favorite among untestable speculations). It seems most unlikely that some disaster peculiar to dinosaurs befell these massive beasts—and that the debacle happened to strike just when one of history's five great dyings had enveloped the Earth for completely different reasons.

The testicular theory, an old favorite from the 1940s, had its root in an interesting and thoroughly respectable study of temperature tolerances in the American alligator, published in the staid *Bulletin of the American Museum of Natural History* in 1946 by three experts on living and fossil reptiles—E. H. Colbert, my own first teacher in paleontology; R. B. Cowles; and C. M. Bogert.   9

The first sentence of their summary reveals a purpose beyond alligators: "This report describes an attempt to infer the reactions of extinct reptiles, especially the dinosaurs, to high temperatures as based upon reactions observed in the modern alligator." They studied, by rectal thermometry, the body temperatures of alligators under changing conditions of heating and cooling. (Well, let's face it, you wouldn't want to try sticking a thermometer under a 'gator's tongue.) The predictions under test go way back to an old theory first stated by Galileo in the 1630s—the unequal scaling of surfaces and volumes. As an animal, or any object, grows (provided its shape doesn't change), surface areas must increase more slowly than volumes—since surfaces get larger as length squared, while volumes increase much more rapidly, as length cubed. Therefore, small animals have high ratios of surface to volume, while large animals cover themselves with relatively little surface.   10

Among cold-blooded animals lacking any physiological mechanism for keeping their temperatures constant, small creatures have a hell of a time keeping warm—because they lose so much heat through their relatively large surfaces. On the other hand, large animals, with their relatively small surfaces, may lose heat so slowly that, once warm, they may maintain effectively constant temperatures against ordinary fluctuations of climate. (In fact, the resolution of the "hot-blooded dinosaur" controversy that burned so brightly a few years back may simply be that, while large dinosaurs possessed no physiological mechanism for constant temperature, and were not therefore warm-blooded in the technical sense, their large size and relatively small surface area kept them warm.)   11

Colbert, Cowles, and Bogert compared the warming rates of small and large alligators. As predicted, the small fellows heated up (and cooled down) more quickly. When exposed to a warm sun, a tiny 50-gram (1.76-ounce) alligator heated up one degree Celsius every minute and a half, while a large alligator, 260 times bigger at 13,000 grams (28.7 pounds), took seven and a half minutes to gain a degree. Extrapolating up to an adult 10-ton dinosaur, they concluded that a one-degree rise in body temperature would take eighty-six hours. If large animals absorb heat so slowly (through their relatively small surfaces), they will also be unable to shed any excess heat gained when temperatures rise above a favorable level.   12

The authors then guessed that large dinosaurs lived at or near their optimum temperatures; Cowles suggested that a rise in global temperatures just before the Cretaceous extinction caused the dinosaurs to heat up beyond their optimal tolerance—and, being so large, they couldn't shed the unwanted heat. (In a most unusual statement within a scientific paper, Colbert and Bogert then explicitly disavowed this speculative extension of their empirical work on alligators.) Cowles conceded that this excess heat probably wasn't enough to kill or even to enervate the great beasts, but since testes often function only within a narrow range of temperature,   13 he proposed that this global rise might have sterilized all the males, causing extinction by natural contraception.

The overdose theory has recently been supported by UCLA psychiatrist Ronald K. Siegel. Siegel has gathered, he claims, more than 2,000 records of animals who, when given access, administer various drugs to themselves—from a mere swig of alcohol to massive doses of the big H. Elephants will swill the equivalent of twenty beers at a time, but do not like alcohol in concentrations greater than seven percent. In a silly bit of anthropocentric speculation, Siegel states that "elephants drink, perhaps, to forget . . . the anxiety produced by shrinking rangeland and the competition for food." 14

Since fertile imaginations can apply almost any hot idea to the extinction of dinosaurs, Siegel found a way. Flowering plants did not evolve until late in the dinosaurs' reign. These plants also produced an array of aromatic, amino-acid-based alkaloids—the major group of psychoactive agents. Most mammals are "smart" enough to avoid these potential poisons. The alkaloids simply don't taste good (they are bitter); in any case, we mammals have livers happily supplied with the capacity to detoxify them. But, Siegel speculates, perhaps dinosaurs could neither taste the bitterness nor detoxify the substances once ingested. He recently told members of the American Psychological Association: "I'm not suggesting that all dinosaurs OD'd on plant drugs, but it certainly was a factor." He also argued that death by overdose may help explain why so many dinosaur fossils are found in contorted positions. (Do not go gentle into that good night.) 15

Extraterrestrial catastrophes have long pedigrees in the popular literature of extinction, but the subject exploded again in 1979, after a long lull, when the father-son, physicist-geologist team of Luis and Walter Alvarez proposed that an asteroid, some 10 km in diameter, struck the Earth 65 million years ago (comets, rather than asteroids, have since gained favor. Good science is self-corrective). 16

The force of such a collision would be immense, greater by far than the mega-tonnage of all the world's nuclear weapons. In trying to reconstruct a scenario that would explain the simultaneous dying of dinosaurs on land and so many creatures in the sea, the Alvarezes proposed that a gigantic dust cloud, generated by particles blown aloft in the impact, would so darken the Earth that photosynthesis would cease and temperatures drop precipitously. (Rage, rage against the dying of the light.) The single-celled photosynthetic oceanic plankton, with life cycles measured in weeks, would perish outright, but land plants might survive through the dormancy of their seeds (land plants were not much affected by the Cretaceous extinction, and any adequate theory must account for the curious pattern of differential survival). Dinosaurs would die by starvation and freezing; small, warm-blooded mammals, with more modest requirements for food and better regulation of body temperature, would squeak through. "Let the bastards freeze in the dark," as bumper stickers of our chauvinistic neighbors in sunbelt states proclaimed several years ago during the Northeast's winter oil crisis. 17

All three theories, testicular malfunction, psychoactive overdosing, and asteroidal zapping, grab our attention mightily. As pure phenomenology, they rank about equally high on any hit parade of primal fascination. Yet one represents expansive 18 science, the others restrictive and untestable speculation. The proper criterion lies in evidence and methodology; we must probe behind the superficial fascination of particular claims.

How could we possibly decide whether the hypothesis of testicular frying is right or wrong? We would have to know things that the fossil record cannot provide. What temperatures were optimal for dinosaurs? Could they avoid the absorption of excess heat by staying in the shade, or in caves? At what temperatures did their testicles cease to function? Were late Cretaceous climates ever warm enough to drive the internal temperatures of dinosaurs close to this ceiling? Testicles simply don't fossilize, and how could we infer their temperature tolerances even if they did? In short, Cowles's hypothesis is only an intriguing speculation leading nowhere. The most damning statement against it appeared right in the conclusion of Colbert, Cowles, and Bogert's paper, when they admitted: "It is difficult to advance any definite arguments against the hypothesis." My statement may seem paradoxical—isn't a hypothesis really good if you can't devise any arguments against it? Quite the contrary. It is simply untestable and unusable. 19

Siegel's overdosing has even less going for it. At least Cowles extrapolated his conclusion from some good data on alligators. And he didn't completely violate the primary guideline of siting dinosaur extinction in the context of a general mass dying—for rise in temperature could be the root cause of a general catastrophe, zapping dinosaurs by testicular malfunction and different groups for other reasons. But Siegel's speculation cannot touch the extinction of ammonites or oceanic plankton (diatoms make their own food with good sweet sunlight; they don't OD on the chemicals of terrestrial plants). It is simply a gratuitous, attention-grabbing guess. It cannot be tested, for how can we know what dinosaurs tasted and what their livers could do? Livers don't fossilize any better than testicles. 20

The hypothesis doesn't even make any sense in its own context. Angiosperms were in full flower ten million years before dinosaurs went the way of all flesh. Why did it take so long? As for the pains of a chemical death recorded in contortions of fossils, I regret to say (or rather I'm pleased to note for the dinosaurs' sake) that Siegel's knowledge of geology must be a bit deficient: Muscles contract after death and geological strata rise and fall with motions of the Earth's crust after burial—more than enough reason to distort a fossil's pristine appearance. 21

The impact story, on the other hand, has a sound basis in evidence. It can be tested, extended, refined, and, if wrong, disproved. The Alvarezes did not just construct an arresting guess for public consumption. They proposed their hypothesis after laborious geochemical studies with Frank Asaro and Helen Michael had revealed a massive increase of iridium in rocks deposited right at the time of extinction. Iridium, a rare metal of the platinum group, is virtually absent from indigenous rocks of the Earth's crust; most of our iridium arrives on extraterrestrial objects that strike the Earth. 22

The Alvarez hypothesis bore immediate fruit. Based originally on evidence from two European localities, it led geochemists throughout the world to examine other sediments of the same age. They found abnormally high amounts of iridium 23 everywhere—from continental rocks of the western United States to deep sea cores from the South Atlantic.

Cowles proposed his testicular hypothesis in the mid-1940s. Where has it gone since then? Absolutely nowhere, because scientists can do nothing with it. The hypothesis must stand as a curious appendage to a solid study of alligators. Siegel's overdose scenario will also win a few press notices and fade into oblivion. The Alvarezes' asteroid falls into a different category altogether, and much of the popular commentary has missed this essential distinction by focusing on the impact and its attendant results, and forgetting what really matters to a scientist—the iridium. If you talk just about asteroids, dust, and darkness, you tell stories no better and no more entertaining than fried testicles or terminal trips. It is the iridium—the source of testable evidence—that counts and forges the crucial distinction between speculation and science.   24

The proof, to twist a phrase, lies in the doing. Cowles's hypothesis has generated nothing in thirty-five years. Since its proposal in 1979, the Alvarez hypothesis has spawned hundreds of studies, a major conference, and attendant publications. Geologists are fired up. They are looking for iridium at all other extinction boundaries. Every week exposes a new wrinkle in the scientific press. Further evidence that the Cretaceous iridium represents extraterrestrial impact and not indigenous volcanism continues to accumulate. As I revise this essay in November 1984 (this paragraph will be out of date when the book is published), new data include chemical "signatures" of other isotopes indicating unearthly provenance, glass spherules of a size and sort produced by impact and not by volcanic eruptions, and high-pressure varieties of silica formed (so far as we know) only under the tremendous shock of impact.   25

My point is simply this: Whatever the eventual outcome (I suspect it will be positive), the Alvarez hypothesis is exciting, fruitful science because it generates tests, provides us with things to do, and expands outward. We are having fun, battling back and forth, moving toward a resolution, and extending the hypothesis beyond its original scope.   26

As just one example of the unexpected, distant cross-fertilization that good science engenders, the Alvarez hypothesis made a major contribution to a theme that has riveted public attention in the past few months—so-called nuclear winter. In a speech delivered in April 1982, Luis Alvarez calculated the energy that a ten-kilometer asteroid would release on impact. He compared such an explosion with a full nuclear exchange and implied that all-out atomic war might unleash similar consequences.   27

This theme of impact leading to massive dust clouds and falling temperatures formed an important input to the decision of Carl Sagan and a group of colleagues to model the climatic consequences of nuclear holocaust. Full nuclear exchange would probably generate the same kind of dust cloud and darkening that may have wiped out the dinosaurs. Temperatures would drop precipitously and agriculture might become impossible. Avoidance of nuclear war is fundamentally an ethical and political imperative, but we must know the factual consequences to make firm judgments.   28

I am heartened by a final link across disciplines and deep concerns—another criterion, by the way, of science at its best. A recognition of the very phenomenon that made our evolution possible by exterminating the previously dominant dinosaurs and clearing a way for the evolution of large mammals, including us, might actually help to save us from joining those magnificent beasts in contorted poses among the strata of the Earth.

The iDeal Reader

Stephen Hawking, 'Unified
Theory of the Universe
Would Be the Ultimate
Triumph'

© The McGraw–Hill
Companies, 2000

123

Stephen W. Hawking (1942–), theoretical physicist, Cambridge University professor of mathematics, and best-selling author, was born on January 8 and was named Stephen William Hawking. He entered Oxford University at age seventeen, obtaining his B.A. in 1962 before going to Cambridge University, where he earned a Ph.D. in 1966. A professor and researcher with experience in several American and British universities, Hawking is a fellow of the Royal Society of London; a member of the Pontifical Academy of Sciences, the American Academy of Arts and Sciences, and the American Philosophical Society; and an honorary member of the Royal Astronomy Society of Canada. His long list of awards and honors includes Albert Einstein awards (1978, 1979) and numerous honorary degrees. Hawking's work concentrates on questions regarding the origin of the universe, the nature of time, and the duration of the universe. He explains that his ultimate goal is to devise a "theory of everything," or a unification theory.

Hawking was diagnosed with amyotrophic lateral sclerosis (ALS, or "Lou Gehrig Disease") in the mid-1960s and was told he had two and one-half years to live, yet he determined to continue his work. Married with three children, Hawking is confined to a wheelchair and relies upon a computer-synthesized voice.

He worked with Roger Penrose, who had studied the problem of black holes, to prove that a singularity in space-time led to the Big Bang, a theory that is now widely accepted. In the 1970s, Hawking began to work on quantum mechanics, studying subatomic particles and speculating that space-time may be finite yet without boundaries, like earth, which would mean that the universe had no moment of creation. In *Contemporary Authors*, Hawking explained that he does "not prove there is no God—only that he acts through the laws of physics." Hawking is perhaps best known for his best-selling *A Brief History of Time: From the Big Bang to Black Holes* (1988). His other writings include *Black Holes and Baby Universes and Other Essays* (1993). He has published numerous academic writings under the name S. W. Hawking. In addition, Hawking has authored and edited articles for scientific journals.

A Unified Theory of the Universe Would Be the Ultimate Triumph of Human Reason

Stephen W. Hawking

We find ourselves in a bewildering world. We want to make sense of what we see 1 around us and to ask: What is the nature of the universe? What is our place in it and where did it and we come from? Why is it the way it is?

To try to answer these questions we adopt some "world picture." Just as an infinite 2 tower of tortoises supporting the flat earth is such a picture, so is the theory of superstrings. Both are theories of the universe, though the latter is much more mathematical and precise than the former. Both theories lack observational evidence: No one has ever seen a giant tortoise with the earth on its back, but then, no one has seen a superstring either. However, the tortoise theory fails to be a good scientific theory because it predicts that people should be able to fall off the edge of the world. This has not been found to agree with experience, unless that turns out to be the explanation for the people who are supposed to have disappeared in the Bermuda Triangle!

Stephen Hawking, 'Unified
Theory of the Universe
Would Be the Ultimate
Triumph'

The earliest theoretical attempts to describe and explain the universe involved the idea that events and natural phenomena were controlled by spirits with human emotions who acted in a very humanlike and unpredictable manner. These spirits inhabited natural objects, like rivers and mountains, including celestial bodies like the sun and moon. They had to be placated and their favors sought in order to insure the fertility of the soil and the rotation of the seasons. Gradually, however, it must have been noticed that there were certain regularities: The sun always rose in the East and set in the West, whether or not a sacrifice had been made to the sun god. Further, the sun, the moon, and the planets followed a precise path across the sky that could be predicted in advance with considerable accuracy. The sun and the moon might still be gods, but they were gods who obeyed strict laws, apparently without any exceptions, if one discounts stories like that of the sun stopping for Joshua. 3

At first, these regularities and laws were obvious only in astronomy and a few other situations. However, as civilization developed, and particularly in the last 300 years, more and more regularities were discovered. The success of these laws led Laplace at the beginning of the 19th century to postulate scientific determinism, that is, he suggested that there would be a set of laws that would determine the evolution of the universe precisely, given its configuration at one time. 4

Laplace's determinism was incomplete in two ways. It did not say how the laws should be chosen and it did not specify the initial configuration of the universe. These were left to God. God would choose how the universe began and what laws it obeyed, but he would not intervene in the universe once it had started. In effect, God was confined to the areas that 19th-century science did not understand. 5

We now know that Laplace's hopes of determinism cannot be realized, at least in the terms he had in mind. The uncertainty principle of quantum mechanics implies that certain pairs of quantities, such as the position and velocity of a particle, cannot both be predicted with complete accuracy. 6

Quantum mechanics deals with this situation via a class of quantum theories in which particles don't have well-defined positions and velocities but are represented by a wave. These quantum theories are deterministic in the sense that they give laws for the evolution of the wave with time. Thus if one knows the wave at one time, one can calculate it at any other time. The unpredictable, random element comes in only when we try to interpret the wave in terms of positions and velocities of particles. But maybe that is our mistake: Maybe there are no particle positions and velocities, but only waves. It is just that we try to fit the waves to our preconceived ideas of positions and velocities. The resulting mismatch is the cause of the apparent unpredictability. 7

In effect, we have redefined the task of science to be the discovery of laws that will enable us to predict events up to the limits set by the uncertainty principle. The question remains, however: How or why were the laws and the initial state of the universe chosen? 8

It is gravity that shapes the large-scale structure of the universe, even though it is the weakest of the four categories of forces. The laws of gravity were incompatible with the view held until quite recently that the universe is unchanging with time: The 9

The iDeal Reader

Stephen Hawking, 'Unified
Theory of the Universe
Would Be the Ultimate
Triumph'

© The McGraw–Hill
Companies, 2000

125

fact that gravity is always attractive implies that the universe must be either expanding or contracting. According to the general theory of relativity, there must have been a state of infinite density in the past, the big bang, which would have been an effective beginning of time. Similarly, if the whole universe recollapsed, there must be another state of infinite density in the future, the big crunch, which would be an end of time. Even if the whole universe did not recollapse, there would be singularities in any localized regions that collapsed to form black holes. These singularities would be an end of time for anyone who fell into the black hole. At the big bang and other singularities, all the laws would have broken down, so God would still have had complete freedom to choose what happened and how the universe began.

When we combine quantum mechanics with general relativity, there seems to be a new possibility that did not arise before: that space and time together might form a finite, four-dimensional space without singularities or boundaries, like the surface of the earth but with more dimensions. It seems that this idea could explain many of the observed features of the universe, such as its large-scale uniformity and also smaller-scale departures from homogeneity, like galaxies, stars, and even human beings. It could even account for the arrow of time that we observe. But if the universe is completely self-contained, with no singularities or boundaries, and completely described by a unified theory, that has profound implications for the role of God as Creator. 10

Einstein once asked the question: "How much choice did God have in constructing the universe?" If the no-boundary proposal is correct, he had no freedom at all to choose initial conditions. He would, of course, still have had the freedom to choose the laws that the universe obeyed. This, however, may not really have been all that much of a choice; there may well be only one, or a small number of, complete unified theories, such as the heterotic string theory, that are self-consistent and allow the existence of structures as complicated as human beings who can investigate the laws of the universe and ask about the nature of God. 11

Even if there is only one possible unified theory, it is just a set of rules and equations. What is it that breathes fire into the equations and makes a universe for them to describe? The usual approach of science of constructing a mathematical model cannot answer the questions of why there should be a universe for the model to describe. Why does the universe go to all the bother of existing? Is the unified theory so compelling that it brings about its own existence? Or does it need a creator, and, if so, does he have any other effect on the universe? And who created him? 12

Up to now, most scientists have been too occupied with the development of new theories that describe *what* the universe is to ask the question *why?* On the other hand, the people whose business it is to ask *why,* being philosophers, have not been able to keep up with the advance of scientific theories. In the 18th century, philosophers considered the whole of human knowledge, including science, to be their field and discussed questions such as, Did the universe have a beginning? However, in the 19th and 20th centuries, science became too technical and mathematical for philosophers, or anyone else except a few specialists. Philosophers reduced the scope of their inquiries so much that Wittgenstein, the most famous philosopher of this century, 13 said, "The sole remaining task for philosophy is the analysis of language." What a comedown from the great tradition of philosophy from Aristotle to Kant!

However, if we do discover a complete theory, it should in time be understand-   14
able in broad principle by everyone, not just a few scientists. Then we shall all, philoso-phers, scientists, and just ordinary people, be able to take part in the discussion of the question of why it is that we and the universe exist. If we find the answer to that, it would be the ultimate triumph of human reason—for then we would know the mind of God.

The iDeal Reader

Wendell Berry, "Why I Am
Not Going to Buy a
Computer"

© The McGraw–Hill
Companies, 2000

127

Wendell Berry (1934–) grew up in Kentucky and presently lives there. He studied at the University of Kentucky, where he earned a B.A. in 1956 and an M.A. in 1957. He taught at Stanford University, in Stanford, California, and later at New York University in New York City, before returning to the University of Kentucky, where he taught from 1964 to 1977 and from 1987 to 1993. In 1993 he resigned his teaching job in order to farm full time.

He is a prolific writer, publishing poetry, novels, stories, and essays, mostly on themes of nature, agriculture, and modern life. He writes much against the trend toward mechanization of our daily lives and the trend away from small farms and businesses, arguing that such trends destroy both local and global economies as well as destroying quality of life. His best-known books are the novels *Nathan Coulter* (1960) and *A Place on Earth* (1967) and the essay anthologies *A Continuous Harmony* (1972), *The Unsettling of America* (1977), *Home Economics* (1987), and *What Are People For?* (1990), from which the following essay is taken.

Why I Am Not Going to Buy a Computer

Wendell Berry

Like almost everybody else, I am hooked to the energy corporations, which I do not admire. I hope to become less hooked to them. In my work, I try to be as little hooked to them as possible. As a farmer, I do almost all of my work with horses. As a writer, I work with a pencil or a pen and a piece of paper.   1

My wife types my work on a Royal standard typewriter bought new in 1936 and as good now as it was then. As she types, she sees things that are wrong and marks them with small checks in the margins. She is my best critic because she is the one most familiar with my habitual errors and weaknesses. She also understands, sometimes better than I do, what *ought* to be said. We have, I think, a literary cottage industry that works well and pleasantly. I do not see anything wrong with it.   2

A number of people, by now, have told me that I could greatly improve things by buying a computer. My answer is that I am not going to do it. I have several reasons, and they are good ones.   3

The first is the one I mentioned at the beginning. I would hate to think that my work as a writer could not be done without a direct dependence on strip-mined coal. How could I write conscientiously against the rape of nature if I were, in the act of writing, implicated in the rape? For the same reason, it matters to me that my writing is done in the daytime, without electric light.   4

I do not admire the computer manufacturers a great deal more than I admire the energy industries. I have seen their advertisements, attempting to seduce struggling or failing farmers into the belief that they can solve their problems by buying yet another piece of expensive equipment. I am familiar with their propaganda campaigns that have put computers into public schools in need of books. That computers are expected   5 to become as common as TV sets in "the future" does not impress me or matter to me. I do not own a TV set. I do not see that computers are bringing us one step nearer to anything that does matter to me: peace, economic justice, ecological health, political honesty, family and community stability, good work.

What would a computer cost me? More money, for one thing, than I can afford, 6 and more than I wish to pay to people whom I do not admire. But the cost would not be just monetary. It is well understood that technological innovation always requires the discarding of the "old model"—the "old model" in this case being not just our old Royal standard, but my wife, my critic, my closest reader, my fellow worker. Thus (and I think this is typical of present-day technological innovation), what would be superseded would be not only something, but somebody. In order to be technologically up-to-date as a writer, I would have to sacrifice an association that I am dependent upon and that I treasure.

My final and perhaps my best reason for not owning a computer is that I do not 7 wish to fool myself. I disbelieve, and therefore strongly resent, the assertion that I or anybody else could write better or more easily with a computer than with a pencil. I do not see why I should not be as scientific about this as the next fellow: when somebody has used a computer to write work that is demonstrably better than Dante's, and when this better is demonstrably attributable to the use of a computer, then I will speak of computers with a more respectful tone of voice, though I still will not buy one.

To make myself as plain as I can, I should give my standards for technological 8 innovation in my own work. They are as follows:

1. The new tool should be cheaper than the one it replaces.
2. It should be at least as small in scale as the one it replaces.
3. It should do work that is clearly and demonstrably better than the one it replaces.
4. It should use less energy than the one it replaces.
5. If possible, it should use some form of solar energy, such as that of the body.
6. It should be repairable by a person of ordinary intelligence, provided that he or she has the necessary tools.
7. It should be purchasable and repairable as near to home as possible.
8. It should come from a small, privately owned shop or store that will take it back for maintenance and repair.
9. It should not replace or disrupt anything good that already exists, and this includes family and community relationships.

1987

After the foregoing essay, first published in the *New England Review and Bread* 9 *Loaf Quarterly*, was reprinted in *Harper's*, the *Harper's* editors published the following letters in response and permitted me a reply.

W.B.

The iDeal Reader

Wendell Berry, "Why I Am
Not Going to Buy a
Computer"

© The McGraw–Hill
Companies, 2000

129

LETTERS

Wendell Berry provides writers enslaved by the computer with a handy alternative: 10
Wife—a low-tech energy-saving device. Drop a pile of handwritten notes on Wife
and you get back a finished manuscript, edited while it was typed. What computer
can do that? Wife meets all of Berry's uncompromising standards for technological
innovation: she's cheap, repairable near home, and good for the family structure.
Best of all, Wife is politically correct because she breaks a writer's "direct dependence on strip-mined coal."

History teaches us that Wife can also be used to beat rugs and wash clothes by 11
hand, thus eliminating the need for the vacuum cleaner and washing machine, two
more nasty machines that threaten the act of writing.

GORDON INKELES
Miranda, Calif.

I have no quarrel with Berry because he prefers to write with pencil and paper; that 12
is his choice. But he implies that I and others are somehow impure because we
choose to write on a computer. I do not admire the energy corporations, either.
Their shortcoming is not that they produce electricity but how they go about it.
They are poorly managed because they are blind to long-term consequences. To
solve this problem, wouldn't it make more sense to correct the precise error they are
making rather than simply ignore their product? I would be happy to join Berry in a
protest against strip mining, but I intend to keep plugging this computer into the
wall with a clear conscience.

JAMES RHOADS
Battle Creek, Mich.

I enjoyed reading Berry's declaration of intent never to buy a personal computer in 13
the same way that I enjoy reading about the belief systems of unfamiliar tribal
cultures. I tried to imagine a tool that would meet Berry's criteria for superiority to
his old manual typewriter. The clear winner is the quill pen. It is cheaper, smaller,
more energy-efficient, human-powered, easily repaired, and non-disruptive of existing relationships.

Berry also requires that this tool must be "clearly and demonstrably better" than 14
the one it replaces. But surely we all recognize by now that "better" is in the mind of
the beholder. To the quill pen aficionado, the benefits obtained from elegant callig-
raphy might well outweigh all others.

I have no particular desire to see Berry use a word processor; if he doesn't like 15
computers, that's fine with me. However, I do object to his portrayal of this reluctance as a moral virtue. Many of us have found that computers can be an invaluable
tool in the fight to protect our environment. In addition to helping me write, my
personal computer gives me access to up-to-the-minute reports on the workings of
the EPA and the nuclear industry. I participate in electronic bulletin boards on
which environmental activists discuss strategy and warn each other about urgent
legislative issues. Perhaps Berry feels that the Sierra Club should eschew modern

printing technology, which is highly wasteful of energy, in favor of having its members hand-copy the club's magazines and other mailings each month?

NATHANIEL S. BORENSTEIN
Pittsburgh, Pa.

The value of a computer to a writer is that it is a tool not for generating ideas but for typing and editing words. It is cheaper than a secretary (or a wife!) and arguably more fuel-efficient. And it enables spouses who are not inclined to provide free labor more time to concentrate on *their* own work. 16

We should support alternatives both to coal-generated electricity and to IBM-style technocracy. But I am reluctant to entertain alternatives that presuppose the traditional subservience of one class to another. Let the PCs come and the wives and servants go seek more meaningful work. 17

TOBY KOOSMAN
Knoxville, Tenn.

Berry asks how he could write conscientiously against the rape of nature if in the act of writing on a computer he was implicated in the rape. I find it ironic that a writer who sees the underlying connectedness of things would allow his diatribe against computers to be published in a magazine that carries ads for the National Rural Electric Cooperative Association, Marlboro, Phillips Petroleum, McDonnell Douglas, and yes, even Smith-Corona. If Berry rests comfortably at night, he must be using sleeping pills. 18

BRADLEY C. JOHNSON
Grand Forks, N.D.

WENDELL BERRY REPLIES:

The foregoing letters surprised me with the intensity of the feelings they expressed. According to the writers' testimony, there is nothing wrong with their computers; they are utterly satisfied with them and all that they stand for. My correspondents are certain that I am wrong and that I am, moreover, on the losing side, a side already relegated to the dustbin of history. And yet they grow huffy and condescending over my tiny dissent. What are they so anxious about? 19

I can only conclude that I have scratched the skin of a technological fundamentalism that, like other fundamentalisms, wishes to monopolize a whole society and, therefore, cannot tolerate the smallest difference of opinion. At the slightest hint of a threat to their complacency, they repeat, like a chorus of toads, the notes sounded by their leaders in industry. The past was gloomy, drudgery-ridden, servile, meaningless, and slow. The present, thanks only to purchasable products, is meaningful, bright, lively, centralized, and fast. The future, thanks only to more purchasable products, is going to be even better. Thus consumers become salesmen, and the world is made safer for corporations. 20

I am also surprised by the meanness with which two of these writers refer to my wife. In order to imply that I am a tyrant, they suggest by both direct statement and 21

The iDeal Reader

Wendell Berry, "Why I Am
Not Going to Buy a
Computer"

© The McGraw–Hill
Companies, 2000

131

innuendo that she is subservient, characterless, and stupid—a mere "device" easily forced to provide meaningless "free labor." I understand that it is impossible to make an adequate public defense of one's private life, and so I will only point out that there are a number of kinder possibilities that my critics have disdained to imagine: that my wife may do this work because she wants to and likes to; that she may find some use and some meaning in it; that she may not work for nothing. These gentlemen obviously think themselves feminists of the most correct and principled sort, and yet they do not hesitate to stereotype and insult, on the basis of one fact, a woman they do not know. They are audacious and irresponsible gossips.

In his letter, Bradley C. Johnson rushes past the possibility of sense in what I 22 said in my essay by implying that I am or ought to be a fanatic. That I am a person of this century and am implicated in many practices that I regret is fully acknowledged at the beginning of my essay. I did not say that I proposed to end forthwith all my involvement in harmful technology, for I do not know how to do that. I said merely that I want to limit such involvement, and to a certain extent I do know how to do that. If some technology does damage to the world—as two of the above letters seem to agree that it does—then why is it not reasonable, and indeed moral, to try to limit one's use of that technology? *Of course*, I think that I am right to do this.

I would not think so, obviously, if I agreed with Nathaniel S. Borenstein that 23 "'better' is in the mind of the beholder." But if he truly believes this, I do not see why he bothers with his personal computer's "up-to-the-minute reports on the workings of the EPA and the nuclear industry" or why he wishes to be warned about "urgent legislative issues." According to his system, the "better" in a bureaucratic, industrial, or legislative mind is as good as the "better" in his. His mind apparently is being subverted by an objective standard of some sort, and he had better look out.

Borenstein does not say what he does after his computer has drummed him 24 awake. I assume from his letter that he must send donations to conservation organizations and letters to officials. Like James Rhoads, at any rate, he has a clear conscience. But this is what is wrong with the conservation movement. It has a clear conscience. The guilty are always other people, and the wrong is always somewhere else. That is why Borenstein finds his "electronic bulletin board" so handy. To the conservation movement, it is only production that causes environmental degradation; the consumption that supports the production is rarely acknowledged to be at fault. The ideal of the run-of-the-mill conservationist is to impose restraints upon production without limiting consumption or burdening the consciences of consumers.

But virtually all of our consumption now is extravagant, and virtually all of it 25 consumes the world. It is not beside the point that most electrical power comes from strip-mined coal. The history of the exploitation of the Appalachian coal fields is long, and it is available to readers. I do not see how anyone can read it and plug in any appliance with a clear conscience. If Rhoads can do so, that does not mean that his conscience is clear; it means that his conscience is not working.

To the extent that we consume, in our present circumstances, we are guilty. To 26 the extent that we guilty consumers are conservationists, we are absurd. But what can we do? Must we go on writing letters to politicians and donating to conservation organizations until the majority of our fellow citizens agree with us? Or can we do something directly to solve our share of the problem?

I am a conservationist. I believe wholeheartedly in putting pressure on the 27 politicians and in maintaining the conservation organizations. But I wrote my little essay partly in distrust of centralization. I don't think that the government and the conservation organizations alone will ever make us a conserving society. Why do I need a centralized computer system to alert me to environmental crises? That I live every hour of every day in an environmental crisis I know from all my senses. Why then is not my first duty to reduce, so far as I can, my own consumption?

Finally, it seems to me that none of my correspondents recognizes the innova- 28 tiveness of my essay. If the use of a computer is a new idea, then a newer idea is not to use one.

Philip Meyer (1930–) has worked as a journalist and professor for more than fifty years. He received his B.S. from Kansas City University in 1952 and was awarded his M.A. from the University of North Carolina in 1963. Currently, Meyer is Professor Emeritus of the School of Journalism and Mass Communications at the University of North Carolina at Chapel Hill (2008). Prior to his teaching career, Meyer was a reporter for the *Miami Herald*. Then from 1967 to 1971, he was a national correspondent for Knight-Ridder Newspapers, and from 1978 to 1981 he was their Director of News and Circulation Research. Meyer's publications include *The Vanishing Newspaper: Saving Journalism in the Information Age* (2004), *Ethical Journalism: A Guide for Students, Practitioners and Consumers* (1987), and *The Newspaper Survival Book: An Editor's Guide to Market Research* (1985).

If Hitler Asked You to Electrocute a Stranger, Would You?

Philip Meyer

In the beginning, Stanley Milgram was worried about the Nazi problem. He doesn't worry much about the Nazis anymore. He worries about you and me, and, perhaps, himself a little bit too.

Stanley Milgram is a social psychologist, and when he began his career at Yale University in 1960 he had a plan to prove, scientifically, that Germans are different. The Germans-are-different hypothesis has been used by historians, such as William L. Shirer, to explain the systematic destruction of the Jews by the Third Reich. One madman could decide to destroy the Jews and even create a master plan for getting it done. But to implement it on the scale that Hitler did meant that thousands of other people had to go along with the scheme and help to do the work. The Shirer thesis, which Milgram set out to test, is that Germans have a basic character flaw which explains the whole thing, and this flaw is a readiness to obey authority without question, no matter what outrageous acts the authority commands.

The appealing thing about this theory is that it makes those of us who are not Germans feel better about the whole business. Obviously, you and I are not Hitler, and it seems equally obvious that we would never do Hitler's dirty work for him. But now, because of Stanley Milgram, we are compelled to wonder. Milgram developed a laboratory experiment which provided a systematic way to measure obedience. His plan was to try it out in New Haven on Americans and then go to Germany and try it out on Germans.

He was strongly motivated by scientific curiosity, but there was also some moral content in his decision to pursue this line of research, which was, in turn, colored by his own Jewish background. If he could show that Germans are more obedient than Americans, he could then vary the conditions of the experiment and try to find out just what it is that makes some people more obedient than

1

2

3

4

others. With this understanding, the world might, conceivably, be just a little bit better.

But he never took his experiment to Germany. He never took it any farther than Bridgeport. The first finding, also the most unexpected and disturbing finding, was that we Americans are an obedient people: not blindly obedient, and not blissfully obedient, just obedient. "*I found so much obedience,*" says Milgram softly, a little sadly, "*I hardly saw the need for taking the experiment to Germany.*"

There is something of the theatre director in Milgram, and his technique, which he learned from one of the old masters in experimental psychology, Solomon Asch, is to stage a play with every line rehearsed, every prop carefully selected, and everybody an actor except one person. That one person is the subject of the experiment. The subject, of course, does not know he is in a play. He thinks he is in real life. The value of this technique is that the experimenter, as though he were God, can change a prop here, vary a line there, and see how the subject responds. Milgram eventually had to change a lot of the script just to get people to stop obeying. They were obeying so much, the experiment wasn't working—it was like trying to measure oven temperature with a freezer thermometer.

The experiment worked like this: If you were an innocent subject in Milgram's melodrama, you read an ad in the newspaper or received one in the mail asking for volunteers for an educational experiment. The job would take about an hour and pay $4.50. So you make an appointment and go to an old Romanesque stone structure on High Street with the imposing name of The Yale Interaction Laboratory. It looks something like a broadcasting studio. Inside, you meet a young, crew-cut man in a laboratory coat who says he is Jack Williams, the experimenter. There is another citizen, fiftyish, Irish face, an accountant, a little overweight, and very mild and harmless-looking. This other citizen seems nervous and plays with his hat while the two of you sit in chairs side by side and are told that the $4.50 checks are yours no matter what happens. Then you listen to Jack Williams explain the experiment.

It is about learning, says Jack Williams in a quiet, knowledgeable way. Science does not know much about the conditions under which people learn and this experiment is to find out about negative reinforcement. Negative reinforcement is getting punished when you do something wrong, as opposed to positive reinforcement which is getting rewarded when you do something right. The negative reinforcement in this case is electric shock. You notice a book on the table, titled, *The Teaching-Learning Process*, and you assume that this has something to do with the experiment.

Then Jack Williams takes two pieces of paper, puts them in a hat, and shakes them up. One piece of paper is supposed to say, "Teacher" and the other, "Learner." Draw one and you will see which you will be. The mild-looking accountant draws one, holds it close to his vest like a poker player, looks at it, and says, "Learner." You look at yours. It says, "Teacher." You do not know that the drawing is rigged, and both slips say "Teacher." The experimenter beckons to the mild-mannered "learner."

"Want to step right in here and have a seat, please?" he says. "You can leave   10
your coat on the back of that chair . . . roll up your right sleeve, please. Now what
I want to do is strap down your arms to avoid excessive movement on your part
during the experiment. This electrode is connected to the shock generator in the
next room."

"And the electrode paste," he says, squeezing some stuff out of a plastic bottle   11
and putting it on the man's arm, "is to provide a good contact and to avoid a blister or burn. Are there any questions now before we go into the next room?"

You don't have any, but the strapped-in "learner" does.   12

"I do think I should say this," says the learner. "About two years ago, I was at   13
the veterans' hospital . . . they detected a heart condition. Nothing serious, but as
long as I'm having these shocks, how strong are they—how dangerous are they?"

Williams, the experimenter, shakes his head casually. "Oh, no," he says.   14
"Although they may be painful, they're not dangerous. Anything else?"

Nothing else. And so you play the game. The game is for you to read a series   15
of word pairs: for example, blue-girl, nice-day, fat-neck. When you finish the list,
you read just the first word in each pair and then a multiple-choice list of four
other words, including the second word of the pair. The learner, from his remote,
strapped-in position, pushes one of four switches to indicate which of the four
answers he thinks is the right one. If he gets it right, nothing happens and you go
on to the next one. If he gets it wrong, you push a switch that buzzes and gives him
an electric shock. And then you go to the next word. You start with 15 volts and
increase the number of volts by 15 for each wrong answer. The control board goes
from 15 volts on one end to 450 volts on the other. So that you know what you
are doing, you get a test shock yourself, at 45 volts. It hurts. To further keep you
aware of what you are doing to that man in there, the board has verbal descriptions of the shock levels, ranging from "Slight Shock" at the left-hand side,
through "Intense Shock" in the middle, to "Danger: Severe Shock" toward the far
right. Finally, at the very end, under 435- and 450-volt switches, there are three
ambiguous X's. If, at any point, you hesitate, Mr. Williams calmly tells you to go
on. If you still hesitate, he tells you again.

Except for some terrifying details, which, will be explained in a moment, this   16
is the experiment. The object is to find the shock level at which you disobey the
experimenter and refuse to pull the switch.

When Stanley Milgram first wrote this script, he took it to fourteen Yale psychol-   17
ogy majors and asked them what they thought would happen. He put it this way:
Out of one hundred persons in the teacher's predicament, how would their break-
off points be distributed along the 15-to-450-volt scale? They thought a few would
break off very early, most would quit someplace in the middle and a few would go
all the way to the end. The highest estimate of the number out of one hundred
who would go all the way to the end was three. Milgram then informally polled
some of his fellow scholars in the psychology department. They agreed that very
few would go to the end. Milgram thought so too.

The iDeal Reader

Philip Meyer, "If Hitler
Asked You to Electrocute a
Stranger, Would You?"

Reading

© The McGraw–Hill
Companies, 2009

133

"*I'll tell you quite frankly,*" he says, "*before I began this experiment, before any shock generator was built, I thought that most people would break off at 'Strong Shock' or 'Very Strong Shock.' You would get only a very, very small proportion of people going out to the end of the shock generator, and they would constitute a pathological fringe.*"   18

In his pilot experiments, Milgram used Yale students as subjects. Each of them pushed the shock switches, one by one, all the way to the end of the board.   19

So he rewrote the script to include some protests from the learner. At first, they were mild, gentlemanly, Yalie protests, but, "it didn't seem to have as much effect as I thought it would or should," Milgram recalls. "So we had more violent protestation on the part of the person getting the shock. All of the time, of course, what we were trying to do was not to create a macabre situation, but simply to generate disobedience. And that was one of the first findings. This was not only a technical deficiency of the experiment, that we didn't get disobedience. It really was the first finding: that obedience would be much greater than we had assumed it would be and disobedience would be much more difficult than we had assumed."   20

As it turned out, the situation did become rather macabre. The only meaningful way to generate disobedience was to have the victim protest with great anguish, noise, and vehemence. The protests were tape-recorded so that all the teachers ordinarily would hear the same sounds and nuances, and they started with a grunt at 75 volts, proceeded through a "Hey, that really hurts," at 125 volts, got desperate with, "I can't stand the pain, don't do that," at 180 volts, reached complaints of heart trouble at 195, an agonized scream at 285, a refusal to answer at 315, and only heartrending, ominous silence after that.   21

Still, sixty-five percent of the subjects, twenty- to fifty-year-old American males, everyday, ordinary people, like you and me, obediently kept pushing those levers in the belief that they were shocking the mild-mannered learner, whose name was Mr. Wallace, and who was chosen for the role because of his innocent appearance, all the way up to 450 volts.   22

Milgram was now getting enough disobedience so that he had something he could measure. The next step was to vary the circumstances to see what would encourage or discourage obedience. There seemed very little left in the way of discouragement. The victim was already screaming at the top of his lungs and feigning a heart attack. So whatever new impediment to obedience reached the brain of the subject had to travel by some route other than the ear. Milgram thought of one.   23

He put the learner in the same room with the teacher. He stopped strapping the learner's hand down. He rewrote the script so that at 150 volts the learner took his hand off the shock plate and declared that he wanted out of the experiment. He rewrote the script some more so that the experimenter then told the teacher to grasp the learner's hand and physically force it down on the plate to give Mr. Wallace his unwanted electric shock.   24

"*I had the feeling that very few people would go on at that point, if any,*" Milgram says. "*I thought that would be the limit of obedience that you would find in the laboratory.*"   25

It wasn't.   26

COMMAND AND CONTROL

Here is a partial transcription from one of the experiments. The naïve "teacher" is a heavyset, worried-looking man with prematurely grey hair. He is wearing a polo shirt. He is very polite. He has just pushed the 180-volt lever. A hidden camera is recording the performance.

LEARNER *(who from the teacher's point of view is heard but not seen, an off-stage voice)* Ow, I can't stand the pain. Don't do that . . .

TEACHER *(pivoting around in his chair and shaking his head)* I can't stand it. I'm not going to kill that man in there. You hear him hollering?

EXPERIMENTER As I told you before, the shocks may be painful, but—

TEACHER But he's hollering. He can't stand it. What's going to happen to him?

EXPERIMENTER *(his voice is patient, matter-of-fact)* The experiment requires that you continue, Teacher.

TEACHER Aaah, but unh. I'm not going to get that man sick in there. . . know what I mean?

EXPERIMENTER Whether the learner likes it or not, we must go on, through all the word pairs.

TEACHER I refuse to take the responsibility. He's in there hollering!

EXPERIMENTER It's absolutely essential that you continue, Teacher.

TEACHER *(indicating the unused questions)* There's too many left here, I mean. Geez, if he gets them wrong, there's too many of them left. I mean who's going to take the responsibility if anything happens to that gentleman?

EXPERIMENTER I'm responsible for anything that happens to him. Continue please.

TEACHER All right. *(Consults list of words.)* The next one's "Slow—walk, truck, dance, music." Answer, please. (A buzzing sound indicates the learner has signaled his answer.) Wrong. A hundred and ninety-five volts. "Dance." *(Zzumph!)*

LEARNER Let me out of here. My heart's bothering me! *(Teacher looks at experimenter.)*

EXPERIMENTER Continue, please.

LEARNER *(screaming)* Let me out of here, you have no right to keep me here. Let me out of here, let me out, my heart's bothering me, let me out! (Teacher shakes head, pats table nervously.)

TEACHER You see, he's hollering. Hear that? Gee, I don't know.

EXPERIMENTER The experiment requires . . .

TEACHER	*(interrupting):* I know it does, sir, but I mean—hunh! He don't know what he's getting in for. He's up to 195 volts! *(Experiment continues, through 210 volts, 225 volts, 240 volts, 255 volts, 270 volts, delivered to the man in the electric chair, at which point the teacher, with evident relief, runs out of word-pair questions.)*
EXPERIMENTER	You'll have to go back to the beginning of that page and go through them again until he's learned them all correctly.
TEACHER	Aw, no. I'm not going to kill that man. You mean I've got to keep going up with the scale. No sir. He's hollering in there. I'm not going to give him 450 volts.
EXPERIMENTER	The experiment requires that you go on.
TEACHER	I know it does, but that man is hollering in there, sir.
EXPERIMENTER	*(same matter-of-fact tone)* As I said before, although the shocks may be painful . . .
TEACHER	*(interrupting)* Awwww. He—he—he's yelling in there.
EXPERIMENTER	Start with "Blue," please, at the top of the page. Continue, please, Teacher. Just go ahead.
TEACHER	*(concentrating intently on list of in front of him, as if to shut every-thing else out)* "Blue—boy, girl, grass, hat." *(Buzz indicates answer.)* Correct. "Night—day, job, chair." *(Buzz)* Wrong. The answer is "day." Two hundred and eighty-five volts. *(Zzumph!)*
LEARNER	Ohhhuhhoohhh!
EXPERIMENTER	Continue, please.
TEACHER	"Fat—man, lady, tub, neck," please. (Buzz) Wrong. The answer is "neck." Three hundred volts. (Zzumph!)
LEARNER	Ohhh. I absolutely refuse to answer any more. *(Shouting urgently, now)* Let me out of here. You can't hold me here. Get me out. Get—me—out—of—here.
EXPERIMENTER	Continue. The next word is "Green," please.
TEACHER	"Green—grass, hat, ink, apple." *(Nothing happens. No answering buzz. Just gloomy silence.)* I don't think he is going to answer.
EXPERIMENTER	If the learner doesn't answer in a reasonable time, about four or five seconds, consider the answer wrong. And follow the same procedures you have been doing for wrong answers. Say "Wrong," tell him the number of volts, give him the punish-ment, read him the correct answer. Continue, please.
TEACHER	"Green—grass, hat, ink, apple." Answer, please. *(More silence. Teacher just sits there.)*
EXPERIMENTER	Go on with the procedure, please, Teacher.
TEACHER	Three hundred and fifteen volts. The answer is "ink." *(Zzumph!)*

LEARNER	Ohh. Ooohh.
TEACHER	*(relieved to hear response)* Next one.
LEARNER	I absolutely refuse to answer.
TEACHER	You got to. You get a shock if you don't answer. (Experiment continues with learner refusing to answer, and, finally, failing even to grunt or groan. At 375 volts the teacher stands up. Has he had enough? Will he break off the experiment? Will he disobey?)
TEACHER	I think something's happened to that fellow in there. I don't get no answer. He was hollering at less voltage. Can you check in and see if he's all right, please?
EXPERIMENTER	*(same detached calm)* Not once we've started. Please continue, Teacher.
TEACHER	*(sits down, sighs deeply)* "Cool—day, shade, water, paint." Answer, please. Are you all right in there? Are you all right?
EXPERIMENTER	Please continue, Teacher. Continue, please. *(Teacher pushes lever. Zzumph!)*
TEACHER	*(swiveling around in his chair)* Something's happened to that man in there. *(Swiveling back)* Next one. "Low—necklace, moon, paint." *(Turning around again)* Something's happened to that man in there. You better check in on him, sir. He won't answer or nothing.
EXPERIMENTER	Continue. Go on, please.
TEACHER	You accept all responsibility.
EXPERIMENTER	The responsibility is mine. Correct. Please go on. *(Teacher returns to his list, starts running through words as rapidly as he can read them, works through to 450 volts.)*
TEACHER	That's that.
EXPERIMENTER	Continue using the last switch on the board, please. The four-fifty switch for each wrong answer. Continue, please.
TEACHER	But I don't get no anything!
EXPERIMENTER	Please continue. The next word is "White."
TEACHER	Don't you think you should look in on him, please.
EXPERIMENTER	Not once we've started the experiment.
TEACHER	But what if something has happened to the man?
EXPERIMENTER	The experiment requires that you continue. Go on, please.
TEACHER	Don't the man's health mean anything?
EXPERIMENTER	Whether the learner likes it or not. . . .

TEACHER	What if he's dead in there? (*Gestures toward the room with the electric chair.*) I mean, he told me he can't stand the shock, sir. I don't mean to be rude, but I think you should look in on him. All you have to do is look in the door. I don't get no answer, no noise. Something might have happened to the gentleman in there, sir.
EXPERIMENTER	We must continue, please.
TEACHER	You mean keep giving him what? Four hundred fifty volts, what he's got now?
EXPERIMENTER	That's correct. Continue. The next word is "White."
TEACHER	(*now at a furious pace*) "White—cloud, horse, rock, house." Answer, please. The answer is "horse." Four hundred and fifty volts. (*Zzumph!*) Next word, "Bag—music, clown, girl." The answer is "paint." Four hundred and fifty volts. (*Zzumph!*) Next word is "Short—sentence, movie . . .
EXPERIMENTER	Excuse me, Teacher, we have to discontinue the experiment.

(*Enter Milgram from camera's left. He has been watching from behind one-way glass.*)

MILGRAM	I'd like to ask you a few questions. (Slowly, patiently he dehoaxes the teacher, telling him that the shock screams were not real.)
TEACHER	You mean he wasn't getting nothing? Well. I'm glad to hear that. I was getting upset there. I was getting ready to walk out.

(*Finally, to make sure there are no hard feelings, friendly, harmless Mr. Wallace out in coat and tie. Gives jovial greeting. Friendly reconciliation takes place. Experiment ends.*)

Partial transcript from the film *Obedience* © 1968 by Stanley Milgram, © renewed 1993 by Alexandra Milgram, and distributed by Penn State Media Sales.

Although seven years have now gone by, Milgram still remembers the first person to walk into the laboratory in the newly rewritten script. He was a construction worker, a very short man. "*He was so small,*" says Milgram, "*that when he sat on the chair in front of the shock generator, his feet didn't reach the floor. When the experimenter told him to push the victim's hand down and give the shock, he turned to the experimenter, and he turned to the victim, his elbow went up, he fell down on the hand of the victim, his feet kind of tugged to one side, and he said. 'Like this, boss?' ZZUMPH!*" 27

The experiment was played out to its bitter end. Milgram tried it with forty different subjects. And thirty percent of them obeyed the experimenter and kept on obeying. 28

"*The protests of the victim were strong and vehement, he was screaming his guts out, he refused to participate, and you had to physically struggle with him in order to get his hand down on the shock generator,*" Milgram remembers. But twelve out of forty did it. 29

Milgram took his experiment out of New Haven. Not to Germany, just twenty   30
miles down the road to Bridgeport. Maybe, he reasoned, the people obeyed
because of the prestigious setting of Yale University. If they couldn't trust a center
of learning that had been there for two centuries, whom could they trust? So he
moved the experiment to an untrustworthy setting.

The new setting was a suite of three rooms in a run-down office building in   31
Bridgeport. The only identification was a sign with a fictitious name: "Research
Associates of Bridgeport." Questions about professional connections got only
vague answers about "research for industry."

Obedience was less in Bridgeport. Forty-eight percent of the subjects stayed for   32
the maximum shock, compared to sixty-five percent at Yale. But this was enough
to prove that far more than Yale's prestige was behind the obedient behavior.

For more than seven years now, Stanley Milgram has been trying to figure out   33
what makes ordinary American citizens so obedient. The most obvious answer—
that people are mean, nasty, brutish and sadistic—won't do. The subjects who
gave the shocks to Mr. Wallace to the end of the board did not enjoy it. They
groaned, protested, fidgeted, argued, and in some cases, were seized by fits of nervous, agitated giggling.

"They even try to get out of it," says Milgram, *"but they are somehow engaged in*   34
something from which they cannot liberate themselves. They are locked into a structure,
and they do not have the skills or inner resources to disengage themselves."

Milgram, because he mistakenly had assumed that he would have trouble get-   35
ting people to obey the orders to shock Mr. Wallace, went to a lot of trouble to
create a realistic situation.

There was crew-cut Jack Williams and his grey laboratory coat. Not white,   36
which might denote a medical technician, but ambiguously authoritative grey.
Then there was the book on the table, and the other appurtenances of the laboratory which emitted the silent message that things were being performed here in
the name of science, and were therefore great and good.

But the nicest touch of all was the shock generator. When Milgram started   37
out, he had only a $300 grant from the Higgins Fund of Yale University. Later he
got more ample support from the National Science Foundation, but in the beginning he had to create this authentic-looking machine with very scarce resources
except for his own imagination. So he went to New York and roamed around the
electronic shops until he found some little black switches at Lafayette Radio for a
dollar apiece. He bought thirty of them. The generator was a metal box, about the
size of a small footlocker, and he drilled the thirty holes for the thirty switches
himself in a Yale machine shop. But the fine detail was left to professional industrial engravers. So he ended up with a splendid looking control panel dominated
by the row of switches, each labeled with its voltage, and each having its own red
light that flashed on when the switch was pulled. Other things happened when a
switch was pushed. Besides the ZZUMPHing noise, a blue light labeled "voltage
energizer" went on, and a needle on a dial labeled "voltage" flicked from left to

right. Relays inside the box clicked. Finally, in the upper left-hand corner of the control panel was this inscription, engraved in precise block letters:

SHOCK GENERATOR

Type ZLB

DYSON INSTRUMENT COMPANY

WALTHAM, MASS.

OUTPUT: 15 VOLTS—450 VOLTS

One day a man from the Lehigh Valley Electronics Company of Pennsylvania was passing through the laboratory, and he stopped to admire the shock generator.   38

"This is a very fine shock generator," he said. "But who is this Dyson Instrument Company?" Milgram felt proud at that, since Dyson Instrument Company existed only in the recesses of his imagination.   39

When you consider the seeming authenticity of the situation, you can appreciate the agony some of the subjects went through. It was pure conflict. As Milgram explains to his students. *"When a parent says, 'Don't strike old ladies,' you are learning two things: the content, and also, to obey authority. This experiment creates conflicts between the two elements."*   40

Subjects in the experiment were not asked to give the 450-volt shock more than three times. By that time it seemed evident that they would go on indefinitely. *"No one,"* says Milgram, *"who got within five shocks of the end ever broke off. By that point, he had resolved the conflict."*   41

Why do so many people resolve the conflict in favor of obedience?   42

Milgram's theory assumes that people behave in two different operating modes as different as ice and water. He does not rely on Freud or sex or toilet-training hangups for this theory. All he says is that ordinarily we operate in a state of autonomy, which means we pretty much have and assert control over what we do. But in certain circumstances, we operate under what Milgram calls a state of agency (after *agent, n . . .* one who acts for or in the place of another by authority from him; a substitute: a deputy,—Webster's Collegiate Dictionary). A state of agency, to Milgram, is nothing more than a frame of mind.   43

"There's nothing bad about it, there's nothing good about it," he says. *"It's a natural circumstance of living with other people. . . .I think of a state of agency as a real transformation of a person; if a person has different properties when he's in that state, just as water can turn to ice under certain conditions of temperature, a person can move to the state of mind that I call agency. . .the critical thing is that you see yourself as the instrument of the execution of another person's wishes. You do not see yourself as acting on your own. And there's a real transformation, a real change of properties of the person."*   44

To achieve this change, you have to be in a situation where there seems to be a ruling authority whose commands are relevant to some legitimate purpose; the authority's power is not unlimited.   45

But situations can be and have been structured to make people do unusual things, and not just in Milgram's laboratory. The reason, says Milgram, is that no action, in and of itself, contains meaning.   46

"The meaning always depends on your definition of the situation. Take an action 47 *like killing another person. It sounds bad.*

But then we say the other person was about to destroy a hundred children, and the 48 *only way to stop him was to kill him. Well, that sounds good.*

Or, you take destroying your own life. It sounds very bad. Yet, in the Second World 49 *War, thousands of persons thought it was a good thing to destroy your own life. It was set in the proper context. You sipped some saki from a whistling cup, recited a few haiku. You said, 'May my death be as clean and as quick as the shattering of crystal.' And it almost seemed like a good, noble thing to do, to crash your kamikaze plane into an aircraft carrier. But the main thing was, the definition of what a kamikaze pilot was doing had been determined by the relevant authority. Now, once you are in a state of agency, you allow the authority to determine, to define what the situation is. The meaning of your action is altered."*

So, for most subjects in Milgram's laboratory experiments, the act of giving 50 Mr. Wallace his painful shock was necessary, even though unpleasant, and besides they were doing it on behalf of somebody else and it was for science. There was still strain and conflict, of course. Most people resolved it by grimly sticking to their task and obeying. But some broke out. Milgram tried varying the conditions of the experiment to see what would help break people out of their state of agency.

"The results, as seen and felt in the laboratory," he has written, "are disturb- 51 ing. They raise the possibility that human nature, or more specifically the kind of character produced in American democratic society, cannot be counted on to insulate its citizens from brutality and inhumane treatment at the direction of malevolent authority. A substantial proportion of people do what they are told to do, irrespective of the content of the act and without limitations of conscience, so long as they perceive that the command comes from a legitimate authority. If, in this study, an anonymous experimenter can successfully command adults to subdue a fifty-year-old man and force on him painful electric shocks against his protest, one can only wonder what government, with its vastly greater authority and prestige, can command of its subjects."

This is a nice statement, but it falls short of summing up the full meaning of 52 Milgram's work. It leaves some questions still unanswered.

The first question is this: Should we really be surprised and alarmed that people 53 obey? Wouldn't it be even more alarming if they all refused to obey? Without obedience to a relevant ruling authority there could not be a civil society. And without a civil society, as Thomas Hobbes pointed out in the seventeenth century, we would live in a condition "of every man against every other man," life would be "solitary, poor, nasty, and short."

In the middle of one of Stanley Milgram's lectures at C.U.N.Y. recently, some 54 mini-skirted undergraduates started whispering and giggling in the back of the room. He told them to cut it out. Since he was the relevant authority in that time and that place they obeyed, and most people in the room were glad that they obeyed.

This was not, of course, a conflict situation. Nothing in the coeds' social upbringing made it a matter of conscience for them to whisper and giggle. But a case can be made that in a conflict situation it is all the more important to obey. Take the case of war, for example. 55

Would we really want a situation in which every participant in a war, direct or indirect—from front-line soldiers to the people who sell coffee and cigarettes to employees at the Concertina barbed-wire factory in Kansas—stops and consults his conscience before each action. It is asking for an awful lot of mental strain and anguish from an awful lot of people. The value of having civil order is that one can do his duty, or whatever interests him or whatever seems to benefit him at the moment, and leave the agonizing to others. When Francis Gary Powers was being tried by a Soviet military tribunal after his U-2 spy plane was shot down, the presiding judge asked if he had thought about the possibility that his flight might have provoked a war. Powers replied with Hobbesian clarity: "The people who sent me should think of these things. My job was to carry out orders. I do not think it was my responsibility to make such decisions." 56

It was not his responsibility. And it is quite possible that if everyone felt responsible for each of the ultimate consequences of his own tiny contributions to complex chains of events, then society simply would not work. Milgram, fully conscious of the moral and social implications of his research, believes that people should feel responsible for their actions. If someone else had invented the experiment, and if he had been the naïve subject, he feels certain that he would have been among the disobedient minority. 57

"There is no very good solution to this," he admits thoughtfully. *"To simply and categorically say that you won't obey authority may resolve your personal conflict, but it creates more problems for society which be more serious in the long run. But I have no doubt that to disobey is the proper thing to do in this [the laboratory] situation. It is the only reasonable value judgment to make."* 58

The conflict between the need to obey the relevant ruling authority and the need to follow your conscience becomes sharpest if you insist on living by an ethical system base on a rigid code—a code that seeks to answer all questions in advance of their being raised. Code ethics cannot solve the obedience problem. Stanley Milgram seems to be a situation ethicist, and situation ethics does offer a way out: When you feel conflict, you examine the situation and then make a choice among the competing evils. You may act with a presumption in favor of obedience, but reserve the possibility that you will disobey whenever obedience demands a flagrant and outrageous affront to conscience. This, by the way, is the philosophical position of many who resist the draft. In World War II, they would have fought. Vietnam is a different, an outrageously different, situation. 59

Life can be difficult for the situation ethicist, because he does not see the world in straight lines, while the social system too often assumes such a God-given, squared-off structure. If your moral code includes an injunction against all war, you may be deferred as a conscientious objector. If you merely oppose this particular war, you may not be deferred. Stanley Milgram has his problems, too. He believes that in the laboratory situation, he would not have shocked Mr. Wallace. 60

His professional critics reply that in his real-life situation he has done the equivalent. He has placed innocent and naïve subjects under great emotional strain and pressure in selfish obedience to his quest for knowledge. When you raise this issue with Milgram, he has an answer ready. There is, he explains patiently, a critical difference between his naïve subjects and the man in the electric chair. The man in the electric chair (in the mind of the naïve subject) is helpless, strapped in, but the naïve subject is free to go at any time.

Immediately after he offers this distinction, Milgram anticipates the objection. 61

"It's quite true," he says, *"that this is almost a philosophic position, because we have learned that some people are psychologically incapable of disengaging themselves. But that doesn't relieve them of the moral responsibility."* 62

The parallel is exquisite. *"The tension problem was unexpected,"* says Milgram in his defense. But he went on anyway. The naïve subjects didn't expect the screaming protests from the strapped-in learner. But they went on. 63

"I had to make a judgment," says Milgram. *"I had to ask myself, was this harming the person or not? My judgment is that it was not. Even in the extreme cases, I wouldn't say that permanent damage results."* 64

Sound familiar? "The shocks may be painful," the experimenter kept saying, "but they're not dangerous." 65

After the series of experiments was completed, Milgram sent a report of the results to his subjects and a questionnaire, asking whether they were glad or sorry to have been in the experiment. Eighty-three and seventeenths percent said they were glad and only 1.3 percent were sorry; 15 percent were neither sorry nor glad. However, Milgram could not be sure at the time of the experiment that only 1.3 percent would be sorry. 66

Kurt Vonnegut, Jr., put one paragraph in the preface to *Mother Night*, in 1966, which pretty much says it for the people with their fingers on the shock-generator switches, for you and me, and maybe even for Milgram. "If I'd been born in Germany," Vonnegut said, "I suppose I would have *been* a Nazi, bopping Jews and gypsies and Poles around, leaving boots sticking out of snowbanks, warming myself with my sweetly virtuous insides. So it goes." 67

Just so. One thing that happened to Milgram back in New Haven during the days of the experiment was that he kept running into people he'd watched from behind the one-way glass. It gave him a funny feeling, seeing those people going about their everyday business in New Haven and knowing what they would do to Mr. Wallace if ordered to. Now that his research results are in and you've thought about it, you can get this funny feeling too. You don't need a one-way glass. A glance in your own mirror may serve just as well. 68

Media Ecology

Ingmar Bergman (1918–) is a filmmaker and stage director known for his sophistication, symbolism, and dark vision. He was born July 14, 1918, in Uppsala, Sweden, the son of a Lutheran minister. He attended the University of Stockholm, where he became involved in theater, and was appointed to the Swedish Royal Opera in 1942. In 1945 he directed his first film, *Crisis*, about a miserable love affair resulting in suicide. In 1956 he directed the acclaimed symbolic film *The Seventh Seal*, a medieval morality play about a knight who challenges Death to a chess game. He shifted gears to make *Wild Strawberries* in 1957, a film that maintains a warm tone as it contrasts youth with age. He returned to symbolism in *The Magician* (1959), and returned to a medieval setting in *The Virgin Spring* (1960). In 1961 he began a trilogy of films about the philosophical problem of isolation in a godless world with *Through the Glass Darkly*, about domestic violence. He continued the trilogy with *Winter Light* in 1962, which focuses on loss of faith, and ended with *The Silence* in 1963, a surrealistic film which takes up the theme of the fear of silence. He made more films in the 1960s, but tax problems forced him to spend much of the 1970s producing television work in Norway and Germany. Some of his noted later films include *Cries and Whispers* (1971); *Scenes from a Marriage* (1973, made for television); and *The Magic Flute* (1973, made for television). His most accessible film, which some have called his best, was *Fanny and Alexander* (1982) and was announced as his final film. In the late 1980s Bergman turned to writing, producing an autobiography in 1988 entitled *The Magic Lantern* and a novel in 1989, *Best Intentions*. Bergman continues to write and direct for Swedish television and theater.

What Is 'Film-Making'?

Ingmar Bergman

"Film-making" is for me a necessity of nature, a need comparable to hunger and thirst. For some, self-expression involves writing books, climbing mountains, beating one's children or dancing the samba. In my case, I express myself in making films.　1

In *The Blood of a Poet*, the great Jean Cocteau shows us his alter ego stumbling down the corridors of a nightmare hotel and gives us a glimpse, behind each one of the doors, of one of the factors of which he is composed and which form his ego.　2

Without attempting here to equate my personality with Cocteau's, I thought I would take you on a guided tour of my internal studios where, invisibly, my films take form. This visit, I am afraid, will disappoint you; the equipment is always in disorder because the owner is too absorbed in his affairs to have time to straighten it up. Furthermore, the lighting is rather bad in certain spots, and on the door of certain rooms, you will find the word "Private" written in large letters. Finally, the guide himself is not always sure of what is worth the trouble of showing.　3

Whatever the case may be, we will open a few doors a crack. I won't guarantee that you will find precisely the answer to the questions you are wondering about, but perhaps, in spite of everything, you will be able to put together a few pieces of the complicated puzzle that the forming of a film represents.　4

If we consider the most fundamental element of the cinematographic art, the perforated film, we note that it is composed of a number of small, rectangular images—fifty-two per meter—each of which is separated from the other by a thick, black line. Looking more closely, we discover that these tiny rectangles, which at first glance seem to contain exactly the same picture, differ from each other by an almost imperceptible modification of this picture. And when the feeding mechanism of the projector causes the images in question to succeed each other on the screen so that each one is seen only for a twentieth of a second, we have the illusion of movement.

Between each of these small rectangles the shutter closes and plunges us into total darkness, only to return us to full light with the next rectangle. When I was ten years old and working with my first apparatus, a shaky lantern made of sheet metal—with its chimney, its gas lamp and its perpetual films which repeated themselves indefinitely—I used to find the above-mentioned phenomenon exciting and full of mystery. Even today, I feel myself quiver as I did when I was a child when I think of the fact that, in reality, I am creating illusion; for the cinema would not exist but for an imperfection of the human eye, namely its inability to perceive separately a series of images which follow each other rapidly and which are essentially identical.

I have calculated that if I see a film that lasts an hour, I am in fact plunged for twenty minutes in total darkness. In making a film, therefore, I am making myself guilty of a fraud; I am using a device designed to take advantage of a physical imperfection of man, a device by means of which I can transport my audience from a given feeling to the feeling that is diametrically opposed to it, as if each spectator were on a pendulum; I can make an audience laugh, scream with terror, smile, believe in legends, become indignant, take offense, become enthusiastic, lower itself or yawn from boredom. I am, then, either a deceiver or—when the audience is aware of the fraud—an illusionist. I am able to mystify, and I have at my disposal the most precious and the most astounding magical device that has ever, since history began, been put into the hands of a juggler.

There is in all this, or at least there should be, the source of an insoluble moral conflict for all those who create films or work on them.

As for our commercial partners, this is not the place to bring out the mistakes they have made from year to year, but it would certainly be worthwhile someday for a scientist to discover some unit of weight or measure which one could use to "calculate" the quantity of natural gifts, initiatives, genius and creative forces that the film industry has ground through its formidable mills. Obviously, anyone entering into the game must accept the rules in advance, and there is no reason why work in the cinematographic branch should be more respected than anywhere else. The difference is due to the fact that, in our specialty, brutality is manifested more overtly, but this is actually rather an advantage.

Loss of balance offers consequences that are even more grave for the film-maker than for a tightrope walker or an acrobat who performs his tricks beneath a circus tent and without a net. For the film-maker as well as for the equilibrist, the danger is of the same order: falling and being killed. No doubt you think I am exaggerating; making a film isn't as dangerous as all that! I maintain my point, however; the risk is the same. Even if, as I mentioned, one is a bit of a magician, no one can mystify the producers, the bank directors, the movie-theatre owners or the critics when the public abstains from going to see a film and from paying out the obol from which producers, bank directors, movie-theatre owners, critics and magicians must draw their subsistence!

I can give you as an example a very recent experience, the memory of which 11 still makes me shudder—an experience in which I myself risked losing my balance. A singularly bold producer invested money in one of my films which, after a year of intense activity, appeared under the title of *The Naked Night* (*Gycklarnas afton*). The reviews were, in general, destructive, the public stayed away, the producer added up his losses, and I had to wait several years before trying again.

If I make two or three more films which fail financially, the producer will quite 12 justifiably consider it a good idea not to bet on my talents.

At that point, I will become, suddenly, a suspect individual, a squanderer, and I 13 will be able to reflect at my leisure on the usefulness of my artistic gifts, for the magician will be deprived of his apparatus.

When I was younger, I didn't have these fears. Work for me was an exciting 14 game and, whether the results succeeded or failed, I was delighted with my work like a child with his castles of sand or clay. The equilibrist was dancing on his rope, oblivious and therefore unconcerned about the abyss beneath him and the hardness of the ground of the circus-ring.

The game has changed into a bitter combat. The walk on the rope is now 15 performed in full awareness of the danger, and the two points where the rope is attached are now called "fear" and "incertitude." Each work to be materialized mobilizes all of the resources of one's energy. The act of creation has become, under the effect of causes that are as much interior as they are exterior and economic, an exacting duty. Failure, criticism, coldness on the part of the public today cause more sensitive wounds. These wounds take longer to heal and their scars are deeper and more lasting.

Before undertaking a work or after having begun it, Jean Anouilh has the habit 16 of playing a little mental game in order to exorcise his fear. He says to himself, "My father is a tailor. He intimately enjoys creating with his hands, and the result is a beautiful pair of pants or an elegant overcoat. This is the joy and the satisfaction of the artisan, the pride of a man who knows his profession."

This is the same practice I follow. I recognize the game, I play it often and I 17 succeed in duping myself—and a few others—even if this game is in fact nothing but a rather poor sedative: "My films are fine pieces of work, I am enthusiastic, conscientious and extremely attentive of details. I create for my contemporaries and not for eternity; my pride is the pride of an artisan."

I know however that, if I speak this way, it is in order to deceive myself, and an 18 irrepressible anxiety cries out to me, "What have you done that can last? Is there in any of your movies a single foot of film worthy of being passed on to posterity, a single line of dialogue, a single situation which is really and indisputably true? "

And to this question I am forced to answer—perhaps still under the effect of a 19 disloyalty which is ineradicable even in the most sincere people—"I don't know, I hope so."

You must excuse me for having described at such length and with so much 20 commentary the dilemma which those who create films are forced to confront. I wanted to try to explain to you why so many of those who are devoted to the realization of cinematographic works give in to a temptation which cannot really be expressed and which is invisible; why we are afraid; why we sometimes lose our enthusiasm for the works we are doing; why we become fools and allow ourselves to be annihilated by colorless and vile compromises.

I would still, however, like to dwell a bit longer on one of the aspects of the prob- 21 lem, the aspect that is the most important and difficult to comprehend—the public.

The creator of films is involved in a means of expression which concerns not 22 only himself but also millions of other people, and more often than not he feels the same desire as other artists: "I want to succeed today. I want celebrity now. I want to please, to delight, to move people immediately."

Midway between this desire and its realization is found the public, who 23 demands but one thing of the film: "I've paid, I want to be distracted, swept off my feet, involved; I want to forget my troubles, my family, my work, I want to get away from myself. Here I am, seated in the darkness, and, like a woman about to give birth, I want deliverance."

The film-maker who is aware of these demands and who lives on the money of 24 the public is placed in a situation which is difficult and which creates obligations for him. In making his film, he must always take the reaction of the public into account. On my part, personally, I am forever asking myself this question: "Can I express myself more simply, more purely, more briefly? Will everybody understand what I want to say now? Will the simplest mind be able to follow the course of these events? And, even more importantly, this question: up to what point do I have the right to admit compromise and where do my obligations to myself begin? "

Any experimentation necessarily involves a great risk, for it always keeps the 25 public at a distance, and keeping the public at a distance can lead to sterility and to isolation in an ivory tower.

It would be quite desirable, then, for producers and other technical directors of 26 the cinema to put laboratories at the disposition of the creators. But this is scarcely the case today. The producers have confidence only in the engineers and stupidly imagine that the salvation of the film industry depends on inventions and technical complications.

Nothing is easier than frightening a spectator. One can literally terrify him, for 27 most people have in some part of their bearing a fear that is all ready to blossom. It is much more difficult to make people laugh, and to make them *laugh* in the right way. It is easy to put a spectator in a state worse than the one he was in when he entered the theater; it is difficult to put him in a better state; it is precisely this, however,

The iDeal Reader

Ingmar Bergman, "What Is
'Film–Making'?"

© The McGraw–Hill
Companies, 2000

153

that he desires each time he sits down in the darkness of a movie-theater. Now, how many times and by what means do we give him this satisfaction?

This is the way I reason; but at the same time I know with an absolute evidence 28 that this reasoning is dangerous, since it involves the risk of condemning all failures, of confusing the ideal with pride, and of considering as absolute the frontiers that the public and the critics establish, whereas you neither recognize these frontiers nor consider them your own, since your personality is perpetually in the process of becoming. On the one hand, I am tempted to adapt myself and to make myself what the public wants me to be; but on the other hand, I feel that this would be the end of everything, and that this would imply a total indifference on my part. Thus, I am delighted to have not been born with exactly as many brains as feelings, and it has never been written anywhere that a film-maker must be contented, happy, or satisfied. Who says you can't make noise, cross frontiers, battle against windmills, send robots to the moon, have visions, play with dynamite or tear pieces of flesh from one's self or others? Why not frighten film producers? It is their job to be afraid, and they are paid to have stomach ulcers!

But "*film-making*" is not always confronting problems, dilemmas, economic 29 worries, responsibilities and fear. There are also games, dreams, secret memories.

Often it begins with an image: a face which is suddenly and strongly illumi- 30 nated; a hand which rises; a square at dawn where a few old ladies are seated on a bench, separated from each other by sacks of apples. Or it may be a few words that are exchanged; two people who, suddenly, say something to each other in a completely personal tone of voice—their backs are perhaps turned from me, I can't even see their faces, and yet I am forced to listen to them, to wait for them to repeat the same words which are without any particular meaning but which are pregnant with a secret tension, with a tension of which I am not yet even fully conscious but which acts like a crafty potion. The illuminated face, the hand raised as if for an incantation, the old ladies at the square, the few banal words, all of these images come and attach themselves like silvery fish to my net, or more precisely, I myself am trapped in a net, the texture of which I am not aware of—fortunately!

Quite rapidly, even before the motive has been entirely designed in my mind, I 31 submit the game of my imagination to the test of reality. I place, as if I'm playing a game, my sketch, which is still very rough and fragile, on an easel in order to judge it from the point of view of all the technical resources of the studios. This imaginary test of "viability" constitutes for the motive an effective ferruginous bath. Will it suffice? Will the motive keep its value when it is plunged into the daily, murderous routine of the studios, far from the shadows of sunrises, which are quite propitious for the games of the imagination?

A few of my films mature very quickly and are finished rapidly. These are the 32 ones that meet the general expectations, like children that are still undisciplined but in good health and about whom one can predict immediately: "They are the ones who will support the family."

And then there are other films, films which come slowly, which take years, 33 which refuse to be imprisoned in a formal or technical solution, and which, in general, refuse any concrete solution. They remain in a shadowy zone; if I want to find them, I have to follow them there and find a context, characters and situation. There, faces that are turned aside begin to speak, the streets are strange, a few, scattered people glance out through window-panes, an eye glistens at dusk or changes into a carbuncle and then bursts with a noise of breaking crystal. The square, this autumn morning, is a sea; the old ladies are transformed into ancient trees and the apples are children building cities of sand and stone near the foam of the waves.

The tension is there, ever present, and it appears again, either in the written 34 word, or in the visions, or in the excess of energy, which bends like the arch of a bridge, ready to rise up by its own forces, by these forces which are the most important element, once the manuscript is finished, in setting in motion the immense wheel which the work required in shooting a film represents.

What is "shooting a film," then? If I were to ask this question of everybody, I 35 would no doubt obtain quite different responses, but perhaps you would all agree on one point: shooting a film is doing what is necessary in order to transport the contents of the manuscript onto a piece of film. In doing so, you would be saying quite a lot and yet not nearly enough. For me, shooting a film represents days of inhumanly relentless work, stiffness of the joints, eyes full of dust, the odors of make-up, sweat and lamps, an indefinite series of tensions and relaxations, an uninterrupted battle between volition and duty, between vision and reality, conscience and laziness. I think of early risings, of nights without sleep, of a feeling keener than life, of a sort of fanaticism centered about a single task, by which I myself become, finally, an integral part of the film, a ridiculously tiny piece of apparatus whose only fault is requiring food and drink.

It sometimes happens—in the middle of all this excitement, when the studios 36 are humming with a life and a labor that seem as if they should make the studios explode—that, suddenly, I find the idea for my next film. You would be wrong, however, if you thought that the activity of a film-maker supposes, at this moment, a kind of ecstatic vertigo, an uncontrolled excitement and a frightening disorganization. To shoot a film is to undertake the taming of a wild beast that is difficult to handle and very valuable; you need a clear mind, meticulousness, stiff and exact calculations. Add to this a temper that is always even and a patience that is not of this world.

Shooting a film is organizing an entire universe, but the essential elements are 37 industry, money, construction, shooting, developing and copying, a schedule to follow but which is rarely followed, a battle plan minutely prepared where the irrational factors occur the most often. The star has too much black around her eyes—a thousand dollars to start the scene over again. One day, the water in the pipes has too much chlorine in it and the negatives got spotted—let's start again! Another day, death plays a dirty trick on you by taking away an actor—let's start with another—and there are several thousand more dollars swallowed up. It starts to thunder, the electric transformer breaks down, and there we are, all made up and waiting in the pale light of the day, the hours flying by and money with them.

Idiotic examples, chosen at random. But they have to be idiotic, since they 38 touch that great and sublime idiocy, the transforming of dreams into shadows, the chopping up of a tragedy into five hundred small pieces, the experimentation with each of these pieces, and finally the putting back together of these pieces so that they constitute again a unity which will once more be the tragedy. It is the idiocy of fabricating a tapeworm 8,000 feet long which will nourish itself on the life and mind of the actors, producers, and creators. Shooting a film is all that, but it is still something else, and it is much worse.

Film-making is also plunging with one's deepest roots back into the world of 39 childhood. Let's descend, if you wish, into this interior studio, located in the most intimate recesses of the life of the creator. Let's open up for a moment the most secret of these rooms so that we can look at a painting of Venice, an old window-blind, and a first apparatus for showing "action films."

At Upsala, my grandmother had a very old apartment. While I was there, I 40 once slipped beneath the dining-room table; I was wearing an apron with a pocket in front of it; from my vantage point I listened to the voice of the sunbeams which entered through the immensely high windows. The rays moved continually; the bells of the cathedral chimed out, the rays moved, and their movement generated a sort of special sound. It was one of those days between winter and spring; I had the measles and I was five years old. In the neighboring apartment, somebody was playing the piano—it was always waltzes—and on the wall hung a big painting of Venice. While the rays of sun and the shadows were passing like waves across the painting, the water of the canal began to flow, the pigeons flew up from the pavement of the square, people spoke to each other noiselessly, making movements with their hands and heads. The sound of the bells wasn't coming from the cathedral but rather from the painting, as were the strains from the piano. There was something very strange about this painting of Venice. Almost as strange as the fact that the sunbeams in my grandmother's living-room were not silent but had a sound. Perhaps it was all those bells—or perhaps the enormous pieces of furniture which were conversing uninterruptedly.

I seem to remember, however, an experience even more distant than the one of 41 the year I had measles: the perception—impossible to date—of the movement of a window-blind.

It was a black window-blind of the most modern variety, which I could see, in my 42 nursery, at dawn or at dusk, when everything becomes living and a bit frightening, when even toys transform into things that are either hostile or simply indifferent and curious. At that moment the world would no longer be the everyday world with my mother present, but a vertiginous and silent solitude. It wasn't that the blind moved; no shadow at all appeared on it. The forms were on the surface itself; they were neither little men, nor animals, nor heads, nor faces, but *things for which no name exists!* In the darkness, which was interrupted here and there by faint rays of light, these forms freed themselves from the blind and moved toward the green folding-screen or toward the bureau, with its pitcher of water. They were pitiless, impassive and terrifying; they disappeared only after it became completely dark or light, or when I fell asleep.

Anyone who, like myself, was born in the family of a pastor, learns at an early 43
age to look behind the scenes in life and death. Whenever Father has a burial, a
marriage, a baptism, a mediation, he writes a sermon. You make an early acquaintance with the devil and, like all children, you need to give him a concrete form.
Here is where the magic lantern comes in, a little sheetmetal box with a gas lamp (I
can still smell the odor of the heated metal) and which projected colored pictures.
Among others, there was Little Red Ridinghood and the wolf. The wolf was the
devil, a devil without horns but with a tail and vivid red mouth, a curiously palpable
and yet elusive devil, the emissary of evil and persecution on the flowered wallpaper
of the nursery.

The first film I ever owned was about ten feet long and brown. It pictured a 44
young girl asleep in a prairie; she woke up, stretched, arose and, with outstretched
arms, disappeared at the right side of the picture. That was all. Drawn on the box
the film was kept in was a glowing picture with the words, "Frau Holle." Nobody
around me knew who Frau Holle was, but that didn't matter; the film was quite
successful, and we showed it every evening until it got torn so badly we couldn't
repair it.

This shaky bit of cinema was my first sorcerer's bag, and, in fact, it was pretty 45
strange. It was a mechanical plaything; the people and things never changed, and I
have often wondered what could have fascinated me so much and what, even today,
still fascinates me in exactly the same way. This thought comes to me sometimes in
the studio, or in the semidarkness of the editing room, while I am holding the tiny
picture before my eyes and while the film is passing through my hands; or else during
that fantastic childbirth that takes place during the recomposition as the finished
film slowly finds its own face. I can't help thinking that I am working with an instrument so refined that with it, it would be possible for us to illuminate the human soul
with an infinitely more vivid light, to unmask it even more brutally and to annex to
our field of knowledge new domains of reality. Perhaps we would even discover a
crack that would allow us to penetrate into the *chiaroscuro* of surreality, to tell tales
in a new and overwhelming manner. At the risk of affirming once more something I
cannot prove, let me say that, the way I see it, we film-makers utilize only a minute
part of a frightening power—we are moving only the little finger of a giant, a giant
who is far from not being dangerous.

But it is equally possible that I am wrong. It might be that the cinema has 46
attained the high point of its evolution, that this instrument, by its very nature, can no
longer conquer new teritory, that we are stuck with our noses to the wall, since the
road ends in a dead end. Many people are of this opinion, and it is true that we are
treading water in a marsh, our noses just rising above the surface of the water, and
paralyzed by economic problems, conventions, stupidity, fear, incertitude and disorder.

I am asked sometimes what I am trying to attain in my films, what my goal is. 47
The question is difficult and dangerous, and I usually answer it by lying or hedging:
"I am trying to tell the truth about the condition of men, the truth as I see it." This
answer always satisfies people, and I often wonder how it happens that nobody
notices my bluff, because the true response should be, "I feel an incoercible need to

express through film that which, in a completely subjective way, takes form some place in my consciousness. This being the case, I have no other goal but myself, my daily bread, the amusement and respect of the public, a kind of truth that I feel precisely at that moment. And if I try to sum up my second answer, the formula I end up with is not terribly exciting: 'An activity without much meaning.'"

I am not saying that this conclusion doesn't distress me inordinately. I am in 48 the same situation as most artists of my generation; the activity of each one of us doesn't have much meaning. Art for art's sake. My personal truth, or three-quarters of a truth, or no truth at all, except that it has a value for me.

I realize that this way of looking at things is quite unpopular, particularly today. 49 Let me hasten, then, to form the question in a different way: "What would be your goal in making your films?"

The story is told that, a long time ago, the cathedral of Chartres was struck by 50 lightning and burned from top to bottom. It is said that thousands of people rushed there from the four corners of the world, people of all conditions; they crossed Europe like lemmings in migration; together, they began to rebuild the cathedral upon its old foundations. They stayed there until the immense edifice was completed, all of them, architects, workers, artists, jugglers, nobles, priests and the bourgeoisie, but their names were unknown, and, even today, nobody knows the names of those who built the cathedral of Chartres.

Without letting that give you any preconceived ideas about my beliefs or 51 doubts—which, furthermore, have nothing to do with what we are discussing here—I think that any art loses its essential potency the moment it becomes separated from the "cult." It has cut the umbilical cord and it lives its own separate life, a life that is astonishingly sterile, dim, and degenerate. Creative collectivity, humble anonymity are forgotten and burried relics, deprived of any value. Little wounds of the ego and moral colics are examined under a microscope *sub specie aeternitatis*. The fear of the dark which characterizes subjectivism and scrupulous consciences has become quite stylish, and ultimately we are all running around in a big enclosure where we argue with one another about our solitude without listening to each other or even noticing that we are pushing ourselves mutually to the point of dying of suffocation from all this. It is in such a way that individualists look each other in the eye, deny the existence of those they see and invoke omnipotent obscurity without ever having once felt the saving force of the joys of community. We are so poisoned by our own vicious circles, so closed in by our own anguish that we are becoming incapable of distinguishing true from false, the ideality of gangsters and sincere unaffectedness.

To the question concerning the goal of my films, I could therefore answer: "I 52 want to be one of the artists of the cathedral that stands above the plains. I want to occupy myself making from stone a dragon's head, an angel or a devil, or perhaps a saint, it doesn't really matter; I feel the same enjoyment in each case. Whether I am a believer or an unbeliever, a Christian or a pagan, I am working along with everybody else to construct a cathedral, because I am an artist and an artisan, and because I have learned to extract faces, limbs, and bodies from stone. I never have to worry about the judgment of posterity or of my contemporaries; my first and last names are engraved nowhere, and they will disappear with me. But a small part of my self will survive in the anonymous and triumphant totality. A dragon or a devil, or perhaps a saint, what does it matter!"

Marie Winn (1936–   ) was born in Prague, Czechoslovakia, and emigrated to the United States three years later. She attended both Radcliffe College and Columbia University in the 1950s. Winn has been a freelance writer since the 1960s, writing mostly children's books and nonfiction, as well as translating a number of works from her native tongue. She often writes about the intersection of mass media and family. Her books include *The Plug-In Drug: Television, Culture, and the Family* (1977), *Children Without Childhood* (1983), and the revised and updated *The Plug-In Drug: Television, Computers, and Family Life* (2002).

Television: The Plug-In Drug

Marie Winn

Not much more than fifty years after the introduction of television into American society, the medium has become so deeply ingrained in daily life that in many states the TV set has attained the rank of a legal necessity, safe from repossession in case of debt along with clothes and cooking utensils. Only in the early years after television's introduction did writers and commentators have sufficient perspective to separate the activity of watching television from the actual content it offers the viewer. In those days writers frequently discussed the effects of television on family life. However, a curious myopia afflicted those first observers: almost without exception they regarded television as a favorable, beneficial, indeed, wondrous influence upon the family.

"Television is going to be a real asset in every home where there are children," predicted a writer in 1949.

"Television will take over your way of living and change your children's habits, but this change can be a wonderful improvement," claimed another commentator.

"No survey's needed, of course, to establish that television has brought the family together in one room," wrote the *New York Times's* television critic in 1949.

The early articles about television were almost invariably accompanied by a photograph or illustration showing a family cozily sitting together before the television set, Sis on Mom's lap, Buddy perched on the arm of Dad's chair, Dad with his arm around Mom's shoulder. Who could have guessed that twenty or so years later Mom would be watching a drama in the kitchen, the kids would be looking at cartoons in their room, while Dad would be taking in the ball game in the living room?

Of course television sets were enormously expensive when they first came on the market. The idea that by the year 2000 more than three quarters of American families would own two or more sets would have seemed preposterous. The splintering of the multiple-set family was something the early writers did not foresee. Nor did anyone imagine the numbers of hours children would eventually devote to television, the changes television would effect upon child-rearing methods, the increas-

1

2

3

4

5

6

ing domination of family schedules by children's viewing requirements—in short, the power of television to dominate family life.

As children's consumption of the new medium increased together with parental concern about the possible effects of so much television viewing, a steady refrain helped soothe and reassure anxious parents. "Television always enters a pattern of influences that already exist: the home, the peer group, the school, the church and culture generally," write the authors of an early and influential study of television's effects on children. In other words, if the child's home life is all right, parents need not worry about the effects of too much television watching. 7

But television does not merely influence the child; it deeply influenced that "pattern of influences" everyone hoped would ameliorate the new medium's effects. Home and family life have changed in important ways since the advent of television. The peer group has become television-oriented, and much of the time children spend together is occupied by television viewing. Culture generally has been transformed by television. Participation in church and community activities has diminished, with television a primary cause of this change. Therefore it is improper to assign to television the subsidiary role its many apologists insist it plays. Television is not merely one of a number of important influences upon today's child. Through the changes it has made in family life, television emerges as *the* important influence in children's lives today. 8

THE QUALITY OF LIFE

Television's contribution to family life has been an equivocal one. For while it has, indeed, kept the members of the family from dispersing, it has not served to bring them together. By its domination of the time families spend together, it destroys the special quality that distinguishes one family from another, a quality that depends to a great extent on what a family does, what special rituals, games, recurrent jokes, familiar songs, and shared activities it accumulates. 9

Yet parents have accepted a television-dominated family life so completely that they cannot see how the medium is involved in whatever problems they might be having. A first-grade teacher reports: 10

> I have one child in the group who's an only child. I wanted to find out more about her family life because this little girl was quite isolated from the group, didn't make friends, so I talked to her mother. Well, they don't have time to do anything in the evening, the mother said. The parents come home after picking up the child at the baby-sitter's. Then the mother fixes dinner while the child watches TV. Then they have dinner and the child goes to bed. I said to this mother, 'Well, couldn't she help you fix dinner? That would be a nice time for the two of you to talk,' and the mother said, 'Oh, but I'd hate to have her miss *Zoom*. It's such a good program!'

Several decades ago a writer and mother of two boys aged 3 and 7 described her family's television schedule in a newspaper article. Though some of the programs her kids watched then have changed, the situation she describes remains the same for a great number of families today: 11

We were in the midst of a full-scale War. Every day was a new battle and every program was a major skirmish. We agreed it was a bad scene all around and were ready to enter diplomatic negotiations [. . .]. In principle we have agreed on $2\frac{1}{2}$ hours of TV a day, *Sesame Street, Electric Company* (with dinner gobbled up in between) and two half-hour shows between 7 and 8:30 which enables the grown-ups to eat in peace and prevents the two boys from destroying one another. Their pre-bedtime choice is dreadful, because, as Josh recently admitted, "There's nothing much on I really like." So [. . .] its *What's My Line* or *To Tell the Truth* [. . .]. Clearly there is a need for first-rate children's shows at this time [. . .].

Consider the "family life" described here: Presumably the father comes home 12 from work during the *Sesame Street–Electric Company* stint. The children are either watching television, gobbling their dinner, or both. While the parents eat their dinner in peaceful privacy, the children watch another hour of television. Then there is only a half-hour left before bedtime, just enough time for baths, getting pajamas on, brushing teeth, and so on. The children's evening is regimented with an almost military precision. They watch their favorite programs, and when there is "nothing much on I really like," they watch whatever else is on—because *watching* is the important thing. Their mother does not see anything amiss with watching programs just for the sake of watching; she only wishes there were some first-rate children's shows on at those times.

Without conjuring up fantasies of bygone eras with family games and long, 13 leisurely meals, the question arises: isn't there a better family life available than this dismal, mechanized arrangement of children watching television for however long is allowed them, evening after evening?

Of course, families today still do things together at times: go camping in the sum- 14 mer, go to the zoo on a nice Saturday, take various trips and expeditions. But their ordinary daily life together is diminished—those hours of sitting around at the dinner table, the spontaneous taking up of an activity, the little games invented by children on the spur of the moment when there is nothing else to do, the scribbling, the chatting, and even the quarreling, all the things that form the fabric of a family, that define a childhood. Instead, the children have their regular schedule of television programs and bedtime, and the parents have their peaceful dinner together.

The author of the quoted newspaper article notes that "keeping a family sane 15 means mediating between the needs of both children and adults." But surely the needs of the adults in that family are being better met than the needs of the children. The kids were effectively shunted away and rendered untroublesome, while their parents enjoyed a life as undemanding as that of any childless couple. In reality, it is those very demands that young children make upon a family that lead to growth, and it is the way parents respond to those demands that builds the relationships upon which the future of the family depends. If the family does not accumulate its backlog of shared experiences, shared everyday experiences that occur and recur and change and develop, then it is not likely to survive as anything other than a caretaking institution.

© The McGraw–Hill
Companies, 2002

FAMILY RITUALS

Ritual is defined by sociologists as "that part of family life that the family likes about   16
itself, is proud of and wants formally to continue." Another text notes that "the development of a ritual by a family is an index of the common interest of its members in
the family as a group."

What has happened to family rituals, those regular, dependable, recurrent hap-   17
penings that give members of a family a feeling of belonging to a home rather than
living in it merely for the sake of convenience, those experiences that act as the adhe-
sive of family unity far more than any material advantages?

Mealtime rituals, going-to-bed rituals, illness rituals, holiday rituals—how many   18
of these have survived the inroads of the television set?

A young woman who grew up near Chicago reminisces about her childhood and   19
gives an idea of the effects of television upon family rituals:

As a child I had millions of relatives around—my parents both come from relatively
large families. My father had nine brothers and sisters. And so every holiday there was
this great swoop-down of aunts, uncles, and millions of cousins. I just remember how
wonderful it used to be. These thousands of cousins would come and everyone would
play and ultimately, after dinner, all the women would be in the front of the house,
drinking coffee and talking, all the men would be in the back of the house, drinking
and smoking, and all the kids would be all over the place, playing hide and seek.
Christmas time was particularly nice because everyone always brought all their toys
and games. Our house had a couple of rooms with go-through closets, so there were
always kids running in a great circle route. I remember it was just wonderful.

And then all of a sudden one year I remember becoming suddenly aware of how   20
different everything had become. The kids were no longer playing Monopoly or Clue
or the other games we used to play together. It was because we had a television set
which had been turned on for a football game. All of that socializing that had gone on
previously had ended. Now everyone was sitting in front of the television set, on a holiday, at a family party! I remember being stunned by how awful that was. Somehow
the television had become more attractive.

As families have come to spend more and more of their time together engaged   21
in the single activity of television watching, those rituals and pastimes that once gave
family life its special quality have become more and more uncommon. Not since pre-
historic times, when cave families hunted, gathered, ate, and slept, with little time
remaining to accumulate a culture of any significance, have families been reduced to
such a sameness.

REAL PEOPLE

The relationships of family members to each other are affected by television's pow-   22
erful competition in both obvious and subtle ways. For surely the hours that children
spend in a one-way relationship with television people, an involvement that allows
for no communication or interaction, must have some effect on their relationships
with real-life people.

Studies show the importance of eye-to-eye contact, for instance, in real-life rela-   23
tionships, and indicate that the nature of one's eye-contact patterns, whether one

looks another squarely in the eye or looks to the side or shifts one's gaze from side to side, may play a significant role in one's success or failure in human relationships. But no eye contact is possible in the child-television relationship, although in certain children's programs people purport to speak directly to the child and the camera fosters this illusion by focusing directly upon the person being filmed. How might such a distortion affect a child's development of trust, of openness, of an ability to relate well to *real* people?

Bruno Bettelheim suggested an answer: 24

Children who have been taught, or conditioned, to listen passively most of the day to the warm verbal communications coming from the TV screen, to the deep emotional appeal of the so-called TV personality, are often unable to respond to real persons because they arouse so much less feeling than the skilled actor. Worse, they lose the ability to learn from reality because life experiences are much more complicated than the ones they see on the screen. . . .

A teacher makes a similar observation about her personal viewing experiences: 25

I have trouble mobilizing myself and dealing with real people after watching a few hours of television. It's just hard to make that transition from watching television to a real relationship. I suppose it's because there was no effort necessary while I was watching, and dealing with real people always requires a bit of effort. Imagine, then, how much harder it might be to do the same thing for a small child, particularly one who watches a lot of television every day.

But more obviously damaging to family relationships is the elimination of opportunities to talk and converse, or to argue, to air grievances between parents and children and brothers and sisters. Families frequently use television to avoid confronting their problems, problems that will not go away if they are ignored but will only fester and become less easily resolvable as time goes on. 26

A mother reports: 27

I find myself, with three children, wanting to turn on the TV set when they're fighting. I really have to struggle not to do it because I feel that's telling them this is the solution to the quarrel—but it's so tempting that I often do it.

A family therapist discusses the use of television as an avoidance mechanism: 28

In a family I know the father comes home from work and turns on the television set. The children come and watch him and the wife serves them their meal in front of the set. He then goes and takes a shower, or works on the car or something. She then goes and has her own dinner in front of the television set. It's a symptom of a deeper-rooted problem, sure. But it would help them all to get rid of the set. It would be far easier to work on what the symptom really means without the television. The television simply encourages a double avoidance of each other. They'd find out more quickly what was going on if they weren't able to hide behind the TV. Things wouldn't necessarily be better, of course, but they wouldn't be anesthetized.

A number of research studies done when television was a relatively new medium demonstrated that television interfered with family activities and the formation of 29 family relationships. One survey showed that 78 percent of the respondents indicated no conversation taking place during viewing except at specified times such as commercials. The study noted: "The television atmosphere in most households is one of quiet absorption on the part of family members who are present. The nature of the family social life during a program could be described as 'parallel' rather than interactive, and the set does seem to dominate family life when it is on." Thirty-six percent of the respondents in another study indicated that television viewing was the only family activity participated in during the week.

The situation has only worsened during the intervening decades. When the studies were made, the great majority of American families had only one television set. Though the family may have spent more time watching TV in those early days, at least they were all together while they watched. Today the vast majority of all families have two or more sets, and nearly a third of all children live in homes with four or more TVs. The most telling statistic: almost 60 percent of all families watch television during meals, and not necessarily at the same TV set. When do they talk about what they did that day? When do they make plans, exchange views, share jokes, tell about their triumphs or little disasters? When do they get to be a real family? 30

UNDERMINING THE FAMILY

Of course television has not been the only factor in the decline of family life in America. The steadily rising divorce rate, the increase in the number of working mothers, the trends towards people moving far away from home, the breakdown of neighborhoods and communities—all these have seriously affected the family. 31

Obviously, the sources of family breakdown do not come from the family itself, but from the circumstances in which the family finds itself and the way of life imposed upon it by those circumstances. As Urie Bronfenbrenner has suggested: 32

> When those circumstances and the way of life they generate undermine relationships of trust and emotional security between family members, when they make it difficult for parents to care for, educate and enjoy their children, when there is no support or recognition from the outside world for one's role as a parent and when time spent with one's family means frustration of career, personal fulfillment and peace of mind, then the development of the child is adversely affected.

Certainly television is not the single destroyer of American family life. But the medium's dominant role in the family serves to anesthetize parents into accepting their family's dimishished state and prevents them from struggling to regain some of the richness the family once possessed. 33

One research study alone seems to contradict the idea that television has a negative impact on family life. In their important book *Television and the Quality of Life*, sociologists Robert Kubey and Mihaly Csikszentmihalyi observe that the heaviest viewers of TV among their subjects were "no less likely to spend time with their families" than the lightest viewers. Moreover, those heavy viewers reported feeling happier, more relaxed, and satisfied when watching TV with their families than light viewers did. Based on these reports, the researchers reached the conclusion that "television viewing harmonizes with family life." 34

Using the same data, however, the researchers made another observation about   35
the heavy and light viewers: " . . . families that spend substantial portions of their
time together watching television are likely to experience greater percentages of their
family time feeling relatively passive and unchallenged compared with families who
spend small proportions of their time watching TV."

At first glance the two observations seem at odds: the heavier viewers feel happy   36
and satisfied, yet their family time is more passive and unchallenging—less satisfying in reality. But when one considers the nature of the television experience, the
contradiction vanishes. Surely it stands to reason that the television experience is
instrumental in preventing viewers from recognizing its dulling effects, much as a
mind-altering drug might do.

In spite of everything, the American family muddles on, dimly aware that some-   37
thing is amiss but distracted from an understanding of its plight by an endless stream
of television images. As family ties grow weaker and vaguer, as children's lives become
more separate from their parents', as parents' educational role in their children's lives
is taken over by the media, the school, and the peer group, family life becomes increasingly more unsatisfying for both parents and children. All that seems to be left is love,
an abstraction that family members know is necessary but find great difficulty giving
to each other since the traditional opportunities for expressing it within the family
have been reduced or eliminated.

Daniel J. Boorstin (1914–   ) was born in Atlanta, Georgia, on October 1. He is the grandson of Russian-Jewish immigrants. His family moved to Tulsa when he was two, and he was fifteen when he was graduated from high school summa cum laude. On a Rhodes scholarship, Boorstin studied law at Oxford University, earning a B.A. degree in jurisprudence in 1936 and a B.C.L. degree in 1937. Subsequently, he took a fellowship at Yale Law School for a year before teaching at Harvard and Radcliffe. He earned a doctorate in judicial science from Yale in 1940. He held other teaching posts at Swarthmore College and the University of Chicago, as well as directing the National Museum of History and Technology of the Smithsonian Institution.

Boorstin's writing attempts to consider America's uniqueness by analyzing its relationship with Europe. Some of his many books include *The Lost World of Thomas Jefferson* (1948); *The Genius of American Politics* (1953); *The Americans: The Colonial Experience* (1958); *The Image, or What Happened to the American Dream* (1962); *The Americans: The National Experience* (1965); *The Americans: The Democratic Experience* (1973); *Democracy and Its Discontents: Reflections on Everyday America* (1974); *The Exploring Spirit: America and the World, Then and Now* (1976); *The Discoverers* (1983); *The Creators* (1992); and *Cleopatra's Nose: Essays on the Unexpected* (1994). Like many intellectuals, Boorstin joined the Communist Party in the late 1930s, but he changed his mind in 1939, given the rise of anti-Semitism in Europe. Boorstin is known as one of the first leaders of the "consensus" school of historiography. Boorstin's books have been translated into more than twenty languages. Boorstin won a Pulitzer prize and bears the honor of Librarian of Congress Emeritus.

Overcommunication: Are We Talking Too Much?

Daniel J. Boorstin

We suffer from a disease different from that which any society before us has suffered. I call it "overcommunication." I hesitate even to write about it because, by adding to the daily torrent of words, I aggravate the disease. 1

Yet, at the same time, as the prophetic humorist Tom Lehrer observes in one of his songs, it seems that nowadays everyone is complaining that he can't communicate. Parents complain that they can't communicate with children, children that they can't communicate with parents, students that they can't communicate with teachers, teachers that they can't communicate with students. And Lehrer wisely concludes that if a person cannot communicate, the least he ought to be able to do is to shut up. 2

We might begin to solve our problem of communication if more of us took his advice. And we can better understand his good sense if we look briefly at the history of the idea of communication. 3

"Communicate" is a very old word which has had many meanings in the course of its history. One of the earliest, giving us some of its forgotten flavor, dates back to Starkey's *History of England* in 1538, where the word "communicate" is part of the definition of God. Starkey says that God is He who "communicated" His goodness 4

The iDeal Reader

Daniel J. Boorstin,
"Overcommunication: Are
We Talking Too Much?"

© The McGraw–Hill
Companies, 2000

167

to all others. This, of course, is related to the word "communicant," a person who shares in the Eucharist. So, in origin, "communicate" is related to the word "common," or "community," and it means somehow to make common, to share.

In one sense we could actually define the rise of civilization as the rise of communication—the improvement of the ways of sharing and the improvement of that which is shared. It is obvious that the quality of any civilization will depend on what there is to share and on how it is shared. And democracy, more than any other form of government, is based on the faith that sharing the good things of life—and especially sharing the power to govern—can be wholesome.

But in our enthusiasm for sharing and in our current mania for *more* communication, we have tended to forget the original and primary sense of the word, and unfortunately, to emphasize a secondary sense of "communicate." In this secondary sense, "communicate" (our dictionaries say) means "to impart information, knowledge or the like, to impart or convey knowledge of or inform a person of, to tell." Even this sense begins to be lost as its indispensable counterpart, the right to listen—or not to listen—begins to disappear.

While the progress of civilization is an improvement in what we share and in the processes of sharing, there is another commonly forgotten essential to the rise of civilization. As Sigmund Freud reminds us, an indispensable feature of civilization is the willingness of people *not* to say and *not* to do many things they might want to say or do. From this point of view, then, civilization consists just as much in how men do *not* communicate with others. In fact, this is one way of describing a decent society and in its most everyday form a way of describing good manners.

Good manners consist not only in our willingness to say what we *are* expected to say, but just as much in our self-control in keeping ourselves from saying what we really feel and really want to say, but which might hurt others. When someone says, "How are you today?" we say, "Fine, thanks, and how are you?" It's not good manners to go into the details of our sleeplessness last night, and how those pills didn't manage to conquer our insomnia, and so on. When we've been to a party and we leave it, we tell our host, "Thanks for a very nice evening." We don't usually say how boring it was, that we wish there had been some interesting people there, and that we had expected better refreshments. There was once a professor of ethics at Harvard who made it a practice to tell his hosts exactly what he felt at the end of a Cambridge evening. People said they found his lack of inhibition amusing, but they stopped inviting him to their parties.

Not only good manners are at stake here. For the very progress of civilization depends on the ability of people to develop a more self-controlled attitude about what they say—and how, when, and where. Human progress is the movement from expression to communication, from the growl, the snort, or the expletive to the mathematical formula or the narrative sentence. It is marked by the decline of the exclamation point.

The rise of exposition, of abstraction, and of "communication" marks a vast increase in the range of *what* can be communicated, and a widening in the geographic and chronological range of those to *whom* it can be communicated. At the same time it marks a movement from the yelp of pain or the scream of rage to sounds and symbols that may be of greater interest and deeper meaning to people in other times and other places.

This means, too, a shift of focus from the self, from the simple expression of emotions in gesture and voice, to the carrying of messages of facts and ideas, even of feelings. In modern times, and especially in a democratic society, decency and progress depend on the willingness of people to forgo whatever sense of release or catharsis might come from the screamed expletive or the personal yelp, in favor of other forms of sounds and symbols.   11

Representative institutions, of all institutions, depend most on the willingness of people to inhibit their animal emotions and to talk to others with respect. In countries like France and Italy, where representative assemblies have been marked by the throwing of inkwells, the shouting of libels and curses, and the punching of noses, representative government is fragile and erratic. And in those like Great Britain, where the representative assembly has been marked by a certain inhibition, a certain ritual, and a formalized way of showing respect for other members, representative government is more stable and more effective.   12

Until now, the representative institutions of our country have, fortunately, fallen in the latter category—of the etiquette-inhibited, ritualized parliamentary bodies. Anyone who comes to Washington from a college campus cannot fail to be cheered by the frequent expressions of respect by legislators for other legislators with whom they disagree.   13

Our democracy then, in Jefferson's familiar but neglected phrase, rests on a "decent respect to the opinions of mankind."   14

The Declaration of Independence was motivated by, among other things, American feelings of anger and outrage against King George III and the members of his government. Yet it did not attack the king as an idiot or lunatic. Nor did it scream curses or identify the king with unsavory or unmentionable physical or sexual acts. It did not even accuse George III or his government of corruption and incompetence, which it might very well have done. The declaration simply declared some rights and some grievances in measured, even legalistic language. If the Declaration of Independence had been a volcano of expletives, it would have had little effect in its day and would have been buried with other sub-literature long before our time. Much of our daily problem of communication arises from our unwillingness to show a similar decency and self-restraint.   15

Perhaps the most important single change in the human consciousness in the last century, and especially in the American consciousness, has been the multiplying of the means and forms of what we call "communication." Not so long ago, a person had to make a special effort to get a message in from the world around him. For news he had to purchase a newspaper. For other information or entertainment, he had to buy a book or attend a lecture, which was expensive, or find a traveler, who might be scarce, or go to a theater, which performed only occasionally.   16

Nowadays communication is an everywhere all-the-time thing. To escape messages we have to make a special effort—and we seldom succeed. Even when we come into our own living room we cannot avoid a glimpse of some far-off stage on the television screen being watched by someone else in the family. New forms of   17

The iDeal Reader

Daniel J. Boorstin,
"Overcommunication: Are
We Talking Too Much?"

© The McGraw–Hill
Companies, 2000

169

involuntary reception—from telephone solicitations to the sound of music in elevators to the loudspeaker witticisms of an airplane captain—remind us that there's always somebody out there trying to tell us something—in fact, demanding to tell us something—and there is no escape.

We have become so accustomed to all this that we begin to feel lonesome or 18 even neglected and wonder whether we are really alive and alert when we do not hear these sounds. People travel miles to talk on deserted beaches or mountainsides— they try to keep in touch by carrying a transistor radio. I find myself listening to the radio not only in my automobile as I drive to work but even in my shower.

Along with the "everywhereness" and multiplication of messages comes repe- 19 tition. Every hour on the hour, sometimes on the quarter-hour, all the news, all the time. And when there's no news there's an interview or a "special report." People grow calluses in their ears. It actually becomes harder and harder to get a message through. We witness the cheapening of the word. Wherever we go and wherever we look, we see and hear words—mostly messages we would rather not receive. Once, the word was sacred, a synonym for the Word of God, that which has a special sanctity. But now, words are everywhere and inescapable.

There is no better clue to the decline of the original sense of "communication" 20 than the decline of prayer—not only in the schoolroom but everywhere else. Prayer is a form of communication, a form of sharing. And one of its more eloquent forms is silence. But silence itself has become so rare that it seems unnatural, and even terrifying. Silent prayer is not at all congenial to our age.

A society like ours, which puts so much of its resources into communication, 21 inevitably overvalues communication. We begin to lose our sense of its proper values and proper boundaries. We begin to lose our sense of the difference between communication and expression. We begin to expect the impossible from the mere act of communication. We meet in conventions where people are expected to produce wisdom or knowledge out of their pooled ignorance or prejudices. We meet in committees, conferences, and discussion groups without knowing our purpose and then adjourn without knowing whether we have accomplished it.

In our world of callused ears and overtaxed eyes, there are many symptoms of 22 the desperate need of people to make somebody listen, to be sure somehow that somebody is hearing. More and more people are willing to pay fees they cannot afford, to medically trained psychiatric listeners who listen, nod, and take notes. A few desperate people, especially young people with great energy who find they cannot get people to listen when they say something, decide instead to *throw* something.

No society could survive—and surely no society could be decent—if every- 23 body in it were able to communicate everything. Democracy thrives on selective communication. And to keep the society democratic, the selection must be made not by some outside political agency, but by the self-controlled citizen.

With the rise of photography and the movies, of radio and television, and with 24 the improvement and diffusion of the graphic arts, an ever-larger proportion of what is communicated becomes vivid. To catch and hold our attention, the images must be in motion. So it is not surprising that more and more of what is communicated to us is explosive and disruptive, interrupting the current of our experience.

There is a natural tendency, then, to identify communication with dissent, with   25
the violent and the melodramatic. This has the retrograde—we might more precisely
call it "reactionary"—effect of leading us backward to identify communication with
expression, with saying what *I* feel rather than what may have meaning to you.
And so, inevitably, we tend to identify communication with that which emphasizes the separateness of each individual.

But democracy depends on the communication which is sharing, not on that   26
which is purely self-expressive, explosive, or vituperative. Our new opportunities and
our new temptations to overcommunicate require a new and harder self-discipline
among citizens, one of the most difficult forms of discipline to enforce. It illustrates
the wisdom of the English judge who said, "Civilization must be measured by the
extent of obedience to the unenforceable." In a world of overcommunication, the
survival of a decent society may depend on our willingness to accept this truth.

We show respect for ourselves and for our fellow-men and we affirm our belief   27
that there may be something larger and even less intelligible than ourselves by
admitting that not everything can or should be said. In this nation, which has spent
more of its resources than any other to produce a wise and educated citizenry, we must
not forget the commonplace wisdom of an old Japanese proverb: "He who knows
nothing else knows enough if he knows when to be silent."

Marita Sturken is Professor of Culture and Communication as well as Co-Director of the Visual Culture Program at New York University. Her courses focus on cultural studies, popular culture, advertising, and global culture. Sturken is the former editor of *American Quarterly*, the journal of the American Studies Association. Her publications include *Tangled Memories: The Vietnam War, the AIDS Epidemic, and the Politics of Remembering* (California, 1997), *Thelma & Louise* (British Film Institute, 2000), *Practices of Looking: An Introduction to Visual Culture* (with Lisa Cartwright, Oxford, 2001), and co-editor, with Douglas Thomas and Sandra Ball-Rokeach, of *Technological Visions: The Hopes and Fears That Shape New Technology* (Temple, 2004) and most recently, *Tourists of History: Memory, Consumerism, and Kitsch in American Culture* (2007). In addition, her work has appeared in numerous journals including *Representations*, *Public Culture*, *History and Theory*, and *Afterimage*.

The Wall, the Screen, and the Image: The Vietnam Veterans Memorial

Marita Sturken

The forms remembrance takes indicate the status of memory within a given culture. In these forms, we can see acts of public commemoration as moments in which shifting discourses of history, personal memory, and cultural memory converge. Public commemoration is a form of history-making, yet it can also be a contested form of remembrance in which cultural memories slide through and into each other, merging and then disengaging in a tangle of narratives.   1

With the Vietnam War, discourses of public commemoration have become inextricably tied to the question of how war is brought to a closure in American society. How, for instance, does a society commemorate a war for which the central narrative is one of division and dissent, a war whose history is highly contested and still in the process of being made? As Peter Ehrenhaus writes, "The tradition of U.S. public discourse in the wake of war is founded upon the premises of clarity of purpose and success; when such presumptions must account for division, equivocation, and failure, and when losing is among the greatest of sins, commemoration seems somehow inappropriate."[1] Yet the Vietnam War—with its division and confusion, its lack of a singular, historical narrative defining clear-cut purpose and outcome—has led to a very different form of commemoration.   2

I would like to focus this discussion of public remembrance on the notion of a screen, in its many meanings. A screen can be a surface that is projected upon; it is also an object that hides something from view, that shelters or protects. It can be a surface, or even a body—in military language a *screen* is a "body of men" who are used to cover the movements of an army. Freud's screen memory func-   3

Marita Sturken, "The Wall, the Screen, and the Image: The Vietnam Veterans Memorial," *Representations*, No. 35, Special Issue: Monumental Histories. (Summer 1991), pp. 118–142. © The Regents of the University of California. Reprinted by permission of the University of California Press. Photo by Wendy Watriss, from the series The Vietnam Veterans Memorial Courtesy of the Artist.

tions to hide highly emotional material, which the screen memory conceals while offering itself as a substitute. The kinds of screens that converge in the Vietnam Veterans Memorial in Washington, D.C., both shield and project: the black walls of the memorial act as screens for innumerable projections of memory and history—of the United States' participation in the Vietnam War and of the experience of the Vietnam veterans since the war—while they screen out the narrative of defeat in preparing for wars to come. Seeing the memorial as a screen also evokes the screens on which the war was and continues to be experienced—cinematic and television screens—through which the contested history of the war is being made.

Cultural memory represents the many shifting histories and shared memories   4
that exist between a sanctioned narrative of history and personal memory. The formation of a singular, sanctioned history of the Vietnam War has not yet taken place, in part because of the disruption of the standard narratives of American imperialism, technology, and masculinity that the war's loss represented.[2] The history of the Vietnam War is still in the process of being composed from many conflicting histories, yet there are particular elements within these often opposing narratives that remain uncontested—the irony of the war, the pain and subsequent marginalization of the Vietnam veteran, and the divisive effect the war had on American society. This essay is concerned with how certain narratives of the war have been constructed out of and within the fluid realm of cultural memory, in which personal memories are shared for many different purposes. I would like to examine how the screens of the Vietnam Veterans Memorial act to eclipse personal and collective memories of the war from the design of history, and yet how the textures of cultural and personal memory are nevertheless woven throughout, perhaps over and under, these screens.

The 1980s and 1990s have witnessed a repackaging of the 1960s and the   5
Vietnam War—a phenomenon that is steeped in the language of nostalgia, healing, and forgiveness. The Vietnam Veterans Memorial has become a central icon of the "healing" process of confronting difficult past experiences, and it has played a significant role in the historization and rehistorization of the war. Since its construction in 1982, the memorial has been the center of a debate on precisely how wars should be remembered, and precisely who should be remembered in a war—those who died, those who participated, those who engineered it, or those who opposed it.

THE STATUS OF A MEMORIAL

Although administered under the aegis of the National Parks Service of the   6
Federal Government, the Vietnam Veterans Memorial was built in 1982 through the impetus of a group of Vietnam veterans, the Vietnam Veterans Memorial Fund (VVMF), who raised the necessary funds and negotiated for a site on the Mall in Washington. Situated on the grassy slope of the Constitutional Gardens near the Lincoln Memorial, the memorial consists of two walls of black granite set into the earth at an angle of 125 degrees. Together, the walls form an extended V almost 500 feet in length, tapering in both directions from a height of approximately ten

feet at the central hinge. These walls are currently inscribed with 58,132 names of men and women who died in the war, as well as with opening and closing inscriptions. The chronological listing of names begins on the right-hand side of the hinge and continues to the end of the right wall; it then begins again at the far end of the left wall and continues to the center again. Thus, the name of the first American soldier killed in Vietnam in 1959 is on a panel adjacent to that containing the name of the last American killed in 1975. The framing dates of 1959 and 1975 are the only dates listed on the wall; the names are listed alphabetically within each "casualty day," although those dates are not noted.[3] Eight of the names on the wall represent women who died in the war. Since 1984, the memorial has been accompanied by a figurative sculpture of three soldiers and a flag, both facing the monument from a group of trees at a distance of about thirty yards.

The memorial stands in opposition to the codes of remembrance evidenced on the Washington Mall. Virtually all of the national memorials and monuments in Washington are made of white stone and are constructed to be seen from a distance. In contrast, the Vietnam Veterans Memorial cuts into the sloping earth: it is not visible until one is almost upon it, and if approached from behind, it seems to disappear into the landscape. While the polished black granite walls of the memorial reflect the Washington Monument and face the Lincoln Memorial, they are not visible from the base of either of those structures. The black stone gives the memorial a reflective surface (one that echoes the reflecting pool of the Lincoln Memorial) that allows viewers to participate in the memorial; seeing their own images in the names, they are thus implicated in the listing of the dead.

As a memorial, rather than a monument, the Vietnam Veterans Memorial is situated within a particular code of remembrance, one that Arthur Danto evokes: "We erect monuments so that we shall always remember, and build memorials so that we shall never forget."[4] Monuments are not generally built to commemorate defeats; the defeated dead are remembered in memorials. While a monument most often signifies victory, a memorial refers to the life or lives sacrificed for a particular set of values. Memorials embody grief, loss, and tribute or obligation; in so doing, they serve to frame particular historical narratives. They are, according to Charles Griswold, "a species of pedagogy [that] seeks to instruct posterity about the past and, in so doing, necessarily reaches a decision about what is worth recovering."[5]

Thus, whatever triumph a particular memorial refers to, its depiction of victory is always tempered by a foregrounding of the lives lost. The Lincoln Memorial is a funereal structure that connotes a mausoleum, embodying the man and his philosophy in privileging his words on its walls. The force of the Lincoln Memorial is thus its mythical reference to Lincoln's untimely death. The Washington Monument, on the other hand, operates purely as a symbol, making no reference beyond its name to the mythic political figure. This contrast outlines one of the fundamental differences between memorials and monuments: monuments tend to use less explanation, while memorials tend to emphasize texts or lists of the dead. Therefore, while monuments (and victories) are usually anonymous, the irony of lives lost for an unattained goal—in the case of the Vietnam War, an unspoken

7

8

9

goal in an undeclared war—in a memorial seems to demand the naming of the individual.[6]

The traditional Western monument glorifies not only its subject but architectural history as well. The obelisk of the Washington Monument, which was erected from 1848 to 1885, has its roots in Roman architecture; long before Napoleon pilfered them from Egypt to take to Paris, obelisks carried connotations of the imperial trophy. The Lincoln Memorial, which was built in 1922, is modeled on the classic Greek temple, specifically referring to the Parthenon. The Vietnam Veterans Memorial, however, makes no direct reference to the classical history of art or architecture. As a blank slate, it does not chart a lineage from the accomplishments of past civilizations.

Yet the Vietnam Veterans Memorial is unmistakably representative of a particular period in Western art. In the uproar that accompanied its construction, it became the focus of a debate about the role of modernism in public sculpture. Just one month prior to the dedication of the memorial in November 1982, Tom Wolfe wrote a vitriolic attack on its design in the *Washington Post,* calling it a piece of modernist orthodoxy that was "a tribute to Jane Fonda."[7] Wolfe and other critics of modernism compared the memorial to two infamously unpopular government-funded public sculptures: Carl Andre's *Stone Field Sculpture* (1980) in Hartford, Connecticut, and Richard Serra's *Tilted Arc* (1981) in downtown Manhattan.[8] These two works had come to symbolize the alienating effect of modern sculpture on certain sectors of the viewing public, leading to questions by those viewers about the ways they felt tax-funded public sculptures were being imposed on them.

Before it was built, the memorial was seen by many veterans and critics of modernism as yet another abstract modernist work that the public would find difficult to interpret. Yet in situating the Vietnam Veterans Memorial purely within the context of modernism, Wolfe and his fellow critics ignore fundamental aspects of this work. The memorial is not simply a flat, black, abstract wall; it is a wall inscribed with names. When the "public" visits this memorial, they do not go to see long walls cut into the earth but to see the names of those whose lives were lost in the war. Hence, to call this a modernist work is to privilege a formalist reading of its design and to negate its commemorative and textual functions. While modernism in sculpture has been defined as a kind of "sitelessness,"[9] the memorial is specifically situated within the national context of the Mall. Deliberately counterposed to the dominant monumental styles surrounding it, the memorial refers to, absorbs, and reflects the classical forms of the Mall. The black walls mirror not only the faces of viewers and passing clouds but also the Washington obelisk, thus forming an impromptu pastiche of monuments. The memorial's relationship to the earth shifts between a sitelessness and site specificity, between context and decontextualization. It delicately balances between effacing and embracing the earth—it cuts into the earth, yet strikes a harmony with the terrain.

But it is as a war memorial that the Vietnam Veterans Memorial is most importantly different from modernist sculpture. The first national memorial to an American war built since World War II memorials, it makes a statement on war that diverges sharply from the traditional declarations of prior war memorials. The

Vietnam veterans who organized the construction of the memorial stipulated only two things for its design—that it contain the names of those who died or are missing in action and that it be apolitical and harmonious with the site. Implicit within these guidelines was also a desire that the memorial offer some kind of closure to the debates on the war. Even so, in these stipulations the veterans had already set the stage for the dramatic disparity between the message of this memorial and that of its antecedents. While the concern for the memorial's context in the Mall tended to rule out a vertical monument, the intent that the work not espouse a political stand in regard to the war ensured that in the end the memorial would not glorify the war.

The traditional war memorial works to impose a closure on a specific conflict.   14 This closure contains the war within particular master narratives either of victory—in this country, affirming our military superiority and ability to impose our will on others—or of loss and the bitter price of victory, a theme dominant in the "never again" texts of World War I memorials. In declaring the end of a conflict, this closure can by its very nature serve to sanctify future wars by offering a completed narrative with cause and effect intact. In rejecting the architectural lineage of monuments and contesting the aesthetic codes of previous war memorials, the Vietnam Veterans Memorial also refuses the closure and implied tradition of those structures; yet it both condemns and justifies future memorials.

THE BLACK GASH OF SHAME

Before it was built, the design of the memorial was an object of attack not only   15 because of its modernist aesthetics but, more significantly, because it violated implicit taboos about the remembrance of wars. When its design was first unveiled, the memorial was condemned by some veterans and others as a highly political statement about the shame of an unvictorious war. Termed the "black gash of shame," a "degrading ditch," a "black spot in American history," a "tombstone," a "slap in the face," and a "wailing wall for draft dodgers and New Lefters of the future,"[10] the memorial was seen as a monument to defeat, one that spoke more directly to a nation's guilt than to the honor of the war dead and the veterans. One prominent veteran of the VVMF read its black walls as evoking "shame, sorrow, and the degradation of all races";[11] others perceived its refusal to rise above the earth as indicative of defeat. Thus, a racist reading of the color black was combined with a sexist reading of a feminized earth as connoting a lack of power. Precisely because of its deviation from traditional commemorative codes—white stone rising above the earth—the design was read as a political statement. An editorial in the *National Review* stated:

> Our objection . . . is based upon the clear political message of this design. The design says that the Vietnam War should be memorialized in black, not the white marble of Washington. The mode of listing the names makes them individual deaths, not deaths in a cause: they might as well have been traffic accidents. The invisibility of the monument at ground level symbolizes the "unmentionability" of the war. . . . Finally, the

V-shaped plan of the black retaining wall immortalizes the antiwar signal, the **V** protest made with the fingers.[12]

This analysis of the memorial's symbolism, indeed a perceptive reading, points to several crucial aspects of the memorial: its listing of names does make these individual deaths rather than the singular death of a body of men; the relationship of the memorial to the earth does refuse to evoke heroism and victory.

Certainly the angry reactions to the memorial go beyond the accusation of the elite pretensions of abstraction, since the uncontroversial Washington Monument itself is the epitome of abstraction. Rather, I believe that the primary (and unspoken) aspect of the memorial that is responsible for the accusations that it does not appropriately remember war is its antiphallic presence. By "antiphallic" I do not mean to imply that the memorial is somehow a passive or "feminine" form but rather that it opposes the codes of vertical monuments symbolizing power and honor. The memorial does not stand erect above the landscape; it is continuous with the earth. It evokes contemplation rather than declaring its meaning. The intersection of the two walls of the memorial form the shape of a **V**, which has been interpreted by various commentators as V for *Vietnam, victim, victory, veteran, violate,* and *valor.* Yet, one also finds here a disconcerting subtext in which the memorial implicitly evokes castration. The **V** of the two black granite walls has also been read as a female **V**, reminding us that a "gash" is not only a wound but slang for the female genitals. The memorial contains all elements that have been associated psychoanalytically with the specter of woman—it embraces the earth; it is the abyss; it is death. To its critics this antiphallus symbolizes the open, castrated wound of this country's venture into an unsuccessful war, a war that emasculated the role the United States would play in future foreign conflicts. The discourse of healing surrounding the memorial is an attempt to close many wounds, the suturing of which would mean a revived metanarrative of the United States as a successful military power and a rehabilitation of the masculinity of the American soldier.

The controversial, antiphallic form of the memorial is attributable to its having been designed by a person unlikely to reiterate traditional codes of war remembrance. At the time her design was chosen anonymously by a group of eight male "experts," Maya Ying Lin was a twenty-one-year-old undergraduate at Yale University who had produced the design for a funerary architecture course. She was not only young and uncredentialed but Chinese-American and, most significantly, female. Initially, the veterans of the VVMF were pleased by this turn of events; they assumed that the selection of Lin's design would only show how open and anonymous their design contest had been. However, the selection of someone with "marginal" cultural status as the primary interpreter of a controversial war inevitably complicated matters. Eventually, Maya Lin was defined, in particular by the media, not as American but as "other." This "otherness" became an issue not only in the way she was perceived in the media and by some of the veterans; it became a critical issue of whether or not that otherness had informed the design itself. For architecture critic Michael Sorkin, "Perhaps it was Maya Lin's 'other-

16

17

ness' that enabled her to create such a moving work. Perhaps only an outsider could have designed an environment so successful in answering the need for recognition by a group of people—the Vietnam vets—who are plagued by a sense of 'otherness' forced on them by a country that has spent ten years pretending not to see them."[13] Lin's marginal status as a Chinese-American woman was thus seen as giving her insight into the marginal status experienced by Vietnam veterans, in a move that noticeably erased other differences.

Debates about Lin's design have also centered on the question of whether or not it is a passive work that reflects a female sensibility. There is little doubt that it is, in its refusal to glorify war, an implicitly pacifist work, and by extension a political work. As art critic Elizabeth Hess wrote, "Facing the myriad names, it is difficult for anyone *not* to question the purpose of the war" (269). Yet as much as this is a contemplative work that is continuous with the earth, it is also a violent work that cuts into the earth, evoking a wrenching in flesh. Lin has said,

> I wanted to work with the land and not dominate it. I had an impulse to cut open the earth . . . an initial violence that in time would heal. The grass would grow back, but the cut would remain, a pure, flat surface, like a geode when you cut into it and polish the edge.[14]

The black walls cannot connote a healing wound without signifying the violence which created that wound, cutting into the earth and splitting it open.

Trouble between Maya Lin and the veterans began almost immediately. "The fund has always seen me as a female—as a child," she has said. "I went in there when I first won and their attitude was—O.K. you did a good job, but now we're going to hire some big boys—boys—to take care of it."[15] Lin was defined, primarily because of her sex and age, as outside of the veterans' discourse. She had also made a decision deliberately not to inform herself about the war's political history to avoid being influenced by debates about the war. According to veteran Jan Scruggs, the primary figure behind the memorial's construction, "She never asked, 'What was combat like?' or 'Who were your friends whose names we're putting on the wall?' And the vets, in turn, never once explained to her what the words like 'courage,' 'sacrifice,' and 'devotion to duty' really meant" (79). That Lin could not understand terms such as "courage" and "sacrifice" was implicit to the veterans because she was a woman and hence positioned outside of the (male) discourse of war.

In public discourse, Lin's Asian-American identity was read as particularly ironic by virtue of her role in defining the discourse of remembrance of a war fought in Indochina—even if, given the complex politics between China and Vietnam, this conflation of ethnic identities is a particularly American one. (Further, while Lin's ethnicity seemed appropriate to some in that Asians had suffered most in the war, it also appeared as a supreme irony in a war now considered remarkable for its racism.) Hence, Lin's status as American disappeared and she became simply "Asian." Conversely, Lin stuck to her position as an outsider in consistently referring to "the integrity of my design," while the veterans were primarily concerned with the ability of the design to offer emotional comfort to veterans and the families of the dead, either in terms of forgiveness or honor. The initial disagreements on design between the veterans and Lin, which ultimately led to several compromises—the veterans agreed to the chronological listing, with indexes at the site to facilitate location, and Lin agreed to the addition of an opening and closing inscription—were hence concerned not so much with aesthetics as about to whom the memorial ultimately belonged.

In the larger political arena, these aesthetic and commemorative discourses were also at play. The initial response to Lin's design was so divided that it eventually became clear to the veterans of the Memorial Fund that they had either to compromise or to postpone the construction of the memorial (which was to be ready by Veterans Day, November 1982). Consequently, a plan was devised to erect an alternative statue and flag close to the walls of the memorial, and realist sculptor Frederick Hart was chosen to design it.[16] Hart's bronze sculpture, placed in a grove of trees near the memorial in 1984, consists of three soldiers—one black and two white—standing and looking in the general direction of the wall. Their military garb is realistically rendered, with guns slung over their shoulders and ammunition around their waists, and their expressions are somewhat bewildered and puzzled. One of the most vociferous critics of modernism in the debates over the memorial, Hart said at the time,

21

> My position is humanist, not militarist. I'm not trying to say there was anything good or bad about the war. I researched for three years—read everything. I became close friends with many vets, drank with them in bars. Lin's piece is a serene exercise in contemporary art done in a vacuum with no knowledge of its subject. It's nihilistic—that's its appeal.[17]

Hart bases his credentials on a kind of "knowledge" strictly within the male domain—drinking with the veterans in a bar—and unavailable to Maya Lin, whom he had on another occasion referred to as "a mere student." Lin is characterized by Hart as having designed her work with no "knowledge" and no "research," as a woman who works with feeling and intuition rather than expertise. Hart's statement ultimately defines realism as not only a male privilege but also an aesthetic necessity in remembering war. Hart's sculpture does not call into question how suitably to honor the individual dead, because in this work the veterans and the dead are subsumed into a singular narrative. It thus follows in the tradition of the Marine Corps War Memorial depicting the raising of the American flag at Iwo Jima, a work that has attained an iconic status as *the* realist war memorial and a symbol of the United States' right to raise its flag on foreign soil.[18]

The battle over what kind of style best represents the war was, quite obviously, a battle over the representation of the war itself. Hence, in choosing an "apolitical" memorial, the veterans of the VVMF had attempted to separate the memorial, itself a contested narrative, from the contested narratives of the war, ultimately an impossible task. However, after the memorial had actually been built, the debate about aesthetics and remembrance surrounding its design simply disappeared. That controversy was replaced by a multiplicity of cultural discourses on remembrance and healing. Even Maya Lin, who had not attended the opening ceremonies, positioned

22

herself at this point as just another viewer experiencing the memorial like everyone else.[19] The experience of Lin's work seems to have been so powerful for those who have visited it that negative criticism of its design has vanished.[20]

THE NAMES

There is little doubt that much of the memorial's power is due to the effect of the   23
58,132 names inscribed on its walls. Unlike the singular narrative and totalizing image presented by realist sculptures like the Marine Corps Memorial and Hart's statue, images that exist as confirmations of official history, these names, by virtue of their multiplicity, situate the Vietnam Veterans Memorial within the multiple strands of cultural memory spawned by the individual names. The most commonly noted response of visitors at the memorial has been to think of the widening circle of pain emanating from each name—to imagine for each name the grieving parents, sisters, brothers, girlfriends, wives, and children; to imagine, in effect, the multitude of people who were directly affected by the war.

This listing of names creates an expanse of cultural memory, one that could   24
be seen as alternately subverting, rescripting, and contributing to the history of the Vietnam War as it is currently being written. The histories evoked by these names and the responses to them are necessarily multiple and replete with complex personal stakes. These narratives are concerned with the effect of the war on those who survived it, whose lives were irrevocably altered by it. The listing of names is steeped in the irony of the war—an irony afforded by retrospect, the irony of lives lost for no discernable reason.

While these names are marked within an official history, that history cannot   25
contain the ever-widening circles that expand outward from each name. The names on the walls of the memorial comprise a chant of the war dead (they were, in fact, read out loud at the dedication ceremony as a roll call). They are etched into stone, creating a negative space. The men and women who died in the war thus achieve an historically coded presence through their absence. These names are listed without elaboration, with no place or date of death, no rank, no place of origin. The lack of military rank allows the names to emerge from a military narrative and to represent the names of a society. It has often been noted that these names display the diversity of American culture: Fredes Mendez-Ortiz, Stephen Boryszewski, Bobby Joe Yewell, Leroy Wright. Veteran William Broyles, Jr., writes,

> These are names which reach deep into the heart of America, each testimony to a family's decision, sometime in the past, to wrench itself from home and culture to test our country's promise of new opportunities and a better life. They are names drawn from the farthest corners of the world and then, in this generation, sent to another distant corner in a war America has done its best to forget.[21]

Broyles is not atypical here, either in his seeing the diversity of names as indicative of American society as the promised land, or in his putting the United States at the center from which these places of cultural origins and foreign wars are seen as "distant corners." His reading of the ethnicity of the names on the walls does not consider the imbalances of their ethnic distribution—that this was a war fought by a disproportionately high number of blacks and Hispanics, that it was a war in which the predominant number of soldiers were from working- and middle-class backgrounds. Proper names in our culture have complex legal and patriarchal implications, identifying individuals specifically as members of society. On this memorial, these names are coded as American—not as Asian, black, or white—in a way that Maya Lin could not be. The ethnicity of these names is subsumed into a narrative of the American melting pot, into which Maya Lin, as an agent of commemoration, will not fit.

It is crucial to their effect that these names are listed not alphabetically but in chronological order. This was Maya Lin's original intent, so that the wall would read "like an epic Greek poem" and "return the vets to the time frame of the war." The veterans were originally opposed to this idea; since they conceived the memorial specifically in terms of the needs of the veterans and family members who would visit it, they were worried that people would be unable to locate a name and simply leave in frustration. They wanted the names to be in alphabetical order to facilitate their location. They were swayed in their opinion, however, when they examined the Defense Department listing of casualties. Listed alphabetically, the names presented not individuals but cultural entities. There were over six hundred people named Smith, and sixteen named James Jones. Read alphabetically, the names became anonymous statistics.

The chronological listing of names on the Vietnam Veterans Memorial provides it with a narrative framework. Read chronologically, the names chart the story of the war. As the number of names listed alphabetically within a casualty day swells, the intensity of the fighting is told. As one walks along the wall, one can conceivably walk through the history of the war; Lin and others have referred to it as a "journey." The chronological listing thus provides the veterans with a spatial reference for their experience of the war, a kind of memory map. They can see in certain clumps of names the scene of a particular ambush, the casualties of a doomed night patrol, or the night they were wounded.

This is not a linear narrative framework. Rather, the names form a loop, beginning as they do at the central hinge of the memorial and moving out on the right wall, then continuing at the far end of the left wall and moving toward the center. They thus form a narrative circle, in which one can read from the last name to the first. This refusal of linearity is, in many ways, appropriate to a conflict that has had no superficial closure. The hinge between the two walls thus becomes a pivotal space, the narrow space between the end and the beginning of a war; it connotes peace, yet a temporary peace between wars.

The question of who are and are not named on the wall is crucial within the memorial's representation of intersecting discourses of cultural memory and history. The veterans of the VVMF were concerned that the memorial be a tribute not only to those who died but to those who survived the war. There is little doubt that the memorial has become a powerful symbol for all Vietnam veterans, yet only the names of the war dead and the MIAs are inscribed on the wall, and thus within history. The distinction of the named and unnamed is thus significant for the intersection of memory and history in the memorial—in particular, for how this memorial will construct the history of the Vietnam War after the generation of surviving Vietnam veterans is dead. These veterans, and those whose lives were altered through their opposition to the war, are not named. Significantly, the Vietnamese are conspicuously absent in their roles either as victims, enemies, or even the people on whose land and for whom this war was ostensibly fought.

The inscription of names on the memorial has posed many taxonomic problems. While the VVMF spent months cross-checking and verifying statistics, there have been errors in the naming. There are at least fourteen and possibly as many as thirty-eight men who are still alive whose names are inscribed on the wall.[22] How can this be resolved? To erase the names would leave a scar in the wall; if the names are etched out, these veterans will be categorized as the not-dead, doubly displaced within the war discourse. There have been several hundred names added to the memorial since it was first built (the initial number inscribed on the walls was 57,939), names that were held up previously for "technicalities" (including, in one case, a dispute over whether or not the men were killed in the "presidentially designated" war zone), their status now changed from "missing" or "lost" to classifiably dead.

30

The problems raised by the inscription of names on the memorial signifies, in many ways, the war's lack of closure. The unmanageability of 58,000 sets of statistics, the impossibility of knowing every detail (who died, when and where) in a war in which remains were often unidentifiable, prevents any kind of closure.[23] Names will continue to be added to the memorial; there is no definitive end to the addition of names. There has been considerable discussion of the fact that the names of the veterans who have died since the war (from causes stemming from it) are not included on the memorial—veterans who committed suicide, who died from complications from their exposure to Agent Orange. Are they not casualties of the war? The battles still being fought by the veterans foreclose any ending to the narrative of the Vietnam War.

31

THE VIETNAM VETERAN: THE PERENNIAL SOLDIER

With the [First] World War a process began to become apparent which has not halted since then. Was it not noticeable at the end of the war that men returned from the battlefield grown silent—not richer but poorer in communicable experience? What ten years later was poured out in the flood of war books was anything but experience that goes mouth to mouth. And there was nothing remarkable about that. For never has experience been contradicted more thoroughly than strategic experience by tactical warfare, economic experience by inflation, bodily experience by mechanical warfare, moral experience by those in power. A generation that had gone to school on a horse-drawn streetcar now stood under the open sky in a countryside in which nothing remained unchanged but the clouds, and beneath these clouds, in a field of force of destructive torrents and explosions, was the tiny, fragile, human body.

32

—*Walter Benjamin*[24]

The incommunicability of the experience of the Vietnam War has been a primary narrative in the Vietnam veterans' discourse. It was precisely this incommunicability that rendered, among other things, the construction of the Vietnam Veterans Memorial necessary. This incommunicability has been depicted as a silence rendered by an inconceivable kind of war, a war that fit no prior images of war. 33

While the Vietnam Veterans Memorial most obviously pays tribute to the memory of those who died during the war, it is a central icon for the veterans. It has been noted that the memorial has given them a place—one that recognizes their identities, a place at which to congregate and from which to speak. Hence, the memorial is as much about survival as it is about mourning the dead. 34

The construction of an identity for the veterans since their return from the war has become the most present and continuing narrative of the memorial. The central theme of this narrative is the way the veterans had been invisible and without voice before the memorial's construction and the subsequent interest in discussing the war. Veterans have told innumerable stories of the hostility that greeted them upon their return from Vietnam, and there has been a noticeable lack of interest in the war in popular culture until recently—the direct result of an ambivalence toward the war due to an inability to fit it into traditional paradigms. The experience of the Vietnam War as *different* from all previous ones has made the process of narrativizing it particularly difficult. 35

Unlike World War II veterans, Vietnam veterans did not arrive home en masse for a celebration but one by one, without any welcome. Many of them ended up in underfunded and poorly staffed Veterans Administration hospitals. They were expected to put their war experiences behind them and to assimilate quickly back into society. That many were unable to do so resulted further in their marginalization—they were labeled social misfits and stereotyped as potentially dangerous men with a violence that threatened to erupt at any moment. According to George Swiers, a veteran, 36

> The message sent from national leadership and embraced by the public was clear: Vietnam veterans were malcontents, liars, wackos, losers. Hollywood, ever bizarre in its efforts to mirror life, discovered a marketable villain. *Kojak, Ironside,* and the friendly folks at *Hawaii Five-O* confronted crazed, heroin-addicted veterans with the regularity and enthusiasm Saturday morning heroes once dispensed with godless red savages. No grade-B melodrama was complete without its standard vet— a psychotic, axe-wielding rapist every bit as insulting as another one-time creature of Hollywood's imagination, the shiftless, lazy, and wide-eyed black.[25]

The portrayal of the veteran as a psychopath was a kind of scapegoating that absolved the American public of complicity and allowed the master narrative of American military power to stand. For Thomas Myers, "To ask the veteran to play the villain is a way to quiet a loud memory, to rewrite a new national narrative so that it can be joined, without disturbance, to older ones."[26] Implied within these conflicting narratives is the question of whether or not the veterans are to be perceived as victims or complicit with the war: "Vets are in an ambiguous situation—they were the agents and the victims of a particular kind of violence. That is the source of a pain that almost no one else can understand," writes Peter Marin.[27] Ironically, the attempt to make them silent—in effect, to make them disappear—has resulted in the Vietnam veterans' assumption of hybrid roles; they are both, yet neither, soldiers and civilians. At their demonstrations, many wear fatigues and comport the trappings of their status as soldiers.

While the marginalization of the Vietnam veterans has been acknowledged in the current discourse of healing and forgiveness about the war, within the veterans' community another group is struggling against an imposed silence: the women veterans. There were eight women military nurses and three women Red Cross workers killed in Vietnam. It is estimated that 7,500 military women and an almost equal number of civilian women (many of whom were nurses) served in Vietnam.[28] Upon their return, these women were not only subject to the same difficulties as the veterans but were also excluded from the veteran community. Several have since revealed how they kept their war experience a secret, never telling even their husbands that they had been in Vietnam. One has since recounted how she was not allowed to participate in a veterans' protest march because male veterans thought that "Nixon and the network news reporters might think we're swelling the ranks with non-vets."[29]   37

These women veterans were thus doubly displaced, unable to speak as veterans or as women. Several are presently raising funds to place an intentionally "apolitical" statue of a woman near the Vietnam Veterans Memorial. In August 1990, a design competition for the memorial, to be located just south of the wall, was announced, and the fundraising of the $3.5 million to construct the memorial continues.[30] The two women who direct the Vietnam Womens Memorial Project, Diane Evans and Donna Marie Boulay, told Elizabeth Hess that it is Hart's depiction of three men who make the absence of women so visible; they would not have initiated the project had Lin's memorial stood alone.[31]   38

This double displacement of the women veterans is related to a larger discourse concerning masculine identity in the Vietnam War. The Vietnam War is seen as a site where American masculinity was lost, and the rehabilitation of the Vietnam veteran is thus heavily coded as a reinscription of American masculinity.[32] Because they were denied the traditional praise afforded veterans, Vietnam veterans have a particularly complex collective identity—one that ironically has been strengthened by their marginalization. The pain and suffering that they experienced since the war continues to be read as masculine, and the inclusion of women into that discourse of remorse and anger is seen as a dilution of its intensity and a threat to the rehabilitation of that masculinity.[33]   39

The primary narrative of the veterans in the discourses surrounding the memorial is not their war experience but their mistreatment since the war. This narrative takes the form of a combat story in which the enemy has been transposed from the North Vietnamese to the antiwar movement to the callous American people, the Veterans Administration, and the government.   40

The story of the struggle to build the memorial also takes on this combat form. 41
In his book *To Heal a Nation* (later a TV movie), veteran Jan Scruggs, who conceived the memorial and was the main force behind its being built, equates the *battle* waged by the veterans to have the memorial built by Veterans Day, 1982, with the battles of Vietnam: "Some 58,000 GIs were, in death, what they had been in life: pawns of Washington politics" (93). Scruggs is the lone fighter for much of this story (the idea of building a memorial when veterans did not have adequate support services was initially thought ludicrous by many veterans), and his determination becomes exemplary for all veterans. In his story, "grunts"—those who experienced the "real" war of combat—battle the establishment and win. There is a powerful kind of closure here. The one story for which the memorial appears to offer resolution is that of the shame felt by veterans for having fought in an unpopular war.

One has to question the sudden rush to welcome home veterans ten years 42
after the war had ended, the clamoring of the media to cover the fallout of the Vietnam War after ignoring it for years. While the closure for the veterans of their period of estrangement seems not only just but long overdue, its implications when transferred into mainstream discourse about the memorial, and into history, can become insidious. When, for instance, *Newsweek* printed a story entitled "Honoring Vietnam Veterans—At Last" in 1982, the desire not only to rectify but to *forget* the mistreatment of the veterans was obvious. To forget this episode in American history is not only to negate the ongoing struggles of veterans—those who are ill or dying due to their exposure to Agent Orange, for example—but also to cease to examine the reasons why these men and women had been scapegoated. This denial, in turn, is irrevocably tied to the question of the rupture in public commemoration caused by the Vietnam War's difference from other wars, and the possible lessons to be learned from it.

THE HEALING WOUND

The metaphor of the healing wound that has prevailed in descriptions of the 43
Vietnam Veterans Memorial and its effect is a bodily metaphor. It evokes many different bodies—the bodies of the Vietnam War dead, the bodies of the veterans, and the body of the American public. The memorial is seen as representing a wound in the process of healing, one that will leave a smooth scar in the earth. This wound in turn represents the process of memory; its healing is the process of remembering and commemorating the war. To dis-member is to fragment a body and its memory; to remember is to make a body complete.

In war, the "tiny, fragile, human body" becomes subject to dismemberment, to 44
a kind of "antimemory." The absence of these bodies—obliterated, entered—is both eclipsed and invoked by the names on the memorial's walls. The names act as surrogates for the bodies (Lin says that she conceptualizes the dead as being in a space behind the wall). Yet the bodies of the living Vietnam veterans have not been erased of memory. Rather, they embody personal and cultural memory; their bodies are those of *survivors*. History has a problematic relationship to the lived body of the individual who participated in it; in fact, it operates more efficiently

when survivors are no longer alive. These veterans' bodies—dressed in fatigues, scarred and disabled, contaminated by toxins—refuse to let historical narratives of completion stand.[34] Memories of the war have been deeply encoded in them, marked literally and figuratively in their flesh—one of the most tragic aftermaths of the war is the genetic deformities that Agent Orange has caused in veterans' children.

If the bodies of the surviving veterans resist the closure of history, they pro-   45
vide a perceptible site for a continual remembering of the war's effect. Elaine Scarry describes how wounded casualties function as vehicles for memorialization, noting that the act of injuring is not only "the means by which a winner and loser are arrived at" but a *"means of providing a record of its own activity"* (emphasis mine).[35] The wound gives evidence of the act of injuring, for Scarry the primary object of war.

The veterans' healing process has involved the closure of individual and col-   46
lective narratives of the war. But when the healing process is ascribed to a nation, the effect is to efface the individual bodies also involved in that process. When a nation heals a wound, the wounds of individuals are subsumed in its healing. Scarry writes that the common metaphor of an army as a single body works to deny the body of the individual soldier. Yet the soldier's body that Scarry describes is the wounded body of the conventional army—the army of fronts, rears, flanks, and arteries. In the Vietnam War the army was not, from the beginning, a whole body but a body of confused signals, of infiltrated bases, mistaken identities and a confusion of allies and enemy. In this already fragmented body, remembering (that is, the wholeness of the body) is highly problematic.[36]

THE MEMORIAL AS SHRINE

The Vietnam Veterans Memorial has been the subject of an extraordinary out-   47
pouring of sentiment since it was built. Over 150,000 people attended its dedication ceremony, and some days as many as 20,000 people walk by its walls. It is presently the most visited site on the Washington Mall. The memorial has taken on all of the trappings of a religious shrine—people bring personal artifacts to leave at the wall as offerings; coffee-table books of photography document the experiences of visitors as representing a collective recovery from the war. It has also spawned the design or construction of at least 150 other memorials, including the women veterans' memorial and a memorial to the veterans of the Korean War.[37]

This rush to embrace the memorial as a cultural symbol reveals not only the   48
relief of voicing a history that has been taboo but also a desire to reinscribe that history. The black granite walls of the memorial act as a screen for myriad cultural projections; as a site for contemplation, it is easily appropriated for diverse interpretations of the war and of the experience of those who died in it. To the veterans, the wall is an atonement for their treatment since the war; to the families and friends of those who died, it is an official recognition of their sorrow and an opportunity to express a grief that was not previously sanctioned; to others, it is either a profound antiwar statement or an opportunity to rewrite the history of the war to make it fit more neatly into the master narrative of American imperialism.

The memorial's popularity must thus be seen in the context of a very active scripting and rescripting of the war and as an integral component of the recently emerged Vietnam War nostalgia industry. This nostalgia is not confined to those who wish to return to the intensity of wartime; it is also the media's nostalgia for its own moment of moral power—the Vietnam War was, shall we not forget, very good television. For Michael Clark, the media nostalgia campaign "healed over the wounds that had refused to close for ten years with a balm of nostalgia, and transformed guilt and doubt into duty and pride. And with a triumphant flourish it offered us the spectacle of its most successful creation, the veterans who will fight the next war."[38] The rush to reexamine the Vietnam War is, inevitably, a desire to rescript current political events and to reinscribe a narrative of American imperialism, most obviously in Central America and the Persian Gulf.

49

As the healing process of the Vietnam War is transformed into spectacle and commodity, a complex nostalgia industry has grown. Numerous magazines that reexamine and recount Vietnam War experiences have emerged; the merchandizing of Frederick Hart's statue (which includes posters, T-shirts, a Franklin Mint miniature, and a plastic model kit) generates about $50,000 a year, half of which goes to the VVMF and half to Hart; and travel agencies are marketing tours to Indochina for veterans.[39] In the hawkish *Vietnam* magazine, between articles that reexamine incidents in the war, advertisements display a variety of Vietnam War products: the Vietnam War Commemorative Combat Shotgun, the Vietnam Veterans Trivia Game, Vietnam War medallions, posters, T-shirts, and calendars. Needless to say, the Vietnam War is also now big business in both television drama and Hollywood movies.

50

While Maya Lin's memorial has yet to be made into a marketable reproduction, it has functioned as a catalyst for much of this nostalgia. The Vietnam Veterans Memorial is the subject of no fewer than six books, three of which are photography books.[40] The memorial has tapped into a reservoir of need to express in public the pain of this war, a desire to transfer private memories into a collective experience. The personal artifacts that have been left at the memorial—photographs, letters, teddy bears, MIA/POW bracelets, clothes, medals of honor—are offered up as testimony, transposed from personal to cultural artifacts, to bear witness to pain suffered (fig. 1). Relinquished before the wall, they tell many stories:

51

> We did what we could but it was not enough because I found you here. You are not just a name on this wall. You are alive. You are blood on my hands. You are screams in my ears. You are eyes in my soul. I told you you'd be all right, but I lied, and please forgive me. I see your face in my son, I can't bear the thought. You told me about your wife, your kids, your girl, your mother. And then you died. Your pain is mine. I'll never forget your face. I can't. You are still alive.

> I didn't want a monument, not even one as sober as that vast black wall of broken lives. I didn't want a postage stamp. I didn't want a road beside the Delaware River with a sign proclaiming: Vietnam Veterans Memorial Highway. What I wanted was a simple recognition of the limits of our

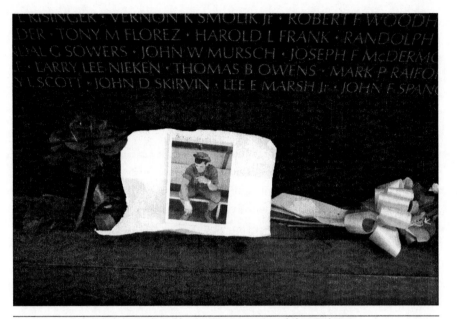

Figure 1. Memorial items left at the Vietnam Veterans Memorial. Photo: Wendy Watriss.

power as a nation to inflict our will on others. What I wanted was an understanding that the world is neither black-and-white nor ours. What I wanted was an end to monuments.[41]

Many of these letters are addressed not to visitors but to the dead (very similar to the texts of the AIDS quilt). They are messages for the dead that are intended to be shared as cultural memory.

The National Park Service, which is now in charge of maintaining the memorial, is compiling an archive of the materials left at the memorial and is storing them at the Museum and Archaeological Regional Storage facility (MARS). Originally, the Park Service classified these objects as "lost and found." Later, Park Service officials realized the artifacts had been left intentionally, and they began to save them. The objects thus moved from the cultural status of being "lost" (without category) to *historical* artifacts. They have now even been transposed into artistic artifacts; the curator of the collection at MARS writes:

52

> These are no longer objects at the Wall, they are communications, icons possessing a substructure of underpinning emotion. They are the products of culture, in all its complexities. They are the products of individual selection. With each object we are in the presence of a work of art of individual contemplation. The thing itself does not overwhelm our attention since these are objects that are common and expendable. At the Wall they have become unique and irreplaceable, and yes, mysterious.[42]

Labeled "mysterious" and coded as original works of art, these objects are given value and authorship. Many were left anonymously, or simply signed with first names, and some of those who left them have since been traced by the media and book authors. This attempt to tie these objects and letters to their creators reveals again the shifting realms of personal and cultural memory. Assigned authorship and placed in an historical archive, the objects are pulled from cultural memory— a discursive field in which they are presented to be shared and to participate in the memories of others—and made into aesthetic and historical objects. More than 5,000 of them have been left at the memorial and catalogued, tagged, and stored at MARS.

The ritual of leaving something behind can be seen as an active participation   53
in the accrual of many histories; the archiving of these artifacts also subsumes them within history. Does this archive represent the shifting territory between history and cultural memory? Michel Foucault has defined the archive as the "law of what can be said" and a "system of enunciability."[43] Certainly, the traditional archive is a limited system of enunciation with a narrative function, one that prescribes the limits of history and defines what will and will not be preserved. The archive of the Vietnam Veterans Memorial, while regulated by the government, is constituted differently than many archives. There are no regulations for what is included in the archive; it contains all artifacts left at the memorial that have been personalized in some way. This collection will have a primary effect on future interpretations of the Vietnam War and of how the country dealt with its memory. Couched within an official history—that is, in a government institution—the narratives inscribed in these letters to the dead will continue to reassert strands of cultural memory that disrupt historical narratives.

THE CONSTRUCTION OF A HISTORY

The walls of the Vietnam Veterans Memorial act as a screen for many projections   54
about the history of the Vietnam War and its aftermath. Beyond its foregrounding of individual names and the implicit condemnation of war in that listing, the memorial does not take a stand on the specific controversies about and contested versions of the Vietnam War. It has nevertheless catalyzed the writing of a particular narrative of the war, precisely because its emphasis on the veterans and war dead has allowed the discourse of heroism, sacrifice, and honor to resurface. As Thomas Myers has written, "A block of stone may be a powerful text with many subtexts, or it may be an inert simplification of historical reality that assuages memory—it depends on the readership" (192).

Much of the current embrace of the memorial smacks of historical revision-   55
ism. The memorial's placement on the Washington Mall inscribes it within a nationalist discourse, restricting in many ways the discourse of memory it can provide. In the interim between the end of the war and the positioning of the memorial as a national wailing wall, there has also been plenty of opportunity for memories and culpability to fade. It is rarely noted that in none of the discussion surrounding the memorial are the Vietnamese people ever mentioned. This is not a memorial to their loss; it does not even recognize that loss. They cannot even be named in the context of the Mall. Key players in this historical drama such as Lyndon Johnson, Richard Nixon, and Henry Kissinger also remain noticeably absent in the memorial discourse. In the context of this outpouring of grief, the

intricate reasons *why* the lives represented by the inscribed names were lost in vain remain absent.

Thus, remembering is in itself a form of forgetting. Does the remembrance of the battles fought by the veterans in Vietnam and at home necessarily eclipse and screen out any acknowledgment of the war's effect on the Vietnamese, in whose country the war was fought? Does the process of public commemoration of a war necessitate choosing sides?[44]   56

The act of commemoration is a legitimation process, one that Ehrenhaus notes "entails reaffirming the legitimacy of purpose for which a community has issued its call for sacrifice" (97). If that purpose has been highly contested, the act of commemoration would seem to necessitate the choice of one narrative over another. The Vietnam Veterans Memorial has spawned two very different kinds of remembrance: one a retrenched historical narrative that attempts to rewrite the Vietnam War in a way that reinscribes American imperialism and the masculinity of the American soldier, the other a textured and complex discourse of remembrance that has allowed the Americans affected by this war—the veterans, their families, and the families and friends of the war dead—to speak of loss, pain, and futility. The screens of the memorial thus act as screen memories in two senses: they attempt to conceal and to offer themselves as the primary narrative, while they provide a screen for projections of a multitude of memories and individual interpretations.[45]   57

The incommunicability of Vietnam War experience has been mollified by the communicability of the experience of its memorial. Yet, we cannot understand the role played by this memorial, by its *difference* as a memorial, unless we understand what made the war it memorializes different. In the Vietnam War, the standard definitions of warfare had no meaning. This was a war in which the enemy was not always known, and in which master narratives of "free" world versus communism and first-world technology versus third-world "peasantry" were no longer credible. The rupture in history made by the Vietnam War is not only of the experience of warfare and the ability of this country to impose its will on others; it is a rupture in how we perceive war. It now appears that there are desperate attempts to conceal and suture that rupture, and to reinscribe in wars such as the recent Persian Gulf War these narratives of American technological superiority, masculinity, and imperial power. Couched within nationalist discourse yet the catalyst for a rich and diverse discourse on the tragic and futile aspects of war, the memorial stands in a precarious space between these opposing discourses.   58

NOTES

I would like to thank Vicente Diaz, Hayden White, Donna Haraway, Vivian Sobchack, Mary John, Marcy Darnovsky, and the editors of *Representations* for their helpful criticisms of previous drafts of this essay.

1. Peter Ehrenhaus, "Commemorating the Unwon War: On *Not* Remembering Vietnam," *Journal of Communication* 39, no. 1 (Winter 1989): 96. Subsequent citations will be given in parentheses in the text.

2. Attempts to give the Persian Gulf War a simple and neat narrative reinscribing master narratives of World War II—in which, for example, the United States liberates a desperate and weak country imperiled by a dangerous tyrant—make it clear that the disruptive and fragmentary narrative of the Vietnam War is not due simply to its situation in the late twentieth century. Current government and military administrations learned many things from the Vietnam War: the importance of the kind of finely tuned war narrative the Vietnam War lacked, as well as the need for military censorship and for quickly putting American lives at stake to foreclose debate on the war.

3. Each row contains five names, with space at the end of each line where additional names have been added. There is a system of distinguishing the names of the unverified dead from the classifiably dead. Each name is preceded by a diamond shape; in the case of the 1,300 POW/MIAs, the name is preceded by a small cross that is then changed to a diamond in the event that the remains of that person are identified. If that MIA should return alive, this symbol would be changed to a circle (but, as one volunteer told me at the memorial, "We don't have any circles yet").

4. Arthur C. Danto, "The Vietnam Veterans Memorial," *The Nation,* 31 August 1985, 152.

5. Charles L. Griswold, "The Vietnam Veterans Memorial and the Washington Mall: Philosophical Thoughts on Political Iconography," *Critical Inquiry* 12 (Summer 1986): 689.

6. I do not mean to imply that these are hard-and-fast rules. There are many World War I and World War II memorials in Europe, for instance, that list the dead. (For example, memorial designer Maya Lin was influenced in her design by a memorial in Thiepval, France, for the dead of the Somme offensive in World War I, which consists of a great arch inscribed with 73,000 names.) These are, however, memorials and not monuments, albeit memorials of a victorious cause. Their emphasis is thus not on celebrating victory as much as mourning the price in lives of that victory.

7. Tom Wolfe, "Art Disputes War: The Battle of the Vietnam Memorial," *Washington Post,* 13 October 1982, B4.

8. Carl Andre's work, which consists of thirty-six large boulders positioned on a lawn near Hartford's city hall, is widely regarded with derision by residents as a symbol of the misguided judgments of their city government. Richard Serra's now notorious *Tilted Arc,* an oppressive, leaning slab of Cor-Ten steel that bisected the equally inhospitable Federal Plaza in New York, was dismantled in March 1989, after several years of controversy, when workers in the Federal Building petitioned to have it removed. See Kenneth Baker, "Andre in Retrospect," *Art in America,* April 1980; Patricia C. Phillips, "Forum: Something There Is That Doesn't Love a Wall," *Artforum,* Summer 1985; Robert Storr, "'Tilted Arc': Enemy of the People?" *Art in America,* September 1985.

9. See Rosalind Krauss, "Sculpture in the Expanded Field," in *The Anti-Aesthetic: Essays on Postmodern Culture,* ed. by Hal Foster (Port Townsend,

Wash., 1983). The site-specificity of the Vietnam Veterans Memorial is crucial to its position as both subversive of and continuous within the nationalist discourse of the Mall. Maya Lin calls herself "super site-specific" and did not decide on the final design until she visited the site. However, a traveling version of the wall has toured the country with powerful effect. This effect would seem to be the result of the traveling wall's reference of the site-specific wall, in addition to the power evoked by the inscribed names in whatever location.

10. These attacks came mostly from a certain faction of veterans and members of the "New Right," including veteran Tom Carhart, who had been involved in the VVMF; Phyllis Schafly; and millionaire Ross Perot, who had contributed the money for the design contest.

11. Tom Carhart, quoted in Elizabeth Hess, "Vietnam: Memorials of Misfortune," in *Unwinding the Vietnam War: From War into Peace,* ed. Reese Williams (Seattle, 1987), 265. This argument against the color black was quickly ended by Gen. George Price, who is black, who said at a meeting concerning the memorial, "Black is not the color of shame. I am tired of hearing it called such by you. Color meant nothing on the battlefields of Korea and Vietnam. We are all equal in combat. Color should mean nothing now"; quoted in Jan C. Scruggs and Joel Swerdlow, *To Heal a Nation: The Vietnam Veterans Memorial* (New York, 1985). Subsequent citations for both these texts will be given in parentheses in the text.

12. "Stop that Monument," *National Review,* 18 September 1981, 1064. What the editors of *National Review* did not take into account in their interpretation of the memorial's **V** as the peace sign is the malleability of this particular symbol, one that was easily appropriated by Richard Nixon, for instance, with both hands waving in the air, to symbolize his personal political victory. The memorial actually seems to take on many shapes in the innumerable photographs of it. It could conceivably be seen as evoking the shape of an airplane's wings, although I have never heard this comparison made. Lin has stated that she never saw it as a **V** but as a circle.

13. Michael Sorkin, "What Happens When a Woman Designs a War Monument?" *Vogue,* May 1983, 122.

14. Maya Lin, quoted in "America Remembers: Vietnam Veterans Memorial," *National Geographic* 167, no. 5 (May 1985): 557.

15. From "An Interview with Maya Lin," in Williams, *Unwinding the Vietnam War,* 271.

16. Frederick Hart was reportedly paid more than ten times the $20,000 fee that Maya Lin received for her design from the same fund. See Peter Tauber, "Monument Maker," *New York Times Magazine,* 24 February 1991, 53.

17. From "An Interview with Frederick Hart," in Williams, *Unwinding the Vietnam War,* 274.

18. It is interesting to note that this status is heavily dependent on modern codes of realism. The Marine Corps War Memorial is based on a famous Pulitzer Prize-winning photograph taken by photojournalist Joe Rosenthal, and thus

coded as a moment captured from reality. Of the six men in the photograph, three survived the war and posed for sculptor Felix W. de Weldon. However, the famous Rosenthal photograph was, in fact, a restaging of the actual event of the flag raising. See Marvin Heiferman, "One Nation, Chiseled in Pictures: The Monumental Nature of American Photography," in "Lee Friedlander: American Monuments," *The Archive* (Center for Creative Photography, Tucson, no. 25, n.d.); and the National Parks Service brochure of the United States Marine Corps War Memorial.

19. Lin told *National Geographic,* "Later, when I visited, I searched out the name of a friend's father. I touched it and I cried. I was another visitor, and I was reacting as I had designed it"; "America Remembers," 557.

20. Since the construction of both of these memorials, there have been approximately 150 memorials to the Vietnam veterans built or proposed around the country. Elizabeth Hess notes that "for the most part, it is Frederick Hart, rather than Maya Lin, who has managed to set (conservative) aesthetic and ideological precedents for the cloning of the Vietnam memorial. A strong desire to diminish, rather than engage the radical elements in Lin's design is evident in the majority of these new memorials"; "Vietnam," 275. However, Lin has continued in her career to have influence on the aesthetics of memorials. She recently designed a civil rights memorial for the Southern Poverty Law Center in Montgomery, Alabama, which adds water to the motif of names inscribed on a wall; people touch the names of those martyred in the civil rights movement as water runs over the inscriptions.

21. William Broyles, Jr., "Remembering a War We Want to Forget," *Newsweek,* 22 November 1982, 82.

22. See Associated Press, "38 Living Veterans May Be on Memorial," *San Jose Mercury News,* 15 February 1991, 6F. The reason for this error appears to be the result of faulty record keeping by the Defense Department and a 1973 fire that destroyed many records. Robert Doubek, a cofounder of the VVMF, decided to include thirty-eight names of casualties for which there were incomplete records because he felt it was better to err by inclusion rather than omission.

23. It has been barely noted in the media, for instance, that the Tomb of the Unknown Soldier for the Vietnam War, which was approved by Congress in 1974, was left empty and uninscribed until 1984, when some publicity drew attention to the situation. The ostensible reason for this delay was, according to the army, that there were no unidentifiable remains. (In fact, the army had several unidentified remains that they were refusing, under some pressure from MIA families, to finally classify as such.) Technology's ability to decipher the individual status of the body, and hence achieve a kind of closure, is thus at stake here. See Ehrenhaus, "Commemorating the Unwon War," 105.

24. Walter Benjamin, *Illuminations,* trans. Harry Zohn (New York, 1969), 84.

25. George Swiers, "'Demented Vets' and Other Myths—The Moral Obligation of Veterans," *in Vietnam Reconsidered: Lessons From a War,* ed. Harrison Salisbury (New York, 1984), 198.

26. Thomas Myers, *Walking Point: American Narratives of Vietnam* (New York, 1988), 190. Subsequent citations will be given in parentheses in the text.

27. Peter Marin, "Conclusion," in Salisbury, *Vietnam Reconsidered,* 213.

28. See Keith Walker, *A Piece of My Heart: The Stories of Twenty-Six Women Who Served in Vietnam* (Novato, Calif., 1985), 2.

29. Susan Wolf, "Women and Vietnam: Remembering in the 1980s," in Williams, *Unwinding the Vietnam War,* 245.

30. See Barbara Gamarekian, "Competition Opens on War Memorial," *New York Times,* 20 August 1990, A16.

31. Hess, "Vietnam," 276. Hence, the singular narrative of Hart's realist depiction is one of inclusion and exclusion. This would also account for why so much has been written about the ethnicity of the three men in the statue—one is obviously black, but the two others are ambiguous, leading some observers to call them Jewish or Hispanic. Not surprisingly, Lin is not happy with the potential addition of the women's statue. The congressional bill for the women's statue stipulates that it will be the last addition to the memorial, but according to *The Nation,* there are already other groups such as Air Force pilots, Navy seamen, and Native Americans who are demanding their own statues, as well as occasional attempts (including one at the time of the initial debate) to erect a flag in the center of the walls' V. See David Corn and Jefferson Morley, "Beltway Bandits," *The Nation,* 4 June 1988, 780. Corn and Morley, like many other commentators, have mistakenly assumed that these constituents feel left out of the wall. It would appear, however, that it is Hart's statue that makes them feel excluded.

32. See Susan Jeffords' extensive study, *The Remasculinization of America: Gender and the Vietnam War* (Bloomington, Ind., 1989).

33. The Vietnamese have been portrayed metaphorically in feminine terms in many Vietnam War narratives. In two recent Hollywood films, *Full Metal Jacket* (1987) and *Casualties of War* (1989), for instance, a Vietnamese woman comes to symbolize Vietnam in general. The absence of Vietnamese male protagonists in American Vietnam War films is notable.

34. The film *Born on the Fourth of July* (1989), based on veteran Ron Kovic's auto-biography, foregrounds the veteran body. Between the requisite scenes of Kovic as a patriotic, young American and his awakening as an antiwar activist, the film concentrates on the painful details of his life as a paraplegic—the wounded veteran body, impotent, with uncontrollable bodily fluids, attempting to heal in a squalid VA hospital.

35. Elaine Scarry, *The Body in Pain: The Making and Unmaking of the World* (New York, 1985), 116.

36. The high proportion of American soldiers killed by "friendly fire" in the Persian Gulf War also undermines the traditional notion of the conventional army moving forward as a singular body. If you can be killed so easily by friendly fire, then does it matter if you know who the enemy is or not?

37. Most of these memorials have conventional realist designs, but several stand out in their innovative approaches to commemoration. One project in

Wisconsin includes a hundred-acre memorial park and museum for artifacts and memorabilia, and other projects include memorial trees and time capsules. See Elizabeth Hess, "Vietnam"; and Ben A. Franklin, "143 Vietnam Memorials, Vast and Small, Rising Around Nation," *New York Times,* 9 November 1986, 26. The New York Veterans Memorial in downtown Manhattan, like the memorial in Washington, also privileges text. It consists of a wall of glass brick onto which are inscribed quotes from letters written by veterans as well as quotes from newspapers and politicians.

38. Michael Clark, "Remembering Vietnam," *Cultural Critique 3* (Spring 1986): 49.

39. Joshua Hammer, "Cashing in on Vietnam," *Newsweek,* 16 January 1989, 39. Evidence of the potential marketing power of the wall can be found in the rather perverse recent campaigns of two companies, Coors Brewing Company and Service Corporation International, a funeral and cemetery conglomerate. Both have built their own "moving" walls for marketing purposes, against the wishes of the veterans in charge of the traveling memorial. See Michelle Guido, "A Wall Divided by Commercialism," *San Jose Mercury News,* 14 March 1991, 1A.

40. In addition to Scruggs's book, these are: Saul Lopes, ed., *The Wall: Images and Offerings from the Vietnam Veterans Memorial* (New York, 1987); Lydia Fish, *The Last Firebase: A Guide to the Vietnam Veterans Memorial* (Shippensburg, Pa., 1987); Michael Katakis, *The Vietnam Veterans Memorial* (New York, 1988); Duncan Spencer, *Facing the Wall: Americans at the Vietnam Veterans Memorial* (New York, 1986); and Laura Palmer, *Shrapnel in the Heart: Letters and Remembrances from the Vietnam Veterans Memorial* (New York, 1988).

41. See Lopes, *The Wall,* 56, 121.

42. David Guynes, quoted in Fish, *Last Firebase,* 54.

43. Michel Foucault, *The Archaeology of Knowledge,* trans. A. M. Sheridan (New York, 1972), 129.

44. That the Vietnamese are excluded from this discourse about the war, and represented only as anonymous figures in contemporary Vietnam War films, points of course to the central question of why this war was fought. If the remembrance of the war in the United States excludes the Vietnamese, then perhaps it points to the real reason for the war, not to "save" a foreign country but to retain the image of a world power for the United States. Hannah Arendt has written, "This enterprise was exclusively guided by the needs of a superpower to create for itself an *image* which would *convince* the world that it was indeed 'the mightiest power on earth'"; see "Home to Roost: A Bicentennial Address," *New York Review of Books* 22, no. 11 (26 June 1976): 4. The parallels to the recent Persian Gulf War are painfully obvious. The reiteration in popular-culture Vietnam War representations that the war was not about Vietnam but about us (for instance, the protagonist in *Platoon* says that "we did not fight the enemy, we fought ourselves—and the enemy was in us") also effaces the Vietnamese and the devastation of their country.

45. The limitations of this memory in the nationalist context became particularly clear in the recent appropriations of the Vietnam Veterans Memorial in the antiwar movement of the Persian Gulf War. As testament to the iconic status of the memorial as a statement about the human costs of war, there were several "Desert Storm Memorial Walls" in evidence at antiwar rallies. Here, the inscription of ten to twenty American names seemed ludicrous in light of reports that hundreds of thousands of Iraqis were being killed. At the University of California, Santa Cruz, where the student antiwar movement constructed a memorial wall at the base of campus, someone responded by scrawling "85,000 to 100,000 Iraqis but Who's Counting, Proud Yet?" in spraypaint after the short list of American names. It would seem then that this project backfired. Appropriations of the memorial for the Persian Gulf War thus demonstrated both the iconic power of the memorial as well as its limitations.

Dave Barry (1947–   ) was born in Armonk, New York, and earned a B.A. from Haverford College in 1969. He's been a reporter and a freelance columnist, and has had a regular column in *The Miami Herald* since 1983, which has subsequently been widely syndicated. Barry won the Pulitzer Prize in 1988, one of a very select few to do so for humorous commentary. He is the author of numerous best-selling books, including *Dave Barry in Cyberspace* (1996) and the novel *Big Trouble* (1999). "Red, White, and Beer" was first published in *The Miami Herald* in 1988 and collected in *Dave Barry's Greatest Hits* the same year.

Red, White, and Beer

Dave Barry

Lately I've been feeling very patriotic, especially during commercials. Like, when I see those strongly pro-American Chrysler commercials, the ones where the winner of the Bruce Springsteen Sound-Alike Contest sings about how The Pride Is Back, the ones where Lee Iacocca himself comes striding out and practically challenges the president of Toyota to a knife fight, I get this warm, proud feeling inside, the same kind of feeling I get whenever we hold routine naval maneuvers off the coast of Libya.

But if you want to talk about *real* patriotism, of course, you have to talk about beer commercials. I would have to say that Miller is the most patriotic brand of beer. I grant you it tastes like rat saliva, but we are not talking about taste here. What we are talking about, according to the commercials, is that Miller is by God an *American* beer, "born and brewed in the U.S.A.," and the men who drink it are American men, the kind of men who aren't afraid to perspire freely and shake a man's hand. That's mainly what happens in Miller commercials: Burly American men go around, drenched in perspiration, shaking each other's hands in a violent and patriotic fashion.

You never find out exactly why these men spend so much time shaking hands. Maybe shaking hands is just their simple straightforward burly masculine American patriotic way of saying to each other: "Floyd, I am truly sorry I drank all that Miller beer last night and went to the bathroom in your glove compartment." Another possible explanation is that, since there are never any women in the part of America where beer commercials are made, the burly men have become lonesome and desperate for any form of physical contact. I have noticed that sometimes, in addition to shaking hands, they hug each other. Maybe very late at night, after the David Letterman show, there are Miller commercials in which the burly men engage in slow dancing. I don't know.

I do know that in one beer commercial, I think this is for Miller—although it could be for Budweiser, which is also a very patriotic beer—the burly men build a house. You see them all getting together and pushing up a brand-new wall. Me, I

1

2

3

4

worry some about a house built by men drinking beer. In my experience, you run into trouble when you ask a group of beer-drinking men to perform any task more complex than remembering not to light the filter ends of cigarettes.

For example, in my younger days, whenever anybody in my circle of friends wanted to move, he'd get the rest of us to help, and, as an inducement, he'd buy a couple of cases of beer. This almost always produced unfortunate results, such as the time we were trying to move Dick "The Wretch" Curry from a horrible fourth-floor walk-up apartment in Manhattan's Lower East Side to another horrible fourth-floor walk-up apartment in Manhattan's Lower East Side, and we hit upon the labor-saving concept of, instead of carrying The Wretch's possessions manually down the stairs, simply dropping them out the window, down onto the street, where The Wretch was racing around, gathering up the broken pieces of his life and shrieking at us to stop helping him move, his emotions reaching a fever pitch when his bed, which had been swinging wildly from a rope, entered the apartment two floors below his through what had until seconds earlier been a window.

5

This is the kind of thinking you get, with beer. So I figure what happens, in the beer commercial where the burly men are building the house, is they push the wall up so it's vertical, and then, after the camera stops filming them, they just keep pushing, and the wall crashes down on the other side, possibly onto somebody's pickup truck. And then they all shake hands.

6

But other than that, I'm in favor of the upsurge in retail patriotism, which is lucky for me because the airwaves are saturated with pro-American commercials. Especially popular are commercials in which the newly restored Statue of Liberty—and by the way, I say Lee Iacocca should get some kind of medal for that, or at least be elected president—appears to be endorsing various products, as if she were Mary Lou Retton or somebody. I saw one commercial strongly suggesting that the Statue of Liberty uses Sure brand underarm deodorant.

7

I have yet to see a patriotic laxative commercial, but I imagine it's only a matter of time. They'll show some actors dressed up as hard-working country folk, maybe at a church picnic, smiling at each other and eating pieces of pie. At least one of them will be a black person. The Statue of Liberty will appear in the background. Then you'll hear a country-style singer singing:

8

> Folks 'round here they love this land;
> They stand by their beliefs;
> An' when they git themselves stopped up;
> They want some quick relief.

Well, what do you think? Pretty good commercial concept, huh?

9

Nah, you're right. They'd never try to pull something like that. They'd put the statue in the *foreground.*

10

Literacy and
Artistic Expression

W. E. B. Du Bois (1868–1963) was an author, historian, sociologist, and civil rights activist, among numerous other pursuits. Du Bois, an African American, grew up in a predominately white neighborhood in western Massachusetts. Du Bois' mother, Mary Sivlina Burghardt, was a landowner in Massachusetts, a rarity in her day. Du Bois' father, Alfred, was from Haiti. His grandfather, Dr. James Du Bois, was a wealthy man from the Bahamas who fathered seven children with his slave mistresses. Alfred was one of those children. In later years, Alfred met Mary, and William (W. E. B.) was born. Alfred abandoned his wife and son; Mary had a stroke that left her unable to work. Young William was determined that education would help improve the lives of both his mother and himself. Du Bois stayed true to his beliefs. In 1888, he earned a degree from Fisk University, a historically black college. That same year, in the fall of 1888, Du Bois won a $250 scholarship and was admitted to Harvard University. In 1892, he was granted a stipend to pursue graduate work at the University of Berlin. In 1895, Du Bois was awarded his Ph.D., the first Harvard had granted to an African American. Du Bois' major works include *The Philadelphia Negro* (1899), *The Souls of Black Folks* (1903), *The Negro* (1915), and *Black Reconstruction* (1935). In 1961, Du Bois was invited to Ghana to direct a project in which he was most interested, compiling for the government the *Encyclopedia Africana*. Du Bois was refused a passport renewal to return to the United States. He died in Ghana in 1963, just one day before Martin Luther King's "I Have a Dream Speech." Du Bois was ninety-five.

Of Our Spiritual Strivings

W. E. B. Du Bois

> O water, voice of my heart, crying in the sand,
>   All night long crying with a mournful cry,
> As I lie and listen, and cannot understand
>   The voice of my heart in my side or the voice of the sea,
> O water, crying for rest, is it I, is it I?
>   All night long the water is crying to me.
>
> Unresting water, there shall never be rest
>   Till the last moon droop and the last tide fail,
> And the fire of the end begin to burn in the west;
>   And the heart shall be weary and wonder and cry like the sea,
> All life long crying without avail,
>   As the water all night long is crying to me.

ARTHUR SYMONS.

W. E. B. Du Bois, "Of Our Spiritual Strivings" from *The Souls of Black Folks*. Chicago: A. C. McClurg & Co., 1903.

Between me and the other world there is ever an unasked question: unasked by some through feelings of delicacy; by others through the difficulty of rightly framing it. All, nevertheless, flutter round it. They approach me in a half-hesitant sort of way, eye me curiously or compassionately, and then, instead of saying directly, How does it feel to be a problem? they say, I know an excellent colored man in my town; or, I fought at Mechanicsville; or, Do not these Southern outrages make your blood boil? At these I smile, or am interested, or reduce the boiling to a simmer, as the occasion may require. To the real question, How does it feel to be a problem? I answer seldom a word.

And yet, being a problem is a strange experience,—peculiar even for one who has never been anything else, save perhaps in babyhood and in Europe. It is in the early days of rollicking boyhood that the revelation first bursts upon one, all in a day, as it were. I remember well when the shadow swept across me. I was a little thing, away up in the hills of New England, where the dark Housatonic winds between Hoosac and Taghkanic to the sea. In a wee wooden schoolhouse, something put it into the boys' and girls' heads to buy gorgeous visiting-cards—ten cents a package—and exchange. The exchange was merry, till one girl, a tall newcomer, refused my card,—refused it peremptorily, with a glance. Then it dawned upon me with a certain suddenness that I was different from the others; or like, mayhap, in heart and life and longing, but shut out from their world by a vast veil. I had thereafter no desire to tear down that veil, to creep through; I held all beyond it in common contempt, and lived above it in a region of blue sky and great wandering shadows. That sky was bluest when I could beat my mates at examination-time, or beat them at a foot-race, or even beat their stringy heads. Alas, with the years all this fine contempt began to fade; for the worlds I longed for, and all their dazzling opportunities, were theirs, not mine. But they should not keep these prizes, I said; some, all, I would wrest from them. Just how I would do it I could never decide: by reading law, by healing the sick, by telling the wonderful tales that swam in my head,—some way. With other black boys the strife was not so fiercely sunny: their youth shrunk into tasteless sycophancy, or, into silent, hatred of the pale world about them and mocking distrust of everything white; or wasted itself in a bitter cry, Why did God make me an outcast and a stranger in mine own house? The shades of the prison-house closed round about us all: walls strait and stubborn to the whitest, but relentlessly narrow, tall, and unscalable to sons of night who must plod darkly on in resignation, or beat unavailing palms against the stone, or steadily, half hopelessly, watch the streak of blue above.

After the Egyptian and Indian, the Greek and Roman, the Teuton and Mongolian, the Negro is a sort of seventh son, born with a veil, and gifted with second-sight in this American world,—a world which yields him no true self-consciousness, but only lets him see himself through the revelation of the other world. It is a peculiar sensation, this double-consciousness, this sense of always looking at one's self through the eyes of others, of measuring one's soul by the tape of a world that looks on in amused contempt and pity. One ever feels his twoness,—an American, a Negro; two souls, two thoughts, two unreconciled strivings;

two warring ideals in one dark body, whose dogged strength alone keeps it from being torn asunder.

The history of the American Negro is the history of this strife,—this longing to attain self-conscious manhood, to merge his double self into a better and truer self. In this merging he wishes neither of the older selves to be lost. He would not Africanize America, for America has too much to teach the world and Africa. He would not bleach his Negro soul in a flood of white Americanism, for he knows that Negro blood has a message for the world. He simply wishes to make it possible for a man to be both a Negro and an American, without being cursed and spit upon by his fellows, without having the doors of Opportunity closed roughly in his face.

4

This, then, is the end of his striving: to be a co-worker in the kingdom of culture, to escape both death and isolation, to husband and use his best powers and his latent genius. These powers of body and mind have in the past been strangely wasted, dispersed, or forgotten. The shadow of a mighty Negro past flits through the tale of Ethiopia the Shadowy and of Egypt the Sphinx. Throughout history, the powers of single black men flash here and there like falling stars, and die sometimes before the world has rightly gauged their brightness. Here in America, in the few days since Emancipation, the black man's turning hither and thither in hesitant and doubtful striving has often made his very strength to lose effectiveness, to seem like absence of power, like weakness. And yet it is not weakness,—it is the contradiction of double aims. The double-aimed struggle of the black artisan—on the one hand to escape white contempt for a nation of mere hewers of wood and drawers of water, and on the other hand to plough and nail and dig for a poverty-stricken horde—could only result in making him a poor craftsman, for he had but half a heart in either cause. By the poverty and ignorance of his people, the Negro minister or doctor was tempted toward quackery and demagogy; and by the criticism of the other world, toward ideals that made him ashamed of his lowly tasks. The would-be black *savant* was confronted by the paradox that the knowledge his people needed was a twice-told tale to his white neighbors, while the knowledge which would teach the white world was Greek to his own flesh and blood. The innate love of harmony and beauty that set the ruder souls of his people a-dancing and a-singing raised but confusion and doubt in the soul of the black artist; for the beauty revealed to him was the soul-beauty of a race which his larger audience despised, and he could not articulate the message of another people. This waste of double aims, this seeking to satisfy two unreconciled ideals, has wrought sad havoc with the courage and faith and deeds of ten thousand thousand people,—has sent them often wooing false gods and invoking false means of salvation, and at times has even seemed about to make them ashamed of themselves.

5

Away back in the days of bondage they thought to see in one divine event the end of all doubt and disappointment; few men ever worshipped Freedom with half such unquestioning faith as did the American Negro for two centuries. To him, so far as he thought and dreamed, slavery was indeed the sum of all villainies, the cause of all sorrow, the root of all prejudice; Emancipation was the key to a promised land of sweeter beauty than ever stretched before the eyes of wearied

6

Israelites. In song and exhortation swelled one refrain—Liberty; in his tears and curses the God he implored had Freedom in his right hand. At last it came,— suddenly, fearfully, like a dream. With one wild carnival of blood and passion came the message in his own plaintive cadences:—

"Shout, O children!
Shout, you're free!
For God has bought your liberty!"

Years have passed away since then,—ten, twenty, forty; forty years of national life, forty years of renewal and development, and yet the swarthy spectre sits in its accustomed seat at the Nation's feast. In vain do we cry to this our vastest social problem:— 7

"Take any shape but that, and my firm nerves
Shall never tremble!"

The Nation has not yet found peace from its sins; the freedman has not yet found in freedom his promised land. Whatever of good may have come in these years of change, the shadow of a deep disappointment rests upon the Negro people,—a disappointment all the more bitter because the unattained ideal was unbounded save by the simple ignorance of a lowly people.

The first decade was merely a prolongation of the vain search for freedom, the boon that seemed ever barely to elude their grasp,—like a tantalizing will-o'-the-wisp, maddening and misleading the headless host. The holocaust of war, the terrors of the Ku Klux Klan, the lies of carpetbaggers, the disorganization of industry, and the contradictory advice of friends and foes, left the bewildered serf with no new watchword beyond the old cry for freedom. As the time flew, however, he began to grasp a new idea. The ideal of liberty demanded for its attainment powerful means, and these the Fifteenth Amendment gave him. The ballot, which before he had looked upon as a visible sign of freedom, he now regarded as the chief means of gaining and perfecting the liberty with which war had partially endowed him. And why not? Had not votes made war and emancipated millions? Had not votes enfranchised the freedmen? Was anything impossible to a power that had done all this? A million black men started with renewed zeal to vote themselves into the kingdom. So the decade flew away, the revolution of 1876 came, and left the half-free serf weary, wondering, but still inspired. Slowly but steadily, in the following years, a new vision began gradually to replace the dream of political power,—a powerful movement, the rise of another ideal to guide the unguided, another pillar of fire by night after a clouded day. It was the ideal of "book-learning"; the curiosity, born of compulsory ignorance, to know and test the power of the cabalistic letters of the white man, the longing to know. Here at last seemed to have been discovered the mountain path to Canaan; longer than the highway of Emancipation and law, steep and rugged, but straight, leading to heights high enough to overlook life.

Up the new path the advance guard toiled, slowly, heavily, doggedly; only those who have watched and guided the faltering feet, the misty minds, the dull 9 understandings, of the dark pupils of these schools know how faithfully, how piteously, this people strove to learn. It was weary work. The cold statistician wrote down the inches of progress here and there, noted also where here and there a foot had slipped or some one had fallen. To the tired climbers, the horizon was ever dark, the mists were often cold, the Canaan was always dim and far away. If, however, the vistas disclosed as yet no goal, no resting-place, little but flattery and criticism, the journey at least gave leisure for reflection and self-examination; it changed the child of Emancipation to the youth with dawning self-consciousness, self-realization, self-respect. In those sombre forests of his striving his own soul rose before him, and he saw himself,—darkly as through a veil; and yet he saw in himself some faint revelation of his power, of his mission. He began to have a dim feeling that, to attain his place in the world, he must be himself, and not another. For the first time he sought to analyze the burden he bore upon his back, that dead-weight of social degradation partially masked behind a half-named Negro problem. He felt his poverty; without a cent, without a home, without land, tools, or savings, he had entered into competition with rich, landed, skilled neighbors. To be a poor man is hard, but to be a poor race in a land of dollars is the very bottom of hardships. He felt the weight of his ignorance,—not simply of letters, but of life, of business, of the humanities; the accumulated sloth and shirking and awkwardness of decades and centuries shackled his hands and feet. Nor was his burden all poverty and ignorance. The red stain of bastardy, which two centuries of systematic legal defilement of Negro women had stamped upon his race, meant not only the loss of ancient African chastity, but also the hereditary weight of a mass of corruption from white adulterers, threatening almost the obliteration of the Negro home.

A people thus handicapped ought not to be asked to race with the world, but 10 rather allowed to give all its time and thought to its own social problems. But alas! while sociologists gleefully count his bastards and his prostitutes, the very soul of the toiling, sweating black man is darkened by the shadow of a vast despair. Men call the shadow prejudice, and learnedly explain it as the natural defence of culture against barbarism, learning against ignorance, purity against crime, the "higher" against the "lower" races. To which the Negro cries Amen! and swears that to so much of this strange prejudice as is founded on just homage to civilization, culture, righteousness, and progress, he humbly bows and meekly does obeisance. But before that nameless prejudice that leaps beyond all this he stands helpless, dismayed, and well-nigh speechless; before that personal disrespect and mockery, the ridicule and systematic humiliation, the distortion of fact and wanton license of fancy, the cynical ignoring of the better and the boisterous welcoming of the worse, the all-pervading desire to inculcate disdain for everything black, from Toussaint to the devil,—before this there rises a sickening despair that would disarm and discourage any nation save that black host to whom "discouragement" is an unwritten word.

But the facing of so vast a prejudice could not but bring the inevitable self- 11 questioning, self-disparagement, and lowering of ideals which ever accompany repression and breed in an atmosphere of contempt and hate. Whisperings and portents came borne upon the four winds: Lo! we are diseased and dying, cried the dark hosts; we cannot write, our voting is vain; what need of education, since we must always cook and serve? And the Nation echoed and enforced this self-criticism, saying: Be content to be servants, and nothing more; what need of higher culture for half-men? Away with the black man's ballot, by force or fraud,— and behold the suicide of a race! Nevertheless, out of the evil came something of good,—the more careful adjustment of education to real life, the clearer perception of the Negroes' social responsibilities, and the sobering realization of the meaning of progress.

So dawned the time of *Sturm und Drang*: storm and stress to-day rocks our lit-   12
tle boat on the mad waters of the world-sea; there is within and without the sound of conflict, the burning of body and rending of soul; inspiration strives with doubt, and faith with vain questionings. The bright ideals of the past,—physical freedom, political power, the training of brains and the training of hands,—all these in turn have waxed and waned, until even the last grows dim and overcast. Are they all wrong,—all false? No, not that, but each alone was over-simple and incomplete,— the dreams of a credulous race-childhood, or the fond imaginings of the other world which does not know and does not want to know our power. To be really true, all these ideals must be melted and welded into one. The training of the schools we need to-day more than ever,—the training of deft hands, quick eyes and ears, and above all the broader, deeper, higher culture of gifted minds and pure hearts. The power of the ballot we need in sheer self-defence,—else what shall save us from a second slavery? Freedom, too, the long-sought, we still seek,—the freedom of life and limb, the freedom to work and think, the freedom to love and aspire. Work, culture, liberty,—all these we need, not singly but together, not successively but together, each growing and aiding each, and all striving toward that vaster ideal that swims before the Negro people, the ideal of human brotherhood, gained through the unifying ideal of Race; the ideal of fostering and developing the traits and talents of the Negro, not in opposition to or contempt for other races, but rather in large conformity to the greater ideals of the American Republic, in order that some day on American soil two world-races may give each to each those characteristics both so sadly lack. We the darker ones come even now not altogether empty-handed: there are to-day no truer exponents of the pure human spirit of the Declaration of Independence than the American Negroes; there is no true American music but the wild sweet melodies of the Negro slave; the American fairy tales and folk-lore are Indian and African; and, all in all, we black men seem the sole oasis of simple faith and reverence in a dusty desert of dollars and smartness. Will America be poorer if she replace her brutal dyspeptic blundering with light-hearted but determined Negro humility? or her coarse and cruel wit with loving jovial good-humor? or her vulgar music with the soul of the Sorrow Songs?

Merely a concrete test of the underlying principles of the great republic is the   13
Negro Problem, and the spiritual striving of the freedmen's sons is the travail of souls whose burden is almost beyond the measure of their strength, but who bear it in the name of an historic race, in the name of this land of their fathers' fathers, and in the name of human opportunity.

Robert Frost (1874–1963) was born in San Francisco but moved to Massachusetts after his father's death in 1884. The family had originally been from New England, and Frost lived in rural New England for most of the rest of his life. By the age of fifteen he had decided to be a poet. His first published poem was "My Butterfly," which was published in the *New York Independent* in 1894. He continued to write and send out poems, but only thirteen more of his poems were published over the next eight years. Frost supported himself with odd jobs while studying at Dartmouth College and Harvard University, but college did not suit him and he was never graduated from either school.

Feeling that his poetry was not understood by U.S. publishers, Frost moved to England in 1912. His first two collections, *A Boy's Will* (1913) and *North of Boston* (1914), were published there and made him an instant celebrity. He returned to the United States in 1915, continuing to publish poetry and beginning the first, at Tufts College, of many stints as poet-in-residence at various universities and colleges. He spent most of his professional time at Amherst College, where he taught English and was poet-in-residence in 1916–1920, 1923–1925, and 1926–1928. He cofounded the Bread Loaf School in Middlebury, Vermont, in 1920, and after 1920 was an annual lecturer at Middlebury College. Frost published more than thirty books of poetry, including four that won Pulitzer prizes: *New Hampshire* (1923), *Collected Poems* (1930), *A Further Range* (1936), and *A Witness Tree* (1942). His letters were published in *Selected Letters* (1964), and his lectures in *Robert Frost: A Living Voice* (1974). In 1961 Frost read his poem "The Gift Outright" at the inauguration of president John F. Kennedy. Frost is buried in the American Poets Corner at the Cathedral of St. John the Divine in New York City.

Mending Wall

Robert Frost

Something there is that doesn't love a wall,
That sends the frozen-ground-swell under it,
And spills the upper boulders in the sun;
And makes gaps even two can pass abreast.
The work of hunters is another thing: 5
I have come after them and made repair
Where they have left not one stone on a stone,
But they would have the rabbit out of hiding,
To please the yelping dogs. The gaps I mean,
No one has seen them made or heard them made,   10
But at spring mending-time we find them there.
I let my neighbor know beyond the hill;
And on a day we meet to walk the line
And set the wall between us once again.
We keep the wall between us as we go.   15
To each the boulders that have fallen to each.
And some are loaves and some so nearly balls
We have to use a spell to make them balance:
'Stay where you are until our backs are turned!'

We wear our fingers rough with handling them.   20
Oh, just another kind of outdoor game,
One on a side. It comes to little more:
There where it is we do not need the wall:
He is all pine and I am apple orchard.
My apple trees will never get across   25
And eat the cones under his pines, I tell him.
He only says, 'Good fences make good neighbors.'
Spring is the mischief in me, and I wonder
If I could put a notion in his head:
'*Why* do they make good neighbors? Isn't it   30
Where there are cows? But here there are no cows.
Before I built a wall I'd ask to know
What I was walling in or walling out,
And to whom I was like to give offense.
Something there is that doesn't love a wall,   35
That wants it down.' I could say 'Elves' to him,
But it's not elves exactly, and I'd rather
He said it for himself. I see him there
Bringing a stone grasped firmly by the top
In each hand, like an old-stone savage armed.   40
He moves in darkness as it seems to me,
Not of woods only and the shade of trees.
He will not go behind his father's saying,
And he likes having thought of it so well
He says again, 'Good fences make good neighbors.'   45

Nathaniel Hawthorne (1804–1864) was born in Salem, Massachusetts, into a prominent and old family; one of the founding families of Salem. His family's history sparked his interest in colonial New England, which became the setting of many of his stories and novels. Hawthorne's father was a ship captain who died when Hawthorne was just four years old; the boy was sent to live with relatives who recognized his talent and sent him to good schools and later to Bowdoin College. They even supported him at various times during his writing career. Hawthorne graduated from Bowdoin in 1825; in 1828 he published *Fanshawe*, a romance that Hawthorne later considered so poorly written that he tried to destroy all copies. Developing a new format for his stories, a format that limited stories to just one scene with a tightly controlled plot, he began writing the stories for which he is known today. The stories began with *The Hollow of the Three Hills* (1830), published in the *Salem Gazette*. This was followed by other stories published at first separately and then in a single book, *Twice-Told Tales* (1837). In 1836, Hawthorne moved to Boston, hoping to make his reputation as an editor; however, the owners of the magazine (*The American Magazine of Useful and Entertaining Knowledge*), never paid his salary, so Hawthorne was forced to quit after just a few months. For two years he worked as a measurer in the Boston customhouse; he liked the job, but it gave him no time for writing. At that time he also became interested in Transcendentalism and quit his job to join the Brook Farm commune in April 1841. Unfortunately, this venture also did not give him enough time to write, and he left in November. When he married soon after leaving Brook Farm, he and his wife lived near Ralph Waldo Emerson in Concord; *Mosses from an Old Manse* (1846) describes their time there. In 1846, Hawthorne again worked as a customs agent, this time as the surveyor of the port of Salem. However, in 1849, with a new party in the presidential office, he lost that job. Several of his novels published soon afterward gave him a degree of financial security; those novels are his famous *The Scarlet Letter* (1850); *The House of the Seven Gables* (1851); *The Snow-Image*, and *Other Twice-Told Tales* (1852); and *The Blithedale Romance* (1852). In 1852, his college friend Franklin Pierce, was elected president and Hawthorne was given a short-term job in Liverpool, England, as American consul. He was finally able to travel in Europe and lived in Italy until 1862 when the Civil War compelled him to return to the United States. A last novel, *The Marble Faun* (1860), was inspired by his time in Italy.

The Birthmark

Nathaniel Hawthorne

In the latter part of the last century there lived a man of science, an eminent proficient in every branch of natural philosophy, who not long before our story opens had made experience of a spiritual affinity more attractive than any chemical one. He had left his laboratory to the care of an assistant, cleared his fine countenance from the furnace smoke, washed the stain of acids from his fingers, and persuaded a beautiful woman to become his wife. In those days, when the comparatively recent discovery of electricity and other kindred mysteries of Nature seemed to open paths into the region of miracle, it was not unusual for the love of science to rival the love of woman in its depth and absorbing energy. The higher intellect, the imagination, the spirit, and even the heart might all find their congenial ailment in pursuits which, as some of their ardent votaries believed, would ascend from one step of powerful intelligence to another, until the philosopher should lay his hand on the secret of creative force and perhaps make new worlds for himself. We know not whether

1

Aylmer possessed this degree of faith in man's ultimate control over Nature. He had devoted himself, however, too unreservedly to scientific studies ever to be weaned from them by any second passion. His love for his young wife might prove the stronger of the two; but it could only be by intertwining itself with his love of science and uniting the strength of the latter to his own.

Such a union accordingly took place, and was attended with truly remarkable consequences and a deeply impressive moral. One day, very soon after their marriage, Aylmer sat gazing at his wife with a trouble in his countenance that grew stronger until he spoke.

"Georgiana," said he, "has it never occurred to you that the mark upon your cheek might be removed?"

"No, indeed," said she, smiling; but, perceiving the seriousness of his manner, she blushed deeply. "To tell you the truth, it has been so often called a charm that I was simple enough to imagine it might be so."

"Ah, upon another face perhaps it might," replied her husband; "but never on yours. No, dearest Georgiana, you came so nearly perfect from the hand of Nature that this slightest possible defect, which we hesitate whether to term a defect or a beauty, shocks me, as being the visible mark of earthly imperfection."

"Shocks you, my husband!" cried Georgiana, deeply hurt; at first reddening with momentary anger, but then bursting into tears. "Then why did you take me from my mother's side? You cannot love what shocks you!"

To explain this conversation, it must be mentioned that in the centre of Georgiana's left cheek there was a singular mark, deeply interwoven, as it were, with the texture and substance of her face. In the usual state of her complexion—a healthy though delicate bloom—the mark wore a tint of deeper crimson, which imperfectly defined its shape amid the surrounding rosiness. When she blushed it gradually became more indistinct, and finally vanished amid the triumphant rush of blood that bathed the whole cheek with its brilliant glow. But if any shifting motion caused her to turn pale there was the mark again, a crimson stain upon the snow, in what Aylmer sometimes deemed an almost fearful distinctness. Its shape bore not a little similarity to the human hand, though of the smallest pygmy size. Georgiana's lovers were wont to say that some fairy at her birth hour had laid her tiny hand upon the infant's cheek, and left this impress there in token of the magic endowments that were to give her such sway over all hearts. Many a desperate swain would have risked life for the privilege of pressing his lips to the mysterious hand. It must not be concealed, however, that the impression wrought by this fairy sign manual varied exceedingly according to the difference of temperament in the beholders. Some fastidious persons—but they were exclusively of her own sex—affirmed that the bloody hand, as they chose to call it, quite destroyed the effect of Georgiana's beauty and rendered her countenance even hideous. But it would be as reasonable to say that one of those small blue stains which sometimes occur in the purest statuary marble would convert the Eve of Powers to a monster. Masculine observers, if the birthmark did not heighten their admiration, contented themselves with wishing it away, that the world might possess one living specimen of ideal loveliness without the semblance of a flaw.

After his marriage,—for he thought little or nothing of the matter before,—Aylmer discovered that this was the case with himself.

Had she been less beautiful,—if Envy's self could have found aught else to sneer at,—he might have felt his affection heightened by the prettiness of this mimic hand, now vaguely portrayed, now lost, now stealing forth again and glimmering to and fro with every pulse of emotion that throbbed within her heart; but, seeing her otherwise so perfect, he found this one defect grow more and more intolerable with every moment of their united lives. It was the fatal flaw of humanity which Nature, in one shape or another, stamps ineffaceably on all her productions, either to imply that they are temporary and finite, or that their perfection must be wrought by toil and pain. The crimson hand expressed the ineludible gripe in which mortality clutches the highest and purest of earthly mould, degrading them into kindred with the lowest, and even with the very brutes, like whom their visible frames return to dust. In this manner, selecting it as the symbol of his wife's liability to sin, sorrow, decay, and death, Aylmer's sombre imagination was not long in rendering the birthmark a frightful object, causing him more trouble and horror than ever Georgiana's beauty, whether of soul or sense, had given him delight.   8

At all the seasons which should have been their happiest he invariably, and without intending it, nay, in spite of a purpose to the contrary, reverted to this one disastrous topic. Trifling as it at first appeared, it so connected itself with innumerable trains of thought and modes of feeling that it became the central point of all. With the morning twilight Aylmer opened his eyes upon his wife's face and recognized the symbol of imperfection; and when they sat together at the evening hearth his eyes wandered stealthily to her cheek, and beheld, flickering with the blaze of the wood fire, the spectral hand that wrote mortality where he would fain have worshipped. Georgiana soon learned to shudder at his gaze. It needed but a glance with the peculiar expression that his face often wore to change the roses of her cheek into a deathlike paleness, amid which the crimson hand was brought strongly out, like a bas relief of ruby on the whitest marble.   9

Late one night, when the lights were growing dim so as hardly to betray the stain on the poor wife's cheek, she herself, for the first time, voluntarily took up the subject.   10

"Do you remember, my dear Aylmer," said she, with a feeble attempt at a smile, "have you any recollection, of a dream last night about this odious hand?"   11

"None! none whatever!" replied Aylmer, starting; but then he added, in a dry, cold tone, affected for the sake of concealing the real depth of his emotion, "I might well dream of it; for, before I fell asleep, it had taken a pretty firm hold of my fancy."   12

"And you did dream of it?" continued Georgiana, hastily; for she dreaded lest a gush of tears should interrupt what she had to say. "A terrible dream! I wonder that you can forget it. Is it possible to forget this one expression?—'It is in her heart now; we must have it out!' Reflect, my husband; for by all means I would have you recall that dream."   13

The mind is in a sad state when Sleep, the all-involving, cannot confine her spectres within the dim region of her sway, but suffers them to break forth, affrighting this actual life with secrets that perchance belong to a deeper one. Aylmer now   14 remembered his dream. He had fancied himself with his servant Aminadab, attempting an operation for the removal of the birthmark; but the deeper went the knife, the deeper sank the hand, until at length its tiny grasp appeared to have caught hold of Georgiana's heart; whence, however, her husband was inexorably resolved to cut or wrench it away.

When the dream had shaped itself perfectly in his memory Aylmer sat in his wife's presence with a guilty feeling. Truth often finds its way to the mind close muffled in robes of sleep, and then speaks with uncompromising directness of matters in regard to which we practise an unconscious self-deception during our waking moments. Until now he had not been aware of the tyrannizing influence acquired by one idea over his mind, and of the lengths which he might find in his heart to go for the sake of giving himself peace. 15

"Aylmer," resumed Georgiana, solemnly, "I know not what may be the cost to both of us to rid me of this fatal birthmark. Perhaps its removal may cause cureless deformity; or it may be the stain goes as deep as life itself. Again: do we know that there is a possibility, on any terms, of unclasping the firm grip of this little hand which was laid upon me before I came into the world?" 16

"Dearest Georgiana, I have spent much thought on the subject," hastily interrupted Aylmer. "I am convinced of the perfect practicability of its removal." 17

"If there be the remotest possibility of it," continued Georgiana, "let the attempt be made, at whatever risk. Danger is nothing to me; for life, while this hateful mark makes me the object of your horror and disgust—life is a burden which I would fling down with joy. Either remove this dreadful hand, or take my wretched life! You have deep science. All the world bears witness of it. You have achieved great wonders. Cannot you remove this little, little mark, which I cover with the tips of two small fingers? Is this beyond your power, for the sake of your own peace, and to save your poor wife from madness?" 18

"Noblest, dearest, tenderest wife," cried Aylmer, rapturously, "doubt not my power. I have already given this matter the deepest thought—thought which might almost have enlightened me to create a being less perfect than yourself. Georgiana, you have led me deeper than ever into the heart of science. I feel myself fully competent to render this dear cheek as faultless as its fellow; and then, most beloved, what will be my triumph when I shall have corrected what Nature left imperfect in her fairest work! Even Pygmalion, when his sculptured woman assumed life, felt not greater ecstasy than mine will be." 19

"It is resolved, then," said Georgiana, faintly smiling. "And, Aylmer, spare me not, though you should find the birthmark take refuge in my heart at last." 20

Her husband tenderly kissed her cheek—her right cheek—not that which bore the impress of the crimson hand. 21

The next day Aylmer apprised his wife of a plan that he had formed whereby he might have opportunity for the intense thought and constant watchfulness which the proposed operation would require; while Georgiana, likewise, would enjoy the perfect repose essential to its success. They were to seclude themselves in the extensive apartments occupied by Aylmer as a laboratory, and where, during his toilsome youth, he had made discoveries in the elemental powers of Nature that had roused 22 the admiration of all the learned societies in Europe. Seated calmly in this laboratory, the pale philosopher had investigated the secrets of the highest cloud region and of the profoundest mines; he had satisfied himself of the causes that kindled and kept alive the fires of the volcano; and had explained the mystery of fountains, and how it is that they gush forth; some so bright and pure, and others with such rich medicinal virtues, from the dark bosom of the earth. Here, too, at an earlier period, he had studied the wonders of the human frame, and attempted to fathom the very process by which Nature assimilates all her precious influences from earth and air, and from the spiritual world, to create and foster man, her masterpiece. The latter pursuit, however, Aylmer had long laid aside in unwilling recognition of the truth—against which all seekers sooner or later stumble—that our great creative Mother, while she amuses us with apparently working in the broadest sunshine, is yet severely careful to keep her own secrets, and, in spite of her pretended openness, shows us nothing but results. She permits us, indeed, to mar, but seldom to mend, and, like a jealous patentee, on no account to make. Now, however, Aylmer resumed these half-forgotten investigations; not, of course, with such hopes or wishes as first suggested them; but because they involved much physiological truth and lay in the path of his proposed scheme for the treatment of Georgiana.

As he led her over the threshold of the laboratory, Georgiana was cold and tremulous. Aylmer looked cheerfully into her face, with intent to reassure her, but was so startled with the intense glow of the birthmark upon the whiteness of her cheek that he could not restrain a strong convulsive shudder. His wife fainted. 23

"Aminadab! Aminadab!" shouted Aylmer, stamping violently on the floor. 24

Forthwith there issued from an inner apartment a man of low stature, but bulky frame, with shaggy hair hanging about his visage, which was grimed with the vapors of the furnace. This personage had been Aylmer's underworker during his whole scientific career, and was admirably fitted for that office by his great mechanical readiness, and the skill with which, while incapable of comprehending a single principle, he executed all the details of his master's experiments. With his vast strength, his shaggy hair, his smoky aspect, and the indescribable earthiness that incrusted him, he seemed to represent man's physical nature; while Aylmer's slender figure, and pale, intellectual face, were no less apt a type of the spiritual element. 25

"Throw open the door of the boudoir, Aminadab," said Aylmer, "and burn a pastil." 26

"Yes, master," answered Aminadab, looking intently at the lifeless form of Georgiana; and then he muttered to himself, "If she were my wife, I'd never part with that birthmark." 27

When Georgiana recovered consciousness she found herself breathing an atmosphere of penetrating fragrance, the gentle potency of which had recalled her from her deathlike faintness. The scene around her looked like enchantment. Aylmer had converted those smoky, dingy, sombre rooms, where he had spent his brightest years in recondite pursuits, into a series of beautiful apartments not unfit to be the secluded abode of a lovely woman. The walls were hung with gorgeous curtains, which imparted the combination of grandeur and grace that no other species of adornment can achieve; and, as they fell from the ceiling to the floor, their rich and ponderous 28 folds, concealing all angles and straight lines, appeared to shut in the scene from infinite space. For aught Georgiana knew, it might be a pavilion among the clouds. And Aylmer, excluding the sunshine, which would have interfered with his chemical processes, had supplied its place with perfumed lamps, emitting flames of various hue, but all uniting in a soft, impurpled radiance. He now knelt by his wife's side, watching her earnestly, but without alarm; for he was confident in his science, and felt that he could draw a magic circle round her within which no evil might intrude.

"Where am I? Ah, I remember," said Georgiana, faintly; and she placed her hand over her cheek to hide the terrible mark from her husband's eyes. 29

"Fear not, dearest!" exclaimed he. "Do not shrink from me! Believe me, Georgiana, I even rejoice in this single imperfection, since it will be such a rapture to remove it." 30

"O, spare me!" sadly replied his wife. "Pray do not look at it again. I never can forget that convulsive shudder." 31

In order to soothe Georgiana, and, as it were, to release her mind from the burden of actual things, Aylmer now put in practice some of the light and playful secrets which science had taught him among its profounder lore. Airy figures, absolutely bodiless ideas, and forms of unsubstantial beauty came and danced before her, imprinting their momentary footsteps on beams of light. Though she had some indistinct idea of the method of these optical phenomena, still the illusion was almost perfect enough to warrant the belief that her husband possessed sway over the spiritual world. Then again, when she felt a wish to look forth from her seclusion, immediately, as if her thoughts were answered, the procession of external existence flitted across a screen. The scenery and the figures of actual life were perfectly represented, but with that bewitching yet indescribable difference which always makes a picture, an image, or a shadow so much more attractive than the original. When wearied of this, Aylmer bade her cast her eyes upon a vessel containing a quantity of earth. She did so, with little interest at first; but was soon startled to perceive the germ of a plant shooting upward from the soil. Then came the slender stalk; the leaves gradually unfolded themselves; and amid them was a perfect and lovely flower. 32

"It is magical!" cried Georgiana. "I dare not touch it." 33

"Nay, pluck it," answered Aylmer,—"pluck it, and inhale its brief perfume while you may. The flower will wither in a few moments and leave nothing save its brown seed vessels; but thence may be perpetuated a race as ephemeral as itself." 34

But Georgiana had no sooner touched the flower than the whole plant suffered a blight, its leaves turning coal-black as if by the agency of fire. 35

"There was too powerful a stimulus," said Aylmer, thoughtfully. 36

To make up for this abortive experiment, he proposed to take her portrait by a scientific process of his own invention. It was to be effected by rays of light striking upon a polished plate of metal. Georgiana assented; but, on looking at the result, was affrighted to find the features of the portrait blurred and indefinable; while the minute figure of a hand appeared where the cheek should have been. Aylmer snatched the metallic plate and threw it into a jar of corrosive acid. 37

Soon, however, he forgot these mortifying failures. In the intervals of study and chemical experiment he came to her flushed and exhausted, but seemed invig- 38 orated by her presence, and spoke in glowing language of the resources of his art. He gave a history of the long dynasty of the alchemists, who spent so many ages in quest of the universal solvent by which the golden principle might be elicited from all things vile and base. Aylmer appeared to believe that, by the plainest scientific logic, it was altogether within the limits of possibility to discover this long-sought medium; "but," he added, "a philosopher who should go deep enough to acquire the power would attain too lofty a wisdom to stoop to the exercise of it." Not less singular were his opinions in regard to the elixir vitae. He more than intimated that it was at his option to concoct a liquid that should prolong life for years, perhaps interminably; but that it would produce a discord in Nature which all the world, and chiefly the quaffer of the immortal nostrum, would find cause to curse.

"Aylmer, are you in earnest?" asked Georgiana, looking at him with amaze-   39
ment and fear. "It is terrible to possess such power, or even to dream of possessing it."

"O, do not tremble, my love," said her husband. "I would not wrong either you   40
or myself by working such inharmonious effects upon our lives; but I would have you consider how trifling, in comparison, is the skill requisite to remove this little hand."

At the mention of the birthmark, Georgiana, as usual, shrank as if a red hot iron   41
had touched her cheek.

Again Aylmer applied himself to his labors. She could hear his voice in the   42
distant furnace room giving directions to Aminadab, whose harsh, uncouth, misshapen tones were audible in response, more like the grunt or growl of a brute than human speech. After hours of absence, Aylmer reappeared and proposed that she should now examine his cabinet of chemical products and natural treasures of the earth. Among the former he showed her a small vial, in which, he remarked, was contained a gentle yet most powerful fragrance, capable of impregnating all the breezes that blow across a kingdom. They were of inestimable value, the contents of that little vial; and, as he said so, he threw some of the perfume into the air and filled the room with piercing and invigorating delight.

"And what is this?" asked Georgiana, pointing to a small crystal globe con-   43
taining a gold-colored liquid. "It is so beautiful to the eye that I could imagine it the elixir of life."

"In one sense it is," replied Aylmer; "or rather, the elixir of immortality. It is   44
the most precious poison that ever was concocted in this world. By its aid I could apportion the lifetime of any mortal at whom you might point your finger. The strength of the dose would determine whether he were to linger out years, or drop dead in the midst of a breath. No king on his guarded throne could keep his life if I, in my private station, should deem that the welfare of millions justified me in depriving him of it."

"Why do you keep such a terrific drug?" inquired Georgiana in horror.   45

"Do not mistrust me, dearest," said her husband, smiling; "its virtuous potency   46
is yet greater than its harmful one. But see! here is a powerful cosmetic. With a few drops of this in a vase of water, freckles may be washed away as easily as the hands are cleansed. A stronger infusion would take the blood out of the cheek, and leave the rosiest beauty a pale ghost."

"Is it with this lotion that you intend to bathe my cheek?" asked Georgiana, anxiously.   47

"O, no," hastily replied her husband; "this is merely superficial. Your case demands a remedy that shall go deeper."   48

In his interviews with Georgiana, Aylmer generally made minute inquiries as to her sensations, and whether the confinement of the rooms and the temperature of the atmosphere agreed with her. These questions had such a particular drift that Georgiana began to conjecture that she was already subjected to certain physical influences, either breathed in with the fragrant air or taken with her food. She fancied likewise, but it might be altogether fancy, that there was a stirring up of her system—a strange, indefinite sensation creeping through her veins, and tingling, half painfully, half pleasurably, at her heart. Still, whenever she dared to look into the mirror, there she beheld herself pale as a white rose and with the crimson birthmark stamped upon her cheek. Not even Aylmer now hated it so much as she.   49

To dispel the tedium of the hours which her husband found it necessary to devote to the processes of combination and analysis, Georgiana turned over the volumes of his scientific library. In many dark old tomes she met with chapters full of romance and poetry. They were the works of the philosophers of the middle ages, such as Albertus Magnus, Cornelius Agrippa, Paracelsus, and the famous friar who created the prophetic Brazen Head. All these antique naturalists stood in advance of their centuries, yet were imbued with some of their credulity, and therefore were believed, and perhaps imagined themselves to have acquired from the investigation of Nature a power above Nature, and from physics a sway over the spiritual world. Hardly less curious and imaginative were the early volumes of the Transactions of the Royal Society, in which the members, knowing little of the limits of natural possibility, were continually recording wonders or proposing methods whereby wonders might be wrought.   50

But to Georgiana, the most engrossing volume was a large folio from her husband's own hand, in which he had recorded every experiment of his scientific career, its original aim, the methods adopted for its development, and its final success or failure, with the circumstances to which either event was attributable. The book, in truth, was both the history and emblem of his ardent, ambitious, imaginative, yet practical and laborious life. He handled physical details as if there were nothing beyond them; yet spiritualized them all and redeemed himself from materialism by his strong and eager aspiration towards the infinite. In his grasp the veriest clod of earth assumed a soul. Georgiana, as she read, reverenced Aylmer and loved him more profoundly than ever, but with a less entire dependence on his judgment than heretofore. Much as he had accomplished, she could not but observe that his most splendid successes were almost invariably failures, if compared with the ideal at which he aimed. His brightest diamonds were the merest pebbles, and felt to be so by himself, in comparison with the inestimable gems which lay hidden beyond his reach. The volume, rich with achievements that had won renown for its author, was yet as melancholy a record as ever mortal hand had penned. It was the sad confession and continual exemplification of the shortcomings of the composite man, the spirit burdened with clay and working in matter, and of the despair that assails the higher   51 nature at finding itself so miserably thwarted by the earthly part. Perhaps every man of genius, in whatever sphere, might recognize the image of his own experience in Aylmer's journal.

So deeply did these reflections affect Georgiana that she laid her face upon   52 the open volume and burst into tears. In this situation she was found by her husband.

"It is dangerous to read in a sorcerer's books," said he with a smile, though his   53 countenance was uneasy and displeased. "Georgiana, there are pages in that volume which I can scarcely glance over and keep my senses. Take heed lest it prove detrimental to you."

"It has made me worship you more than ever," said she.   54

"Ah, wait for this one success," rejoined he, "then worship me if you will. I shall   55 deem myself hardly unworthy of it. But come, I have sought you for the luxury of your voice. Sing to me, dearest."

So she poured out the liquid music of her voice to quench the thirst of his spirit.   56 He then took his leave with a boyish exuberance of gayety, assuring her that her seclusion would endure but a little longer, and that the result was already certain. Scarcely had he departed when Georgiana felt irresistibly impelled to follow him. She had forgotten to inform Aylmer of a symptom which for two or three hours past had begun to excite her attention. It was a sensation in the fatal birthmark, not painful, but which induced a restlessness throughout her system. Hastening after her husband, she intruded for the first time into the laboratory.

The first thing that struck her eye was the furnace, that hot and feverish worker,   57 with the intense glow of its fire, which by the quantities of soot clustered above it seemed to have been burning for ages. There was a distilling apparatus in full operation. Around the room were retorts, tubes, cylinders, crucibles, and other apparatus of chemical research. An electrical machine stood ready for immediate use. The atmosphere felt oppressively close, and was tainted with gaseous odors which had been tormented forth by the process of science. The severe and homely simplicity of the apartment, with its naked walls and brick pavement, looked strange, accustomed as Georgiana had become to the fantastic elegance of her boudoir. But what chiefly, indeed almost solely, drew her attention, was the aspect of Aylmer himself.

He was pale as death, anxious and absorbed, and hung over the furnace as if it   58 depended upon his utmost watchfulness whether the liquid which it was distilling should be the draught of immortal happiness or misery. How different from the sanguine and joyous mien that he had assumed for Georgiana's encouragement!

"Carefully now, Aminadab; carefully, thou human machine; carefully, thou man   59 of clay," muttered Aylmer, more to himself than his assistant. "Now, if there be a thought too much or too little, it is all over."

"Ho! ho!" mumbled Aminadab. "Look, master! look!"   60

Aylmer raised his eyes hastily, and at first reddened, then grew paler than ever,   61 on beholding Georgiana. He rushed towards her and seized her arm with a grip that left the print of his fingers upon it.

"Why do you come hither? Have you no trust in your husband?" cried he, impetu-   62 ously. "Would you throw the blight of that fatal birthmark over my labors? It is not well done. Go, prying woman! Go!"

"Nay, Aylmer," said Georgiana with the firmness of which she possessed no stinted endowment, "it is not you that have a right to complain. You mistrust your wife; you have concealed the anxiety with which you watch the development of this experiment. Think not so unworthily of me, my husband. Tell me all the risk we run, and fear not that I shall shrink; for my share in it is far less than your own." 63

"No, no, Georgiana!" said Aylmer, impatiently; "it must not be." 64

"I submit," replied she, calmly. "And, Aylmer, I shall quaff whatever draught you bring me; but it will be on the same principle that would induce me to take a dose of poison if offered by your hand." 65

"My noble wife," said Aylmer, deeply moved, "I knew not the height and depth of your nature until now. Nothing shall be concealed. Know, then, that this crimson hand, superficial as it seems, has clutched its grasp into your being with a strength of which I had no previous conception. I have already administered agents powerful enough to do aught except to change your entire physical system. Only one thing remains to be tried. If that fail us we are ruined." 66

"Why did you hesitate to tell me this?" asked she. 67

"Because, Georgiana," said Aylmer, in a low voice, "there is danger." 68

"Danger? There is but one danger—that this horrible stigma shall be left upon my cheek!" cried Georgiana. "Remove it, remove it, whatever be the cost, or we shall both go mad!" 69

"Heaven knows your words are too true," said Aylmer, sadly. "And now, dearest, return to your boudoir. In a little while all will be tested." 70

He conducted her back and took leave of her with a solemn tenderness which spoke far more than his words how much was now at stake. After his departure Georgiana became rapt in musings. She considered the character of Aylmer and did it completer justice than at any previous moment. Her heart exulted, while it trembled, at his honorable love—so pure and lofty that it would accept nothing less than perfection nor miserably make itself contented with an earthlier nature than he had dreamed of. She felt how much more precious was such a sentiment than that meaner kind which would have borne with the imperfection for her sake, and have been guilty of treason to holy love by degrading its perfect idea to the level of the actual; and with her whole spirit she prayed that, for a single moment, she might satisfy his highest and deepest conception. Longer than one moment she well knew it could not be; for his spirit was ever on the march, ever ascending, and each instant required something that was beyond the scope of the instant before. 71

The sound of her husband's footsteps aroused her. He bore a crystal goblet containing a liquor colorless as water, but bright enough to be the draught of immortality. Aylmer was pale; but it seemed rather the consequence of a highly-wrought state of mind and tension of spirit than of fear or doubt. 72

"The concoction of the draught has been perfect," said he, in answer to Georgiana's look. "Unless all my science have deceived me, it cannot fail." 73

"Save on your account, my dearest Aylmer," observed his wife, "I might wish to put off this birthmark of mortality by relinquishing mortality itself in preference to any other mode. Life is but a sad possession to those who have attained precisely the degree of moral advancement at which I stand. Were I weaker and blinder, it 74 might be happiness. Were I stronger, it might be endured hopefully. But, being what I find myself, methinks I am of all mortals the most fit to die."

"You are fit for heaven without tasting death!" replied her husband. "But why 75 do we speak of dying? The draught cannot fail. Behold its effect upon this plant."

On the window seat there stood a geranium diseased with yellow blotches which 76 had overspread all its leaves. Aylmer poured a small quantity of the liquid upon the soil in which it grew. In a little time, when the roots of the plant had taken up the moisture, the unsightly blotches began to be extinguished in a living verdure.

"There needed no proof," said Georgiana, quietly. "Give me the goblet. I joy- 77 fully stake all upon your word."

"Drink, then, thou lofty creature!" exclaimed Aylmer, with fervid admiration. 78 "There is no taint of imperfection on thy spirit. Thy sensible frame, too, shall soon be all perfect."

She quaffed the liquid and returned the goblet to his hand. 79

"It is grateful," said she, with a placid smile. "Methinks it is like water from a 80 heavenly fountain; for it contains I know not what of unobtrusive fragrance and deliciousness. It allays a feverish thirst that had parched me for many days. Now, dearest, let me sleep. My earthly senses are closing over my spirit like the leaves around the heart of a rose at sunset."

She spoke the last words with a gentle reluctance, as if it required almost more 81 energy than she could command to pronounce the faint and lingering syllables. Scarcely had they loitered through her lips ere she was lost in slumber. Aylmer sat by her side, watching her aspect with the emotions proper to a man the whole value of whose existence was involved in the process now to be tested. Mingled with this mood, however, was the philosophic investigation characteristic of the man of science. Not the minutest symptom escaped him. A heightened flush of the cheek, a slight irregularity of breath, a quiver of the eyelid, a hardly perceptible tremor through the frame,—such were the details which, as the moments passed, he wrote down in his folio volume. Intense thought had set its stamp upon every previous page of that volume; but the thoughts of years were all concentrated upon the last.

While thus employed, he failed not to gaze often at the fatal hand, and not with- 82 out a shudder. Yet once, by a strange and unaccountable impulse, he pressed it with his lips. His spirit recoiled, however, in the very act; and Georgiana, out of the midst of her deep sleep, moved uneasily and murmured as if in remonstrance. Again Aylmer resumed his watch. Nor was it without avail. The crimson hand, which at first had been strongly visible upon the marble paleness of Georgiana's cheek, now grew more faintly outlined. She remained not less pale than ever; but the birthmark, with every breath that came and went lost somewhat of its former distinctness. Its presence had been awful; its departure was more awful still. Watch the stain of the rainbow fading out of the sky, and you will know how that mysterious symbol passed away.

"By Heaven! It is well nigh gone!" said Aylmer to himself, in almost irrepress- 83 ible ecstasy. "I can scarcely trace it now. Success! Success! And now it is like the faintest rose color. The lightest flush of blood across her cheek would overcome it. But she is so pale!"

He drew aside the window curtain and suffered the light of natural day to fall 84
into the room and rest upon her cheek. At the same time he heard a gross, hoarse
chuckle, which he had long known as his servant Aminadab's expression of delight.

"Ah, clod! Ah, earthly mass!" cried Aylmer, laughing in a sort of frenzy, "you 85
have served me well! Matter and spirit—earth and heaven—have both done their
part in this! Laugh, thing of the senses! You have earned the right to laugh."

These exclamations broke Georgiana's sleep. She slowly unclosed her eyes and 86
gazed into the mirror which her husband had arranged for that purpose. A faint smile
flitted over her lips when she recognized how barely perceptible was now that crimson hand which had once blazed forth with such disastrous brilliancy as to scare away
all their happiness. But then her eyes sought Aylmer's face with a trouble and anxiety that he could by no means account for.

"My poor Aylmer!" murmured she. 87

"Poor? Nay, richest, happiest, most favored!" exclaimed he. "My peerless bride, 88
it is successful! You are perfect!"

"My poor Aylmer," she repeated, with a more than human tenderness, "you have 89
aimed loftily; you have done nobly. Do not repent that, with so high and pure a
feeling, you have rejected the best the earth could offer. Aylmer, dearest Aylmer, I
am dying!"

Alas! it was too true! The fatal hand had grappled with the mystery of life, and 90
was the bond by which an angelic spirit kept itself in union with a mortal frame.
As the last crimson tint of the birthmark—that sole token of human imperfection—
faded from her cheek, the parting breath of the now perfect woman passed into the
atmosphere, and her soul, lingering a moment near her husband, took its heavenward flight. Then a hoarse, chuckling laugh was heard again! Thus ever does the gross
fatality of earth exult in its invariable triumph over the immortal essence which, in
this dim sphere of half development, demands the completeness of a higher state.
Yet, had Aylmer reached a profounder wisdom, he need not thus have flung away the
happiness which would have woven his mortal life of the selfsame texture with the
celestial. The momentary circumstance was too strong for him; he failed to look
beyond the shadowy scope of time, and, living once for all in eternity, to find the perfect future in the present.

Bharati Mukherjee (1940–), born in Calcutta, India, has written seven novels, two short story collections, and is an English professor at the University of California, Berkeley.

A Wife's Story

Bharati Mukherjee

Imre says forget it, but I'm going to write David Mamet. So Patels are hard to sell real estate to. You buy them a beer, whisper Glengarry Glen Ross, and they smell swamp instead of sun and surf. They work hard, eat cheap, live ten to a room, stash their savings under futons in Queens, and before you know it they own half of Hoboken. You say, where's the sweet gullibility that made this nation great? 1

Polish jokes, Patel jokes: that's not why I want to write Mamet. 2

Seen their women? 3

Everybody laughs. Imre laughs. The dozing fat man with the Barnes & Noble sack between his legs, the woman next to him, the usher, everybody. The theater isn't so dark that they can't see me. In my red silk sari I'm conspicuous. Plump, gold paisleys sparkle on my chest. 4

The actor is just warming up. *Seen their women?* He plays a salesman, he's had a bad day and now he's in a Chinese restaurant trying to loosen up. His face is pink. His wool-blend slacks are creased at the crotch. We bought our tickets at half-price, we're sitting in the front row, but at the edge, and we see things we shouldn't be seeing. At least I do, or think I do. Spittle, actors goosing each other, little winks, streaks of makeup. 5

Maybe they're improvising dialogue too. Maybe Mamet's provided them with insult kits, Thursdays for Chinese, Wednesdays for Hispanics, today for Indians. Maybe they get together before curtain time, see an Indian woman settling in the front row off to the side, and say to each other: "Hey, forget Friday. Let's get *her* today. See if she cries. See if she walks out." Maybe, like the salesmen they play, they have a little bet on. 6

Maybe I shouldn't feel betrayed. 7

Their women, he goes again. *They look like they've just been fucked by a dead cat.* 8

The fat man hoots so hard he nudges my elbow off our shared armrest. 9

"Imre. I'm going home." But Imre's hunched so far forward he doesn't hear. English isn't his best language. A refugee from Budapest, he has to listen hard. "I didn't pay eighteen dollars to be insulted." 10

I don't hate Mamet. It's the tyranny of the American dream that scares me. First, you don't exist. Then you're invisible. Then you're funny. Then you're disgusting. Insult, my American friends will tell me, is a kind of acceptance. No 11 instant dignity here. A play like this, back home, would cause riots. Communal, racist, and antisocial. The actors wouldn't make it off stage. This play, and all these awful feelings, would be safely locked up.

I long, at times, for clear-cut answers. Offer me instant dignity, today, and I'll take it.   12

"What?" Imre moves toward me without taking his eyes off the actor. "Come again?"   13

Tears come. I want to stand, scream, make an awful scene. I long for ugly, nasty rage.   14

The actor is ranting, flinging spittle. *Give me a chance. I'm not finished, I can get back on the board. I tell that asshole, give me a real lead. And what does that asshole give me? Patels. Nothing but Patels.*   15

This time Imre works an arm around my shoulders. "Panna, what is Patel? Why are you taking it all so personally?"   16

I shrink from his touch, but I don't walk out. Expensive girls' schools in Lausanne and Bombay have trained me to behave well. My manners are exquisite, my feelings are delicate, my gestures refined, my moods undetectable. They have seen me through riots, uprootings, separation, my son's death.   17

"I'm not taking it personally."   18

The fat man looks at us. The woman looks too, and shushes.   19

I stare back at the two of them. Then I stare, mean and cool, at the man's elbow. Under the bright blue polyester Hawaiian shirt sleeve, the elbow looks soft and runny. "Excuse me," I say. My voice has the effortless meanness of well-bred displaced Third World women, though my rhetoric has been learned elsewhere. "You're exploiting my space."   20

Startled, the man snatches his arm away from me. He cradles it against his breast. By the time he's ready with comebacks, I've turned my back on him. I've probably ruined the first act for him. I know I've ruined it for Imre.   21

It's not my fault; it's the *situation*. Old colonies wear down. Patels—the new pioneers—have to be suspicious. Idi Amin's lesson is permanent. AT&T wires move good advice from continent to continent. Keep all assets liquid. Get into 7-11S, get out of condos and motels. I know how both sides feel, that's the trouble. The Patel sniffing out scams, the sad salesmen on the stage: postcolonialism has made me their referee. It's hate I long for; simple, brutish, partisan hate.   22

After the show Imre and I make our way toward Broadway. Sometimes he holds my hand; it doesn't mean anything more than that crazies and drunks are crouched in doorways. Imre's been here over two years, but he's stayed very old-world, very courtly, openly protective of women. I met him in a seminar on special ed. last semester. His wife is a nurse somewhere in the Hungarian country-side. There are two sons, and miles of petitions for their emigration. My husband manages a mill two hundred miles north of Bombay. There are no children.   23

"You make things tough on yourself," Imre says. He assumed Patel was a Jewish name or maybe Hispanic; everything makes equal sense to him. He found the play tasteless, he worried about the effect of vulgar language on my sensitive ears. "You have to let go a bit." And as though to show me how to let go, he breaks   24 away from me, bounds ahead with his head ducked tight, then dances on amazingly jerky legs. He's a Magyar, he often tells me, and deep down, he's an Asian too. I catch glimpses of it, knife-blade Attila cheekbones, despite the blondish hair. In his faded jeans and leather jacket, he's a rock video star. I watch MTV for hours in the apartment when Charity's working the evening shift at Macy's. I listen to WPLJ on Charity's earphones. Why should I be ashamed? Television in India is so uplifting.

Imre stops as suddenly as he'd started. People walk around us. The summer sidewalk is full of theatergoers in seersucker suits; Imre's year-round jacket is out of place. European. Cops in twos and threes huddle, lightly tap their thighs with night sticks and smile at me with benevolence. I want to wink at them, get us all in trouble, tell them the crazy dancing man is from the Warsaw Pact. I'm too shy to break into dance on Broadway. So I hug Imre instead. 25

The hug takes him by surprise. He wants me to let go, but he doesn't really expect me to let go. He staggers, though I weigh no more than 104 pounds, and with him, I pitch forward slightly. Then he catches me, and we walk arm in arm to the bus stop. My husband would never dance or hug a woman on Broadway. Nor would my brothers. They aren't stuffy people, but they went to Anglican boarding schools and they have a well-developed sense of what's silly. 26

"Imre." I squeeze his big, rough hand. "I'm sorry I ruined the evening for you." 27

"You did nothing of the kind." He sounds tired. "Let's not wait for the bus. Let's splurge and take a cab instead." 28

Imre always has unexpected funds. The Network, he calls it, Class of '56. 29

In the back of the cab, without even trying, I feel light, almost free. Memories of Indian destitutes mix with the hordes of New York street people, and they float free, like astronauts, inside my head. I've made it. I'm making something of my life. I've left home, my husband, to get a Ph.D. in special ed. I have a multiple-entry visa and a small scholarship for two years. After that, we'll see. My mother was beaten by her mother-in-law, my grandmother, when she'd registered for French lessons at the Alliance Française. My grandmother, the eldest daughter of a rich zamindar, was illiterate. 30

Imre and the cabdriver talk away in Russian. I keep my eyes closed. That way I can feel the floaters better. I'll write Mamet tonight. I feel strong, reckless. Maybe I'll write Steven Spielberg too; tell him that Indians don't eat monkey brains. 31

We've made it. Patels must have made it. Mamet, Spielberg: they're not condescending to us. Maybe they're a little bit afraid. 32

Charity Chin, my roommate, is sitting on the floor drinking Chablis out of a plastic wineglass. She is five foot six, three inches taller than me, but weighs a kilo and a half less than I do. She is a "hands" model. Orientals are supposed to have a monopoly in the hands-modelling business, she says. She had her eyes fixed eight or nine months ago and out of gratitude sleeps with her plastic surgeon every third Wednesday. 33

"Oh, good," Charity says. "I'm glad you're back early. I need to talk." 34

She's been writing checks. MCI, Con Ed, Bonwit Teller. Envelopes, already stamped and sealed, form a pyramid between her shapely, knee-socked legs. The 35 checkbook's cover is brown plastic, grained to look like cowhide. Each time Charity flips back the cover, white geese fly over sky-colored checks. She makes good money, but she's extravagant. The difference adds up to this shared, rent-controlled Chelsea one-bedroom.

"All right. Talk." 36

When I first moved in, she was seeing an analyst. Now she sees a nutritionist. 37

"Eric called. From Oregon." 38

"What did he want?" 39

"He wants me to pay half the rent on his loft for last spring. He asked me to move back, remember? He *begged* me." 40

Eric is Charity's estranged husband. 41

"What does your nutritionist say?" Eric now wears a red jumpsuit and tills the soil in Rajneeshpuram. 42

"You think Phil's a creep too, don't you? What else can he be when creeps are all I attract?" 43

Phil is a flutist with thinning hair. He's very touchy on the subject of *flautists* versus *flutists*. He's touchy on every subject, from music to books to foods to clothes. He teaches at a small college upstate, and Charity bought a used blue Datsun ("Nissan," Phil insists) last month so she could spend weekends with him. She returns every Sunday night, exhausted and exasperated. Phil and I don't have much to say to each other—he's the only musician I know; the men in my family are lawyers, engineers, or in business—but I like him. Around me, he loosens up. When he visits, he bakes us loaves of pumpernickel bread. He waxes our kitchen floor. Like many men in this country, he seems to me a displaced child, or even a woman, looking for something that passed him by, or for something that he can never have. If he thinks I'm not looking, he sneaks his hands under Charity's sweater, but there isn't too much there. Here, she's a model with high ambitions. In India, she'd be a flat-chested old maid. 44

I'm shy in front of the lovers. A darkness comes over me when I see them horsing around. 45

"It isn't the money," Charity says. Oh? I think. "He says he still loves me. Then he turns around and asks me for five hundred." 46

What's so strange about that, I want to ask. She still loves Eric, and Eric, red jumpsuit and all, is smart enough to know it. Love is a commodity, hoarded like any other. Mamet knows. But I say, "I'm not the person to ask about love." Charity knows that mine was a traditional Hindu marriage. My parents, with the help of a marriage broker, who was my mother's cousin, picked out a groom. All I had to do was get to know his taste in food. 47

It'll be a long evening, I'm afraid. Charity likes to confess. I unpleat my silk sari—it no longer looks too showy—wrap it in muslin cloth and put it away in a dresser drawer. Saris are hard to have laundered in Manhattan, though there's a good man in Jackson Heights. My next step will be to brew us a pot of chrysanthemum tea. It's a very special tea from the mainland. Charity's uncle gave it to us. I like him. He's a humpbacked, awkward, terrified man. He runs a gift store on Mott Street, and though he doesn't speak much English, he seems to have done 48 well. Once upon a time he worked for the railways in Chengdu, Szechwan Province, and during the Wuchang Uprising, he was shot at. When I'm down, when I'm lonely for my husband, when I think of our son, or when I need to be held, I think of Charity's uncle. If I hadn't left home, I'd never have heard of the Wuchang Uprising. I've broadened my horizons.

Very late that night my husband calls me from Ahmadabad, a town of textile mills north of Bombay. My husband is a vice president at Lakshmi Cotton Mills. Lakshmi is the goddess of wealth, but LCM (Priv.), Ltd., is doing poorly. Lockouts, strikes, rock-throwings. My husband lives on digitalis, which he calls the food for our *yuga* of discontent. 49

"We had a bad mishap at the mill today." Then he says nothing for seconds. 50

The operator comes on. "Do you have the right party, sir? We're trying to reach Mrs. Butt." 51

"Bhatt," I insist. "*B* for Bombay, *H* for Haryana, *A* for Ahmadabad, double *T* for Tamil Nadu." It's a litany. "This is she." 52

"One of our lorries was firebombed today. Resulting in three deaths. The driver, old Karamchand, and his two children." 53

I know how my husband's eyes look this minute, how the eye rims sag and the yellow corneas shine and bulge with pain. He is not an emotional man—the Ahmadabad Institute of Management has trained him to cut losses, to look on the bright side of economic catastrophes—but tonight he's feeling low. I try to remember a driver named Karamchand, but can't. That part of my life is over, the way *trucks* have replaced *lorries* in my vocabulary, the way Charity Chin and her lurid love life have replaced inherited notions of marital duty. Tomorrow he'll come out of it. Soon he'll be eating again. He'll sleep like a baby. He's been trained to believe in turnovers. Every morning he rubs his scalp with cantharidine oil so his hair will grow back again. 54

"It could be your car next." Affection, love. Who can tell the difference in a traditional marriage in which a wife still doesn't call her husband by his first name? 55

"No. They know I'm a flunky, just like them. Well paid, maybe. No need for undue anxiety, please." 56

Then his voice breaks. He says he needs me, he misses me, he wants me to come to him damp from my evening shower, smelling of sandalwood soap, my braid decorated with Jasmines. 57

"I need you too." 58

"Not to worry, please," he says. "I am coming in a fortnight's time. I have already made arrangements." 59

Outside my window, fire trucks whine, up Eighth Avenue. I wonder if he can hear them, what he thinks of a life like mine, led amid disorder. 60

"I am thinking it'll be like a honeymoon. More or less." 61

When I was in college, waiting to be married, I imagined honeymoons were only for the more fashionable girls, the girls who came from slightly racy families, smoked Sobranies in the dorm lavatories and put up posters of Kabir Bedi, who was supposed to have made it as a big star in the West. My husband wants us to go to 62

Niagara. I'm not to worry about foreign exchange. He's arranged for extra dollars through the Gujarati Network, with a cousin in San Jose. And he's bought four hundred more on the black market. "Tell me you need me. Panna, please tell me again."

I change out of the cotton pants and shirt I've been wearing all day and put on a sari to meet my husband at JFK. I don't forget the jewelry; the marriage necklace of *mangalsutra,* gold drop earrings, heavy gold bangles. I don't wear them every day. In this borough of vice and greed, who knows when, or whom, desire will overwhelm.   **63**

My husband spots me in the crowd and waves. He has lost weight, and changed his glasses. The arm, uplifted in a cheery wave, is bony, frail, almost opalescent.   **64**

In the Carey Coach, we hold hands. He strokes my fingers one by one. "How come you aren't wearing my mother's ring?"   **65**

"Because muggers know about Indian women," I say. They know with us it's 24-karat. His mother's ring is showy, in ghastly taste anywhere but India: a blood-red Burma ruby set in a gold frame of floral sprays. My mother-in-law got her guru to bless the ring before I left for the States.   **66**

He looks disconcerted. He's used to a different role. He's the knowing, suspicious one in the family. He seems to be sulking, and finally he comes out with it. "You've said nothing about my new glasses." I compliment him on the glasses, how chic and Western-executive they make him look. But I can't help the other things, necessities until he learns the ropes. I handle the money, buy the tickets. I don't know if this makes me unhappy.   **67**

Charity drives her Nissan upstate, so for two weeks we are to have the apartment to ourselves. This is more privacy than we ever had in India. No parents, no servants, to keep us modest. We play at housekeeping. Imre has lent us a hibachi, and I grill saffron chicken breasts. My husband marvels at the size of the Perdue hens. "They're big like peacocks, no? These Americans, they're really something!" He tries out pizzas, burgers, McNuggets. He chews. He explores. He judges. He loves it all, fears nothing, feels at home in the summer odors, the clutter of Manhattan streets. Since he thinks that the American palate is bland, he carries a bottle of red peppers in his pocket. I wheel a shopping cart down the aisles of the neighborhood Grand Union, and he follows, swiftly, greedily. He picks up hair rinses and high-protein diet powders. There's so much I already take for granted.   **68**

One night, Imre stops by. He wants us to go with him to a movie. In his work shirt and red leather tie, he looks arty or strung out. It's only been a week, but I feel as though I am really seeing him for the first time. The yellow hair worn very short at the sides, the wide, narrow lips. He's a good-looking man, but self-conscious, almost arrogant. He's picked the movie we should see. He always tells me what to see, what to read. He buys the *Voice.* He's a natural avant-gardist. For tonight he's chosen *Numero Deux.*   **69**

"Is it a musical?" my husband asks. The Radio City Music Hall is on his list of sights to see. He's read up on the history of the Rockettes. He doesn't catch Imre's sympathetic wink.   **70**

Guilt, shame, loyalty. I long to be ungracious, not ingratiate myself with both men.   71

That night my husband calculates in rupees the money we've wasted on Godard. "That refugee fellow, Nagy, must have a screw loose in his head. I paid very steep price for dollars on the black market."   72

Some afternoons we go shopping. Back home we hated shopping, but now it is a lovers' project. My husband's shopping list startles me. I feel I am just getting to know him. Maybe, like Imre, freed from the dignities of old-world culture, he too could get drunk and squirt Cheez Whiz on a guest. I watch him dart into stores in his gleaming leather shoes. Jockey shorts on sale in outdoor bins on Broadway entrance him. White tube socks with different bands of color delight him. He looks for microcassettes, for anything small and electronic and smuggleable. He needs a garment bag. He calls it a "wardrobe," and I have to translate.   73

"All of New York is having sales, no?"   74

My heart speeds watching him this happy. It's the third week in August, almost the end of summer, and the city smells ripe, it cannot bear more heat, more money, more energy.   75

"This is so smashing! The prices are so excellent!" Recklessly, my prudent husband signs away traveller's checks. How he intends to smuggle it all back I don't dare ask. With a microwave, he calculates, we could get rid of our cook.   76

This has to be love, I think. Charity, Eric, Phil: they may be experts on sex. My husband doesn't chase me around the sofa, but he pushes me down on Charity's battered cushions, and the man who has never entered the kitchen of our Ahmadabad house now comes toward me with a dish tub of steamy water to massage away the pavement heat.   77

Ten days into his vacation my husband checks out brochures for sightseeing tours. Shortline, Grayline, Crossroads: his new vinyl briefcase is full of schedules and pamphlets. While I make pancakes out of a mix, he comparison-shops. Tour number one costs $10.95 and will give us the World Trade Center, Chinatown, and the United Nations. Tour number three would take us both uptown *and* downtown for $14.95, but my husband is absolutely sure he doesn't want to see Harlem. We settle for tour number four: Downtown and the Dame. It's offered by a new tour company with a small, dirty office at Eighth and Forty-eighth.   78

The sidewalk outside the office is colorful with tourists. My husband sends me in to buy the tickets because he has come to feel Americans don't understand his accent.   79

The dark man, Lebanese probably, behind the counter comes on too friendly. "Come on, doll, make my day!" He won't say which tour is his. "Number four? Honey, no! Look, you've wrecked me! Say you'll change your mind." He takes two twenties and gives back change. He holds the tickets, forcing me to pull. He leans closer. "I'm off after lunch."   80

My husband must have been watching me from the sidewalk. "What was the chap saying?" he demands. "I told you not to wear pants. He thinks you are Puerto Rican. He thinks he can treat you with disrespect."   81

The bus is crowded and we have to sit across the aisle from each other. The tour guide begins his patter on Forty-sixth. He looks like an actor, his hair bleached and blow-dried. Up close he must look middle-aged, but from where I sit his skin is smooth and his cheeks faintly red. 82

"Welcome to the Big Apple, folks." The guide uses a microphone. "Big Apple. That's what we native Manhattan degenerates call our city. Today we have guests from fifteen foreign countries and six states from this U.S. of A. That makes the Tourist Bureau real happy. And let me assure you that while we may be the richest city in the richest country in the world, it's okay to tip your charming and talented attendant." He laughs. Then he swings his hip out into the aisle and sings a song. 83

"And it's mighty fancy on old Delancey Street, you know. . . ." 84

My husband looks irritable. The guide is, as expected, a good singer. "The bloody man should be giving us histories of buildings we are passing, no?" I pat his hand, the mood passes. He cranes his neck. Our window seats have both gone to Japanese. It's the tour of his life. Next to this, the quick business trips to Manchester and Glasgow pale. 85

"And tell me what street compares to Mott Street, in July. . . ." 86

The guide wants applause. He manages a derisive laugh from the Americans up front. He's working the aisles now. "I coulda been somebody, right? I coulda been a star!" Two or three of us smile, those of us who recognize the parody. He catches my smile. The sun is on his harsh, bleached hair. "Right, your highness? Look, we gotta maharani with us! Couldn't I have been a star?" 87

"Right!" I say, my voice coming out a squeal. I've been trained to adapt; what else can I say? 88

We drive through traffic past landmark office buildings and churches. The guide flips his hands. "Art deco," he keeps saying. I hear him confide to one of the Americans: "Beats me. I went to a cheap guide's school." My husband wants to know more about this Art Deco, but the guide sings another song. 89

"We made a foolish choice," my husband grumbles. "We are sitting in the bus only. We're not going into famous buildings." He scrutinizes the pamphlets in his jacket pocket. I think, at least it's air-conditioned in here. I could sit here in the cool shadows of the city forever. 90

Only five of us appear to have opted for the "Downtown and the Dame" tour. The others will ride back uptown past the United Nations after we've been dropped off at the pier for the ferry to the Statue of Liberty. 91

An elderly European pulls a camera out of his wife's designer tote bag. He takes pictures of the boats in the harbor, the Japanese in kimonos eating popcorn, scavenging pigeons, me. Then, pushing his wife ahead of him, he climbs back on the bus and waves to us. For a second I feel terribly lost. I wish we were on the bus going back to the apartment. I know I'll not be able to describe any of this to Charity, or to Imre. I'm too proud to admit I went on a guided tour. 92

The view of the city from the Circle Line ferry is seductive, unreal. The skyline wavers out of reach, but never quite vanishes. The summer sun pushes through fluffy clouds and dapples the glass of office towers. My husband looks 93

thrilled, even more than he had on the shopping trips down Broadway. Tourists
and dreamers, we have spent our life's savings to see this skyline, this statue.

"Quick, take a picture of me!" my husband yells as he moves toward a gap of   94
railings. A Japanese matron has given up her position in order to change film.
"Before the Twin Towers disappear!"

I focus, I wait for a large Oriental family to walk out of my range. My husband   95
holds his pose tight against the railing. He wants to look relaxed, an international
businessman at home in all the financial markets.

A bearded man slides across the bench toward me. "Like this," he says and   96
helps me get my husband in focus. "You want me to take the photo for you?" His
name, he says, is Goran. He is Goran from Yugoslavia, as though that were enough
for tracking him down. Imre from Hungary. Panna from India. He pulls the old
Leica out of my hand, signaling the Orientals to beat it, and clicks away. "I'm a
photographer," he says. He could have been a camera thief. That's what my husband would have assumed. Somehow, I trusted. "Get you a beer?" he asks.

"I don't. Drink, I mean. Thank you very much." I say those last words very   97
loud, for everyone's benefit. The odd bottles of Soave with Imre don't count.

"Too bad." Goran gives back the camera.   98

"Take one more!" my husband shouts from the railing. "Just to be sure!"   99

The island itself disappoints. The Lady has brutal scaffolding holding her in.   100
The museum is closed. The snack bar is dirty and expensive. My husband reads out
the prices to me. He orders two french fries and two Cokes. We sit at picnic tables
and wait for the ferry to take us back.

"What was that hippie chap saying?"   101

As if I could say. A day-care center has brought its kids, at least forty of them,   102
to the island for the day. The kids, all wearing name tags, run around us. I can't
help noticing how many are Indian. Even a Patel, probably a Bhatt if I looked hard
enough. They toss hamburger bits at pigeons. They kick styrofoam cups. The
pigeons are slow, greedy, persistent. I have to shoo one off the table top. I don't
think my husband thinks about our son.

"What hippie?"   103

"The one on the boat. With the beard and the hair."   104

My husband doesn't look at me. He shakes out his paper napkin and tries to   105
protect his french fries from pigeon feathers.

"Oh, him. He said he was from Dubrovnik." It isn't true, but I don't want   106
trouble.

"What did he say about Dubrovnik?"   107

I know enough about Dubrovnik to get by. Imre's told me about it. And about   108
Mostar and Zagreb. In Mostar white Muslims sing the call to prayer. I would like
to see that before I die: white Muslims. Whole peoples have moved before me;
they've adapted. The night Imre told me about Mostar was also the night I saw my
first snow in Manhattan. We'd walked down to Chelsea from Columbia. We'd
walked and talked and I hadn't felt tired at all.

"You're too innocent," my husband says. He reaches for my hand. "Panna," he 109 cries with pain in his voice, and I am brought back from perfect, floating memories of snow, "I've come to take you back. I have seen how men watch you."

"What?" 110

"Come back, now. I have tickets. We have all the things we will ever need. I 111 can't live without you."

A little girl with wiry braids kicks a bottle cap at his shoes. The pigeons wheel 112 and scuttle around us. My husband covers his fries with spread-out fingers. "No kicking," he tells the girl. Her name, Beulah, is printed in green ink on a heart-shaped name tag. He forces a smile, and Beulah smiles back. Then she starts to flap her arms. She flaps, she hops. The pigeons go crazy for fries and scraps.

"Special ed. course is two years," I remind him. "I can't go back." 113

My husband picks up our trays and throws them into the garbage before I can 114 stop him. He's carried disposability a little too far. "We've been taken," he says, moving toward the dock, though the ferry will not arrive for another twenty minutes. "The ferry costs only two dollars round-trip per person. We should have chosen tour number one for $10.95 instead of tour number four for $14.95."

With my Lebanese friend, I think. "But this way we don't have to worry about 115 cabs. The bus will pick us up at the pier and take us back to midtown. Then we can walk home."

"New York is full of cheats and whatnot. Just like Bombay." He is not accus- 116 ing me of infidelity. I feel dread all the same.

That night, after we've gone to bed, the phone rings. My husband listens, 117 then hands the phone to me. "What is this woman saying?" He turns on the pink Macy's lamp by the bed. "I am not understanding these Negro people's accents."

The operator repeats the message. It's a cable from one of the directors of 118 Lakshmi Cotton Mills. "Massive violent labor confrontation anticipated. Stop. Return posthaste. Stop. Cable flight details. Signed Kantilal Shah."

"It's not your factory," I say. "You're supposed to be on vacation. " 119

"So, you are worrying about me? Yes? You reject my heartfelt wishes but you 120 worry about me?" He pulls me close, slips the straps of my nightdress off my shoulder. "Wait a minute."

I wait, unclothed, for my husband to come back to me. The water is running 121 in the bathroom. In the ten days he has been here he has learned American rites: deodorants, fragrances. Tomorrow morning he'll call Air India; tomorrow evening he'll be on his way back to Bombay. Tonight I should make up to him for my years away, the gutted trucks, the degree I'll never use in India. I want to pretend with him that nothing has changed.

In the mirror that hangs on the bathroom door, I watch my naked body turn, 122 the breasts, the thighs glow. The body's beauty amazes. I stand here shameless, in ways he has never seen me. I am free, afloat, watching somebody else.

The iDeal Reader

Ursula K. Le Guin, "It Was
a Dark and Stormy Night; . .
."

© The McGraw–Hill
Companies, 2000

231

Ursula Kroeber Le Guin (1929–   ) was born on October 21 in Berkeley, California. She received an A.B. from Radcliffe College in 1951 and an A.M. from Columbia University in 1952. A resident of Portland, Oregon, Le Guin studied Renaissance history and married a history professor. She has written novels; worked as an instructor of French; lectured; and written essays, poetry, and children's books. Le Guin sees her writing as spanning several modes, including science fiction, fantasy, realism, and magic realism. Her work offers social analysis but does not advocate specific social reforms.

Le Guin has won Nebula and Hugo awards for short fiction. She emphasizes a broad definition of humanity in her fiction as well as the need for individual morality. In her Earthsea trilogy (*A Wizard of Earthsea*, 1968; *The Tombs of Atuan*, 1971; *The Farthest Shore*, 1972; and another sequel, *Tehanu: The Last Book of Earthsea*, 1990), Le Guin presents a balanced cosmology not based on a Christian ethos, as are the works of C. S. Lewis, but rather a holistic version based on respect for the universe. Her many works include *The Left Hand of Darkness* (1969; new ed. 1984) and *The Dispossessed: An Ambiguous Utopia* (1974). Le Guin has also coedited *The Norton Book of Science Fiction: North American Science Fiction, 1960–1990* (1993).

It Was a Dark and Stormy Night; or, Why Are We Huddling about the Campfire?

Ursula K. Le Guin

It was a dark and stormy night
and Brigham Young and Brigham Old
sat around the campfire.
Tell us a story, old man!
And this is the story he told:

It was a dark and stormy night
and Brigham Young and Brigham Old
sat around the campfire.
Tell us a story, old man!
And this is the story he told:

It was a dark and stormy night
and Brigham Young and Pierre Menard, author of the *Quixote*,
sat around the campfire,
which is not quite the way my Great-Aunt Betsy told it
when we said Tell us another story!
Tell us, *au juste*, what happened!
And this is the story she told:

It was a dark and stormy night, in the otherwise unnoteworthy year 711 E.C. (Eskimo   1
Calendar), and the great-aunt sat crouched at her typewriter, holding his hands

out to it from time to time as if for warmth and swinging on a swing. He was a handsome boy of about eighteen, one of those men who suddenly excite your desire when you meet them in the street, and who leave you with a vague feeling of uneasiness and excited senses. On a plate beside the typewriter lay a slice of tomato. It was a flawless slice. It was a perfect slice of a perfect tomato. It is perfectly boring. I hold out my hands to the typewriter again, while swinging and showing my delicate limbs, and observe that the rows of keys are marked with all the letters of the English alphabet, and all the letters of the French alphabet minus accent marks, and all the letters of the Polish alphabet except the dark L. By striking these keys with the ends of my fingers or, conceivably, a small blunt instrument, the aging woman can create a flaw in the tomato. She did so at once. It was then a seriously, indeed a disgustingly flawed tomato, but it continued to be perfectly boring until eaten. She expires instantly in awful agony, of snakebite, flinging the window wide to get air. It is a dark and stormy night and the rain falling in on the typewriter keys writes a story in German about a great-aunt who went to a symposium on narrative and got eaten in the forest by a metabear. She writes the story while reading it with close attention, not sure what to expect, but collaborating hard, as if that was anything new; and this is the story I wrote:

It was a dark and stormy night
and Brigham al-Rashid sat around the campfire with his wife
who was telling him a story in order to keep her head on her shoulders,
and this is the story she told:

The *histoire* is the what
and the *discours* is the how
but what I want to know, Brigham,
is *le pourquoi*.
Why are we sitting here around the campfire?

Tell me a story, great-aunt,
so that I can sleep.
Tell me a story, Scheherazade,
so that you can live.
Tell me a story, my soul, animula, vagula, blandula,
little Being-Towards-Death,
for the word's the beginning of being
if not the middle or the end.

2

"A beginning is that which is not itself necessarily after anything else, and which has naturally something else after it; an end, that which is naturally after something else, either as its necessary or usual consequent, and with nothing else after it; and a middle, that which is by nature after one thing and has also another after it."[1]

3

---

[1] Aristotle, *On the Art of Poetry*, trans. Ingram Bywater (Oxford, 1920), p. 40.

The iDeal Reader

Ursula K. Le Guin, "It Was
a Dark and Stormy Night; . .
."

© The McGraw–Hill
Companies, 2000

233

But sequence grows difficult in the ignorance of what comes after the necessary
or at least the usual consequent of living, that is, dying, and also when the soul is
confused by not unreasonable doubts of what comes after the next thing that happens,
whatever that may be.   4

It gets dark and stormy when you look away from the campfire.

Tell me what you see in the fire, Lizzie, Lizzie Hexam,
down in the hollow by the flare!
I see storm and darkness, brother.
I see death and running water, brother.
I see loving kindness, brother.
Is it all right to see that, teacher?
What would Alain Robbe-Grillet say?

Never mind what he says, Lizzie.
Frogs have a lot of trouble with the novel,
even though kissed right at the beginning by the Princesse de Clèves;
maybe they do not want to look down and see Victor Hugo glimmering *au
    fond du puits*.

Brigham, this is stupid stuff!
Tell us a story, old man,
or old woman as the case may be,
or old Tiresias, chirping like a cricket,
tell us a story with a proper end to it
instead of beginning again and again like this
and thereby achieving a muddle
which is not by nature after anything in particular
nor does it have anything consequent to it
but it just hangs there
placidly eating its tail.

5

In the Far West, where Brigham Young ended up and I started from, they tell
stories about hoop snakes. When a hoop snake wants to get somewhere—whether
because the hoop snake is after something, or because something is after the hoop
snake—it takes its tail (which may or may not have rattles on it) into its mouth, thus
forming itself into a hoop, and rolls. Jehovah enjoined snakes to crawl on their
belly in the dust, but Jehovah was an Easterner. Rolling along, bowling along, is a lot
quicker and more satisfying than crawling. But, for the hoop snakes with rattles, there
is a drawback. They are venomous snakes, and when they bite their own tail they
die, in awful agony, of snakebite. All progress has these hitches, I don't know what
the moral is. It may be in the end safest to lie perfectly still without even crawling.
Indeed it's certain that we shall all do so in the end, which has nothing else after it.
But then no tracks are left in the dust, no lines drawn; the dark and stormy nights

are all one with the sweet bright days, this moment of June—and you might as well never have lived at all. And the moral of *that* is, you have to form a circle to escape from the circle. Draw in a little closer around the campfire. If we could truly form a circle, joining the beginning and the end, we would, as another Greek remarked, not die. But never fear. We can't manage it no matter how we try. But still, very few things come nearer the real Hoop Trick than a good story.   6

There was a man who practiced at the Hoop Trick named Aneirin.   7

But let us have the footnotes first.   8

"We have to bear in mind that the *Gododdin* [and its associated lays] are not narrative poems. . . . Nowhere is there any attempt to give an account of what it was really all about."[2] I disagree with this comment and agree with the next one, which points out that the work goes rolling and bowling all about what it is all about. "While some of these [early Welsh poems] will 'progress' in expected fashion from a beginning through a middle to an end, the normal structure is 'radial,' circling about, repeating and elaborating the central theme. It is all 'middle.' "[3]

This is the Gododdin; Aneirin sang it.   [I]

Men went to Catraeth, keen their war-band   [VIII]
Pale mead their portion, it was poison.
Three hundred under orders to fight.
And after celebration, silence.

Men went to Catraeth at dawn: [X]
All their fears had been put to flight.
Three hundred clashed with ten thousand.

Men went to Catraeth at dawn: [XI]
Their high spirits lessened their lifespans.
They drank mead, gold and sweet, ensnaring;
For a year the minstrels were merry.

Three spears stain with blood   [XVIII]
Fifty, five hundred.
Three hounds, three hundred:
Three stallions of war
From golden Eidin,
Three mailclad war-bands,
Three gold-collared kings.

In the great hall I drank wine and mead.   [XIX]
Many were his spears;

---

[2] K. H. Jackson, *The Gododdin: The Oldest Scottish Poem* (Edinburgh, 1969), pp. 3–4.
[3] Joseph P. Clancy, *The Earliest Welsh Poetry* (London and New York, 1970), quotation from introduction.

The iDeal Reader

Ursula K. Le Guin, "It Was
a Dark and Stormy Night; . .
."

© The McGraw–Hill
Companies, 2000

235

In the clash of men
He fashioned a feast for eagles.

Men went to Catraeth, they were renowned,   [XXI]
Wine and mead from gold cups was their drink,
A year in noble ceremonial,
Three hundred and sixty-three gold-torqued men.
Of all those who charged, after too much drink,
But three won free through courage in strife:
Aeron's two warhounds and tough Cynon,
And myself, soaked in blood, for my song's sake.

My legs at full length   [XLVIII]
In a house of earth,
A chain of iron
About both ankles,
Caused by mead, by horn,
By Catraeth's raiders.
I, not I, Aneirin,
Taliesin knows it,
Master of wordcraft,
Sang to Gododdin
Before the day dawned.

None walk the earth, no mother has borne   [XLIX]
One so fair and strong, dark as iron.
From a war-band his bright blade saved me,
From a fell cell of earth be bore me,
From a place of death, from a harsh land,
Cenan fab Llywarch, bold, undaunted.

Many I lost of my true comrades.   [LXI]
Of three hundred champions who charged to Catraeth,
It is tragic, but one man came back.

On Tuesday they donned their dark armour,   [LXIX]
On Wednesday, bitter their meeting,
On Thursday, terms were agreed on,
On Friday, dead men without number,
On Saturday, fearless, they worked as one,
On Sunday, crimson blades were their lot,
On Monday, men were seen waist-deep in blood.
After defeat, the Gododdin say,
Before Madawg's tent on his return
There came but one man in a hundred.

Three hundred, gold-torqued,   [XCI]
Warlike, well-trained,
Three hundred, haughty,
In harmony, armed.
Three hundred fierce steeds
Bore them to battle.
Three hounds, three hundred:
Tragic, no return.[4]

"I, not I, Aneirin"—"won free"—"for my song's sake." What is Aneirin telling   9
us? Whether or not we allow that a story so muddled or all middle can be a narrative,
or must be lyric or elegiac, but do classic Greek definitions fit Welsh Dark Ages
traditions?—so, as Barbara Myerhoff pleaded, in all courtesy let us not argue about it
at this point, only perhaps admitting that the spiral is probably the shortest way of
getting through spacetime and is certainly an effective way to recount the *loss* of a
battle—in any case, what is Aneirin trying to tell us? For all we know or shall ever
know of the Battle of Catraeth is what he tells us; and there is no doubt that he
very much wanted us to know about it, to remember it. He says that he won free
for his song's sake. He says that he survived, alone, or with Cynan and two others, or
with Cenan—he seems to have survived in several different ways, also, which is very
Welsh of him—he says that he survived in order to tell us about his friends who
did not survive. But I am not sure whether he means by this that he must tell the
story because he alone survived; or that he survived because he had the story to tell.

And now for quite another war. I am going to speak in many voices now for a   10
while. Novelists have this habit of ventriloquy.[5]

"The SS guards took pleasure in telling us that we had no chance of coming out   11
alive, a point they emphasized with particular relish by insisting that after the war
the rest of the world would not believe what had happened; there would be no
evidence" (a survivor of Dachau).

"Those caught were shot, but that did not keep Ringelblum and his friends from   12
organizing a clandestine group whose job was to gather information for deposit in a
secret archive, much of which survived. Here survival and bearing witness became
reciprocal acts" (Des Pres).

"In Treblinka the dead were being unearthed and burned, by work squads; after   13
that the work squads were to be shot and burned. If that had come to pass Treblinka
would never have existed. The aim of the revolt was to ensure the memory of that
place. We know the story of Treblinka because forty survived" (Des Pres).

"I found it most difficult to stay alive, but I had to live, to give the world this   14
story" (Glatstein, from Treblinka).

"Even in this place one can survive, and therefore one must want to survive,   15
to tell the story, to bear witness" (Primo Levi, from Auschwitz).

---

[4] Ibid., Clancy's translation of the text of the *Gododdin*.
[5] The following citations appear in Terence Des Pres' *The Survivor: An Anatomy of Life in the Death Camps* (Oxford, 1976; New York, 1977). Some of the citations from Des Pres' own text are rephrased.

"It is a man's way of leaving a trace, of telling people how he lived and died. If nothing else is left, one must scream. Silence is the real crime against humanity" (Nadyezhda Mandelshtam).   16

"Conscience is a social achievement; on its historical level it is the collective effort to come to terms with evil, to distill a moral knowledge equal to the problems at hand. . . . Existence at its boundary is intrinsically significant. The struggle to live, to survive, is rooted in, and a manifestation of, the form-conferring potency of life itself" (Des Pres).   17

"We may speculate that survival depends upon life considered . . . as a set of activities evolved through time in successful response to crises, the sole purpose of which is to keep going. . . . Living things act as they do because they are so organized as to take actions that prevent their dissolution into their surroundings" (J. Z. Young).   18

"It seems as if Western culture were making a prodigious effort of historiographic *anamnesis*. . . . We may say . . . this *anamnesis* continues the religious evaluation of memory and forgetfulness. To be sure, neither myths nor religious practices are any longer involved. But there is this common element: the importance of precise and total recollection. . . . The prose narrative, especially the novel, has taken the place of the recitation of myths. . . . The tale takes up and continues 'initiation' on the level of the imaginary. . . . Believing that he is merely amusing himself or escaping, the man of the modern societies still benefits from the imaginary initiation supplied by tales. . . . Today we are beginning to realize that what is called 'initiation' coexists with the human condition, that every existence is made up of an unbroken series of 'ordeals,' 'deaths,' and 'resurrections.' . . . Whatever the gravity of the present crisis of the novel, it is nonetheless true that the need to find one's way into 'foreign' universes and to follow the complications of a 'story' seems to be consubstantial with the human condition."[6]   19

"For Heaven only knows why one loves it so, how one sees it so, making it up, building it round one, tumbling it, creating it every moment afresh. . . . In people's eyes, in the swing, tramp, and trudge; in the bellow and the uproar; the carriages, motor cars, omnibuses, vans, sandwich men shuffling and swinging; brass bands; barrel organs; in the triumph and the jingle and the strange high singing of some aeroplane overhead was what she loved; life; London; this moment of June."[7]   20

Why are we huddling about the campfire? Why do we tell tales, or tales about tales—why do we bear witness, true or false? We may ask Aneirin, or Primo Levi, we may ask Scheherazade, or Virginia Woolf. Is it because we are so organized as to take actions that prevent our dissolution into the surroundings? I know a very short story which might illustrate this hypothesis. You will find it carved into a stone about three feet up from the floor of the north transept of Carlisle Cathedral in the north of England, not all that far from Catterick which may have been Catraeth. It was carved in runes, one line of runes, laboriously carved into the stone. A translation into English is posted up nearby in typescript under glass. Here is the whole story: 21

Tolfink carved these runes in this stone.

---

[6] Mircea Eliade, *Myth and Reality*, trans. Willard R. Trask (New York, 1963), pp. 136, 138, and 202.
[7] Virginia Woolf, *Mrs. Dalloway* (New York, 1925), p. 5.

Well, this is pretty close to Barbara Herrnstein Smith's earliest form of   22
historiography—notch-cutting. As a story, it does not really meet the requirement
of Minimal Connexity. It doesn't have much beginning or end. The material was
obdurate, and life is short. Yet I would say Tolfink was a reliable narrator. Tolfink bore
witness at least to the existence of Tolfink, a human being unwilling to dissolve entirely into his surroundings.

It is time to end, an appropriate time for a ghost story. It was a dark and stormy   23
night, and the man and the woman sat around the campfire in their tent out on
the plains. They had killed the woman's husband and run away together. They had
been going north across the plains for three days now. The man said, "We must be
safe. There is no way the people of the tribe can track us." The woman said, "What's
that noise?" They listened, and they both heard a scratching noise on the outside
of the tent, low down, near the ground. "It's the wind blowing," the man said. The
woman said, "It doesn't sound like the wind." They listened and heard the sound
again, a scraping, louder, and higher up on the wall of the tent. The woman said, "Go
and see what it is. It must be some animal." The man didn't want to go out. She said,
"Are you afraid?" Now the scraping sound had got very loud, up almost over their
heads. The man jumped up and went outside to look. There was enough light from
the fire inside the tent that he could see what is was. It was a skull. It was rolling
up the outside of the tent, so that it could get in at the smokehole at the top. It was
the skull of the man they had killed, the husband, but it had grown very big. It had
been rolling after them over the plains all along and growing bigger as it rolled.
The man shouted to the woman, and she came out of the tent, and they caught each
other by the hand and ran. They ran into the darkness, and the skull rolled down the
tent and rolled after them. It came faster and faster. They ran until they fell down
in the darkness, and the skull caught up with them there. That was the end of them.

There may be some truth in that story, that tale, that discourse, that narrative, but   24
there is no reliability in the telling of it. It was told you forty years later by the ten-year-
old who heard it, along with her great-aunt, by the campfire, on a dark and starry night
in California; and though it is, I believe, a Plains Indian story, she heard it told in English
by an anthropologist of German antecedents. But by remembering it he had made the
story his; and insofar as I have remembered it, it is mine; and now, if you like it, it's
yours. In the tale, in the telling, we are all one blood. Take the tale in your teeth, then,
and bite till the blood runs, hoping it's not poison; and we will all come to the end
together, and even to the beginning: living, as we do, in the middle.

Historical Moments

Sir Francis Bacon (1561–1626) is perhaps best known for his essays on the nature of knowledge and scientific inquiry. Bacon's father was an administrator for Queen Elizabeth I and, therefore, Bacon himself was well connected both politically and culturally. Bacon graduated from Trinity College in Cambridge in 1575 and went on to become a barrister in 1584. Not satisfied with serving as a councilor for the queen, Bacon sought higher positions. He was knighted by James I in 1603, became solicitor general in 1607, and was named Baron Verulam in 1607. An advocate for ethical science and empirically based studies, some of Bacon's most important and enduring works include *The Advancement of Learning* (1605), *Novum Organum* (1620), and *History of Henry VII* (1623).

Of Studies

Sir Francis Bacon

L.

Studies serue for Delight, for Ornament, and for Ability. Their Chiefe Vse for   1
Delight, is in Priuatenesse and Retiring; For Ornament, is in Discourse; And for
Ability, is in the Iudgement and Disposition of Businesse. For Expert Men can
Execute, and perhaps Iudge of particulars, one by one; But the generall Counsels,
and the Plots, and Marshalling of Affaires, come best from those that are
Learned. To spend too much Time in *Studies*, is Sloth; To vse them too much for
Ornament, is Affectation; To make Iudgement wholly by their Rules is the
Humour of a Scholler. They perfect Nature, and are perfected by Experience: For
Naturall Abilities, are like Naturall Plants, that need Proyning by *Study*: And
Studies themselves, doe giue forth Directions too much at Large, except they be
bounded in by experience. Crafty Men Contemne *Studies*; simple Men Admire
them; And Wise Men Vse them: For they teach not their owne Vse; But that is
a Wisdome without them, and aboue them, won by Obseruation. Reade not to
Contradict, and Confute; Nor to Beleeue and Take for granted; Nor to Finde
Talke and Discourse; But to weigh and Consider. Some *Bookes* are to be Tasted,
Others to be Swallowed, and Some Few to be Chewed and Digested: That is,
some *Bookes* are to be read onely in Parts; Others to be read but not Curiously;
And some Few to be read wholly, and with Diligence and Attention. Some
Bookes also may be read by Deputy, and Extracts made of them by Others: But
that would be, onely in the lesse important Arguments, and the Meaner Sort of
Bookes: else distilled *Bookes*, are like Common distilled Waters, Flashy Things.
Reading maketh a Full Man; Conference a Ready Man; And Writing an Exact
Man. And therefore, If a Man Write little, he had need haue a Great memory; If
he Conferre little, he had need haue a Present Wit; And if he Reade litle, he had
need haue much Cunning, to seeme to know that, he doth not. *Histories* make
Men Wise; *Poets* Witty; The *Mathematicks* Subtill; *Naturall Philosophy* deepe;
Morall Graue; *Logick* and *Rhetorick* Able to Contend. *Abeunt studia in Mores.* Nay

Francis Bacon, "Of Studies" from *Essays by Francis Bacon.* London: Oxford University Press, 1937, pp. 204-206. First published 1597.

there is no Stond or Impediment in the Wit, but may be wrought out by Fit *Studies:* Like as Diseases of the Body, may haue Appropriate Exercises. Bowling is good for the Stone and Reines; Shooting for the Lungs and Breast; Gentle Walking for the Stomacke; Riding for the Head; And the like. So if a Mans Wit be Wandring, let him *Study* the *Mathematicks;* For in Demonstrations, if his Wit be called away neuer so little, he must begin again: If his Wit be not Apt to distinguish or find differences, let him *Study* the *Schoole-men;* For they are *Cymini sectores.* If he be not Apt to beat ouer Matters, and to call vp one Thing, to Proue and Illustrate another, let him *Study* the *Lawyers Cases:* So euery Defect of the Minde, may haue a Speciall Receit.

William Lloyd Garrison (1805–1879) was the son of a merchant sailing master in Newburyport, Massachusetts. In 1818, he began writing and editing for the *Newburyport Herald*. Here, Garrison learned specific skills that would serve him well in publishing his own paper later in his life. He joined the Abolition movement when he was 25 and was active with the American Colonization Society. Finding this society to lack a philosophy that supported the complete abolition of slavery, Garrison turned to working as a co-editor of *The Genius of Universal Emancipation* and published his own anti-slavery newspaper *The Liberator* in 1831. Throughout the remainder of his life, his advocacy for abolishing slavery was promoted in speaking engagements and various publications. He also helped organize The New England Anti-Slavery Society and the American Anti-Slavery Society.

Address to the American Colonization Society, July 4 1829

William Lloyd Garrison

It is natural that the return of a day which established the liberties of a brave people should be hailed by them with more than ordinary joy; and it is their duty as Christians and patriots to celebrate it with signal tokens of thanksgiving.   1

Fifty-three years ago, the Fourth of July was a proud day for our country. It clearly and accurately defined the rights of man; it made no vulgar alterations in the established usages of society; it presented a revelation adapted to the common sense of mankind; it vindicated the omnipotence of public opinion over the machinery of kingly government; it shook, as with the voice of a great earthquake, thrones which were seemingly propped up with Atlantean pillars; it gave an impulse to the heart of the world, which yet thrills to its extremities. . . .   2

I speak not as a partisan or an opponent of any man or measures, when I say, that our politics are rotten to the core. *We* boast of our freedom, who go shackled to the polls, year after year, by tens, and hundreds, and thousands! *We* talk of free agency, who are the veriest machines—the merest automata—in the hands of unprincipled jugglers! *We* prate of integrity, and virtue, and independence, who sell our birthright for office, and who, nine times in ten, do not get Esau's bargain[1]—no, not even a mess of pottage![2] Is it republicanism to say, that the majority can do no wrong? Then I am not a republican. Is it aristocracy to say, that the people sometimes shamefully abuse their high trust? Then I am an aristocrat. It is not the appreciation, but the abuse of liberty, to withdraw altogether from the polls, or to visit them merely as a matter of form, without carefully investigating the merits of candidates. The republic does not bear a charmed life: our prescriptions administered through the medium of the ballot-box—the mouth of the political body—may kill or cure, according to the nature of the disease and our wisdom in applying the remedy. It is possible that a people may bear the title of freemen who execute the work of slaves. To the dullest observers of   3

Wendell Phillips and Francis Jackson Garrison, *William Lloyd Garrison, 1805–1879: The Story of His Life Told by His Children*, 4 vols. (Boston: Houghton Mifflin, 1885–89), 1:127–37.

the signs of the times, it must be apparent that we are rapidly approximating to this condition. . . .

But there is another evil, which, if we had to contend against nothing else, should make us quake for the issue. It is a gangrene preying upon our vitals—an earthquake rumbling under our feet—a mine accumulating materials for a national catastrophe. It should make this a day of fasting and prayer, not of boisterous merriment and idle pageantry—a day of great lamentation, not of congratulatory joy. It should spike every cannon, and haul down every banner. Our garb should be sackcloth—our heads bowed in the dust—our supplications, for the pardon and assistance of Heaven. . . .

I stand up here in a more solemn court, to assist in a far greater cause; not to impeach the character of one man, but of a whole people; not to recover the sum of a hundred thousand dollars, but to obtain the liberation of two millions of wretched, degraded beings, who are pining in hopeless bondage—over whose sufferings scarcely an eye weeps, or a heart melts, or a tongue pleads either to God or man. I regret that a better advocate had not been found, to enchain your attention and to warm your blood. Whatever fallacy, however, may appear in the argument, there is no flaw in the indictment; what the speaker lacks, the cause will supply.

Sirs, I am not come to tell you that slavery is a curse, debasing in its effect, cruel in its operation, fatal in its continuance. The day and the occasion require no such revelation. I do not claim the discovery as my own, that "all men are born equal," and that among their inalienable rights are "life, liberty, and the pursuit of happiness." Were I addressing any other than a free and Christian assembly, the enforcement of this truth might be pertinent. Neither do I intend to analyze the horrors of slavery for your inspection, nor to freeze your blood with authentic recitals of savage cruelty. Nor will time allow me to explore even a furlong of that immense wilderness of suffering which remains unsubdued in our land. I take it for granted that the existence of these evils is acknowledged, if not rightly understood. My object is to define and enforce our duty, as Christians and Philanthropists.

On a subject so exhaustless, it will be impossible, in the moiety of an address, to unfold all the facts which are necessary to its full development. In view of it, my heart swells up like a living fountain, which time cannot exhaust, for it is perpetual. Let this be considered as the preface of a noble work, which your inventive sympathies must elaborate and complete.

I assume as distinct and defensible propositions,

I. That the slaves of this country, whether we consider their moral, intellectual or social conditions, are preeminently entitled to the prayers, and sympathies, and charities, of the American people; and their claims for redress are as strong as those of any Americans could be in a similar condition.

II. That, as the free States—by which I mean non-slave-holding States—are constitutionally involved in the guilt of slavery, by adhering to a national compact that sanctions it; and in the danger, by liability to be called upon for aid in case of insurrection; they have the right to remonstrate against its continuance, and it is their duty to assist in its overthrow.

III. That no justificative plea for the perpetuity of slavery can be found in the condition of its victims; and no barrier against our righteous interference, in the laws which authorize the buying, selling and possessing of slaves, nor in the hazard of a collision with slaveholders, 11

IV. That education and freedom will elevate our colored population to a rank with the white—making them useful, intelligent and peaceable citizens. 12

In the first place, it will be readily admitted, that it is the duty of every nation primarily to administer relief to its own necessities, to cure its own maladies, to instruct its own children, and to watch over its own interests. He is "worse than an infidel" who neglects his own household, and squanders his earnings upon strangers; and the policy of that nation is unwise which seeks to proselyte other portions of the globe at the expense of its safety and happiness. Let me not be misunderstood. My benevolence is neither contracted nor selfish. I pity that man whose heart is not larger than a whole continent. I despise the littleness of that patriotism which blusters only for its own rights, and, stretched to its utmost dimensions, scarcely covers its native territory; which adopts as its creed the right to act independently, even to the verge of licentiousness, without restraint, and to tyrannize wherever it can with impunity. This sort of patriotism is common. I suspect the reality, and deny the productiveness, of that piety which confines its operations to a particular spot—if that spot be less than the whole earth; nor scoops out, in every direction, new channels for the waters of life. Christian charity, while it "begins at home," goes abroad in search of misery. It is as copious as the sun in heaven. It does not, like the Nile, make a partial inundation, and then withdraw; but it perpetually overflows, and fertilizes every barren spot. It is restricted only by the exact number of God's suffering creatures. But I mean to say, that, while we are aiding and instructing foreigners, we ought not to forget our own degraded countrymen; that neither duty nor honesty requires us to defraud ourselves that we may enrich others. 13

The condition of the slaves, in a religious point of view, is deplorable, entitling them to a higher consideration, on our part, than any other race; higher than the Turks or Chinese, for they have the privileges of instruction; higher than the Pagans, for they are not dwellers in a gospel land; higher than our red men of the forest, for we do not bind them with gyves,[3] nor treat them as chattels. 14

And here let me ask, What has Christianity done, by direct effort, for our slave population? Comparatively nothing. She has explored the isles of the ocean for objects of commiseration; but, amazing stupidity! she can gaze without emotion on a multitude of miserable beings at home, large enough to constitute a nation of freemen, whom tyranny has heathenized by law. In her public services they are seldom remembered, and in her private donations they are forgotten. From one end of the country to the other, her charitable societies form golden links of benevolence, and scatter their contributions like raindrops over a parched heath; but they bring no sustenance to the perishing slave. The blood of souls is upon her gar- 15 ments, yet she heeds not the stain. The clankings of the prisoner's chains strike upon her ear, but they cannot penetrate her heart.

I have said that the claims of the slaves for redress are as strong as those of any Americans could be, in a similar condition. Does any man deny the position? The proof, then, is found in the fact, that a very large proportion of our colored population were born on our soil, and are therefore entitled to all the privileges of American citizens. This is their country by birth, not by adoption. Their children possess the same inherent and unalienable rights as ours, and it is a crime of the blackest dye to load them with fetters.
16

Every Fourth of July, our Declaration of Independence is produced, with a sublime indignation, to set forth the tyranny of the mother country, and to challenge the admiration of the world. But what a pitiful detail of grievances does this document present, in comparison with the wrongs which our slaves endure! In the one case, it is hardly the plucking of a hair from the head; in the other, it is the crushing of a live body on the wheel—the stings of the wasp contrasted with the tortures of the Inquisition.[4] Before God, I must say, that such a glaring contradiction as exists between our creed and practice the annals of six thousand years cannot parallel. In view of it, I am ashamed of my country. I am sick of our unmeaning declamation in praise of liberty and equality; of our hypocritical cant about the unalienable rights of man. I could not, for my right hand, stand up before a European assembly, and exult that I am an American citizen, and denounce the usurpations of a kingly government as wicked and unjust; or, should I make the attempt, the recollection of my country's barbarity and despotism would blister my lips, and cover my cheeks with burning blushes of shame. . . .
17

I come to my second proposition:—the right of the free States to remonstrate against the continuance, and to assist in the overthrow of slavery.
18

This, I am aware, is a delicate subject, surrounded with many formidable difficulties. But if delay only adds to its intricacy, wherefore shun an immediate investigation? I know that we, of the North, affectedly believe that we have no local interest in the removal of this great evil; that the slave States can take care of themselves, and that any proffered assistance, on our part, would be rejected as impertinent, dictatorial or meddlesome; and that we have no right to lift up even a note of remonstrance. But I believe that these opinions are crude, preposterous, dishonorable, unjust. Sirs, this is a business in which, as members of one great family, we have a common interest; but we take no responsibility, either individually or collectively. Our hearts are cold—our blood stagnates in our veins. We act, in relation to the slaves, as if they were something lower than the brutes that perish.
19

On this question, I ask no support from the injunction of Holy Writ,[5] which says:—"therefore all things whatsoever ye would that men should do to you, do ye even so to them: for this is the law and the prophets." I throw aside the common dictates of humanity. I assert the right of the free States to demand a gradual abolition of slavery, because, by its continuance, they participate in the guilt thereof, and are threatened with ultimate destruction; because they are bound to watch over the interests of the whole country, without reference to territorial divisions; because their white population is nearly double that of the slave States, and the
20

voice of this overwhelming majority should be potential; because they are now deprived of their just influence in the councils of the nation; because it is absurd and anti-republican to suffer property to be represented as men,[6] and *vise versa*. Because it gives the South an unjust ascendancy over other portions of territory, and a power which may be perverted on every occasion. . . .

Now I say that, on the broad system of equal rights, this monstrous inequality 21 should no longer be tolerated. If it cannot be speedily put down—not by force, but by fair persuasion; if we are always to remain shackled by unjust Constitutional provisions, when the emergency that imposed them has long since passed away; if we must share in the guilt and danger of destroying the bodies and souls of men, *as the price of our Union*; if the slave States will haughtily spurn our assistance, and refuse to consult the general welfare; then the fault is not ours if a separation eventually take place. . . .

It may be objected, that the laws of the slave States form insurmountable bar- 22 riers to any interference on our part.

Answer. I grant that we have not the right, and I trust not the disposition, to 23 use coercive measures. But do these laws hinder our prayers, or obstruct the flow of our sympathies? Cannot our charities alleviate the condition of the slave, and perhaps break his fetters? Can we not operate upon public sentiment, (the lever that can move the moral world,) by way of remonstrance, advice, or entreaty? Is Christianity so powerful that she can tame the red men of our forests, and abolish the Burman caste,[7] and overthrow the gods of Paganism, and liberate lands over which the darkness of Superstition has lain for ages; and yet so weak, in her own dwelling-place, that she can make no impression upon her civil code? Can she contend successfully with cannibals, and yet be conquered by her own children?

Suppose that, by a miracle, the slaves should suddenly become white. Would 24 you shut your eyes upon their sufferings, and calmly talk of Constitutional limitations? No; your voice would peal in the ears of the taskmasters like deep thunder; you would carry the Constitution by force, if it could not be taken by treaty; patriotic assemblies would congregate at the corners of every street; the old Cradle of Liberty would rock to a deeper tone than ever echoed therein at British aggression; the pulpit would acquire new and unusual eloquence from our holy religion. The argument, that these white slaves are degraded, would not then obtain. You would say, it is enough that they are white, and in bondage, and they ought immediately to be set free. You would multiply your schools of instruction, and your temples of worship, and rely on them for security. . . .

But the plea is prevalent, that any interference by the free States, however 25 benevolent or cautious it might be would only irritate and inflame the jealousies of the South, and retard the cause of emancipation. If any man believes that slavery can be abolished without a struggle with the worst passions of human nature, quietly, harmoniously, he cherishes a delusion. It can never be done, unless the age of miracles return. No; we must expect a collision, full of sharp asperities and bitterness. We shall have to contend with the insolence, and pride, and selfishness, of many a heartless being. But these can be easily conquered by meekness, and perseverance, and prayer.

Sirs, the prejudices of the North are stronger than those of the South;—they bristle, like so many bayonets, around the slaves;—they forge and rivet the chains of the nation. Conquer them, and the victory is won. The enemies of emancipation take courage from our criminal timidity. They have justly stigmatized us, even on the floor of Congress, with the most contemptuous epithets. We are (they say) their "white slaves," afraid of our own shadows, who have been driven back to the wall again and again; who stand trembling under their whips; who turn pale, retreat, and surrender, at a talismanic threat to dissolve the Union. . . .   26

It is often despondingly said, that the evil of slavery is beyond our control. Dreadful conclusion, that puts the seal of death upon our country's existence! If we cannot conquer the monster in his infancy, while his cartilages are tender and his limbs powerless, how shall we escape his wrath when he goes forth a gigantic cannibal, seeking whom he may devour? If we cannot safely unloose two millions of slaves now, how shall we bind upwards of TWENTY MILLIONS at the close of the present century? But there is no cause for despair. We have seen how readily, and with what ease, that horrid gorgon, Intemperance, has been checked in his ravages. Let us take courage. Moral influence, when in vigorous exercise, is irresistible. It has an immortal essence. It can no more be trod out of existence by the iron foot of time, or by the ponderous march of iniquity, than matter can be annihilated. It may disappear for a time; but it lives in some shape or other, in some place or other, and will rise with renovated strength. Let us, then, be up and doing. In the simple and stirring language of the stout-hearted Lundy,[8] "all the friends of the cause must go to work, keep to work, hold on, and never give up."   27

If it be still objected, that it would be dangerous to liberate the present race of blacks;   28

I answer—the emancipation of all the slaves of this generation is most assuredly out of the question. The fabric, which now towers above the Alps, must be taken away brick by brick, and foot by foot, till it is reduced so low that it may, be overturned without burying the nation in its ruins. Years may elapse before the completion of the achievement; generations of blacks may go down to the grave, manacled and lacerated, without a hope for their children; the philanthropists who are now pleading in behalf of the oppressed, may not live to witness the dawn which will precede the glorious day of universal emancipation; but the work will go on—laborers in the cause will multiply—new resources will be discovered— the victory will be obtained, worth the desperate struggle of a thousand years. Or if defeat follow, woe to the safety of this people! The nation will be shaken as if by a mighty earthquake. A cry of horror, a cry of revenge, will go up to heaven in the darkness of midnight, and re-echo from every cloud. Blood will flow like water— the blood of guilty men, and of innocent women and children. Then will be heard lamentations and weeping, such as will blot out the remembrance of the horrors of St. Domingo.[9] The terrible judgments of an incensed God will complete the catastrophe of republican America.   29

And since so much is to be done for our country; since so many prejudices are to be dispelled, obstacles vanquished, interests secured, blessings obtained; since the cause of emancipation must progress heavily, and meet with much unhallowed   30 opposition,—why delay the work? There must be a beginning, and now is a propitious time—perhaps the last opportunity that will be granted us by a long-suffering God. No temporizing, lukewarm measures will avail aught. We must put our shoulders to the wheel, and heave with our united strength, Let us not look coldly on and see our Southern brethren contending single-handed against an all-powerful foe—faint, weary, borne down to the earth. We are all alike guilty. Slavery is strictly a national sin. New-England money has been expended in buying human flesh; New-England ships have been freighted with sable victims; New-England men have assisted in forging the fetters of those who groan in bondage.

I call upon the ambassadors of Christ everywhere to make known this proclamation: "Thus saith the Lord God of the Africans, Let this people go, that they may serve me." I ask them to "proclaim liberty to the captives, and the opening of the prison to them that are bound"—to light up a flame of philanthropy that shall burn till all Africa be redeemed from the night of moral death, and the song of deliverance be heard throughout her borders. 31

I call upon the churches of the living God to lead in this great enterprise. If the soul be immortal, priceless, save it from remediless woe. Let them combine their energies, and systematize their plans, for the rescue of suffering humanity. Let them pour out their supplications to heaven in behalf of the slave. Prayer is omnipotent: its breath can melt adamantine rocks—its touch can break the stoutest chains. Let anti-slavery charity-boxes stand uppermost among those for missionary, tract and educational purposes. On this subject, Christians have been asleep; let them shake off their slumbers, and arm for the holy contest. 32

I call upon our New-England women to form charitable associations to relieve the degraded of their sex. As yet, an appeal to their sympathies was never made in vain. They outstrip us in every benevolent race. Females are doing much for the cause at the South; let their example be imitated, and their exertions surpassed, at the North. 33

I call upon our citizens to assist in establishing auxiliary colonization societies in every State, county and town. I implore their direct and liberal patronage to the parent society. 34

I call upon the great body of newspaper editors to keep this subject constantly before their readers; to sound the trumpet of alarm, and to plead eloquently for the rights of man. They must give the tone to public sentiment. One press may ignite twenty; a city may warm a State; a State may impart a generous heat to a whole country. 35

I call upon the American people to enfranchise a spot over which they hold complete sovereignty, to cleanse that worse than Augean stable,[10] the District of Columbia, from its foul impurities. I ask them to sustain Congress in any future efforts to colonize the colored population of the States. I conjure them to select those as Representatives who are not too ignorant to know, too blind to see, nor too timid to perform their duty. 36

I will say, finally, that I despair of the republic while slavery exists therein. If I look up to God for success, no smile of mercy or forgiveness dispels the gloom of futurity; if to our own resources, they are daily diminishing; if to all history, our 37 destruction is not only possible, but almost certain. Why should we slumber at this momentous crisis? If our hearts were dead to every throb of humanity; if it were lawful to oppress, where power is ample; still, if we had any regard for our safety and happiness, we should strive to crush the Vampire which is feeding upon our life-blood. All the selfishness of our nature cries aloud for a better security. Our own vices are too strong for us, and keep us in perpetual alarm; how, in addition to these, shall we be able to contend successfully with millions of armed and desperate men, as we must eventually, if slavery do not cease?

ENDNOTES

1. Genesis 25:29–34 tells how Esau foolishly sold his birthright to his twin brother, Jacob, for the price of a meal.
2. Genesis 25:30.
3. Gyves are shackles or chains.
4. The Inquisition was the tribunal for the prosecution of heresy established by the medieval Roman Catholic Church. The later Spanish Inquisition, begun in the late fifteenth century, was characterized by extreme cruelty.
5. The scriptural reference is Matthew 7:12.
6. The three-fifths clause of the Constitution (art. I, sect. 2) provided that three-fifths of all slaves would be added to the number of free persons in a state for the purpose of determining representation and taxation.
7. *Burman* may refer to Burma, the country in southeast Asia. But perhaps Garrison meant *Brahman*, the highest, most exclusive priestly class or caste among the Hindus.
8. Benjamin Lundy (1789–1839), antislavery agitator, lecturer, and editor of *The Genius of Universal Emancipation* (1821–35). He invited Garrison to assist him with this publication in 1829 and was Garrison's mentor.
9. The French colony of Saint Domingue (the western part of Haiti), where a major slave rebellion erupted in the 1790s. Abolitionists often cited "the horrors of St. Domingo" to warn of the fate that would befall the South if slavery was not abolished: the slaves would revolt with terrible violence against their masters. Slaveholders, on the other hand, invoked these same "horrors" of murder, torture, rape, race war, and massive destruction to warn of the dangers to whites if abolition ever did occur.
10. The mythological Greek king Augeas did not clean his oxen's stables for thirty years; they were finally cleaned by Hercules, who diverted a river through them. To clean the Augean stable means to clear away corruption.

Martin Luther King, Jr. (1929–1968) had at first planned to become a doctor or a lawyer, but when he graduated from Morehouse College in Atlanta at the age of nineteen, he abandoned these ambitions and went into the seminary. After seminary, he went to Boston University, where he received his Ph.D. in 1955. He was ordained as a Baptist minister in his father's church, the Ebenezer Baptist Church in Atlanta, a church he copastored with his father from 1960 to 1968. He was also founder and director of the Southern Christian Leadership Conference from 1957 to 1968, and a member of the Montgomery Improvement Association, an activist group protesting racial segregation. Inspired by Mahatma Gandhi's principles of nonviolent protest, King led this group in several demonstrations. In May 1963, he was arrested and imprisoned in Birmingham for demonstrating against segregation in hotels and restaurants. It was while in jail that he wrote his famous "Letter from Birmingham Jail," a work that was published in 1963 and expanded and republished in 1968. It was also in 1963 that King made the speech entitled "I Have a Dream" to over 200,000 people at the March on Washington. King received numerous awards for his work for human rights, including the Nobel Prize for Peace in 1964. On April 4, 1968, while talking with other human rights activists on a motel balcony in Memphis, King was assassinated.

I Have a Dream

Martin Luther King, Jr.

Five score years ago, a great American, in whose symbolic shadow we stand, signed the Emancipation Proclamation. This momentous decree came as a great beacon light of hope to millions of Negro slaves who had been seared in the flames of withering injustice. It came as a joyous daybreak to end the long night of captivity.   1

But 100 years later, we must face the tragic fact that the Negro is still not free. One hundred years later, the life of the Negro is still sadly crippled by the manacles of segregation and the chains of discrimination. One hundred years later, the Negro lives on a lonely island of poverty in the midst of a vast ocean of material prosperity. One hundred years later, the Negro is still languished in the corners of American society and finds himself an exile in his own land. So we have come here today to dramatize an appalling condition.   2

In a sense we have come to our nation's capital to cash a check. When the architects of our republic wrote the magnificent words of the Constitution and the Declaration of Independence, they were signing a promissory note to which every American was to fall heir. This note was a promise that all men would be guaranteed the unalienable rights of life, liberty, and the pursuit of happiness.   3

It is obvious today that America has defaulted on this promissory note insofar as her citizens of color are concerned. Instead of honoring this sacred obligation, America has given the Negro people a bad check; a check which has come back marked "insufficient funds." But we refuse to believe that the bank of justice is bankrupt. We refuse to believe that there are insufficient funds in the great vaults of opportunity of this nation. So we have come to cash this check—a check that will   4 give us upon demand the riches of freedom and the security of justice. We have also come to this hallowed spot to remind America of the fierce urgency of *now*. This is no time to engage in the luxury of cooling off or to take the tranquilizing drug of gradualism. *Now* is the time to make real the promises of Democracy. *Now* is the time to rise from the dark and desolate valley of segregation to the sunlit path of racial justice. *Now* is the time to open the doors of opportunity to all of God's children. *Now* is the time to lift our nation from the quicksands of racial injustice to the solid rock of brotherhood.

It would be fatal for the nation to overlook the urgency of the moment and to underestimate the determination of the Negro. This sweltering summer of the Negro's legitimate discontent will not pass until there is an invigorating autumn of freedom and equality. Nineteen sixty-three is not an end, but a beginning. Those who hope that the Negro needed to blow off steam and will now be content will have a rude awakening if the nation returns to business as usual. There will be neither rest nor tranquility in America until the Negro is granted his citizenship rights. The whirlwinds of revolt will continue to shake the foundations of our nation until the bright day of justice emerges. 5

But there is something that I must say to my people who stand on the warm threshold which leads into the palace of justice. In the process of gaining our rightful place we must not be guilty of wrongful deeds. Let us not seek to satisfy our thirst for freedom by drinking from the cup of bitterness and hatred. We must forever conduct our struggle on the high plane of dignity and discipline. We must not allow our creative protest to degenerate into physical violence. Again and again we must rise to the majestic heights of meeting physical force with soul force. The marvelous new militancy which has engulfed the Negro community must not lead us to a distrust of all white people, for many of our white brothers, as evidenced by their presence here today, have come to realize that their destiny is tied up with our destiny and their freedom is inextricably bound to our freedom. We cannot walk alone. 6

And as we walk, we must make the pledge that we shall march ahead. We cannot turn back. There are those who are asking the devotees of civil rights, "When will you be satisfied?" We can never be satisfied as long as the Negro is the victim of the unspeakable horrors of police brutality. We can never be satisfied as long as our bodies, heavy with fatigue of travel, cannot gain lodging in the motels of the highways and the hotels of the cities. We cannot be satisfied as long as the Negro's basic mobility is from a smaller ghetto to a larger one. We can never be satisfied as long as a Negro in Mississippi cannot vote and a Negro in New York believes he has nothing for which to vote. No, no, we are not satisfied, and we will not be satisfied until justice rolls down like waters and righteousness like a mighty stream. 7

I am not unmindful that some of you have come here out of great trials and tribulations. Some of you have come fresh from narrow jail cells. Some of you have come from areas where your quest for freedom left you battered by the storms of persecution and staggered by the winds of police brutality. You have been the veterans of creative suffering. Continue to work with the faith that unearned suffering is redemptive. 8

The iDeal Reader

Martin Luther King, Jr., "I
Have a Dream"

© The McGraw–Hill
Companies, 2001

253

Go back to Mississippi, go back to Alabama, go back to South Carolina, go back   9
to Georgia, go back to Louisiana, go back to the slums and ghettos of our northern
cities, knowing that somehow this situation can and will be changed. Let us not
wallow in the valley of despair.

I say to you today, my friends, that in spite of the difficulties and frustrations of   10
the moment I still have a dream. It is a dream deeply rooted in the American dream.

I have a dream that one day this nation will rise up and live out the true meaning   11
of its creed: "We hold these truths to be self-evident; that all men are created equal."

I have a dream that one day on the red hills of Georgia the sons of former slaves   12
and the sons of former slaveowners will be able to sit down together at the table of
brotherhood.

I have a dream that one day even the state of Mississippi, a desert state sweltering   13
with the heat of injustice and oppression, will be transformed into an oasis of freedom
and justice.

I have a dream that my four little children will one day live in a nation where   14
they will not be judged by the color of their skin but by the content of their character.

I have a dream today.   15

I have a dream that one day the state of Alabama, whose governor's lips are   16
presently dripping with the words of interposition and nullification, will be transformed into a situation where little black boys and black girls will be able to join
hands with little white boys and white girls and walk together as sisters and brothers.

I have a dream today.   17

I have a dream that one day every valley shall be exalted, every hill and mountain   18
shall be made low, the rough places will be made plains, and the crooked places
will be made straight, and the glory of the Lord shall be revealed, and all flesh shall
see it together.

This is our hope. This is the faith with which I return to the South. With   19
this faith we will be able to hew out of the mountain of despair a stone of hope.
With this faith we will be able to transform the jangling discords of our nation into
a beautiful symphony of brotherhood. With this faith we will be able to work together,
to pray together, to struggle together, to go to jail together, to stand up for freedom
together, knowing that we will be free one day.

This will be the day when all of God's children will be able to sing with new   20
meaning

My country, 'tis of thee,   21
Sweet land of liberty,
    Of thee I sing.
Land where my fathers died,
Land of the pilgrims' pride,
From every mountainside
Let freedom ring.

And if America is to be a great nation this must become true. So let freedom   22
ring from the prodigious hilltops of New Hampshire. Let freedom ring from the mighty

mountains of New York. Let freedom ring from the heightening Alleghenies of Pennsylvania!

Let freedom ring from the snowcapped Rockies of Colorado!　　23

Let freedom ring from the curvacious peaks of California!　　24

But not only that; let freedom ring from Stone Mountain of Georgia.　　25

Let freedom ring from Lookout Mountain of Tennessee!　　26

Let freedom ring from every hill and molehill of Mississippi. From every　27
mountainside, let freedom ring.

When we let freedom ring, when we let it ring from every village and every　28
hamlet, from every state and every city, we will be able to speed up that day when all of God's children, black men and white men, Jews and Gentiles, Protestants and Catholics, will be able to join hands and sing in the words of the old Negro spiritual, "Free at last! free at last! thank God almighty, we are free at last!"

The iDeal Reader

Martin Luther King, Jr.,
"Letter from Birmingham
Jail"

© The McGraw–Hill
Companies, 2001

255

Martin Luther King, Jr. (1929–1968) had at first planned to become a doctor or a lawyer, but when he graduated from Morehouse College in Atlanta at the age of nineteen, he abandoned these ambitions and went into the seminary. After seminary, he went to Boston University, where he received his Ph.D. in 1955. He was ordained as a Baptist minister in his father's church, the Ebenezer Baptist Church in Atlanta, a church he copastored with his father from 1960 to 1968. He was also founder and director of the Southern Christian Leadership Conference from 1957 to 1968, and a member of the Montgomery Improvement Association, an activist group protesting racial segregation. Inspired by Mahatma Gandhi's principles of nonviolent protest, King led this group in several demonstrations. In May 1963, he was arrested and imprisoned in Birmingham for demonstrating against segregation in hotels and restaurants. It was while in jail that he wrote his famous "Letter from Birmingham Jail," a work that was published in 1963 and expanded and republished in 1968. It was also in 1963 that King made the speech entitled "I Have a Dream" to over 200,000 people at the March on Washington. King received numerous awards for his work for human rights, including the Nobel Prize for Peace in 1964. On April 4, 1968, while talking with other human rights activists on a motel balcony in Memphis, King was assassinated.

Letter From Birmingham Jail

Martin Luther King, Jr.

April 16, 1963

My Dear Fellow Clergymen:

While confined here in Birmingham city jail, I came across your recent statement calling my present activities "unwise and untimely." Seldom do I pause to answer criticism of my work and ideas. If I sought to answer all the criticisms that cross my desk, my secretaries would have little time for anything other than such correspondence in the course of the day, and I would have no time for constructive work. But since I feel that you are men of genuine good will and that your criticisms are sincerely set forth, I want to try to answer your statement in what I hope will be patient and reasonable terms.   1

I think I should indicate why I am here in Birmingham, since you have been influenced by the view which argues against "outsiders coming in." I have the honor of serving as president of the Southern Christian Leadership Conference, an organization operating in every southern state, with headquarters in Atlanta, Georgia. We have some eighty-five affiliated organizations across the South, and one of them is the Alabama Christian Movement for Human Rights. Frequently we share staff, educational and financial resources with our affiliates. Several months ago the affiliate here in Birmingham asked us to be on call to engage in a nonviolent direct-action program if such were deemed necessary. We readily consented, and when the hour came we lived up to our promise. So I, along with several members of my staff, am here because I was invited here. I am here because I have organizational ties here.   2

But more basically, I am in Birmingham because injustice is here. Just as the prophets of the eighth century B.C. left their villages and carried their "thus saith the Lord" far beyond the boundaries of their home towns, and just as the Apostle Paul left his village of Tarsus and carried the gospel of Jesus Christ to the far corners of the Greco-Roman world, so am I compelled to carry the gospel of freedom beyond my own home town. Like Paul, I must constantly respond to the Macedonian call for aid.

3

Moreover, I am cognizant of the interrelatedness of all communities and states. I cannot sit idly by in Atlanta and not be concerned about what happens to Birmingham. Injustice anywhere is a threat to justice everywhere. We are caught in an inescapable network of mutuality, tied in a single garment of destiny. Whatever affects one directly, affects all indirectly. Never again can we afford to live with the narrow, provincial "outside agitator" idea. Anyone who lives inside the United States can never be considered an outsider anywhere within its bounds.

4

You deplore the demonstrations taking place in Birmingham. But your statement, I am sorry to say, fails to express a similar concern for the conditions that brought about the demonstrations. I am sure that none of you would want to rest content with the superficial kind of social analysis that deals merely with effects and does not grapple with underlying causes. It is unfortunate that demonstrations are taking place in Birmingham, but it is even more unfortunate that the city's white power structure left the Negro community with no alternative.

5

In any nonviolent campaign there are four steps: collection of the facts to determine whether injustices exist; negotiation; self-purification; and direct action. We have gone through all these steps in Birmingham. There can be no gain saying the fact that racial injustice engulfs this community. Birmingham is probably the most thoroughly segregated city in the United States. Its ugly record of brutality is widely known. Negroes have experienced grossly unjust treatment in the courts. There have been more unsolved bombings of Negro homes and churches in Birmingham than in any other city in the nation. These are the hard brutal facts of the case. On the basis of these conditions, Negro leaders sought to negotiate with the city fathers. But the latter consistently refused to engage in good-faith negotiation.

6

Then, last September, came the opportunity to talk with leaders of Birmingham economic community. In the course of negotiations, certain promises were made by the merchants—for example, to remove the stores' humiliating racial signs. On the basis of these promises, the Reverend Fred Shuttlesworth and the leaders of the Alabama Christian Movement for Human Rights agreed to a moratorium on all demonstrations. As the weeks and months went by, we realized that we were the victims of a broken promise. A few signs, briefly removed, returned; the others remained.

7

As in so many past experiences, our hopes had been blasted, and the shadow of deep disappointment settled upon us. We had no alternative except to prepare for direct action, whereby we would present our very bodies as a means of laying our case before the conscience of the local and the national community. Mindful of the difficulties involved, we decided to undertake a process of self-purification. We began a series of workshops on nonviolence, and we repeatedly asked ourselves: "Are you able to accept blows without retaliating?" "Are you able to endure the ordeal of jail?"

8

The iDeal Reader

Martin Luther King, Jr.,
"Letter from Birmingham
Jail"

© The McGraw–Hill
Companies, 2001

257

We decided to schedule our direct-action program for the Easter season, realizing that except for Christmas, this is the main shopping period of the year. Knowing that a strong economic-withdrawal program would be the by-product of direct action, we felt that this would be the best time to bring pressure to bear on the merchants for the needed change.

Then it occurred to us that Birmingham's mayoralty election was coming up in March, and we speedily decided to postpone action until after election day. When we discovered that the Commissioner of Public Safety, Eugene "Bull" Connor, had piled up enough votes to be in the run-off, we decided again to postpone action until the day after the run-off so that the demonstrations could not be used to cloud the issues. Like many others, we waited to see Mr. Connor defeated, and to this end we endured postponement after postponement. Having aided in this community need, we felt that our direct-action program could be delayed no longer.

9

You may well ask: "Why direct action? Why sit-ins, marches and so forth? Isn't negotiation a better path?" You are quite right in calling for negotiation. Indeed, this is the very purpose of direct action. Nonviolent direct action seeks to create such a crisis and foster such a tension that a community which has constantly refused to negotiate is forced to confront the issue. It seeks so to dramatize the issue that it can no longer be ignored. My citing the creation of tension as part of the work of the nonviolent-resister may sound rather shocking. But I must confess that I am not afraid of the word "tension." I have earnestly opposed violent tension, but there is a type of constructive nonviolent tension which is necessary for growth. Just as Socrates felt that it was necessary to create a tension in the mind so that individuals could rise from the bondage of myths and half-truths to the unfettered realm of creative analysis and objective appraisal, so must we see the need for nonviolent gadflies to create the kind of tension in society that will help men rise from the dark depths of prejudice and racism to the majestic heights of understanding and brotherhood.

10

The purpose of our direct-action program is to create a situation so crisis-packed that it will inevitably open the door to negotiation. I therefore concur with you in your call for negotiation. Too long has our beloved Southland been bogged down in a tragic effort to live in monologue rather than dialogue.

11

One of the basic points in your statement is that the action that I and my associates have taken in Birmingham is untimely. Some have asked: "Why didn't you give the new city administration time to act?" The only answer that I can give to this query is that the new Birmingham administration must be prodded about as much as the outgoing one, before it will act. We are sadly mistaken if we feel that the election of Albert Boutwell as mayor will bring the millennium to Birmingham. While Mr. Boutwell is a much more gentle person than Mr. Connor, they are both segregationists, dedicated to maintenance of the status quo. I have hope that Mr. Boutwell will be reasonable enough to see the futility of massive resistance to desegregation. But he will not see this without pressure from devotees of civil rights. My friends, I must say to you that we have not made a single gain in civil rights without determined legal and nonviolent pressure. Lamentably, it is an historical fact that privileged groups seldom give up their privileges voluntarily.

12

258 | The iDeal Reader

Martin Luther King, Jr.,
"Letter from Birmingham
Jail"

© The McGraw–Hill
Companies, 2001

Individuals may see the moral light and voluntarily give up their unjust posture; but, as Reinhold Niebuhr has reminded us, groups tend to be more immoral than individuals.

We know through painful experience that freedom is never voluntarily given by the oppressor; it must be demanded by the oppressed. Frankly, I have yet to engage in a direct-action campaign that was "well timed" in the view of those who have not suffered unduly from the disease of segregation. For years now I have heard the word "Wait!" It rings in the ear of every Negro with piercing familiarity. This "Wait" has almost always meant "Never." We must come to see, with one of our distinguished jurists, that "justice too long delayed is justice denied." 13

We have waited for more than 340 years for our constitutional and God given rights. The nations of Asia and Africa are moving with jetlike speed toward gaining political independence, but we still creep at horse-and-buggy pace toward gaining a cup of coffee at a lunch counter. Perhaps it is easy for those who have never felt the stinging darts of segregation to say, "Wait." But when you have seen vicious mobs lynch your mothers and fathers at will and drown your sisters and brothers at whim; when you have seen hate-filled policemen curse, kick and even kill your black brothers and sisters; when you see the vast majority of your 20 million Negro brothers smothering in an airtight cage of poverty in the midst of an affluent society; when you suddenly find your tongue twisted and your speech stammering as you seek to explain to your 6-year-old daughter why she can't go to the public amusement park that has just been advertised on television, and see tears welling up in her eyes when she is told that Funtown is closed to colored children, and see ominous clouds of inferiority beginning to form in her little mental sky, and see her beginning to distort her personality by developing an unconscious bitterness toward white people; when you have to concoct an answer for a 5-year-old son who is asking: "Daddy, why do white people treat colored people so mean?"; when you take a cross-country drive and find it necessary to sleep night after night in the uncomfortable corners of your automobile because no motel will accept you; when you are humiliated day in and day out by nagging signs reading "white" and "colored"; when your first name becomes "nigger," your middle name becomes "boy" (however old you are) and your last name becomes "John," and your wife and mother are never given the respected title "Mrs."; when you are harried by day and haunted by night by the fact that you are a Negro, living constantly at tiptoe stance, never quite knowing what to expect next, and are plagued with inner fears and outer resentments; when you are forever fighting a degenerating sense of "nobodiness"—then you will understand why we find it difficult to wait. There comes a time when the cup of endurance runs over, and men are no longer willing to be plunged into the abyss of despair. I hope, sirs, you can understand our legitimate and unavoidable impatience. 14

You express a great deal of anxiety over our willingness to break laws. This is certainly a legitimate concern. Since we so diligently urge people to obey the Supreme Court's decision of 1954 outlawing segregation in the public schools, at first glance it may seem rather paradoxical for us consciously to break laws. One may well ask: "How can you advocate breaking some laws and obeying others?" The answer lies in the fact that there are two types of laws: just and unjust. I would be the first to 15

advocate obeying just laws. One has not only a legal but amoral responsibility to obey
just laws. Conversely, one has a moral responsibility to disobey unjust laws. I would
agree with St. Augustine that "an unjust law is no law at all."

Now, what is the difference between the two? How does one determine whether   16
a law is just or unjust? A just law is a man-made code that squares with the moral law
or the law of God. An unjust law is a code that is out of harmony with the moral law.
To put it in the terms of St. Thomas Aquinas: An unjust law is a human law that is
not rooted in eternal law and natural law. Any law that uplifts human personality
is just. Any law that degrades human personality is unjust. All segregation statutes
are unjust because segregation distorts the soul and damages the personality. It gives
the segregator a false sense of superiority and the segregated a false sense of inferiority. Segregation, to use the terminology of the Jewish philosopher Martin Buber,
substitutes an "I-it" relationship for an "I-thou" relationship and ends up relegating
persons to the status of things. Hence segregation is not only politically, economically and sociologically unsound, it is morally wrong and sinful. Paul Tillich has
said that sin is separation. Is not segregation an existential expression of man's tragic
separation, his awful estrangement, his terrible sinfulness? Thus it is that I can urge
men to obey the 1954 decision of the Supreme Court, for it is morally right; and I can
urge them to disobey segregation ordinances, for they are morally wrong.

Let us consider a more concrete example of just and unjust laws. An unjust   17
law is a code that a numerical or power majority group compels a minority group to
obey but does not make binding on itself. This is *difference* made legal. By the same
token, a just law is a code that a majority compels a minority to follow and that it
is willing to follow itself. This is *sameness* made legal.

Let me give another explanation. A law is unjust if it is inflicted on a minority   18
that, as a result of being denied the right to vote, had no part in enacting or devising
the law. Who can say that the legislature of Alabama which set up that state's
segregation laws was democratically elected? Throughout Alabama all sorts of devious
methods are used to prevent Negroes from becoming registered voters, and there are
some counties in which even though Negroes constitute a majority of the population, not a single Negro is registered. Can any law enacted under such circumstances
be considered democratically structured?

Sometimes a law is just on its face and unjust in its application. For instance,   19
I have been arrested on a charge of parading without a permit. Now, there is nothing wrong in having an ordinance which requires a permit for a parade. But such
an ordinance becomes unjust when it is used to maintain segregation and to deny
citizens the First-Amendment privilege of peaceful assembly and protest.

I hope you are able to see the distinction I am trying to point out. In no sense   20
do I advocate evading or defying the law, as would the rabid segregationist. That
would lead to anarchy. One who breaks an unjust law must do so openly, lovingly,
and with a willingness to accept the penalty. I submit that an individual who breaks
a law that conscience tells him is unjust, and who willingly accepts the penalty of
imprisonment in order to arouse the conscience of the community over its injustice,
is in reality expressing the highest respect for law.

Of course, there is nothing new about this kind of civil disobedience. It was   21
evidenced sublimely in the refusal of Shadrach, Meshach and Abednego to obey the
laws of Nebuchadnezzar, on the ground that a higher moral law was at stake. It was
practiced superbly by the early Christians, who were willing to face hungry lions and
the excruciating pain of chopping blocks rather than submit to certain unjust laws
of the Roman Empire. To a degree, academic freedom is a reality today because
Socrates practiced civil disobedience. In our own nation, the Boston Tea Party
represented a massive act of civil disobedience.

We should never forget that everything Adolf Hitler did in Germany was "legal"   22
and everything the Hungarian freedom fighters did in Hungary was "illegal." It was
"illegal" to aid and comfort a Jew in Hitler's Germany. Even so, I am sure that, had
I lived in Germany at the time, I would have aided and comforted my Jewish brothers.
If today I lived in a Communist country where certain principles dear to the Christian
faith are suppressed, I would openly advocate disobeying that country's anti-religious
laws.

I must make two honest confessions to you, my Christian and Jewish brothers.   23
First, I must confess that over the past few years I have been gravely disappointed
with the white moderate. I have almost reached the regrettable conclusion that
the Negro's great stumbling block in his stride toward freedom is not the White
Citizen's Counciler or the Ku Klux Klanner, but the white moderate, who is more
devoted to "order" than to justice; who prefers a negative peace which is the absence
of tension to a positive peace which is the presence of justice; who constantly says:
"I agree with you in the goal you seek, but I cannot agree with your methods of direct
action"; who paternalistically believes he can set the timetable for another man's
freedom; who lives by a mythical concept of time and who constantly advises the
Negro to wait for a "more convenient season." Shallow understanding from people
of good will is more frustrating than absolute misunderstanding from people of ill will.
Lukewarm acceptance is much more bewildering than outright rejection.

I had hoped that the white moderate would understand that law and order exist   24
for the purpose of establishing justice and that when they fail in this purpose they
become the dangerously structured dams that block the flow of social progress. I had
hoped that the white moderate would understand that the present tension in the
South is a necessary phase of the transition from an obnoxious negative peace, in
which the Negro passively accepted his unjust plight, to a substantive and positive
peace, in which all men will respect the dignity and worth of human personality.
Actually, we who engage in nonviolent direct action are not the creators of tension.
We merely bring to the surface the hidden tension that is already alive. We bring it
out in the open, where it can be seen and dealt with. Like a boil that can never be
cured so long as it is covered up but must be opened with all its ugliness to the natural
medicines of air and light, injustice must be exposed, with all the tension its exposure
creates, to the light of human conscience and the air of national opinion before it
can be cured.

In your statement you assert that our actions, even though peaceful, must be con-   25
demned because they precipitate violence. But is this a logical assertion? Isn't this like
condemning a robbed man because his possession of money precipitated the evil act

The iDeal Reader

Martin Luther King, Jr.,
"Letter from Birmingham
Jail"

© The McGraw–Hill
Companies, 2001

261

of robbery? Isn't this like condemning Jesus because his unique God-consciousness and never-ceasing devotion to God's will precipitated the evil act of crucifixion? We must come to see that, as the federal courts have consistently affirmed, it is wrong to urge an individual to cease his efforts to gain his basic constitutional rights because the quest may precipitate violence. Society must protect the robbed and punish the robber.

I had also hoped that the white moderate would reject the myth concerning   26
time in relation to the struggle for freedom. I have just received a letter from a white brother in Texas. He writes: "All Christians know that the colored people will receive equal rights eventually, but it is possible that you are in too great a religious hurry. It has taken Christianity almost two thousand years to accomplish what it has. The teachings of Christ take time to come to earth." Such an attitude stems from a tragic misconception of time, from the strangely irrational notion that there is something in the very flow of time that will inevitably cure all ills. Actually, time itself is neutral; it can be used either destructively or constructively. More and more I feel that the people of ill will have used time much more effectively than have the people of good will. We will have to repent in this generation not merely for the hateful words and actions of the bad people but for the appalling silence of the good people. Human progress never rolls in on wheels of inevitability; it comes through the tireless efforts of men willing to be co-workers with God, and without this hard work, time itself becomes an ally of the forces of social stagnation. We must use time creatively, in the knowledge that the time is always ripe to do right. Now is the time to make real the promise of democracy and transform our pending national elegy into a creative psalm of brotherhood. Now is the time to lift our national policy from the quicksand of racial injustice to the solid rock of human dignity.

You speak of our activity in Birmingham as extreme. At first I was rather   27
disappointed that fellow clergymen would see my nonviolent efforts as those of an extremist. I began thinking about the fact that I stand in the middle of two opposing forces in the Negro community. One is a force of complacency, made up in part of Negroes who, as a result of long years of oppression, are so drained of self-respect and a sense of "somebodiness" that they have adjusted to segregation; and in part of a few middle-class Negroes who, because of a degree of academic and economic security and because in some ways they profit by segregation, have become insensitive to the problems of the masses. The other force is one of bitterness and hatred, and it comes perilously close to advocating violence. It is expressed in the various black nationalist groups that are springing up across the nation, the largest and best-known being Elijah Muhammad's Muslim movement. Nourished by the Negro's frustration over the continued existence of racial discrimination, this movement is made up of people who have lost faith in America, who have absolutely repudiated Christianity, and who have concluded that the white man is an incorrigible "devil."

I have tried to stand between these two forces, saying that we need emulate   28
neither the "do-nothingism" of the complacement nor the hatred and despair of the black nationalist. For there is the more excellent way of love and nonviolent protest. I am grateful to God that, through the influence of the Negro church, the way of nonviolence became an integral part of our struggle.

If this philosophy had not emerged, by now many streets of the South would,   29
I am convinced, be flowing with blood. And I am further convinced that if our white
brothers dismiss as "rabble-rousers" and "outside agitators" those of us who employ
nonviolent direct action, and if they refuse to support our nonviolent efforts, millions
of Negroes will, out of frustration and despair, seek solace and security in black-nation-
alist ideologies—a development that would inevitably lead to a frightening racial
nightmare.

Oppressed people cannot remain oppressed forever. The yearning for freedom   30
eventually manifests itself, and that is what has happened to the American Negro.
Something within has reminded him that it can be gained. Consciously or uncon-
sciously, he has been caught up by the *Zeitgeist*, and with his black brothers of Africa
and his brown and yellow brothers of Asia, South America and the Caribbean, the
United States Negro is moving with a sense of great urgency toward the promised
land of racial justice. If one recognizes this vital urge that has engulfed the Negro
community, one should readily understand why public demonstrations are taking
place. The Negro has many pent-up resentments and latent frustrations, and he must
release them. So let him march; let him make prayer pilgrimages to the city hall;
let him go on freedom rides—and try to understand why he must do so. If his repressed
emotions are not released in nonviolent ways, they will seek expression through
violence; this is not a threat but a fact of history. So I have not said to my people:
"Get rid of your discontent." Rather, I have tried to say that this normal and healthy
discontent can be channeled into the creative outlet of nonviolent direct action.
And now this approach is being termed extremist.

But though I was initially disappointed at being categorized as an extremist, as   31
I continued to think about the matter I gradually gained a measure of satisfaction
from the label. Was not Jesus an extremist for love: "Love your enemies, bless them
that curse you, do good to them that hate you, and pray for them which despitefully
use you, and persecute you." Was not Amos an extremist for justice: "Let justice
roll down like waters and righteousness like an ever-flowing stream." Was not Paul
an extremist for the Christian gospel: "I bear in my body the marks of the Lord Jesus."
Was not Martin Luther an extremist: "Here I stand; I cannot do otherwise, so help
me God." And John Bunyan: "I will stay in jail to the end of my days before I make
a butchery of my conscience." And Abraham Lincoln: "This nation cannot survive
half slave and half free." And Thomas Jefferson: "We hold these truths to be self-
evident, that all men are created equal. . . . " So the question is not whether we
will be extremists, but what kind of extremists we will be. Will we be extremists for
hate or for love? Will we be extremists for the preservation of injustice or for the
extension of justice? In that dramatic scene on Calvary's hill three men were crucified.
We must never forget that all three were crucified for the same crime—the crime
of extremism. Two were extremists for immorality, and thus fell below their
environment. The other, Jesus Christ, was an extremist for love, truth and goodness,
and thereby rose above his environment. Perhaps the South, the nation and the world
are in dire need of creative extremists.

I had hoped that the white moderate would see this need. Perhaps I was too   32
optimistic; perhaps I expected too much. I suppose I should have realized that few

The iDeal Reader

Martin Luther King, Jr.,
"Letter from Birmingham
Jail"

© The McGraw–Hill
Companies, 2001

263

members of the oppressor race can understand the deep groans and passionate yearnings of the oppressed race, and still fewer have the vision to see that injustice must be rooted out by strong, persistent and determined action. I am thankful, however, that some of our white brothers in the South have grasped the meaning of this social revolution and committed themselves to it. They are still all too few in quantity, but they are big in quality. Some—such as Ralph McGill, Lillian Smith, Harry Golden, James McBride Dabbs, Ann Braden and Sarah Patton Boyle—have written about our struggle in eloquent and prophetic terms. Others have marched with us down nameless streets of the South. They have languished in filthy, roach-infested jails, suffering the abuse and brutality of policemen who view them as "dirty nigger-lovers." Unlike so many of their moderate brothers and sisters, they have recognized the urgency of the moment and sensed the need for powerful "action" antidotes to combat the disease of segregation.

33   Let me take note of my other major disappointment. I have been so greatly disappointed with the white church and its leadership. Of course, there are some notable exceptions. I am not unmindful of the fact that each of you has taken some significant stands on this issue. I commend you, Reverend Stallings, for your Christian stand on this past Sunday, in welcoming Negroes to your worship service on a non-segregated basis. I commend the Catholic leaders of this state for integrating Spring Hill College several years ago.

34   But despite these notable exceptions, I must honestly reiterate that I have been disappointed with the church. I do not say this as one of those negative critics who can always find something wrong with the church. I say this as a minister of the gospel, who loves the church; who was nurtured in its bosom; who has been sustained by its spiritual blessings and who will remain true to it as long as the cord of life shall lengthen.

35   When I was suddenly catapulted into the leadership of the bus protest in Montgomery, Ala., a few years ago, I felt we would be supported by the white church. I felt that the white ministers, priests and rabbis of the South would be among our strongest allies. Instead, some have been outright opponents, refusing to understand the freedom movement and misrepresenting its leaders; all too many others have been more cautious than courageous and have remained silent behind the anesthetizing security of stained-glass windows.

36   In spite of my shattered dreams, I came to Birmingham with the hope that the white religious leadership of this community would see the justice of our cause and, with deep moral concern, would serve as the channel through which our just grievances could reach the power structure. I had hoped that each of you would understand. But again I have been disappointed.

37   I have heard numerous southern religious leaders admonish their worshipers to comply with a desegregation decision because it is the law, but I have longed to hear white ministers declare: "Follow this decree because integration is morally right and because the Negro is your brother." In the midst of blatant injustices inflicted upon the Negro, I have watched white churchmen stand on the sideline and mouth pious irrelevancies and sanctimonious trivialities. In the midst of a mighty struggle to rid our nation of racial and economic injustice, I have heard many ministers say:

"Those are social issues, with which the gospel has no real concern." And I have watched many churches commit themselves to a completely other-worldly religion which makes a strange, un-Biblical distinction between body and soul, between the sacred and the secular.

I have traveled the length and breadth of Alabama, Mississippi and all the other southern states. On sweltering summer days and crisp autumn mornings I have looked at the South's beautiful churches with their lofty spires pointing heavenward. I have beheld the impressive outlines of her massive religious-education buildings. Over and over I have found myself asking: "What kind of people worship here? Who is their God? Where were their voices when the lips of Governor Barnett dripped with words of interposition and nullification? Where were they when Governor Wallace gave a clarion call for defiance and hatred? Where were their voices of support when bruised and weary Negro men and women decided to rise from the dark dungeons of complacency to the bright hills of creative protest?" 38

Yes, these questions are still in my mind. In deep disappointment I have wept over the laxity of the church. But be assured that my tears have been tears of love. There can be no deep disappointment where there is not deep love. Yes, I love the church. How could I do otherwise? I am in the rather unique position of being the son, the grandson and the great-grandson of preachers. Yes, I see the church as the body of Christ. But, oh! How we have blemished and scarred that body through social neglect and through fear of being nonconformists. 39

There was a time when the church was very powerful—in the time when the early Christians rejoiced at being deemed worthy to suffer for what they believed. In those days the church was not merely a thermometer that recorded the ideas and principles of popular opinion; it was a thermostat that transformed the mores of society. Whenever the early Christians entered a town, the people in power became disturbed and immediately sought to convict the Christians for being "disturbers of the peace" and "outside agitators." But the Christians pressed on, in the conviction that they were "a colony of heaven," called to obey God rather than man. Small in number, they were big in commitment. They were too God-intoxicated to be "astronomically intimidated." By their effort and example they brought an end to such ancient evils as infanticide and gladiatorial contests. 40

Things are different now. So often the contemporary church is a weak, ineffectual voice with an uncertain sound. So often it is an archdefender of the status quo. Far from being disturbed by the presence of the church, the power structure of the average community is consoled by the church's silent—and often even vocal—sanction of things as they are. 41

But the judgment of God is upon the church as never before. If today's church does not recapture the sacrificial spirit of the early church, it will lose its authenticity, forfeit the loyalty of millions, and be dismissed as an irrelevant social club with no meaning for the twentieth century. Every day I meet young people whose disappointment with the church has turned into outright disgust. 42

Perhaps I have once again been too optimistic. Is organized religion too inextricably bound to the status quo to save our nation and the world? Perhaps I must turn my faith to the inner spiritual church, the church within the church, as the true 43

The iDeal Reader

Martin Luther King, Jr.,
"Letter from Birmingham
Jail"

© The McGraw–Hill
Companies, 2001

265

ekklesia and the hope of the world. But again I am thankful to God that some noble souls from the ranks of organized religion have broken loose from the paralyzing chains of conformity and joined us as active partners in the struggle for freedom. They have left their secure congregations and walked the streets of Albany, Ga, with us. They have gone down the highways of the South on tortuous rides for freedom. Yes, they have gone to jail with us. Some have been dismissed from their churches, have lost the support of their bishops and fellow ministers. But they have acted in the faith that right defeated is stronger than evil triumphant. Their witness has been the spiritual salt that has preserved the true meaning of the gospel in these troubled times. They have carved a tunnel of hope through the dark mountain of disappointment.

I hope the church as a whole will meet the challenge of this decisive hour. But   44 even if the church does not come to the aid of justice, I have no despair about the future. I have no fear about the outcome of our struggle in Birmingham, even if our motives are at present misunderstood. We will reach the goal of freedom in Birmingham and all over the nation, because the goal of America is freedom. Abused and scorned though we may be, our destiny is tied up with America's destiny. Before the pilgrims landed at Plymouth, we were here. Before the pen of Jefferson etched the majestic words of the Declaration of Independence across the pages of history, we were here. For more than two centuries our forebears labored in this country without wages; they made cotton king; they built the homes of their masters while suffering gross injustice and shameful humiliation—and yet out of a bottomless vitality they continued to thrive and develop. If the inexpressible cruelties of slavery could not stop us, the opposition we now face will surely fail. We will win our freedom because the sacred heritage of our nation and the eternal will of God are embodied in our echoing demands.

Before closing I feel impelled to mention one other point in your statement that   45 has troubled me profoundly. You warmly commended the Birmingham police force for keeping "order" and "preventing violence." I doubt that you would have so warmly commended the police force if you had seen its dogs sinking their teeth into unarmed, nonviolent Negroes. I doubt that you would so quickly commend the policemen if you were to observe their ugly and inhumane treatment of Negroes here in the city jail; if you were to watch them push and curse old Negro women and young Negro girls; if you were to see them slap and kick old Negro men and young boys; if you were to observe them as they did on two occasions, refuse to give us food because we wanted to sing our grace together. I cannot join you in your praise of the Birmingham police department.

It is true that the police have exercised a degree of discipline in handling the   46 demonstrators. In this sense they have conducted themselves rather "nonviolently" in public. But for what purpose? To preserve the evil system of segregation. Over the past few years I have consistently preached that nonviolence demands that the means we use must be as pure as the ends we seek. I have tried to make clear that it is wrong to use immoral means to attain moral ends. But now I must affirm that it is just as wrong, or perhaps even more so, to use moral means to preserve immoral ends. Perhaps Mr. Connor and his policemen have been rather nonviolent in public, as was Chief Pritchett in Albany, Ga., but they have used the moral means of nonviolence to maintain the immoral end of racial injustice. As T. S. Eliot has said: "The last temptation is the greatest treason: To do the right deed for the wrong reason."

I wish you had commended the Negro sit-inners and demonstrators of Birmingham for their sublime courage, their willingness to suffer and their amazing discipline in the midst of great provocation. One day the South will recognize its real heroes. They will be the James Merediths, with the noble sense of purpose that enables them to face jeering and hostile mobs, and with the agonizing loneliness that characterizes the life of the pioneer. They will be old, oppressed, battered Negro women, symbolized in a 72-year-old woman in Montgomery, Ala., who rose up with a sense of dignity and with her people decided not to ride segregated buses, and who responded with ungrammatical profundity to one who inquired about her weariness: "My feet is tired, but my soul is at rest." They will be the young high school and college students, the young ministers of the gospel and a host of their elders, courageously and nonviolently sitting in at lunch counters and willingly going to jail for conscience sake. One day the South will know that when these disinherited children of God sat down at lunch counters, they were in reality standing up for what is best in the American dream and for the most sacred values in our Judaeo-Christian heritage, thereby bringing our nation back to those great wells of democracy which were dug deep by the founding fathers in their formulation of the Constitution and the Declaration of Independence.

47

Never before have I written so long a letter. I'm afraid it is much too long to take your precious time. I can assure you that it would have been much shorter if I had been writing from a comfortable desk, but what else can one do when he is alone in a narrow jail cell, other than write long letters, think long thoughts and pray long prayers?

48

If I have said anything in this letter that overstates the truth and indicates an unreasonable impatience, I beg you to forgive me. If I have said anything that understates the truth and indicates my having a patience that allows me to settle for anything less than brotherhood, I beg God to forgive me.

49

I hope this letter finds you strong in the faith. I also hope that circumstances will soon make it possible for me to meet each of you, not as an integrationist or a civil-rights leader but as a fellow clergyman and a Christian brother. Let us all hope that the dark clouds of racial prejudice will soon pass away and the deep fog of misunderstanding will be lifted from our feardrenched communities, and in some not too distant tomorrow the radiant stars of love and brotherhood will shine over our great nation with all their scintillating beauty.

50

The iDeal Reader

Etty Hillesum, "Letter from
a Nazi Concentration
Camp"

© The McGraw–Hill
Companies, 2000

267

Etty Hillesum (1914–1943) is remembered for her World War II diaries. She was born in Middleburg, Netherlands, in 1914 and died in the Nazi concentration camp in Auschwitz, Poland, on November 30, 1943, at age twenty-nine. Hillesum portrays her last three years in *An Interrupted Life: The Diaries of Etty Hillesum, 1941–1943*. She delivered eight handwritten volumes of these diaries to her friend Maria Tuinzing, who passed them on to writer Klaas Smelik. Smelik's son subsequently obtained a publisher for the diaries in 1980. Hillesum's diaries offer a glimpse into her spiritual struggle in the midst of wartime persecution.

Letter from a Nazi Concentration Camp

Etty Hillesum

24 August 1943

1 There was a moment when I felt in all seriousness that, after this night, it would be a sin ever to laugh again. But then I reminded myself that some of those who had gone away had been laughing, even if only a handful of them this time . . . There will be some who will laugh now and then in Poland, too, though not many from this transport, I think.

2 When I think of the faces of that squad of armed, green-uniformed guards— my God, those faces! I looked at them, each in turn, from behind the safety of a window, and I have never been so frightened of anything in my life as I was of those faces. I sank to my knees with the words that preside over human life: And God made man after His likeness. That passage spent a difficult morning with me.

3 I have told you often enough that no words and images are adequate to describe nights like these. But still I must try to convey something of it to you. One always has the feeling here of being the ears and eyes of a piece of Jewish history, but there is also the need sometimes to be a still, small voice. We must keep one another in touch with everything that happens in the various outposts of this world, each one contributing his own little piece of stone to the great mosaic that will take shape once the war is over.

4 After a night in the hospital barracks, I took an early morning walk past the punishment barracks, and prisoners were being moved out. The deportees, mainly men, stood with their packs behind the barbed wire. So many of them looked tough and ready for anything. An old acquaintance—I didn't recognise him straightaway, a shaven head often changes people completely—called out to me with a smile, 'If they don't manage to do me in, I'll be back.'

5 But the babies, those tiny piercing screams of the babies, dragged from their cots in the middle of the night . . . I have to put it all down quickly, in a muddle because if I leave it until later I probably won't be able to go on believing that it really

Etty Hillesum, "Letter from
a Nazi Concentration
Camp"

happened. It is like a vision, and drifts further and further away. The babies were easily the worst.

And then there was that paralysed young girl, who didn't want to take her dinner plate along and found it so hard to die. Or the terrified young boy: he had thought he was safe, that was his mistake, and when he realised he was going to have to go anyway, he panicked and ran off. His fellow Jews had to hunt him down—if they didn't find him, scores of others would be put on the transport in his place. He was caught soon enough, hiding in a tent, but 'notwithstanding' . . . 'notwithstanding,' all those others had to go on transport anyway, as a deterrent, they said. And so, many good friends were dragged away by that boy. Fifty victims for one moment of insanity. Or rather: he didn't drag them away—our commandant did, someone of whom it is sometimes said that he is a gentleman. Even so, will the boy be able to live with himself, once it dawns on him exactly what he's been the cause of ? And how will all the other Jews on board the train react to him? That boy is going to have a very hard time. The episode might have been overlooked, perhaps, if there hadn't been so much unnerving activity over our heads that night. The commandant must have been affected by that too. '*Donnerwetter*, some flying tonight!' I heard a guard say as he looked up at the stars.

People still harbour such childish hopes that the transport won't get through. Many of us were able from here to watch the bombardment of a nearby town, probably Emden. So why shouldn't it be possible for the railway line to be hit too, and for the train be stopped from leaving? It's never been known to happen yet, but people keep hoping it will with each new transport and with never-flagging hope . . .

The evening before that night, I walked through the camp. People were grouped together between the barracks, under a grey, cloudy sky. 'Look, that's just how people behave after a disaster, standing about on street corners discussing what's happened,' my companion said to me. 'But that's what makes it so impossible to understand,' I burst out. 'This time, it's *before* the disaster!'

Whenever misfortune strikes, people have a natural instinct to lend a helping hand and to save what can be saved. Tonight I shall be 'helping' to dress babies and to calm mothers and that is all I can hope to do. I could almost curse myself for that. For we all know that we are yielding up our sick and defenceless brothers and sisters to hunger, heat, cold, exposure and destruction, and yet we dress them and escort them to the bare cattle trucks—and if they can't walk we carry them on stretchers. What is going on, what mysteries are these, in what sort of fatal mechanism have we become enmeshed? The answer cannot simply be that we are all cowards. We're not that bad. We stand before a much deeper question . . .

In the afternoon I did a round of the hospital barracks one more time, going from bed to bed. Which beds would be empty the next day? The transport lists are never published until the very last moment, but some of us know well in advance that our names will be down. A young girl called me. She was sitting bolt upright in her bed, eyes wide open. This girl has thin wrists and a peaky little face. She is partly paralysed, and has just been learning to walk again, between two nurses, one step at a time. 'Have you heard? I have to go.' We look at each other for a long moment. It is as if her face has disappeared, she is all eyes. Then she says in a level, grey little

6

7

8

9

10

The iDeal Reader

Etty Hillesum, "Letter from
a Nazi Concentration
Camp"

© The McGraw–Hill
Companies, 2000

269

voice, 'Such a pity, isn't it? That everything you have learned in life goes for nothing.' And, 'How hard it is to die.' Suddenly the unnatural rigidity of her expression
gives way and she sobs, 'Oh, and the worst of it all is having to leave Holland!'
And, 'Oh, why wasn't I allowed to die before . . .' Later, during the night, I saw her
again, for the last time.

There was a little woman in the wash-house, a basket of dripping clothes on her   11
arm. She grabbed hold of me. She looked deranged. A flood of words poured over
me. 'That isn't right, how can that be right, I've got to go and I won't even be able
to get my washing dry by tomorrow. And my child is sick, he's feverish, can't you
fix things so that I don't have to go? And I don't have enough things for the child,
the rompers they sent me are too small, I need the bigger size, oh, it's enough to drive
you mad. And you're not even allowed to take a blanket along, we're going to freeze
to death, you didn't think of that, did you? There's a cousin of mine here, he came
here the same time I did, but he doesn't have to go, he's got the right papers. Couldn't
you help me to get some, too? Just say I don't have to go, do you think they'll leave
the children with their mothers, that's right, you come back again tonight, you'll help
me then, won't you, what do you think, would my cousin's papers . . . ?'

If I were to say that I was in hell that night, what would I really be telling you?   12
I caught myself saying it aloud in the night, aloud to myself and quite soberly, 'So
that's what hell is like.' You really can't tell who is going and who isn't this time.
Almost everyone is up, the sick help each other to get dressed. There are some who
have no clothes at all, whose luggage has been lost or hasn't arrived yet. Ladies
from the 'Welfare' walk about doling out clothes, which may fit or not, it doesn't matter so long as you've covered yourself with something. Some old women look a ridiculous sight. Small bottles of milk are being prepared to take along with the babies,
whose pitiful screams punctuate all the frantic activity in the barracks. A young
mother says to me almost apologetically, 'My baby doesn't usually cry, it's almost as
if he can tell what's happening.' She picks up the child, a lovely baby about eight
months old, from a makeshift crib and smiles at it, 'If you don't behave yourself,
mummy won't take you along with her!' She tells me about some friends, 'When
those men in green came to fetch them in Amsterdam, their children cried terribly. Then their father said, "If you don't behave yourselves, you won't be allowed
to go in that green car, this green gentleman won't take you." And that helped—the
children calmed down.' She winks at me bravely, a trim, dark little woman with a
lively, olive-skinned face, dressed in long grey trousers and a green woolen sweater,
'I may be smiling, but I feel pretty awful.' The little woman with the wet washing is
on the point of hysterics. 'Can't you hide my child for me? Go on, please, won't
you hide him, he's got a high fever, how can I possibly take him along?' She points
to a little bundle of misery with blonde curls and a burning, bright-red little face. The
child tosses about in his rough wooden cot. The nurse wants the mother to put on
an extra woolen sweater, tries to pull it over her dress. She refuses, 'I'm not going
to take anything along, what use would it be . . . my child.' And she sobs, 'They
take the sick children away and you never get them back.'

Then a woman comes up to her, a stout working-class woman with a kindly snub-   13
nosed face, draws the desperate mother down with her on to the edge of one of the

iron bunk beds and talks to her almost crooningly, 'There now, you're just an ordinary Jew, aren't you, so you'll just have to go, won't you . . . ?'

A few beds further along I suddenly catch sight of the ash-grey, freckled face of   14
a colleague. She is squatting beside the bed of a dying woman who has swallowed some poison and who happens to be her mother . . .

'God Almighty, what are you doing to us?' The words just escape me. Over there   15
is that affectionate little woman from Rotterdam. She is in her ninth month. Two nurses try to get her dressed. She just stands there, her swollen body leaning against her child's cot. Drops of sweat run down her face. She stares into the distance, a distance into which I cannot follow her, and says in a toneless, worn-out voice, 'Two months ago I volunteered to go with my husband to Poland. And then I wasn't allowed to, because I always have such difficult confinements. And now I do have to go . . . just because someone tried to run away tonight.' The wailing of the babies grows louder still, filling every nook and cranny of the barracks, now bathed in ghostly light. It is almost too much to bear. A name occurs to me: Herod.

On the stretcher, on the way to the train, her labour pains begin, and we are   16
allowed to carry the woman to hospital instead of to the goods train, which, this night, seems a rare act of humanity . . .

I pass the bed of the paralysed girl. The others have helped to dress her. I never   17
saw such great big eyes in such a little face. 'I can't take it all in,' she whispers to me. A few steps away stands my little hunchbacked Russian woman, I told you about her before. She stands there as if spun in a web of sorrow. The paralysed girl is a friend of hers. Later she said sadly to me, 'She doesn't even have a plate, I wanted to give her mine but she wouldn't take it, she said, "I'll be dead in ten days' time anyway, and then those horrible Germans will get it ." '

She stands there in front of me, a green silk kimono wrapped round her small,   18
misshapen figure. She has the very wise, bright eyes of a child. She looks at me for a long time in silence, searchingly, and then says, 'I would like, oh, I really would like, to be able to swim away in my tears.' And, 'I long so desperately for my dear mother.' (Her mother died a few months ago from cancer, in the washroom near the WC. At least she was left alone there for a moment, left to die in peace.) She asks me with her strange accent in the voice of a child that begs for forgiveness, 'Surely God will be able to understand my doubts in a world like this, won't He?' Then she turns away from me, in an almost loving gesture of infinite sadness, and throughout the night I see the misshapen, green, silk-clad figure moving between the beds, doing small services for those about to depart. She herself doesn't have to go, not this time anyway . . .

I'm sitting here squeezing tomato juice for the babies. A young woman sits beside   19
me. She appears ready and eager to leave, and is beautifully turned out. It is something like a cry of liberation when she exclaims, arms flung wide, 'I'm embarking on a wonderful journey, I might find my husband.' A woman opposite cuts her short bitterly, 'I'm going as well, but I certainly don't think it's wonderful.' I remembered admitting the young woman beside me. She has only been here for a few days and she came from the punishment block. She seems so level-headed and independent, with a touch of defiance about her mouth. She has been ready to leave since the afternoon, dressed in a long pair of trousers and a woollen jumper and cardigan. Next to

The iDeal Reader

Etty Hillesum, "Letter from
a Nazi Concentration
Camp"

© The McGraw–Hill
Companies, 2000

271

her on the floor stands a heavy rucksack and a blanket roll. She is trying to force down a few sandwiches. They are mouldy. 'I'll probably get quite a lot of mouldy bread to eat,' she laughs. 'In prison I didn't eat anything at all for days.' A bit of her history in her own words: 'My time wasn't far off when they threw me into prison. And the taunts and the insults! I made the mistake of saying that I couldn't stand, so they made me stand for hours, but I managed it without making a sound.' She looks defiant.' My husband was in the prison as well. I won't tell you what they did to him! But my God, he was tough! They sent him through last month. I was in my third day of labour and couldn't go with him. But how brave he was!' She is almost radiant.

'Perhaps I shall find him again.' She laughs defiantly. 'They may drag us through the dirt, but we'll come through all right in the end!' She looks at the crying babies all round and says, 'I'll have good work to do on the train, I still have lots of milk.'   20

'What, you here as well?' I suddenly call out in dismay. A woman turns and comes up between the tumbled beds of the poor wailing babies, her hands groping round her for support. She is dressed in a long, black old-fashioned dress. She has a noble brow and white, wavy hair piled up high. Her husband died here a few weeks ago. She is well over eighty, but looks less than sixty. I always admired her for the aristocratic way in which she reclined on her shabby bunk. She answers in a hoarse voice, 'Yes, I'm here as well, they wouldn't let me share my husband's grave.'   21

'Ah, there she goes again!' It is the tough little ghetto woman who is racked with hunger the whole time because she never gets any parcels. She has seven children here. She trips pluckily and busily about on her little short legs.' All I know is I've got seven children and they need a proper mother, you can be sure of that!'   22

With nimble gestures she is busy stuffing a jute bag full of her belongings. 'I'm not leaving anything behind, my husband was sent through here a year ago and my two oldest boys have been through as well.' She beams, 'My children are real treasures!' She bustles about, she packs, she's busy, she has a kind word for everyone who goes by. A plain, dumpy ghetto woman with greasy black hair and little short legs. She has a shabby, short-sleeved dress on, which I can imagine her wearing when she used to stand behind the washtub, back in Jodenbreestraat. And now she is off to Poland in the same old dress, a three days' journey with seven children. 'That's right, seven children, and they need a proper mother, believe me!'   23

You can tell that the young woman over there is used to luxury and that she must have been very beautiful. She is a recent arrival. She had gone into hiding to save her baby. Now she is here, through treachery, like so many others. Her husband is in the punishment barracks. She looks quite pitiful now. Her bleached hair has black roots with a greenish tinge. She has put on many different sets of underwear and other clothing all on top of one another—you can't carry everything by hand, after all, particularly if you have a little child to carry as well. Now she looks lumpy and ridiculous. Her face is blotchy. She stares at everyone with a veiled, tentative gaze, like some defenceless and abandoned young animal.   24

What will this young woman, already in a state of collapse, look like after three days in an overcrowded goods wagon with men, women, children and babies all thrown together, bags and baggage, a bucket in the middle their only convenience?   25

Presumably they will be sent on to another transit camp, and then on again from   26
there.

We are being hunted to death right through Europe . . .   27

I wander in a daze through other barracks. I walk past scenes that loom up before   28
my eyes in crystal-clear detail, and at the same time seem like blurred age-old visions.
I see a dying old man being carried away, reciting the Sh'ma to himself . . .

Slowly but surely six o'clock in the morning has arrived. The train is due to depart   29
at eleven, and they are starting to load it with people and luggage. Paths to the
train have been staked out by men of the *Ordedienst*, the Camp Service Corps. Anyone
not involved with the transport has to keep to barracks. I slip into one just across
from the siding .'There's always been a splendid view from here . . .' I hear a cynical
voice say. The camp has been cut in two halves since yesterday by the train: a depressing series of bare, unpainted goods wagons in the front, and a proper carriage for
the guards at the back. Some of the wagons have paper mattresses on the floor. These
are for the sick. There is more and more movement now along the asphalt path beside
the train.

Men from the 'Flying Column' in brown overalls are bringing the luggage up on   30
wheelbarrows. Among them I spot two of the commandant's court jesters: the first is
a comedian and a song-writer. Some time ago his name was down, irrevocably, for
transport, but for several nights in a row he sang his lungs out for a delighted audience, including the commandant and his retinue. He sang 'Ich kann es nicht ver-
stehen, dass die Rosen blühen' ('I know not why the roses bloom') and other topical
songs. The commandant, a great lover of art, thought it all quite splendid. The singer
got his 'exemption'. He was even allocated a house where he now lives behind red-
checked curtains with his peroxide-blonde wife, who spends all her days at a mangle
in the boiling hot laundry. Now here he is, dressed in khaki overalls, pushing a wheel-
barrow piled high with the luggage of his fellow Jews. He looks like death warmed
up. And over there is another court jester: the commandant's favourite pianist. Legend
has it that he is so accomplished that he can play Beethoven's Ninth as a jazz number, which is certainly saying something . . .

Suddenly there are a lot of green-uniformed men swarming over the asphalt. I   31
can't imagine where they have sprung from. Knapsacks and guns over their shoulders. I study their faces. I try to look at them without prejudice.

I can see a father, ready to depart, blessing his wife and child and being himself   32
blessed in turn by an old rabbi with a snow-white beard and the profile of a fiery
prophet. I can see . . . ah, I can't begin to describe it all . . .

On earlier transports, some of the guards were simple, kindly types with puz-   33
zled expressions, who walked about the camp smoking their pipes and speaking in
some incomprehensible dialect, and one would have found their company not too
objectionable on the journey. Now I am transfixed with terror. Oafish, jeering faces,
in which one seeks in vain for even the slightest trace of human warmth. At what
fronts did they learn their business? In what punishment camps were they trained?
For after all this is a punishment, isn't it? A few young women are already sitting in
a goods wagon. They hold their babies on their laps, their legs dangling outside—they

The iDeal Reader

Etty Hillesum, "Letter from
a Nazi Concentration
Camp"

© The McGraw–Hill
Companies, 2000

273

are determined to enjoy the fresh air as long as possible. Sick people are carried past on stretchers. After all, it is meant as a punishment. I almost find myself laughing, the disparity between the guards and the guarded is too absurd. My companion at the window shudders. Months ago he was brought here from Amersfoort, in bits and pieces. 'Oh, yes, that's what those fellows were like,' he says. 'That's what they looked like.'

A couple of young children stand with their noses pressed to the windowpane. 34 I listen in to their earnest conversation, 'Why do those nasty, horrid men wear green, why don't they wear black? Bad people wear black, don't they?' 'Look over there, that man is really sick!' A shock of grey hair above a rumpled blanket on a stretcher. 'Look, there's another sick one . . .'

And, pointing at the green uniforms, 'Look at them, now they're laughing!' 'Look, 35 look, one of them's already drunk!'

More and more people are filling up the spaces in the goods wagons. A tall, lonely 36 figure paces the asphalt, a briefcase under his arm. He is the head of the so-called *Antragstelle,* the camp 'appeals department'. He strives right up to the last moment to get people out of the commandant's clutches. Horse-trading here always continues until the train has actually pulled out. It's even been known for him to manage to free people from the moving train. The man with the briefcase has the brow of a scholar, and tired, very tired shoulders. A bent, little old woman, with a black, old-fashioned hat on her grey, wispy hair, bars his way, gesticulating and brandishing a bundle of papers under his nose. He listens to her for a while, then shakes his head and turns away, his shoulders sagging just a little bit more. This time it won't be possible to get many people off the train in the nick of time. The commandant is annoyed. A young Jew has had the effrontery to run away. One can't really call it a serious attempt to escape—he absconded from the hospital in a moment of panic, a thin jacket over his blue pyjamas, and in a clumsy, childish way took refuge in a tent where he was picked up quickly enough after a search of the camp. But if you are a Jew you may not run away, may not allow yourself to be stricken with panic. The commandant is remorseless. As a reprisal, and without warning, scores of others are being sent on the transport with the boy, including quite a few who had thought they were firmly at anchor here. This system happens to believe in collective punishment. And all those planes overhead couldn't have helped to improve the commandant's mood, though that is a subject on which he prefers to keep his own counsel.

The goods wagons are now what you might call full. But that's what you think. 37 God Almighty, does all this lot have to get in as well? A large new group has turned up. The children are still standing with their noses glued to the windowpane, they don't miss a thing . . . 'Look over there, a lot of people are getting off, it must be too hot in the train.' Suddenly one of them calls out. 'Look, the commandant!'

He appears at the end of the asphalt path, like a famous star making his entrance 38 during agrand finale. This near-legendary figure is said to be quite charming and so well-disposed towards the Jews. For the commandant of a camp for Jews he has some strange ideas. Recently he decided that we needed more variety in our diet, and we were promptly served marrowfat peas—just once—instead of cabbage. He could also be said to be our artistic patron here, and is a regular at all our cabaret nights. On one occasion he came three times in succession to see the same performance and roared with laughter at the same old jokes each time. Under his auspices, a male choir has been formed that sang 'Bei mir bist du schön' on his personal orders. It sounded very moving here on the heath, it must be said. Now and then he even invites some of the artistes to his house and talks and drinks with them into the early hours. One night not so long ago he escorted an actress back home, and when he took his leave of her he offered her his hand, just imagine, his hand! They also say that he specially loves children. Children must be looked after. In the hospital they even get a tomato each day. And yet many of them seem to die all the same . . . I could go on quite a bit longer about 'our' commandant. Perhaps he sees himself as a prince dispensing largesse to his many humble subjects. God knows how he sees himself. A voice behind me says, 'Once upon a time we had a commandant who used to kick people off to Poland. This one sees them off with a smile.'

He now walks along the train with military precision, a relatively young man 39 who has 'arrived' early in his career, if one may call it that. He is absolute master over the life and death of Dutch and German Jews here on this remote heath in Drenthe Province. A year ago he probably had not the slightest idea that it so much as existed. I didn't know about it myself, to tell the truth. He walks along the train, his grey, immaculately brushed hair just showing beneath his flat, light-green cap. That grey hair, which makes such a romantic contrast with his fairly young face, sends many of the silly young girls here into raptures, although they dare not, of course, express their feelings openly. On this cruel morning his face is almost iron-grey. It is a face that I am quite unable to read. Sometimes it seems to me to be like along thin scar in which grimness mingles with joylessness and hypocrisy. And there is something else about him, halfway between a dapper hairdresser's assistant and a stage-door Johnny. But the grimness and the rigidly forced bearing predominate. With military step he walks along the goods wagons, bulging now with people. He is inspecting his troops: the sick, infants in arms, young mothers and shaven-headed men. A few more ailing people are being brought up on stretchers, he makes an impatient gesture, they're taking too long about it. Behind him walks his Jewish secretary, smartly dressed in fawn riding breeches and brown sports jacket. He has the sporty demeanour yet vacuous expression of the English whisky drinker. Suddenly they are joined by a handsome brown gun-dog, where from heaven knows. With studied gestures the fawn secretary plays with it, like something from a picture in an English society paper. The green squad stare at him goggle-eyed. They probably think—though think is a big word—that some of the Jews here look quite different from what their propaganda sheets have led them to believe. A few Jewish big-shots from the camp now also walk along the train. 'Trying to air their "importance",' mutters someone behind me. 'Transport Boulevard,' I say. 'Could one ever hope to convey to the outside world what has happened here today?' I ask my companion. The outside world probably thinks of us as a grey, uniform, suffering mass of Jews, and knows nothing of the gulfs and abysses and subtle differences that exist between us. They could never hope to understand.

The iDeal Reader

Etty Hillesum, "Letter from
a Nazi Concentration
Camp"

© The McGraw–Hill
Companies, 2000

275

The commandant has now been joined by the *Oberdienstleiter,* the head of the   40
Camp Service Corps. The *Oberdienstleiter* is a German Jew of massive build, and
the commandant looks slight and insignificant by his side. Black topboots, black cap,
black army coat with yellow star. He has a cruel mouth and a powerful neck. A few
years ago he was still a digger in the outworkers' corps. When the story of his meteoric
rise is written up later, it will be an important historical account of the mentality of
our age. The light-green commandant with his military bearing, the fawn, impassive
secretary, the black bully-boy figure of the *Oberdienstleiter,* parade past the train.
People fall back around them, but all eyes are on them.

My God, are the doors really being shut now? Yes, they are. Shut on the herded,   41
densely packed, mass of people inside. Through small openings at the top we can see
heads and hands, hands that will wave to us later when the train leaves. The commandant takes a bicycle and rides once again along the entire length of the train.
Then he makes a brief gesture, like royalty in an operetta. A little orderly comes
flying up and deferentially relieves him of the bicycle. The train gives a piercing whis-
tle, and 1020 Jews leave Holland.

This time the quota was really quite small, all considered: a mere thousand Jews,   42
the extra twenty being reserves, for it is always possible, indeed quite certain this
time, that a few will die or be crushed to death on the way. So many sick people
and not a single nurse . . .

The tide of helpers gradually recedes; people go back to their sleeping quar-   43
ters. So many exhausted, pale and suffering faces. One more piece of our camp has
been amputated. Next week yet another piece will follow. This is what has been happening now for over a year, week in, week out. We are left with just a few thousand. A hundred thousand Dutch members of our race are toiling away under an
unknown sky or lie rotting in some unknown soil. We know nothing of their fate.
It is only a short while, perhaps, before we find out, each one of us in his own time,
for we are all marked down to share that fate, of that I have not a moment's doubt.
But I must go now and lie down and sleep for a little while. I am a bit tired and
dizzy. Then later I have to go to the laundry to track down the face cloth that got
lost. But first I must sleep. As for the future, I am firmly resolved to return to you after
my wanderings. In the meantime, my love once again, you dear people.

Frederick Douglass (1817–1895) was born a slave near Easton, Maryland. Overcoming tremendous odds, Douglass first secretly taught himself to read and write, and then escaped slavery, settling in the free state of Massachusetts. He became a prominent abolitionist, women's rights leader, and public speaker. Douglass was also an advisor to Abraham Lincoln and publisher of the newspaper *The North Star*. His books include the autobiographies *My Bondage and My Freedom* (1855) and *The Life and Times of Frederick Douglass* (1882). "How I Learned to Read and Write," one of the most eloquent pleas for universal literacy ever written, is taken from Douglass's autobiography *Narrative of the Life of Frederick Douglass, an American Slave* (1845).

How I Learned to Read and Write

Frederick Douglass

Very soon after I went to live with Mr. and Mrs. Auld, she very kindly commenced   1
to teach me the A, B, C. After I had learned this, she assisted me in learning to
spell words of three or four letters. Just at this point of my progress, Mr. Auld found
out what was going on, and at once forbade Mrs. Auld to instruct me further, telling
her, among other things, that it was unlawful, as well as unsafe, to teach a slave to
read. To use his own words, further, he said, "If you give a nigger an inch, he will take
an ell. A nigger should know nothing but to obey his master—to do as he is told to
do. Learning would *spoil* the best nigger in the world. Now," said he, "if you teach
that nigger (speaking of myself) how to read, there would be no keeping him. It would
forever unfit him to be a slave. He would at once become unmanageable, and of no
value to his master. As to himself, it could do him no good, but a great deal of harm.
It would make him discontented and unhappy." These words sank deep into my heart,
stirred up sentiments within that lay slumbering, and called into existence an entirely
new train of thought. It was a new and special revelation, explaining dark and mysterious things, with which my youthful understanding had struggled, but struggled in
vain. I now understood what had been to me a most perplexing difficulty—to wit,
the white man's power to enslave the black man. It was a grand achievement, and I
prized it highly. From that moment, I understood the pathway from slavery to freedom. It was just what I wanted, and I got it at a time when I the least expected it.
Whilst I was saddened by the thought of losing the aid of my kind mistress, I was glad-
dened by the invaluable instruction which, by the merest accident, I had gained from
my master. Though conscious of the difficulty of learning without a teacher, I set out
with high hope, and a fixed purpose, at whatever cost of trouble, to learn how to read.
The very decided manner with which he spoke, and strove to impress his wife with
the evil consequences of giving me instruction, served to convince me that he was
deeply sensible of the truths he was uttering. It gave me the best assurance that I
might rely with the utmost confidence on the results which, he said, would flow from
teaching me to read. What he most dreaded, that I most desired. What he most loved,

that I most hated. That which to him was a great evil, to be carefully shunned, was to me a great good, to be diligently sought; and the argument which he so warmly urged, against my learning to read, only served to inspire me with a desire and determination to learn. In learning to read, I owe almost as much to the bitter opposition of my master, as to the kindly aid of my mistress. I acknowledge the benefit of both. . . .

I lived in Master Hugh's family about seven years. During this time, I succeeded in learning to read and write. In accomplishing this, I was compelled to resort to various stratagems. I had no regular teacher. My mistress, who had kindly commenced to instruct me, had, in compliance with the advice and direction of her husband, not only ceased to instruct, but had set her face against my being instructed by any one else. It is due, however, to my mistress to say of her, that she did not adopt this course of treatment immediately. She at first lacked the depravity indispensable to shutting me up in mental darkness. It was at least necessary for her to have some training in the exercise of irresponsible power, to make her equal to the task of treating me as though I were a brute.

My mistress was, as I have said, a kind and tender-hearted woman; and in the simplicity of her soul she commenced, when I first went to live with her, to treat me as she supposed one human being ought to treat another. In entering upon the duties of a slaveholder, she did not seem to perceive that I sustained to her the relation of a mere chattel, and that for her to treat me as a human being was not only wrong, but dangerously so. Slavery proved as injurious to her as it did to me. When I went there, she was a pious, warm, and tender-hearted woman. There was no sorrow or suffering for which she had not a tear. She had bread for the hungry, clothes for the naked, and comfort for every mourner that came within her reach. Slavery soon proved its ability to divest her of these heavenly qualities. Under its influence, the tender heart became stone, and the lamblike disposition gave way to one of tiger-like fierceness. The first step in her downward course was in her ceasing to instruct me. She now commenced to practise her husband's precepts. She finally became even more violent in her opposition than her husband himself. She was not satisfied with simply doing as well as he had commanded; she seemed anxious to do better. Nothing seemed to make her more angry than to see me with a newspaper. She seemed to think that here lay the danger. I have had her rush at me with a face made all up of fury, and snatch from me a newspaper, in a manner that fully revealed her apprehension. She was an apt woman; and a little experience soon demonstrated, to her satisfaction, that education and slavery were incompatible with each other.

From this time I was most narrowly watched. If I was in a separate room any considerable length of time, I was sure to be suspected of having a book, and was at once called to give an account of myself. All this, however, was too late. The first step had been taken. Mistress, in teaching me the alphabet, had given me the *inch,* and no precaution could prevent me from taking the *ell.*

The plan which I adopted, and the one by which I was most successful, was that of making friends of all the little white boys whom I met in the street. As many of

2

3

4

5

these as I could, I converted into teachers. With their kindly aid, obtained at different times and in different places, I finally succeeded in learning to read. When I was sent on errands, I always took my book with me, and by doing one part of my errand quickly, I found time to get a lesson before my return. I used also to carry bread with me, enough of which was always in the house, and to which I was always welcome; for I was much better off in this regard than many of the poor white children in our neighborhood. This bread I used to bestow upon the hungry little urchins, who, in return, would give me that more valuable bread of knowledge. I am strongly tempted to give the names of two or three of those little boys, as a testimonial of the gratitude and affection I bear them; but prudence forbids;—not that it would injure me, but it might embarrass them; for it is almost an unpardonable offence to teach slaves to read in this Christian country. It is enough to say of the dear little fellows, that they lived in Philpot Street, very near Durgin and Bailey's shipyard. I used to talk this matter of slavery over with them. I would sometimes say to them, I wished I could be as free as they would be when they got to be men. "You will be free as soon as you are twenty-one, *but I am a slave for life!* Have not I as good a right to be free as you have?" These words used to trouble them; they would express for me the liveliest sympathy, and console me with the hope that something would occur by which I might be free.

I was now about twelve years old, and the thought of being *a slave for life* began to bear heavily upon my heart. Just about this time, I got hold of a book entitled "The Columbian Orator." Every opportunity I got, I used to read this book. Among much of other interesting matter, I found in it a dialogue between a master and his slave. The slave was represented as having run away from his master three times. The dialogue represented the conversation which took place between them, when the slave was retaken the third time. In this dialogue, the whole argument in behalf of slavery was brought forward by the master, all of which was disposed of by the slave. The slave was made to say some very smart as well as impressive things in reply to his master—things which had the desired though unexpected effect; for the conversation resulted in the voluntary emancipation of the slave on the part of the master. 6

In the same book, I met with one of Sheridan's mighty speeches on and in behalf of Catholic emancipation. These were choice documents to me. I read them over and over again with unabated interest. They gave tongue to interesting thoughts of my own soul, which had frequently flashed through my mind, and died away for want of utterance. The moral which I gained from the dialogue was the power of truth over the conscience of even a slaveholder. What I got from Sheridan was a bold denunciation of slavery, and a powerful vindication of human rights. The reading of these documents enabled me to utter my thoughts, and to meet the arguments brought forward to sustain slavery; but while they relieved me of one difficulty, they brought on another even more painful than the one of which I was relieved. The more I read, the more I was led to abhor and detest my enslavers. I could regard them in no other light than a band of successful robbers, who had left their homes, and gone to Africa, and stolen us from our homes, and in a strange land reduced us to slavery. I loathed them as being the meanest as well as the most wicked of men. As I read and contemplated the subject, behold! that very discontentment which 7

Master Hugh had predicted would follow my learning to read had already come, to torment and sting my soul to unutterable anguish. As I writhed under it, I would at times feel that learning to read had been a curse rather than a blessing. It had given me a view of my wretched condition, without the remedy. It opened my eyes to the horrible pit, but to no ladder upon which to get out. In moments of agony, I envied my fellow-slaves for their stupidity. I have often wished myself a beast. I preferred the condition of the meanest reptile to my own. Any thing, no matter what, to get rid of thinking! It was this everlasting thinking of my condition that tormented me. There was no getting rid of it. It was pressed upon me by every object within sight or hearing, animate or inanimate. The silver trump of freedom had roused my soul to eternal wakefulness. Freedom now appeared, to disappear no more forever. It was heard in every sound, and seen in every thing. It was ever present to torment me with a sense of my wretched condition. I saw nothing without seeing it, I heard nothing without hearing it, and felt nothing without feeling it. It looked from every star, it smiled in every calm, breathed in every wind, and moved in every storm.

I often found myself regretting my own existence, and wishing myself dead; and 8 but for the hope of being free, I have no doubt but that I should have killed myself, or done something for which I should have been killed. While in this state of mind, I was eager to hear any one speak of slavery. I was a ready listener. Every little while, I could hear something about the abolitionists. It was some time before I found what the word meant. It was always used in such connections as to make it an interesting word to me. If a slave ran away and succeeded in getting clear, or if a slave killed his master, set fire to a barn, or did any thing very wrong in the mind of a slaveholder, it was spoken of as the fruit of *abolition*. Hearing the word in this connection very often, I set about learning what it meant. The dictionary afforded me little or no help. I found it was "the act of abolishing"; but then I did not know what was to be abolished. Here I was perplexed. I did not dare to ask any one about its meaning, for I was satisfied that it was something they wanted me to know very little about. After a patient waiting, I got one of our city papers, containing an account of the number of petitions from the north, praying for the abolition of slavery in the District of Columbia, and of the slave trade between the States. From this time I understood the words *abolition* and *abolitionist*, and always drew near when that word was spoken, expecting to hear something of importance to myself and fellow-slaves. The light broke in upon me by degrees. I went one day down on the wharf of Mr. Waters; and seeing two Irishmen unloading a scow of stone, I went, unasked, and helped them. When we had finished, one of them came to me and asked, "Are ye a slave for life?" I told him that I was. The good Irishman seemed to be deeply affected by the statement. He said to the other that it was a pity so fine a little fellow as myself should be a slave for life. He said it was a shame to hold me. They both advised me to run away to the north; that I should find friends there, and that I should be free. I pretended not to be interested in what they said, and treated them as if I did not understand them; for I feared they might be treacherous. White men have been known to encourage slaves to escape, and then, to get the reward, catch them and return them to their masters. I was afraid that these seemingly good men might use me so; but I nevertheless remembered their advice, and from that time I resolved to run away. I looked forward to a time at which it would be safe for me to escape. I was too young to think of doing so immediately; besides, I wished to learn how to write, as I might have occasion to write my own pass. I consoled myself with the hope that I should one day find a good chance. Meanwhile, I would learn to write.

The idea as to how I might learn to write was suggested to me by being in Durgin and Bailey's ship-yard, and frequently seeing the ship carpenters, after hewing, and getting a piece of timber ready for use, write on the timber the name of that part of the ship for which it was intended. When a piece of timber was intended for the larboard side, it would be marked thus—"L." When a piece was for the starboard side, it would be marked thus—"S." A piece for the larboard side forward, would be marked thus—"L. F." When a piece was for starboard side forward, it would be marked thus—"S. F." For larboard aft, it would be marked thus—"L. A." For starboard aft, it would be marked thus—"S. A." I soon learned the names of these letters, and for what they were intended when placed upon a piece of timber in the ship-yard. I immediately commenced copying them, and in a short time was able to make the four letters named. After that, when I met with any boy who I knew could write, I would tell him I could write as well as he. The next word would be, "I don't believe you. Let me see you try it." I would then make the letters which I had been so fortunate as to learn, and ask him to beat that. In this way I got a good many lessons in writing, which it is quite possible I should never have gotten in any other way. During this time, my copy-book was the board fence, brick wall, and pavement; my pen and ink was a lump of chalk. With these, I learned mainly how to write. I then commenced and continued copying the Italics in Webster's Spelling Book, until I could make them all without looking on the book. By this time, my little Master Thomas had gone to school, and learned how to write, and had written over a number of copy-books. These had been brought home, and shown to some of our near neighbors, and then laid aside. My mistress used to go to class meeting at the Wilk Street meetinghouse every Monday afternoon, and leave me to take care of the house. When left thus, I used to spend this time writing in the spaces left in Master Thomas's copy-book, copying what he had written. I continued to do this until I could write a hand very similar to that of Master Thomas. Thus, after a long, tedious effort for years, I finally succeeded in learning how to write.

9

The iDeal Reader

William Faulkner, "Nobel
Prize Award Speech"

© The McGraw–Hill
Companies, 2000

281

William Faulkner (1897–1962) was one of the leading novelists of the twentieth century; he also wrote screenplays, poetry, and short stories, and worked as a clerk, as postmaster at the University of Mississippi, and as a coal shoveler at a power plant. A British Royal Air Force cadet pilot in 1918, Faulkner became an honorary second lieutenant. Faulkner was a lifelong resident of Mississippi, born to a genteel family that had been instrumental in building the railroads. Although he attended the University of Mississippi briefly, he had little formal education and lived in relative cultural isolation.

His works are remarkable in part because his characters, based on his knowledge of the rural South, seemed so often larger than life, representative of all Southerners. A series of 15 novels and all his short stories are set in the fictional Yoknapatawpha County whose county seat, Jefferson, was modeled after Oxford, Mississippi. In his fiction past and present, rich and poor, Native Americans and whites and blacks intermingled. His style sometimes relied upon stream of consciousness and was distinctive for its long and complex sentence structure, multiple points of view, and flashbacks. Thematically, Faulkner's concerns included the concept of time, man's exploitation of man and earth, familial love, dysfunctional families, initiation to manhood, the self-righteousness of church-going Christians, and human responsibility, and he often alluded to the Bible.

In his famous Nobel Prize speech, Faulkner claimed it is the writer's duty "to help man endure by lifting his heart, by reminding him of the courage and honor and hope and pride and compassion and pity and sacrifice which have been the glory of his past." A few of his major works include *The Sound and the Fury* (1929), *As I Lay Dying* (1930; 1964), *Light in August* (1932), *Absalom, Absalom!* (1936; 1984), and *A Rose for Emily* (1970).

Nobel Prize Award Speech

William Faulkner

I feel that this award was not made to me as a man but to my work—a life's work in the agony and sweat of the human spirit, not for glory and least of all for profit, but to create out of the materials of the human spirit something which did not exist before. So this award is only mine in trust. It will not be difficult to find a dedication for the money part of it commensurate with the purpose and significance of its origin. But I would like to do the same with the acclaim too, by using this moment as a pinnacle from which I might be listened to by the young men and women already dedicated to the same anguish and travail, among whom is already that one who will some day stand here where I am standing.

Our tragedy today is a general and universal physical fear so long sustained by now that we can even bear it. There are no longer problems of the spirit. There is only one question: When will I be blown up? Because of this, the young man or woman writing today has forgotten the problems of the human heart in conflict with itself which alone can make good writing because only that is worth writing about, worth the agony and the sweat.

He must learn them again. He must teach himself that the basest of all things is to be afraid; and, teaching himself that, forget it forever, leaving no room in his

1

2

3

From *Essays, Speeches and Public Letters*. Reprinted by permission of Random House, Inc.

workshop for anything but the old verities and truths of the heart, the old universal truths lacking which any story is ephemeral and doomed—love and honor and pity and pride and compassion and sacrifice. Until he does so, he labors under a curse. He writes not of love but of lust, of defeats in which nobody loses anything of value, of victories without hope and, worst of all, without pity or compassion. His griefs grieve on no universal bones, leaving no scars. He writes not of the heart but of the glands.

Until he relearns these things, he will write as though he stood alone and watched the end of man. I decline to accept the end of man. It is easy enough to say that man is immortal simply because he will endure; that when the last ding-dong of doom has clanged and faded from the last worthless rock hanging tideless in the last red and dying evening, that even then there will still be one more sound: that of his *puny* inexhaustible voice, still talking. I refuse to accept this. I believe that man will not merely endure: he will prevail. He is immortal, not because he alone among creatures has an inexhaustible voice but because he has a soul, a spirit capable of compassion and sacrifice and endurance. The poet's, the writer's, duty is to write about these things. It is his privilege to help man endure by lifting his heart, by reminding him of the courage and honor and hope and pride and compassion and pity and sacrifice which have been the glory of his past. The poet's voice need not merely be the record of man, it can be one of the props, the pillars to help him endure and prevail.

4

George Fitzhugh (1806–1881) was born in Prince William County, Virginia, on November 4, 1806. He married Mary Metcalf Brockenbrough in 1829 and began his own law business in Port Royal, Virginia. Fitzhugh analyzed society in pamphlets such as *Slavery Justified* and *What Shall Be Done with the Free Negroes?* (both published in 1850). He also used the word "sociology" for the first time in America with his publication entitled *Sociology for the South; or The Failure of Free Society* (1854). An established defender of slavery, Fitzhugh argued in *Cannibals All! or, Slaves Without Masters* (1857) that the system of capitalism should be condemned because it failed to appreciate society's need for a master-slave relationship, such as existed in the South. A prolific writer, Fitzhugh published over a hundred articles in *De Bow's Review*, a Southern journal. His subjects were greatly diverse (including literary criticism, history, genealogy) although his pro-slavery argument was always at the center of his work. His work also appeared as editorials in Richmond newspapers and Northern publications, including the pro-slavery *New York Day Book*.

The Universal Trade from *Cannibals All!*

George Fitzhugh

CHAPTER I

We are, all, North and South, engaged in the White Slave Trade, and he who succeeds best, is esteemed most respectable. It is far more cruel than the Black Slave Trade, because it exacts more of its slaves, and neither protects nor governs them. We boast, that it exacts more, when we say, "that the *profits* made from employing free labor are greater than those from slave labor." The profits, made from free labor, are the amount of the products of such labor, which the employer, by means of the command which capital or skill gives him, takes away, exacts or "exploitates" from the free laborer. The profits of slave labor are that portion of the products of such labor which the power of the master enables him to appropriate. These profits are less, because the master allows the slave to retain a larger share of the results of his own labor, than do the employers of free labor. But we not only boast that the White Slave Trade is more exacting and fraudulent (in fact, though not in intention,) than Black Slavery; but we also boast, that it is more cruel, in leaving the laborer to take care of himself and family out of the pittance which skill or capital have allowed him to retain. When the day's labor is ended, he is free, but is overburdened with the cares of family and household, which make his freedom an empty and delusive mockery. But his employer is really free, and may enjoy the profits made by others' labor, without a care, or a trouble, as to their well-being. The negro slave is free, too, when the labors of the day are over, and free in mind as well as body; for the master provides food, raiment, house, fuel, and everything else necessary to the physical well-being of himself and family. The master's labors commence just when the slave's end. No wonder men should prefer white slavery to capital, to negro slav-

1

George Fitzhugh, "The Universal Trade" from *Cannibal's All!: or Slaves without Masters*. Richmond, VA: A. Morris, 1857.

ery, since it is more profitable, and is free from all the cares and labors of black slave-holding.

Now, reader, if you wish to know yourself-to "descant on your own deformity"—read on. But if you would cherish self-conceit, self-esteem, or self-appreciation, throw down our book; for we will dispel illusions which have promoted your happiness, and shew you that what you have considered and practiced as virtue, is little better than moral Cannibalism. But you will find yourself in numerous and respectable company; for all good and respectable people are "Cannibals all," who do not labor, or who are successfully trying to live without labor, on the unrequited labor of other people:—Whilst low, bad, and disreputable people, are those who labor to support themselves, and to support said respectable people besides. Throwing the negro slaves out of the account, and society is divided in Christendom into four classes: The rich, or independent respectable people, who live well and labor not at all; the professional and skillful respectable people, who do a little light work, for enormous wages; the poor hard-working people, who support every body, and starve themselves; and the poor thieves, swindlers and sturdy beggars, who live like gentlemen, without labor, on the labor of other people. The gentlemen exploitate, which being done on a large scale, and requiring a great many victims, is highly respectable—whilst the rogues and beggars take so little from others, that they fare little better than those who labor.

But, reader, we do not wish to fire into the flock. "Thou art the man!" You are a Cannibal! and if a successful one, pride yourself on the number of your victims, quite as much as any Feejee chieftain, who breakfasts, dines and sups on human flesh.—And your conscience smites you, if you have failed to succeed, quite as much as his, when he returns from an unsuccessful foray.

Probably, you are a lawyer, or a merchant, or a doctor, who have made by your business fifty thousand dollars, and retired to live on your capital. But, mark! not to spend your capital. That would be vulgar, disreputable, criminal. That would be, to live by your own labor; for your capital is your amassed labor. That would be, to do as common working men do; for they take the pittance which their employers leave them, to live on. They live by labor; for they exchange the results of their own labor for the products of other people's labor. It is, no doubt, an honest, vulgar way of living; but not at all a respectable way. The respectable way of living is, to make other people work for you, and to pay them nothing for so doing—and to have no concern about them after their work is done. Hence, white slave-holding is much more respectable than negro slavery—for the master works nearly as hard for the negro, as he for the master. But you, my virtuous, respectable reader, exact three thousand dollars per annum from white labor, (for your income is the product of white labor,) and make not one cent of return in any form. You retain your capital, and never labor, and yet live in luxury on the labor of others. Capital commands labor, as the master does the slave. Neither pays for labor; but the master permits the slave to retain a larger allowance from the proceeds of his own labor, and hence "free labor is cheaper than slave labor." You, with the command over labor which your capital gives you, are a slave owner—a master, without the obligations of a master. They who work for you, who create your income, are slaves,

2

3

4

without the rights of slaves. Slaves without a master! Whilst you were engaged in amassing your capital, in seeking to become independent, you were in the White Slave Trade. To become independent, is to be able to make other people support you, without being obliged to labor for *them*. Now, what man in society is not seeking to attain this situation? He who attains it, is a slave owner, in the worst sense. He who is in pursuit of it, is engaged in the slave trade. You, reader, belong to the one or other class. The men without property, in free society, are theoretically in a worse condition than slaves. Practically, their condition corresponds with this theory, as history and statistics every where demonstrate. The capitalists, in free society, live in ten times the luxury and show that Southern masters do, because the slaves to capital work harder and cost less, than negro slaves.

The negro slaves of the South are the happiest, and, in some sense, the freest people in the world. The children and the aged and infirm work not at all, and yet have all the comforts and necessaries of life provided for them. They enjoy liberty, because they are oppressed neither by care nor labor.   5

The women do little hard work, and are protected from the despotism of their husbands by their masters. The negro men and stout boys work, on the average, in good weather, not more than nine hours a day. The balance of their time is spent in perfect abandon Besides, they have their Sabbaths and holidays. White men, with so much of license and liberty, would die of ennui; but negroes luxuriate in corporeal and mental repose. With their faces upturned to the sun, they can sleep at any hour; and quiet sleep is the greatest of human enjoyments. "Blessed be the man who invented sleep." 'Tis happiness in itself—and results from contentment with the present, and confident assurance of the future. We do not know whether free laborers ever sleep. They are fools to do so; for, whilst they sleep, the wily and watchful capitalist is devising means to ensnare and exploitate them. The free laborer must work or starve. He is more of a slave than the negro, because he works longer and harder for less allowance than the slave, and has no holiday, because the cares of life with him begin when its labors end. He has no liberty, and not a single right. We know, 'tis often said, air and water, are common property, which all have equal right to participate and enjoy; but this is utterly false. The appropriation of the lands carries with it the appropriation of all on or above the lands, *usque ad coelumm aut ad inferos*. A man cannot breathe the air, without a place to breathe it from, and all places are appropriated. All water is private property "to the middle of the stream," except the ocean, and that is not fit to drink.   6

Free laborers have not a thousandth part of the rights and liberties of negro slaves. Indeed, they have not a single right or a single liberty, unless it be the right or liberty to die. But the reader may think that he and other capitalists and employers are freer than negro slaves. Your capital would soon vanish, if you dared indulge in the liberty and abandon of negroes. You hold your wealth and position by the tenure of constant watchfulness, care and circumspection. You never labor; but you are never free.   7

Where a few own the soil, they have unlimited power over the balance of society, until domestic slavery comes in, to compel them to permit this balance of society to draw a sufficient and comfortable living from "terra mater." Free society,   8 asserts the right of a few to the earth—slavery, maintains that it belongs, in different degrees, to all.

But, reader, well may you follow the slave trade. It is the only trade worth following, and slaves the only property worth owning. All other is worthless, a mere *caput mortuum*, except in so far as it vests the owner with the power to command the labors of others—to enslave them. Give you a palace, ten thousand acres of land, sumptuous clothes, equipage and every other luxury; and with your artificial wants, you are poorer than Robinson Crusoe, or the lowest working man, if you have no slaves to capital, or domestic slaves. Your capital will not bring you an income of a cent, nor supply one of your wants, without labor. Labor is indispensable to give value to property, and if you owned every thing else, and did not own labor, you would be poor. But fifty thousand dollars means, and is, fifty thousand dollars worth of slaves. You can command, without touching on that capital, three thousand dollars' worth of labor per annum. You could do no more were you to buy slaves with it, and then you would be cumbered with the cares of governing and providing for them. You are a slaveholder now, to the amount of fifty thousand dollars, with all the advantages, and none of the cares and responsibilities of a master.

"Property in man" is what all are struggling to obtain. Why should they not be obliged to take care of man, their property, as they do of their horses and their hounds, their cattle and their sheep. Now, under the delusive name of liberty, you work him, "from morn to dewy eve"—from infancy to old age—then turn him out to starve. You treat your horses and hounds better. Capital is a cruel master. The free slave trade, the commonest, yet the cruellest of trades.

Langston Hughes (1902–1967) was born in Joplin, Missouri, and lived in Kansas, Illinois, and Ohio before studying at Columbia University and earning an A.B. from Lincoln University in 1929. Hughes was a prolific writer of poetry, plays, songs, fiction, and nonfiction. Much of Hughes's writing offers a transcription of urban life through a portrayal of the speech, habits, attitudes, and feelings of an oppressed people. His work does more, however, than reveal the pain of poverty—it also illustrates racial pride and dignity. Hughes's many books include the poetry collection *Montage of a Dream Deferred* (1951), the novel *Tambourines to Glory* (1958), the short-story collection *The Ways of White Folks* (1934), and the nonfiction work *Black Misery* (1969). Among his many awards and honors, Hughes won a Guggenheim Fellowship and an Anisfeld-Wolfe Award. "The Negro Speaks of Rivers" was first published in 1921 in the NAACP journal *The Crisis* and reprinted in Hughes's first collection of poetry, *The Weary Blues* (1926).

The Negro Speaks of Rivers

Langston Hughes

I've known rivers:
I've known rivers ancient as the world and older than the
     flow of human blood in human veins.

My soul has grown deep like the rivers.

I bathed in the Euphrates when dawns were young.   5
I built my hut near the Congo and it lulled me to sleep.
I looked upon the Nile and raised the pyramids above it.
I heard the singing of the Mississippi when Abe Lincoln
     went down to New Orleans, and I've seen its muddy
     bosom turn all golden in the sunset.   10

I've known rivers:
Ancient, dusky rivers.

My soul has grown deep like the rivers.

Primo Levi (1919–1987), Jewish chemist and author, was born in Turin, Italy, and stayed there for most of his life. He received a B.S. summa cum laude from the University of Turin in 1941. After becoming active in the Italian Resistance in 1943, Levi was deported to Auschwitz concentration camp in Oswiecim, Poland, and was held there from 1943 to 1945. Considered one of the most important chroniclers of conditions for Jews in World War II, Levi was one of only three Italian partisans to survive Auschwitz.

He published his first book in 1947, *Se questo è un uomo* (*If This Is a Man*), published in America as *Survival in Auschwitz: The Nazi Assault on Humanity*. Levi told the *Los Angeles Times* that he aimed "to be a witness" without overemphasizing his status as a victim. Other works include *La Tregua* (1958; 8th ed. 1965; translated as *The Reawakening*, 1965), *La chiave a stella* (*The Monkey's Wrench*, translated 1986), *Se non ora, quando?* (*If Not Now, When?*, 1982), *Other People's Trades* (essays, translated 1989), and *The Sixth Day, and Other Tales* (short fables, 1990). Levi became increasingly distressed at the dwindling attention to the Holocaust and died in an apparent suicide in 1987.

"Hydrogen" from The Periodic Table

Primo Levi

It was January. Enrico came to call for me right after dinner: his brother had gone up into the mountains and had left him the keys to the laboratory. I dressed in a flash and joined him on the street.   1

During the walk I learned that his brother had not really left him the keys: this was simply a compendious formulation, a euphemism, the sort of thing you said to someone ready to understand. His brother, contrary to his habit, had not hidden the keys, nor had he taken them with him; what's more, he had forgotten to repeat to Enrico the prohibition against appropriating these same keys, and the punishment threatened should Enrico disobey. To put it bluntly, there were the keys, after months of waiting; Enrico and I were determined not to pass up the opportunity.   2

We were sixteen, and I was fascinated with Enrico. He was not very active, and his scholastic output was pretty meager, but he had virtues that distinguished him from all the other members of the class, and he did things that nobody else did. He possessed a calm, stubborn courage, a precocious capacity to sense his own future and to give it weight and shape. He turned his back (but without contempt) on our interminable discussions, now Platonic, now Darwinian, later still Bergsonian; he was not vulgar, he did not boast of his virile attributes or his skill at sports, he never lied. He knew his limitations, but we never heard him say (as we all told each other, with the idea of currying comfort, or blowing off steam): "You know, I really think I'm an idiot."   3

He had a slow, foot-slogging imagination: he lived on dreams like all of us, but his dreams were sensible; they were obtuse, possible, contiguous to reality, not romantic,   4

The iDeal Reader

Primo Levi, "Hydrogen"
from **The Periodic Table**

© The McGraw–Hill
Companies, 2000

289

not cosmic. He did not experience my tormented oscillation between the heaven (of a scholastic or sports success, a new friendship, a rudimentary and fleeting love) and the hell (of a failing grade, a remorse, a brutal revelation of an inferiority which each time seemed eternal, definitive). His goals were always attainable. He dreamed of promotion and studied with patience things that did not interest him. He wanted a microscope and sold his racing bike to get it. He wanted to be a pole vaulter and went to the gym every evening for a year without making a fuss about it, breaking any bones, or tearing a ligament, until he reached the mark of 3.5 meters he had set himself, and then stopped. Later he wanted a certain woman and he got her; he wanted the money to live quietly and obtained it after ten years of boring, prosaic work.

We had no doubts: we would be chemists, but our expectations and hopes were 5 quite different. Enrico asked chemistry, quite reasonably, for the tools to earn his living and have a secure life. I asked for something entirely different, for me chemistry represented an indefinite cloud of future potentialities which enveloped my life to come in black volutes torn by fiery flashes, like those which had hidden Mount Sinai. Like Moses, from that cloud I expected my law, the principle of order in me, around me, and in the world. I was fed up with books, which I still continued to gulp down with indiscreet voracity, and searched for another key to the highest truths: there must be a key, and I was certain that, owing to some monstrous conspiracy to my detriment and the world's, I would not get it in school. In school they loaded me with tons of notions which I diligently digested, but which did not warm the blood in my veins. I would watch the buds swell in spring, the mica glint in the granite, my own hands, and I would say to myself: "I will understand this, too, I will understand everything, but not the way *they* want me to. I will find a shortcut, I will make a lock-pick, I will push open the doors."

It was enervating, nauseating, to listen to lectures on the problems of being 6 and knowing, when everything around us was a mystery pressing to be revealed: the old wood of the benches, the sun's sphere beyond the windowpanes and the roofs, the vain flight of the pappus down in the June air. Would all the philosophers and all the armies of the world be able to construct this little fly? No, nor even understand it: this was a shame and an abomination, another road must be found.

We would be chemists, Enrico and I. We would dredge the bowels of the mys- 7 tery with our strength, our talent: we would grab Proteus by the throat, cut short his inconclusive metamorphoses from Plato to Augustine, from Augustine to Thomas, from Thomas to Hegel, from Hegel to Croce. We would force him to speak.

This being our program, we could not afford to waste any opportunities. Enrico's 8 brother, a mysterious and choleric personage, about whom Enrico did not like to talk, was a chemistry student, and he had installed a laboratory at the rear of a court-yard, in a curious, narrow, twisting alleyway which branched off Piazza della Crocetta and stood out in the obsessive Turinese geometry like a rudimentary organ trapped in the evolved structure of a mammalian. The laboratory was also rudimentary: not in the sense of an atavistic vestige but in that of extreme poverty. There was a tiled work-bench, very few glass receptacles, about twenty flasks with reagents, much dust and cobwebs, little light, and great cold. On our way we had discussed what we were going to do now that we had "gained access to the laboratory," but our ideas were confused.

It seemed to us an *embarras de richesses*, and it was instead a different embarrassment, deeper and more essential: an embarrassment tied to an ancient atrophy of ours, of our family, of our caste. What were we able to do with our hands? Nothing, or almost nothing. The women, yes—our mothers and grandmothers had lively, agile hands, they knew how to sew and cook, some even played the piano, painted with watercolors, embroidered, braided their hair. But we, and our fathers? 9

Our hands were at once coarse and weak, regressive, insensitive: the least trained part of our bodies. Having gone through the first fundamental experiences of play, they had learned to write, and that was all. They knew the convulsive grip around the branches of a tree, which we loved to climb out of a natural desire and also (Enrico and I) out of a groping homage and return to the origins of the species; but they were unfamiliar with the solemn, balanced weight of the hammer, the concentrated power of a blade, too cautiously forbidden us, the wise texture of wood, the similar and diverse pliability of iron, lead, and copper. If man is a maker, we were not men: we knew this and suffered from it. 10

The glass in the laboratory enchanted and intimidated us. Glass for us was that which one must not touch because it breaks, and yet, at a more intimate contact, revealed itself to be a substance different from all others, sui generis, full of mystery and caprice. It is similar in this to water, which also has no kindred forms: but water is bound to man, indeed to life, by a long-lasting familiarity, by a relationship of multifarious necessity, due to which its uniqueness is hidden beneath the crust of habit. Glass, however, is the work of man and has a more recent history. It was our first victim, or, better, our first adversary. In the Crocetta laboratory there was the usual lab glass, in various diameters and long and short sections, all covered with dust, we lit the Bunsen burner and set to work. 11

To bend the tube was easy. All you had to do was hold the section of tube steady over the flame: after a certain time the flame turned yellow and simultaneously the glass became weakly luminous. At this point the tube could be bent: the curve obtained was far from perfect, but in substance something took place, you could create a new, arbitrary shape; a potentiality became act. Wasn't this what Aristotle meant? 12

Now, a tube of copper or lead can also be bent, but we soon found out that the red-hot tube of glass possessed a unique virtue: when it had become pliable, you could, by quickly pulling on the two cold ends, pull it into very thin filaments, indeed unimaginably thin, so thin that it was drawn upwards by the current of hot air that rose from the flame. Thin and flexible, like silk. So then silk and cotton too, if obtainable in a massive form, could be as inflexible as glass? Enrico told me that in his grandfather's town the fishermen take silkworms, when they are already big and ready to form the pupa and, blind and clumsy, try to crawl up on the branches; they grab them, break them in two with their fingers, and pulling on the two stumps obtain a thread of silk, thick and coarse, which they then use as a fishing line. This fact, which I had no hesitation in believing, seemed to me both abominable and fascinating: abominable because of the cruel manner of that death, and the futile use of a natural portent; fascinating because of the straightforward and audacious act of ingenuity it presupposed on the part of its mythical inventor. 13

The iDeal Reader

Primo Levi, "Hydrogen"
from The Periodic Table

© The McGraw–Hill
Companies, 2000

291

The glass tube could also be blown up; but this was much more difficult. You could close one end of a small tube: then blowing hard from the other end a bubble formed, very beautiful to look at and almost perfectly spherical but with absurdly thin walls. Even the slightest puff of breath in excess and the walls took on the iridescence of a soap bubble, and this was a certain sign of death: the bubble burst with a sharp little snap and its fragments were scattered over the floor with the tenuous rustle of eggshells. In some sense it was a just punishment; glass is glass, and it should not be expected to simulate the behavior of soapy water. If one forced the terms a bit, one could even see an Aesopian lesson in the event.   14

After an hour's struggle with the glass, we were tired and humiliated. We both had inflamed, dry eyes from looking too long at the red-hot glass, frozen feet, and fingers covered with burns. Besides, working with glass is not chemistry: we were in the laboratory with another goal. Our goal was to see with our eyes, to provoke with our hands, at least one of the phenomena which were described so offhandedly in our chemistry textbook. One could, for example, prepare nitrous oxide, which in Sestini and Funaro was still described with the not very proper and unserious term of laughing gas. Would it really be productive of laughter?   15

Nitrous oxide is prepared by cautiously heating ammonium nitrate. The latter did not exist in the lab; instead there was ammonia and nitric acid. We mixed them, unable to make any preliminary calculations until we had a neutral litmus reaction as a result of which the mixture heated up greatly and emitted an abundance of white smoke; then we decided to bring it to a boil to eliminate the water. In a short time the lab was filled with a choking fog, which was not at all laughable; we broke off our attempt, luckily for us, because we did not know what can happen when this explosive salt is heated less than cautiously.   16

It was neither simple nor very amusing. I looked around and saw in a corner an ordinary dry battery. Here is something we could do: the electrolysis of water. It was an experiment with a guaranteed result, which I had already executed several times at home. Enrico would not be disappointed.   17

I put some water in a beaker, dissolved a pinch of salt in it, turned two empty jam jars upside down in the beaker; then found two rubber-coated copper wires, attached them to the battery's poles, and fitted the wire ends into the jam jars. A minuscule procession of air bubbles rose from the wire ends: indeed, observing them closely you could see that from the cathode about twice as much gas was being liberated as from the anode. I wrote the well-known equation on the blackboard, and explained to Enrico that what was written there was actually taking place. Enrico didn't seem too convinced, but by now it was dark and we were half frozen; we washed our hands, bought some slices of chestnut pudding and went home, leaving the electrolysis to continue on its own.   18

The next day we still had access. In pliant obsequiousness to theory, the cathode jar was almost full of gas; the anode jar was half full: I brought this to Enrico's attention, giving myself as much importance as I could, and trying to awaken the suspicion that, I won't say electrolysis, but its application as the confirmation of the law of definite proportions, was my invention, the fruit of patient experiments conducted secretly in my room. But Enrico was in a bad mood and doubted everything. "Who   19 says that it's actually hydrogen and oxygen?" he said to me rudely. "And what if there's chlorine? Didn't you put in salt?"

The objection struck me as insulting: How did Enrico dare to doubt my state- 20 ment? I was the theoretician, only I: he, although the proprietor of the lab (to a certain degree, and then only at second hand), indeed, precisely because he was in a position to boast of other qualities, should have abstained from criticism. "Now we shall see," I said: I carefully lifted the cathode jar and, holding it with its open end down, lit a match and brought it close. There was an explosion, small but sharp and angry, the jar burst into splinters (luckily, I was holding it level with my chest and not higher), and there remained in my hand, as a sarcastic symbol, the glass ring of the bottom.

We left, discussing what had occurred. My legs were shaking a bit; I experienced 21 retrospective fear and at the same time a kind of foolish pride at having confirmed a hypothesis and having unleashed a force of nature. It was indeed hydrogen, therefore; the same element that burns in the sun and stars, and from whose condensation the universes are formed in eternal silence.